The Hurricane II Manual

A.P. 1564 B | VOL. I | FRONTISPIECE

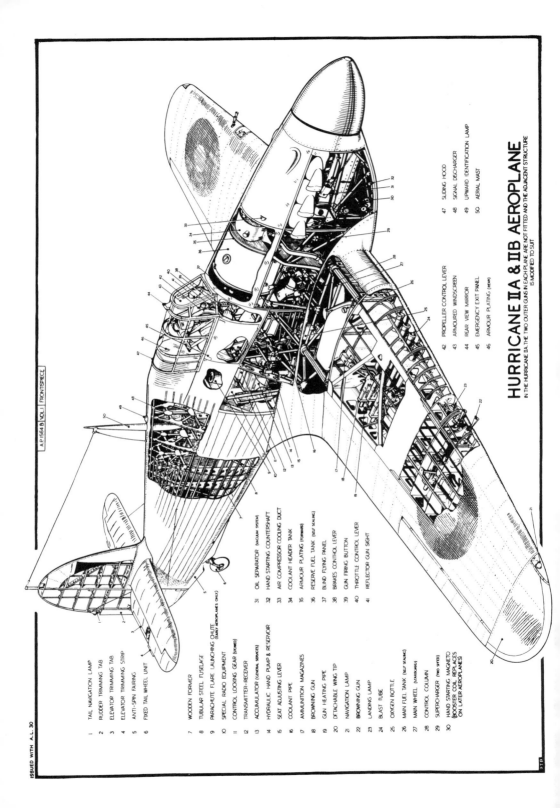

HURRICANE IIA & IIB AEROPLANE

IN THE HURRICANE IIA THE TWO OUTER GUNS IN EACH PLANE ARE NOT FITTED AND THE ADJACENT STRUCTURE IS MODIFIED TO SUIT

1 TAIL NAVIGATION LAMP
2 RUDDER TRIMMING TAB
3 ELEVATOR TRIMMING TAB
4 ELEVATOR TRIMMING STRIP
5 ANTI-SPIN FAIRING
6 FIXED TAIL WHEEL UNIT

7 WOODEN FORMER
8 TUBULAR STEEL FUSELAGE
9 PARACHUTE FLARE LAUNCHING CHUTE (EARLY AEROPLANES ONLY)
10 SPECIAL RADIO EQUIPMENT (STOWED)
11 CONTROL LOCKING GEAR (STOWED)
12 TRANSMITTER-RECEIVER
13 ACCUMULATOR (GENERAL SERVICES)
14 HYDRAULIC HAND PUMP & RESERVOIR
15 SEAT ADJUSTING LEVER
16 COOLANT PIPE
17 AMMUNITION MAGAZINES
18 BROWNING GUN
19 GUN HEATING PIPE
20 DETACHABLE WING TIP
21 NAVIGATION LAMP
22 BROWNING GUN
23 LANDING LAMP
24 BLAST TUBE
25 OXYGEN BOTTLE
26 MAIN FUEL TANK (SELF SEALING)
27 MAIN WHEEL (STAINLESS)
28 CONTROL COLUMN
29 SUPERCHARGER (TWO SPEED)
30 HAND STARTING MAGNETO (BOOSTER COIL REPLACES ON LATER AEROPLANES)

31 OIL SEPARATOR (VACUUM SYSTEM)
32 HAND STARTING COUNTERSHAFT
33 AIR COMPRESSOR COOLING DUCT
34 COOLANT HEADER TANK
35 ARMOUR PLATING (FORWARD)
36 RESERVE FUEL TANK (SELF SEALING)
37 BLIND FLYING PANEL
38 BRAKES CONTROL LEVER
39 GUN FIRING BUTTON
40 THROTTLE CONTROL LEVER
41 REFLECTOR GUN SIGHT

42 PROPELLER CONTROL LEVER
43 ARMOURED WINDSCREEN
44 REAR VIEW MIRROR
45 EMERGENCY EXIT PANEL
46 ARMOUR PLATING (REAR)

47 SLIDING HOOD
48 SIGNAL DISCHARGER
49 UPWARD IDENTIFICATION LAMP
50 AERIAL MAST

The Hurricane II Manual

The Official Air Publication for the Hurricane IIA, IIB, IIC,
IID, IV and Sea Hurricane IIB and IIC, 1941–1945

RAF MUSEUM SERIES

General Editor: Dr Michael A Fopp
Director General, RAF Museum, Hendon

Greenhill Books, London
Stackpole Books, Pennsylvania

This edition of *The Hurricane II Manual* first published 2003 by
Greenhill Books
Lionel Leventhal Limited
Park House
1 Russell Gardens
London NW11 9NN
and
Stackpole Books
5067 Ritter Road, Mechanicsburg, PA 17055, USA

The Hurricane II Manual is Crown Copyright and published by permission of the Controller of Her Majesty's Stationary Office. The material contained in this publication originally appeared under the air publication reference 1564B, C & D, Volume I entitled HURRICANE IIA, IIB and IIC AIRCRAFT, Merlin XX Engine; ADDENDUM I, Sea Hurricane IIB and IIC and Hurricane IIB and IIC (with arrester hook); ADDENDUM II, Hurricane IID and IV. This edition contains a new Foreword and photographs of the RAF Museum's Hurricane I.

The original Air Publication was produced for official and internal purposes by the Air Ministry.

The quality of the illustrations in the original of this volume falls short of the high standard of reproduction normally expected in modern books; they have of necessity been reproduced to complete this facsimile edition.

British Library Cataloguing in Publication Data

The Hurricane II manual. – (RAF museum series)
1. Hurricane (Fighter planes) – Handbooks, manuals, etc.
623.7′464′0941

Library of Congress Cataloging-in-Publication Data available

ISBN 1-85367-544-X

Printed and bound in Thailand by Imago

Contents

* This section in the original Air Publications was allotted to "Equipment at crew stations"; it did not apply to this manual.

Foreword

by Dr Michael Fopp MA PhD FMA FRAeS
Director General, Royal Air Force Museum, Hendon

Sydney Camm's best-known design is rightly famous for its part in the Battle of Britain where it proved very effective against the Luftwaffe's bombers. The type's subsequent service is less well known, but was equally valuable.

The Hurricane is descended from a long line of Camm designs, notably the Hawker Hart and the single-seat Fury biplane fighter. In 1933 Camm began work on a monoplane fighter, and although no official funds were available the project proceeded as a private venture by the company. A contract was issued in February 1935 for a prototype, which flew on 6 November. The company decided in April 1936, before a contract had been issued, to prepare for production of 1000 aircraft and an order for 600 was received on 3 June.

The Hurricane entered RAF service in December 1937, and hit the headlines when Squadron Leader J.W. Gillan of No. 111 Squadron made a flight from Edinburgh to Northolt at an average speed of 408 mph, albeit with the aid of a strong tail wind. By the outbreak of war Hurricanes equipped 18 squadrons. They served in France in 1939 and 1940, with the Advanced Air Striking Force and the Air Component of the British Expeditionary Force, and this brought valuable experience for pilots such as 'Ginger' Lacey, who went on to become key players in the Battle of Britain. Although the Hurricane may have been the 'workhorse' of the Battle in comparison to the 'thoroughbred' Spitfire, it bore the brunt of the fighting and shot down more enemy aircraft than any other form of defence. Nevertheless, the need for heavier armament was becoming clear, and the Mark II Hurricane was developed in response. The Mark IIA retained the eight .303" machine guns of the Mark I, but the IIB mounted twelve guns and could carry bombs or drop tanks externally. The IIC featured four 20mm cannon, and fought on many fronts in several roles, whilst the IID was a tank destroyer armed with two 40mm Vickers Type S anti-tank guns. Many Hurricanes were converted for service with the Royal Navy, fighting over the Atlantic and Mediterranean, and protecting convoys bound for Russia. Other Hurricanes – mostly Mark Is – were launched by catapult from the decks of merchant ships, with their pilots either ditching the aircraft or descending by parachute to await rescue.

Critics of the Hurricane point out that it was not developed in the way that the Spitfire was, but the Typhoon and Tempest – and their operational use – owe much to lessons learned from the Hurricane. The Hurricane IIC was the variant built in the largest numbers – nearly two thirds of those built were IICs or their Canadian derivatives the Marks X, XI, XII and XIIA. The Mark IV, also covered by this manual, was introduced in February 1943. It featured a 'universal armament wing' capable of mounting two 40mm guns, or eight rockets, or 500lb of bombs, or long-range tanks. It was a specialised ground attack version, with extra armour and served in Tunisia, Italy and Burma. The RAF's last Hurricane squadron – No. 6 – operated Hurricane IVs in Palestine until January 1947.

The RAF Museum's Hurricane IIC LF738

The RAF Museum's Hurricane IIC was part of the final production batch, built by Hawker at Langley in 1944. Delivered to No. 22 Maintenance Unit at Silloth on 19 March it did not see front-line service, being issued to No. 1682 Bomber Defence Training Flight at Enstone on 10 April. This unit was responsible for providing training facilities for bomber crews by performing dummy attacks, and was in the process of replacing its Curtiss Tomahawks with Hurricanes. It was disbanded in August 1944 and LF738 was reallocated to No. 22. Operational Training Unit at Wellesbourne Mountford, probably for similar duties. The end of the war meant that fewer aircrew were needed, and the unit disbanded on 24 July 1945.

LF738 was allocated to ground instructional duties at RAF Biggin Hill, and on Sunday 19 September 1954, a drumhead service was held to dedicate the Hurricane – together with Spitfire SL674 – as a permanent memorial to stand outside the station's Battle of Britain chapel. The two aircraft remained there (apart from refurbishment work undertaken at St Athan in 1969 and at Bicester in 1974) until February 1984 when LF738 moved to Rochester to await restoration work by the Medway Aircraft Preservation Society. Many components had been removed over the years, probably to keep the RAF's airworthy Hurricanes flying, and corrosion had taken a heavy toll. Work started in earnest in 1993 and the completed Hurricane, in the colour scheme it wore whist with 1682 BDTF, was handed over to the RAF on 28 June 1995. It has been displayed at the Museum's Cosford site since August 1995.

Section 1:
Leading particulars. Introduction. Pilot's controls and equipment.

LEADING PARTICULARS

Name	Hurricane II
Duty	Day and night fighting
Type	Single seater, single-engined, low-wing monoplane

MAIN DIMENSIONS

Complete aircraft

(Datum line horizontal except where otherwise stated)

Length, approximately	32 ft. 3 in.
Span	40 ft. 0 in.
Ground angle, tail down	10°
Overall heights—	
One blade vertically upwards	12 ft. 0½ in.
One blade vertically downwards	11 ft. 10 in.
One blade vertically upwards, tail down ...	13 ft. 3 in.
One blade vertically downwards, tail down ...	10 ft. 5 in.

Fuselage

Length (propeller shaft to rear fin-post)	28 ft. 10½ in.
Height, maximum	6 ft. 7½ in.
Width, maximum	3 ft. 3¼ in.

Wings

Aerofoil section—at root	Clark Y.H. 19% modified
Aerofoil section—at tip	Clark Y.H. 12·2% modified
Chord at root	8 ft. 0¼ in.
Chord at tip, ignoring washout	3 ft. 11¼ in.
Incidence (aerofoil to fuselage datum lines) ...	2°
Dihedral (outer plane datum lines)	3½°
Sweepback on front spar	3°
Sweepback on leading edge	5° 6′

Centre section

Span (joint pin centres)	9 ft. 1½ in.
Chord	8 ft. 0¼ in.
Incidence (aerofoil to fuselage datum lines) ...	2°
Dihedral	Nil
Sweepback	Nil

Tail plane

Span	11 ft. 0 in.
Chord (maximum), including elevator	4 ft. 2½ in.
▌Incidence (aerofoil to fuselage datum lines) ...	1½°
Dihedral	Nil
Sweepback	Nil

AREAS

Main plane, with ailerons and flaps	257·6 sq. ft.
Ailerons, total	20·4 sq. ft.
Flaps, total	25·11 sq. ft.
Tail plane, with elevator and trimming tabs ...	33·26 sq. ft.
	or
	33·50 sq. ft.
Elevator and trimming tabs	13·46 sq. ft.
	or
	13·70 sq. ft.
Trimming tabs (two), each	0·38 sq. ft.
	or
	0·50 sq. ft.
Fin with rudder and tab	21·89 sq. ft.
	or
	21·98 sq. ft.
Rudder, with tab	13·06 sq. ft.
	or
	13·15 sq. ft.
Tab	0·36 sq. ft.
	or
	0·45 sq. ft.

CONTROL SURFACES—SETTINGS AND RANGE OF MOVEMENT

Tail plane	Fixed
Fin—leading edge offset to port	1½°
Aileron droop (at inner end)	Nil to ¼ in.
Aileron movement	22° up
	21° down
Elevator	27° up
	26° down
Trimming tabs, movable	23° up and down
Trimming tabs, fixed	5° up
Rudder	28° each way
▌Rudder tab—	
Trimming movement	15° port only
Balance movement	20° each way
Flaps	80° down ± 5°
Tolerances on ranges of all movements, except flaps	± 1°

UNDERCARRIAGE

Main wheel units

Type	Two separate shock-absorber struts and pneumatic wheel units retracting inwards and backwards
Track	7 ft. 10 in.

Shock-absorber struts—

Type	Vickers oleo-pneumatic
Air pressure	*See* Sect. 4, Chap. 3
Fluid	Specification D.T.D.44D (Stores Ref. 34A/43 and 141)

Wheels—

Type	A.H.O.10019 or A.H.8123
Tyre	I.V.V.12, I.V.V 13 or I.V.V.17, 8 in. × 10¼ in.
Tube	I.V.V.8
Air pressure	*See* Sect. 4, Chap. 2, fig. 1
Brakes	Dunlop pneumatic

Tail wheel unit

(i) Type	Non-retractable shock-absorber strut with fully castoring pneumatic wheel

Shock-absorber strut—

Type	Dowty compression coil spring

Wheel—

Type	Dunlop A.H.O.5000/IX
Tyre	"Ecta" W.J.11, 4 in. for 3½ in. wheel
Air pressure	*See* Sect. 4, Chap. 2, fig. 1
(ii) Type	Non-retractable shock-absorber strut with fully castoring pneumatic wheel

Shock-absorber strut—

Type	Dowty oleo-pneumatic C.6595 or C.7941
Air pressure	Type C.6595—630 lb./sq. in. (Full extension —no load) Type C.7941—990 lb./sq. in. (Full extension —no load)
Fluid	Specification D.T.D.44D (Stores Ref. 34A/43 and 141)

Wheel—
Type	...	...	...	...	Dunlop A.H.O.5048
Tyre	...	...	...	...	"Ecta" W.M.11. or W.M.14, 4·95 in. for 3½ in. wheel
Air pressure	...	...	...	...	*See* Sect. 4, Chap. 2, fig. 1
(iii) Type	...	...	...	...	Non-retractable shock-absorber strut with fully castoring pneumatic wheel

Shock-absorber strut—
Type	...	...	...	...	Lockheed oleo-pneumatic
Air pressure	...	...	...	...	385 lb./sq. in. (Full extension—no load)
Fluid	...	...	...	...	Specification D.T.D.388 (Stores Ref. 34A/82 and 83)

Wheel—
Type	...	...	...	...	Dunlop A.H.O.5048
Tyre	...	...	...	...	"Ecta" W.M.11, or W.M.14, 4·95 in. for 3½ in. wheel
Air pressure	...	...	...	...	*See* Sect. 4, Chap. 2, fig. 1

ENGINE

Name	...	...	...	...	...	Merlin XX
Type	...	...	...	...	...	12-cylinder 60°, two-speed supercharged, geared, liquid-cooled

Direction of rotation—
Crankshaft	...	...	...	...	Left hand
Propeller shaft	...	...	...	...	Right hand
Fuel and oil	...	...	...	...	*See* A.P.1464, Leaflet C.37

Fuel pumps—
Type	...	...	...	...	EP2
Mk.	...	...	...	...	II–1
Coolant	...	...	...	...	70% distilled water + 30% ethylene-glycol D.T.D.344A (Stores Ref. 33C/559)

PROPELLER

Type	...	...	...	...	...	Rotol variable-pitch external cylinder group (*see* A.P.1538E, Vol. I) or D.H. bracket type (*see* A.P.1538B, Vol. I)
Diameter	...	...	...	...	...	11 ft. 3 in.
Control	...	...	...	...	...	Constant speed
Pitch settings	...	...	...	...	...	*See* relevant Air Publication

Continued on next leaf

TANK CAPACITIES

Fuel -	Each tank		Total	
	Actual	Effective	Actual	Effective
(i) Normal capacity -			97 gals.	94 gals.
Main tanks (2)	34½ gals.	33 gals.		
Reserve tank	28 gals.	28 gals.		
(ii) With fixed long-range tanks (2)	44 gals.	43 gals.	185 gals.	180 gals.
(iii) With jettisonable 45 gal. tanks (2)	45 gals.	43½ gals.	187 gals.	183 gals.
(iv) With jettisonable 90 gal. tanks (2)	90 gals.	90 gals.	277 gals.	274 gals.

Oil -				
(i) Normal capacity, main tank only -			10½ gals.	9 gals.
(ii) With auxiliary tank (in conjunction with jettisonable 90 gal. fuel tanks) -			14½ gals.	12 gals.
Main tank	10½ gals.	8 gals.		
Aux. tank	4 gals.	4 gals.		

OIL DILUTION SYSTEM

Valve .... Stores Ref.5U/1566
Voltage 12
Fuel pressure .... 8 to 10 lb./sq.in.
Size of orifice .... 0.046 in. or 0.089 in.
Jet .... Stores Ref.5U/1561

DE-ICING SYSTEM

Windscreen de-icing -
Tank capacity .... ½ gallon
Fluid .... Specification D.T.D.406A
(Stores Ref.33C/621) or
Ethyl-alcohol B.S.S.3D9
(Stores Ref.33C/720)

INTRODUCTION

1.   The Hurricane II is a single-seater, low wing, cantilever land monoplane with retractable main wheel units and enclosed cockpit.   It is
powered by a Merlin XX engine fitted with a right-hand tractor propeller
of the Rotol or D.H. variable-pitch type with constant-speed control.
The main dimensions of the aeroplane are: span 40 ft., length 32 ft. 3 in.

2.   Hurricanes Mk.IIA, Mk.IIB and Mk.IIC differ mainly in the armament
carried, as follows :-

Mk.IIA	8 Browning guns	(.303 in.)
Mk.IIB	12 Browning guns	(.303 in.)
Mk.IIC	4 Hispano guns	(20 mm.)

The Mk.IIA has the Hurricane I 8-gun stressed-skin main plane, and there
are two versions: the Series I can only be fitted with the 8-gun main
plane, but the Series II has a fuselage incorporating strengthened longerons
which enable conversion to a later Mk. to be made, by substitution of the
appropriate main plane. (<u>Note</u>.- In this publication the Mk.IIA is only
described where it is important to do so, as for example, in the Loading
and C.G.data given in Sect.4, Chap.1.   The 8-gun main plane is practically
identical with the 12-gun main plane if the outboard guns are disregarded;
consequently, description of the IIB gun installation covers the IIA
installation).   In the case of the Mk.IIA Series 2, Mk.IIB and Mk.IIC, two
bombs may be carried, one under each outer plane.

3.   The cockpit is heated indirectly from the radiator circuit and is
totally enclosed under a transparent hood which slides towards the rear for
entry and exit purposes; the pilot's seat is adjustable vertically at any
time; the pilot is protected by armour plating against attack from front
and rear.   An emergency exit panel is provided in the starboard side of
the decking and the sliding hood is jettisonable; a knock-out panel is incorporated in the hood at its port front bottom corner to give clear vision
under difficult conditions.   Flying controls are of the conventional stick
type, with a rudder bar which is adjustable horizontally for leg reach; the
cockpit is fitted with a normal set of instruments as well as with those
necessary for instrument flying.

4.   The fuselage structure consists of four tubular steel longerons, of
steel and light-alloy tubes, and plan and bulkhead bracing of tubes and
swaged wires; the tubular members are rolled to rectangular section in the
vicinity of the joints.   The engine and front fuselage are covered with
light-alloy panels, the decking with fabric-covered plywood and the rear
fuselage with fabric on wooden formers and stringers.

5.   The cantilever main plane is built in three sections: port and
starboard outer planes and centre section, the last-named being integral
with the fuselage and faired into it; the underside of the centre section is
flush with the bottom of the fuselage.   The outer planes are of the
stressed-skin type, and those of the Mk.IIA are interchangeable with
Hurricane I stressed-skin outer planes.   The fabric-covered mass-balanced
ailerons have a differential action and hydraulically-operated split flaps
are fitted to the trailing edges of the outer planes and centre section;
the flaps extend between the inner ends of the ailerons except at the
position of the radiator fairing.

F.S./1

6.   The tail unit components are all of metal construction and are
fabric-covered.   The non-adjustable cantilever tail plane is attached to
the top rear end of the fuselage;   longitudinal trimming is obtained by
elevator tabs adjusted from the cockpit through an irreversible gear
mounted within each horn balanced elevator.   The rudder has a small horn
balance, which houses the mass-balanced weight, and it is fitted with a
tab controllable from the cockpit and also operated automatically
from the rudder hinge so as to produce a servo action.   The fin is offset
to counteract engine and propeller torque.   The tail unit surfaces are
faired into the fuselage and into each other, no external bracing being
employed.   Some aeroplanes have slightly larger elevator and rudder tabs
than others.

7.   The main wheel units consist of two oleo-pneumatic shock-absorber
struts which retract inwards and backwards into a well between the centre-
section spars, the units being hydraulically operated and fitted with
mechanical locking and electrical indicating devices; an audible warning
device operates when the units are not locked down and the throttle is
less than one-third open.   Each shock-absorber strut carries a stub axle
with a medium-pressure pneumatic wheel fitted with a pneumatically-
operated brake controlled by a lever on the control column;   differential
action of the brakes, in conjunction with the rudder bar, is provided.
When on the ground, the tail is supported by a non-retractable shock-
absorber strut which carries a fully-castoring and self-centring wheel
with a self-earthing tyre.

8.   The main fuel tanks are housed within the centre section between
the spars, one on each side of the fuselage, and, above the longerons, a
reserve fuel tank is carried between the firewall and the instrument
panel;   these tanks are protected by self-sealing coverings.   Long-range
fuel tanks can be fitted if required, one under each outer plane;   they
can be of either operational or non-operational fixed type or of
jettisonable type.   The oil tank forms the port leading edge of the
centre section and an auxiliary oil tank is fitted when the larger
jettisonable-type fuel tanks are installed.   To prevent aeration of the
fuel and oil, air pressure is permanently maintained in the oil tank and
is applied to the fuel tanks at high altitudes.   A combined oil and coolant
radiator is hung beneath the fuselage behind the main-wheels well and is
contained in a low-velocity cowling duct, which has a flap shutter hand-
operated from the cockpit.

9.   In every case the guns carried fire forward and are mounted in the
outer planes, half the total number in each.   They are pneumatically-
controlled from a single pushbutton on the control column spade grip.

10.   A remotely-controlled radio-telephone transmitter-receiver is
situated behind the pilot's seat;   on early aeroplanes a flare
launching tube is fitted behind this instrument.   A mounting for an

upward-firing recognition device is incorporated adjacent to the aerial
mast in the rear fuselage.   Oxygen equipment is also installed and a
camera gun (pneumatically-operated from the gun-firing button on the
control column) is mounted in the leading edge of the starboard outer
plane.   The electrical installation, by means of an engine-driven
generator, provides power for navigation, identification, landing,
formation-keeping (if fitted) and cockpit lamps, fuel gauge, engine
starting, heated pressure head, radio supply, reflector gun sight,
heated clothing and camera gun.   Windscreen de-icing equipment is
fitted, and port fires are installed to enable the pilot to destroy the
aeroplane should circumstances necessitate.

SECTION I

PILOT'S CONTROLS AND EQUIPMENT

LIST OF CONTENTS

INTRODUCTION

1.   The Hurricane Mks. II and IV are each fitted with a
Merlin 20 engine and a Rotol 35° propeller. The
Mks. IID and IV are low-level attack versions of the
earlier Marks and are equipped to carry various
alternative armaments. The aircraft controls,
including the undercarriage, flaps and brakes are
identical with those on Mark I aircraft.

FUEL, OIL AND COOLANT SYSTEMS

2.   Fuel tanks (See Figs.5 and 5A). -

(i) Main and Reserve tanks. - The main tanks are housed
within the centre section, one on each side of the
fuselage, and a reserve tank is carried between the
fireproof bulkhead and the instrument panel. Fuel is
delivered to the engine by an engine-driven pump.
These tanks are self-sealing and their effective
capacities are as follows:

            Main tanks: 33 gallons each.
            Reserve tank: 28 gallons.

To meet the possibility of engine cutting due to fuel
boiling in warm weather at high altitudes, these
tanks can be pressurised (operative above 20,000 feet).
Pressurising, however, impairs the self-sealing of
tanks and should, therefore, be used only when the
fuel pressure warning light comes on, or when
auxiliary drop tanks are used (see below).

(ii) Auxiliary tanks: When not fitted with under-wing
armament or containers, a pair of auxiliary tanks may
be carried, one under each wing. The types of tank
and their capacities are as follows:

            Fixed: 44 gallons each.
            Drop: 45 or 90 gallons each.

With the exception of some fixed tanks which are used
for combat duties, these tanks are non-self-sealing.
Fuel in the fixed tanks is delivered to the main
tanks by electrically driven immersed pumps, but
fuel in the drop tanks is supplied direct to the
engine fuel pump by air pressure.

3.   Fuel cocks.-

   (i) The main fuel cock control (48) on the left-hand
       side of the cockpit has a spring safety plate which
       prevents the fuel supply being turned off inadver-
       tently. The control can only be turned to the OFF
       position whilst the safety plate is held depressed.

  (ii) A switch for the electric pump in each fixed auxil-
       iary tank is fitted on the left-hand side of the
       cockpit, either just above the elevator trimming tab
       control, or on the lower part of the electrical panel.

 (iii) The fuel cock control (73) and jettison lever (74)
       for the drop tanks are mounted together on the right-
       hand side of the cockpit, below the windscreen de-
       icing pump. The cock control has three positions:
       OFF, PORT and STARBOARD. The pressurising cock must
       be turned on when the tanks are used. The jettison
       lever is pulled down to jettison both tanks
       simultaneously, but cannot be moved until the fuel
       cock is set to OFF. When the lever is operated, the
       air pressure supply is automatically cut off.

  (iv) The tank pressurising cock (22) is fitted on the
       left-hand side of the cockpit, below the throttle
       quadrant, and is marked ATMOSPHERE and PRESSURE.

4.   Fuel contents gauge.- A gauge (49) on the right-
     hand side of the instrument panel indicates
     selectively the contents of each of the three main
     tanks. A switch unit (48), comprising a combined
     selector and pushbutton, is fitted above the gauge.

5.   Fuel pressure warning light.- The warning light (50)
     on the right-hand side of the instrument panel comes
     on if the pressure drops to 6 lb/sq.in.

6.   Oil system.- The self-sealing oil tank, which has
     an effective capacity of 9 gallons, forms the port
     leading edge of the centre section. The oil passes
     through a filter before entering the engine and
     then through a cooler inside the coolant radiator.
     Pressure (54) and temperature (53) gauges are fitted
     on the instrument panel. When 90-gallon fuel drop
     tanks are carried, an auxiliary oil tank of 4
     gallons capacity is fitted behind the seat, the cock
     control for which is on the left-hand side of the
     seat, above the radiator flap control quadrant.

7.   Coolant system.- The system is thermostatically controlled, the radiator being by-passed until the coolant reaches a certain temperature. The header tank is mounted on the fireproof bulkhead and is fitted with a pressure relief valve. The air flow through the radiator is controlled by a flap lever in the cockpit.

MAIN SERVICES

8.   Hydraulic system.- An engine-driven hydraulic pump supplies the power for operating the undercarriage and flaps. The system is automatic, selection of the desired operation of the undercarriage or flaps, by means of the selector lever, being sufficient to commence the operation. A handpump (71) is provided for use in the event of engine failure or engine-driven pump failure.

9.   Electrical system.- A 12-volt generator, controlled by a switch (3) on the left-hand side of the cockpit, supplies an accumulator which in turn supplies the whole of the electrical installation. There is a voltmeter (31) on the left-hand side of the cockpit. and a red light (36) marked POWER FAILURE on the instrument panel comes on when the generator is not charging the accumulator.

10.   Pneumatic system.- The wheel brakes and the gun-firing mechanism are operated pneumatically, air being supplied by an engine-driven compressor and stored in a cylinder at a maximum pressure of 300 lb/sq.in.

AIRCRAFT CONTROLS

11.   Flying controls.- The control column is of the spade-grip pattern and incorporates a gun-firing pushbutton and the brake lever. The rudder bar is adjustable for leg reach by means of a star-wheel midway between the two pedals.

12.   Trimming tabs.- The elevator trimming tabs are controlled by a handwheel (24) on the left-hand side of the cockpit and an indicator is fitted next to it. Forward rotation of the hand-wheel corrects tail heaviness. The automatic balance tab on the rudder can be set for trimming purposes by means of a small control wheel (23) on the left-hand side of the cockpit, which is turned clockwise to apply right rudder.

13. <u>Undercarriage and flap control</u>.- The selector lever
(76) for the undercarriage and flaps is on the
right-hand side of the cockpit and works in a gate,
having a neutral position and an UP and DOWN
position for both undercarriage and flaps, the
positions for operating the flaps being outboard.
The catch on the side of the lever must be pressed in
order to release it for movement from an operative
position, but the lever can be moved from the neutral
position without first releasing the catch. To
obviate inadvertent selection on the ground of the
wheels up position, a safety catch (77) is provided
on the gate which must be turned in a clockwise
direction to permit entry of the selector lever into
the wheels UP slot. For emergency lowering of the
undercarriage see Para.35.

14. <u>Undercarriage indicator</u>.- The electrical indicator
(41) is on the left-hand side of the instrument panel
and has duplicate pairs of lamps, the green lamps
indicating when the undercarriage is locked in the
DOWN position, and the red lamps when the undercarriage is fully retracted and locked. There are
two switches to the left of the indicator, the left-
hand one (38) being the ON-OFF switch for the green
lamps, and the right-hand one (39) being the change-
over switch for the duplicate sets of lamps. A
dimmer switch is provided in the centre of the
indicator. When the undercarriage is retracted, the
wheels are visible through two small windows in the
bottom of the cockpit.

15. <u>Undercarriage warning light</u>.- A red light on the
instrument panel comes on at any time when the
throttle lever is less than one-third open and the
undercarriage is not locked down. When the throttle
is opened again or the undercarriage is lowered
the light goes out.

16. <u>Flap indicator</u>.- This (72) is mechanically operated,
the pointer moving along a graduated scale marked UP
and DOWN at its extremities. It is situated
immediately below the hydraulic selector lever.

17. <u>Wheel brakes</u>.- The brake lever is fitted on the
control column spade-grip and a catch for retaining
it in the on position for parking is fitted below
the lever pivot. A triple pressure gauge, showing
the air pressure in the pneumatic system cylinder
and at each brake, is mounted forward of the foot
of the control column.

18.   <u>Flying control locking gear</u>.- The locking struts,
        interference bar and bracket are stowed in a canvas
        bag in the starboard side of the wireless bay. The
        bracket clips on to·the control column, just below
        the spade grip, for locking of the aileron control
        and the two struts, attached to the bracket by
        shackles, lock the rudder bar and control column.
        The spring loaded interference bar fits on to the
        bracket and is inserted in a slot in the back of the
        seat.

        ENGINE CONTROLS

19.   <u>Throttle</u>.- The throttle lever (7) works in a slot in
        the decking shelf on the left-hand side of the cock-
        pit. The take-off position is gated. There is a
        friction adjuster (16) on the inboard end of the
        lever spindle. The mixture control is fully
        automatic and there is no pilot's control lever.

20.   <u>Boost control cut-out</u>.- The automatic boost control
        may be cut out by pulling the knob (34) on the left-
        hand side of the instrument panel.

21.   <u>Propeller control</u>.- The speed control lever (10) on
        the left-hand side of the cockpit varies the governed
        rpm from 3,000 down to 1,800. A friction adjuster
        is fitted on the inboard side of the control.

22.   <u>Supercharger control</u>.- The push-pull control (17)
        is fitted below the left-hand side of the
        instrument panel, and must be pushed in for low
        (M) gear and pulled out for high (S) gear.

23.   <u>Radiator flap control</u>.- The airflow through the
        coolant radiator and oil cooler is controlled by a
        lever (26) on the left-hand side of the pilot's
        seat. In order to release the lever for operation
        the thumb-button must be depressed.

24.   <u>Slow-running cut-out</u>.- The control on the
        carburettor is operated by pulling out the knob
        (64) immediately to the right of the undercarriage
        and flap selector lever.

25.   <u>Cylinder priming pump</u>.- The priming pump (59)
        is fitted below the right-hand side of the
        instrument panel.

26. **Engine starting.** - The starter and booster coil pushbuttons (32 & 33) are to the left of the ignition switches (58) on the instrument panel. An external supply socket for the starter motor is accessible through a removable panel in the starboard engine cowling, and two handles for hand starting are stowed in the undercarriage wheel recess under the centre section.

27. **Oil dilution.** - The pushbutton (4) for operating the solenoid valve is on the left-hand side of the cockpit.

    OTHER CONTROLS

28. **Gun controls.** - The machine guns and cannon are normally fired by the pushbutton on the control column spade grip. The two 40 mm guns on Mk.IID and IV aircraft are fired electro-pneumatically by the pushbutton in the throttle lever; they cannot be fired, however, until the master switch (11) on the decking shelf, forward of the throttle quadrant, is switched on. The cocking lever (28) on the electrical panel to the left of the seat should be pushed down in the event of a misfire.

29. **R.P.controls.** - The projectiles are fired by the pushbutton in the throttle lever and a selector switch (40) below the left-hand side of the windscreen enables them to be fired in PAIRS or as a SALVO. They must not be fired with the flaps lowered.

30. **Bomb controls.** - There are two selector switches and two nose and tail fusing switches on a small panel (67) on the right-hand side of the cockpit. The bombs are released by the pushbutton in the throttle lever.

31. **S.C.I. controls.** - These are operated by the pushbutton in the throttle lever and there is a container jettison pushbutton (63) on the right-hand side of the cockpit.

32. **Camera gun control.** - The camera gun operates only when the guns and cannon or the R.P. are fired, or when the lower pushbutton on the control column spade grip is depressed.

33.   **Landing lamps.-** The landing lamps, one in the
leading edge of each wing, are controlled by a two-
way switch (15) to the left of the instrument panel,
which enables either lamp to be used; both lamps are
off when the switch is in the upright position. A
dipping lever (5) on the left-hand side of the cockpit can be held in any position by tightening the
knurled wheel; when the wheel is unscrewed, the lever
is pulled aft into the UP position by a return spring
in each of the lamp units.

34.   **Recognition device.-** The flares are selected and
released by a single lever (25) immediately aft of
the trimming tab control. The slot is marked SELECT
and FIRE.

     EMERGENCIES

35.   **Undercarriage emergency operation.-**

   (i) In the event of failure of the engine-driven
hydraulic pump, the undercarriage may be lowered by
moving the selector lever to the WHEELS DOWN position
and then operating the handpump.

   (ii) If the handpump fails to lower the undercarriage the
selector lever should still be left in the WHEELS
DOWN position and the red-painted foot pedal (21),
outboard of the port heelrest, should be firmly
pushed forward. The wheels should then fall and lock
down under their own weight.

  (iii) If difficulty is experienced in operating the undercarriage and flap selector lever it may be overcome
by first selecting the opposite to that which is
required. If, for example, the selection of undercarriage down is found to be difficult, the lever
should first be moved into the undercarriage up
position and then immediately moved to the down
position.

36.   **Hood jettisoning.-** To jettison the hood the lever aft
of the radiator flap control should be pulled sharply
forward and upwards. If the hood does not readily
leave the aircraft it should be assisted by pushing it
upwards, or failing that, by releasing the emergency
exit panel (see below) in addition to operating the
jettison control.
    <u>Note</u>: When jettisoning the hood it is advisable to
       lower one's head as far as possible so as to
       avoid injury when it leaves the aircraft.

37.   Emergency exit panel.- The large detachable panel
      on the starboard side of the cockpit is secured by
      horizontal spring-loaded plungers and a bolt
      operated by the cockpit hood. To jettison the panel,
      the hood must first be fully opened and the release
      lever (66) then moved aft and upwards.

38.   Abandoning by parachute.- When abandoning the
      aircraft by parachute it is important to decrease
      speed and then dive over the side immediately. The
      pilot must not stand on the seat and delay in
      jumping or he will hit either the aerial mast or
      the tailplane.

39.   Forced landing.- In the event of having to make a
      forced landing the glide may be lengthened consider-
      ably by moving the propeller speed control fully
      back and gliding at about 130 mph IAS. With under-
      carriage and flaps up the gliding angle at speeds of
      120-140 mph IAS is very flat.

40.   Ditching (See A.P.2095, Pilot's Notes General)

   (i) In general, the pilot should if possible abandon the
       aircraft by parachute.

  (ii) In the event of having to ditch, auxiliary drop
       tanks, bombs, or containers (if fitted) should be
       jettisoned and the following procedure should be
       observed:

       (a) The cockpit hood should be jettisoned.

       (b) Flaps should be lowered fully in order to reduce
           landing speed as much as possible.

       (c) The undercarriage should be retracted.

       (d) Safety harness should be kept on, with straps
           tight, and the R/T plug disconnected.

       (e) The engine, if available should be used to help
           make the touch-down in a tail-down attitude at
           as low a speed as possible.

       (f) When about to touch the water a normal banked
           turn, with full rudder, should be made so as to
           prevent "hooking" the radiator into the water.

41.   First-aid outfit.- The first-aid outfit is attached
        to the inside of a detachable panel on the port side
        of the cockpit and is accessible by kicking in the
        panel, breaking the stringers, and tearing the
        fabric.

42.   Crowbar.- A crowbar, for use in an emergency, is
        stowed in clips to the right of the seat.

KEY TO FIG.1

1. Radio contactor master switch.
2. Cockpit light dimmer switch.
3. Generator switch.
4. Oil dilution pushbutton.
5. Landing lamp control lever.
6. Oxygen supply cock.
7. Throttle lever (incorporating pushbutton).
8. Socket for footage indicator plug.
9. Wedge plate for camera gun footage indicator.
10. Propeller speed control.
11. Cannon master switch.
12. Compass light dimmer switch.
13. Cockpit light.
14. Cockpit light dimmer switch.
15. Landing lamp switch.
16. Friction adjuster.
17. Supercharger control.
18. Fuel cock control.
19. T.R.9D contactor switch.
20. Radio contactor.
21. Undercarriage emergency release lever.
22. Fuel tank pressurising control.
23. Rudder trimming tab control.
24. Elevator trimming tab control.
25. Recognition device selector lever.
26. Radiator flap control lever.
27. Heated clothing socket.
28. Cannon cocking lever.
29. Microphone/telephone socket.
30. Hood catch control.
31. Voltmeter.

COCKPIT – PORT SIDE

FIG
1

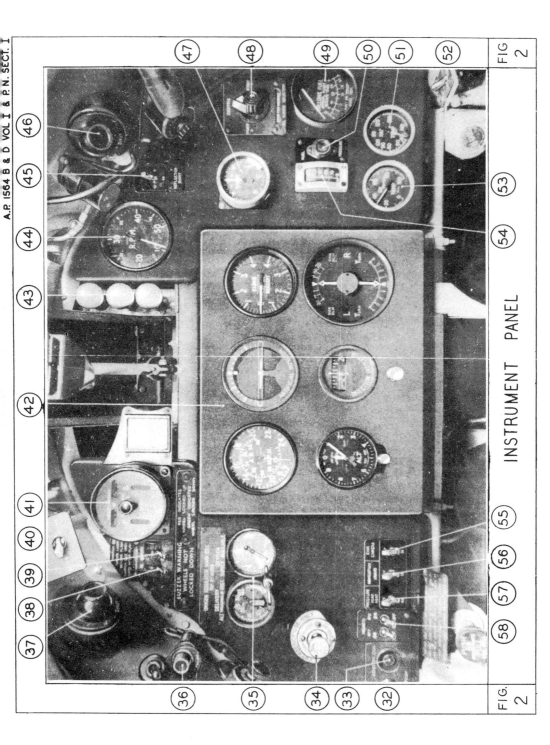

INSTRUMENT PANEL

FIG. 2

FIG 2

KEY TO FIG.2

32.   Engine starter pushbutton.
33.   Booster coil pushbutton.
34.   Boost control cut-out.
35.   Oxygen regulator.
36.   Power failure warning light.
37.   Cockpit ventilator.
38.   Undercarriage indicator ON-OFF switch.
39.   Undercarriage indicator change-over switch.
40.   R.P. selector switch.
41.   Undercarriage indicator.
42.   Instrument flying panel.
43.   Reflector sight spare lamps.
44.   Engine speed indicator.
45.   Reflector sight switch.
46.   Cockpit ventilator.
47.   Boost gauge.
48.   Fuel contents gauge selector switch.
49.   Fuel contents gauge.
50.   Fuel pressure warning light.
51.   Radiator temperature gauge.
52.   Beam approach master switch.
53.   Oil temperature gauge.
54.   Oil pressure gauge.
55.   Camera gun switch.
56.   Navigation lights switch.
57.   Pressure head heater switch.
58.   Ignition switches.

KEY TO FIG.3

59. Cylinder priming pump.
60. Cockpit light.
61. Cockpit light dimmer switch.
62. Signalling switch box.
63. Container jettison pushbutton.
64. Slow-running cut-out.
65. Windscreen de-icing pump.
66. Emergency exit panel jettison lever.
67. Bomb fusing and selector switches.
68. Sutton harness release.
69. I.F.F. master switch.
70. I.F.F. pushbuttons.
71. Hydraulic handpump.
72. Flap indicator.
73. Drop tank fuel cock control.
74. Drop tank jettison control.
75. Seat adjustment lever.
76. Undercarriage and flap selector lever.
77. Undercarriage selector safety catch.

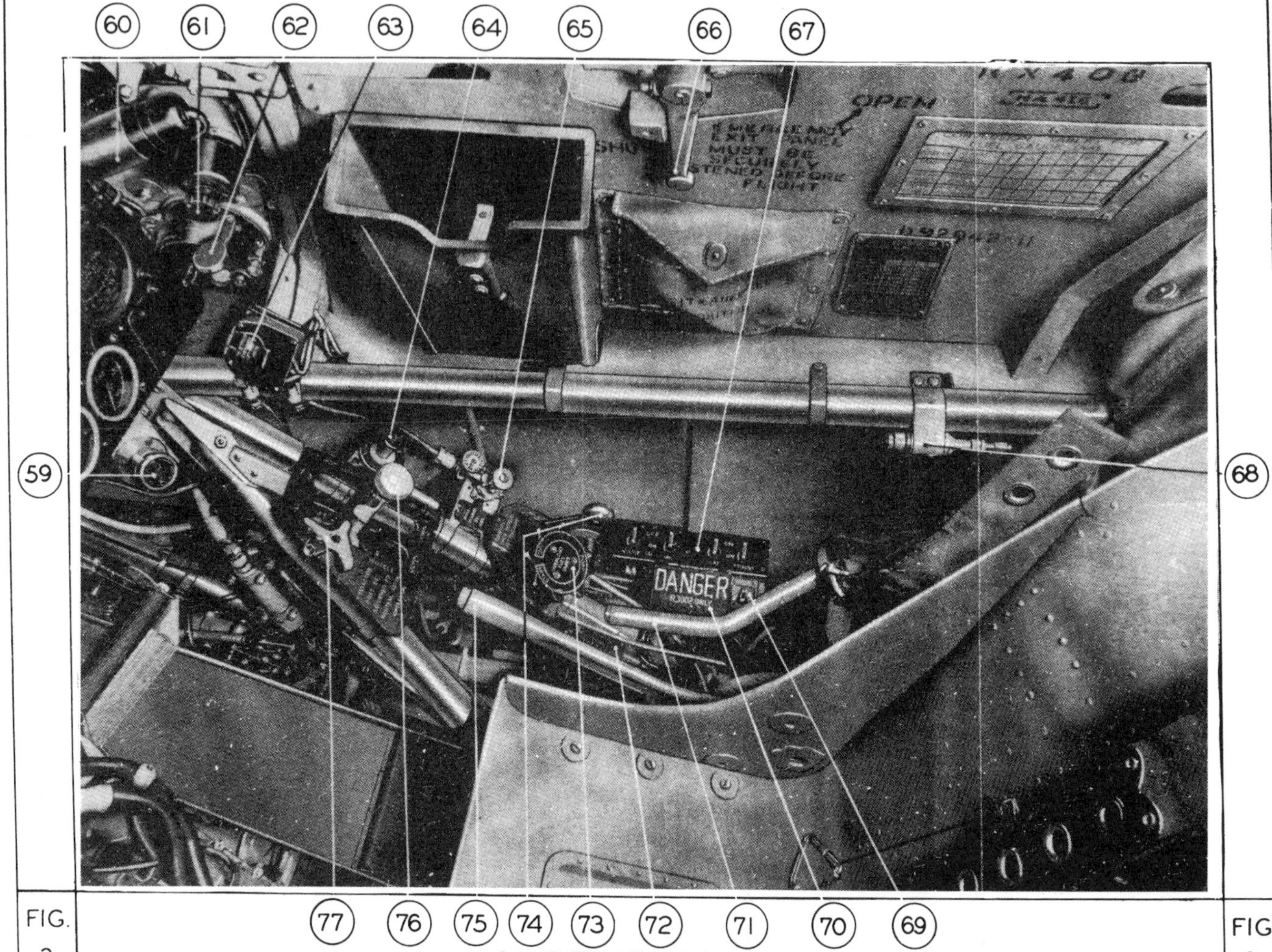

COCKPIT - STARBOARD SIDE

FIG. 3

FIG. 3

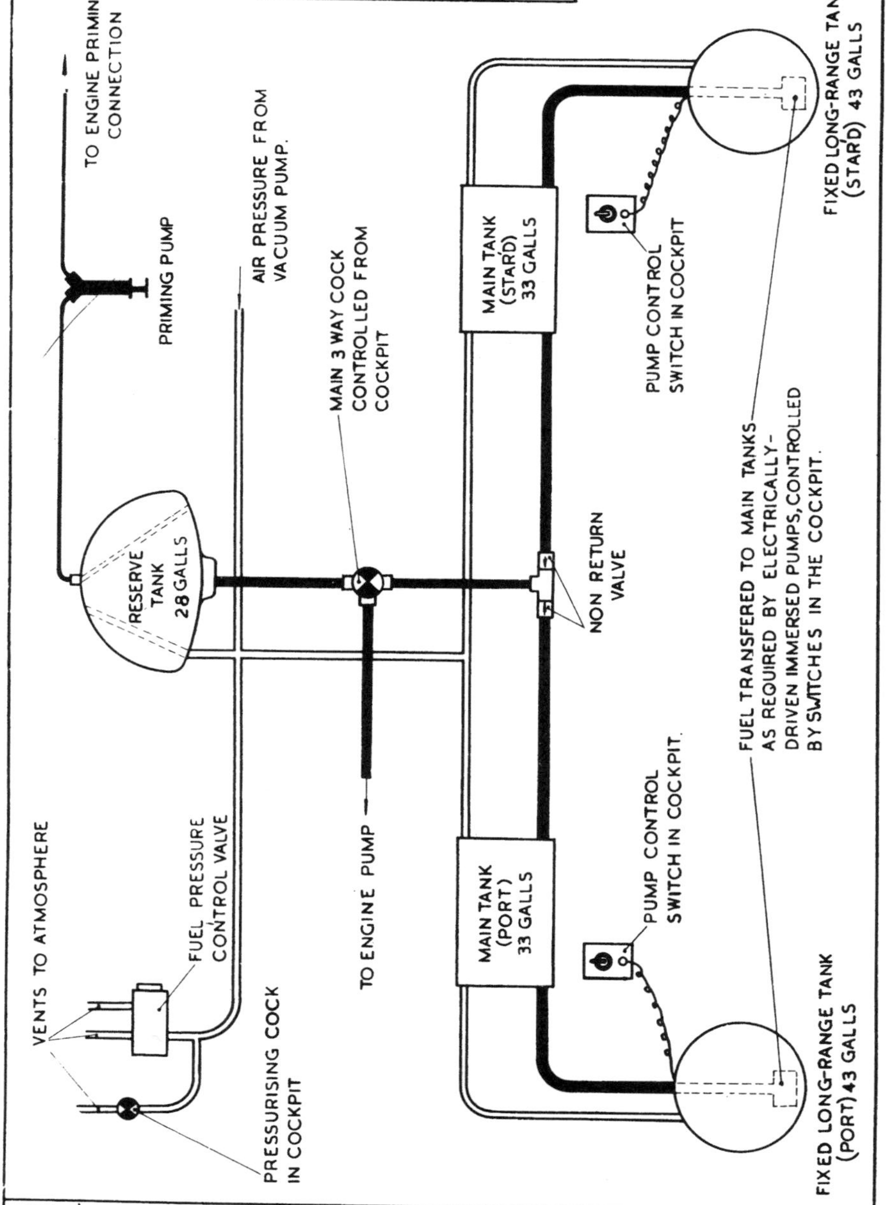

A.P.1564B VOL.I SECT.I.

TO ENGINE PRIMING CONNECTION

PRIMING PUMP

AIR PRESSURE FROM VACUUM PUMP.

MAIN 3 WAY COCK CONTROLLED FROM COCKPIT

RESERVE TANK 28 GALLS

VENTS TO ATMOSPHERE

FUEL PRESSURE CONTROL VALVE

TO ENGINE PUMP

PRESSURISING COCK IN COCKPIT

MAIN TANK (STAR'D) 33 GALLS

PUMP CONTROL SWITCH IN COCKPIT

FIXED LONG-RANGE TANK (STAR'D) 43 GALLS

NON RETURN VALVE

FUEL TRANSFERED TO MAIN TANKS AS REQUIRED BY ELECTRICALLY-DRIVEN IMMERSED PUMPS, CONTROLLED BY SWITCHES IN THE COCKPIT.

MAIN TANK (PORT) 33 GALLS

PUMP CONTROL SWITCH IN COCKPIT.

FIXED LONG-RANGE TANK (PORT) 43 GALLS

FIG. 5

FUEL SYSTEM DIAGRAM —
WITH FIXED LONG-RANGE TANKS.

FIG. 5

F.S/11

A.P. 1564 B | VOL. 1 | SECT I.

TO ENGINE PRIMING CONNECTION

PRIMING PUMP

JETTISONABLE TANK (STAR'D) 44½ OR 90 GALLS

MAIN TANK (STAR'D) 33 GALLS

AIR PRESSURE FROM VACUUM PUMP

NON RETURN VALVES

COCK INTER-CONNECTED WITH TANK JETTISON LEVER

FUEL FORCED OUT OF THE JETTISONABLE TANKS BY AIR FROM THE TANK PRESSURISING SYSTEM

RESERVE TANK 28 GALLS

MAIN 3 WAY COCK CONTROLLED FROM COCKPIT

TO ENGINE PUMP

MAIN TANK (PORT) 33 GALLS

JETTISONABLE TANK FUEL CONTROL COCK

VENTS TO ATMOSPHERE

FUEL PRESSURE CONTROL VALVE

PRESSURISING COCK IN COCKPIT

JETTISONABLE TANK (PORT) 44½ OR 90 GALLS

| FIG. 5A | FUEL SYSTEM DIAGRAM-WITH JETTISONABLE LONG-RANGE TANKS | FIG. 5A |

Section 2: Handling and flying notes for pilot.

SECTION 2

HANDLING AND FLYING NOTES FOR PILOT

1.   ENGINE DATA: MERLIN XX

   (i) <u>Fuel</u>:   100 octane only.

  (ii) <u>Oil</u>:   See A.P.1464/C.37.

 (iii) <u>Engine limitations</u>:

		R.p.m.	Boost lb/sq.in.	Temp. ^{o}C Clnt.	Oil
MAX.TAKE-OFF TO 1,000 FEET	M	3,000	+12	–	–
MAX.CLIMBING 1 HR. LIMIT	M) S)	2,850	+ 9	125	90
MAX.RICH CONTINUOUS	M) S)	2,650	+ 7	105^{1}	90
MAX.WEAK CONTINUOUS	M) S)	2,650	+ 4	105^{1}	90
COMBAT 5 MINS LIMIT	M S	3,000 3,000	+14* +16*	135 135	105 105

<u>Note</u>:

   * Combat boost is obtained by operating the
boost control cut-out.

   ^{1} 115°C coolant temperature is permitted
for short periods at cruising rpm.

OIL PRESSURE: NORMAL: 60-80 lb/sq.in.
                                 MINIMUM: 45   "

MINM. TEMP. FOR TAKE-OFF: OIL: 15°C
                         COOLANT: 60°C

FUEL PRESSURE: 8-10 lb/sq.in.

2.   FLYING LIMITATIONS

(i) Maximum speeds (mph IAS):

Diving:	390
Undercarriage down:	120
Flaps down:	120

(ii) At AUWs in excess of 8,750 lbs. care is necessary in ground handling and the aircraft should be taken off only from concrete or equivalent runways.

(iii) Spinning is prohibited at all times of Mark IID and IV aircraft, and of Mark IIA, B and C aircraft only when carrying 90-gallon drop tanks, bombs, SCI, containers, or RP.

(iv) Aerobatics are prohibited and violent manoeuvres must be avoided when carrying 90-gallon drop tanks, bombs, SCI, containers, or RP (Mk.IIA, B and C aircraft only).

(v) Aircraft carrying drop tanks should not be dived.

(vi) Mark III containers must not be dropped at speeds in excess of 150 mph IAS and at heights lower than 500 feet.

(vii) Bombs should be jettisoned and RP fired, if possible, before landing.

3.   POSITION ERROR CORRECTIONS

From	100	120	150	180	210	270	mph	IAS
To	120	150	180	210	270	320	mph	IAS
Add	4	2	0				mph	
Subtract			0	2	4	6	mph	

4.   MANAGEMENT OF FUEL AND OIL SYSTEMS

(i) The Main Tanks should be used first, but if the Reserve Tank is used before the Main Tanks, the following precautions must be observed:

(a) Change over to MAIN TANKS ON before emptying the Reserve tank.

(b) If this has not been done and the engine cuts, close the throttle (to avoid over-revving when the engine picks up) and change over to MAIN TANKS ON at once.

(c) In order to displace air drawn into the fuel
system from the empty reserve tank, the engine
must be windmilled at high speed, when it will
pick up after a few seconds. It is emphasised
that the pick-up will not be immediate after
the change-over.

(ii) If fitted with fixed auxiliary tanks:

(a) Start and take-off in the normal way on the
main tanks.

(b) As soon as the contents gauge registers only
5 gallons in the main tanks, switch ON the
auxiliary tank pumps.

(c) Switch OFF the pumps immediately the contents
gauge registers 25 gallons.

(d) When the contents of the MAIN TANKS are again
reduced to 5 gallons, switch ON the pumps until
the contents gauge again registers 25 gallons
and then switch OFF the pumps. The auxiliary
tanks will then be practically empty.

(iii) If fitted with drop tanks:

(a) Start and take-off in the normal way on the
main tanks.

(b) At a safe height (say 2,000 feet) change over
to a drop tank and turn the pressurising cock
to PRESSURE. Turn OFF the main tanks.

(c) When the drop tank is empty and the fuel
pressure warning light comes on, change-over
to the second drop tank and at the same time
turn ON the reserve tank, which should still
be full. This will enable the engine to
pick up more quickly and when it does so,
turn OFF the reserve tank and change-over to
the second drop tank.

(d) When the second drop tank is empty and the
fuel pressure warning light comes on, turn
ON the main tanks and turn OFF the drop tank.
If the engine does not pick up on the main
tanks, prime the system by using the reserve
tank as before.

(e) The cock for the auxiliary oil tank (if
fitted) should be turned on about $3\frac{1}{2}$ hours
after take-off, but not before this time.
After having been turned on, the cock cannot
afterwards be turned off during flight.

(f) On reinforcing flights, under maximum range
engine conditions (2,650 rpm and +4 lb/sq.in.
boost on climb to height, and level flight at
190 mph IAS reducing to 160 mph IAS after
jettisoning tanks) oil consumption is consider-
ably reduced and, therefore, the auxiliary oil
tank should not be turned on until after
approximately 5 hours flight, when there will be
sufficient space in the main tank to accommodate
the extra 4 gallons. The normal oil tank should
be filled to 8 gallons only.

5.   PRELIMINARIES

(i) If fitted with R.P. and a drop tank or A.P. and
a bomb, the aircraft should be trimmed carefully
to relieve stick load.
The recommended aileron tab setting is neutral
at full load. Then with a drop tank fitted
under the port wing, changes in load will cause
the following alterations in trim:

Tank empty: Slightly right wing low
Tank empty and R.P. fired: Trim satisfactory.
Tank jettisoned and
          R.P. fired: Slightly right wing low
Tank jettisoned,
          R.P. not fired: Right wing low.

(ii) Switch on the undercarriage indicator and check
green lights. Test the change-over switch.

(iii) See that the short (lower) arm of the hydraulic
selector safety catch is across the wheels up slot
of the gate.

(iv) Check that the throttle pushbutton master switch
is OFF.

(v) Check contents of fuel tanks. If fitted with
auxiliary tanks see that the pump switches or
cock control are OFF.

(vi) Test operation of flying controls.

(vii) See that the cockpit hood is locked open.

6.   STARTING THE ENGINE AND WARMING UP

   (i) Set fuel cock to MAIN TANKS ON.

   (ii) Set the controls as follows:

Throttle	-	½ inch open
Propeller control	-	Fully forward
Supercharger control	-	MODERATE
Radiator shutter	-	OPEN

   (iii) If an external priming connection is fitted, high
         volatility fuel (Stores ref. 34A/111) should be used
         for priming at air temperatures below freezing.
         Work the priming pump until the fuel reaches the
         priming nozzles; this may be judged by a sudden
         increase in resistance.

   (iv) Switch ON the ignition and press the starter and
        booster coil pushbuttons. Turning periods must not
        exceed 20 seconds, with a 30 seconds wait between
        each. Work the priming pump as rapidly and vigorously
        as possible while the engine is being turned; it
        should start after the following number of strokes
        if cold:

Air temperature °C:	+30	+20	+10	0	-10	-20
Normal fuel:		3	4	7	12	
High volatility fuel:				4	8	18

   (v) At temperatures below freezing it will probably be
       necessary to continue priming after the engine has
       fired and until it picks up on the carburettor.

   (vi) Release the starter button as soon as the engine
        starts and as soon as it is running satisfactorily
        release the booster coil pushbutton and screw down
        the priming pump.

   (vii) Open up slowly to 1,000 rpm, then warm up at
         this speed.

7.   TESTING THE ENGINE AND INSTALLATIONS

       While warming up:

   (i) Check temperatures and pressures, and test operation
       of hydraulic system by lowering and raising the flaps.

<u>After warming up, with two men on the tail:</u>

<u>Note</u>: The following tests constitute a comprehensive check to be carried out after inspection or repair, or at the pilot's discretion. In normal circumstances they may be reduced in accordance with local instructions.

(ii) Open up to +4 lb/sq.in. boost and exercise and check operation of the two-speed supercharger. Rpm should fall when S ratio is engaged.

(iii) At +4 lb/sq.in. boost exercise and check operation of the constant speed propeller. Rpm should fall to 1,800 with the control fully back. Check that the generator is charging; the power failure light should be out and the voltage 14 or over.

(iv) With the propeller control fully forward open the throttle up to +12 lb/sq.in. boost and check static boost and rpm which should be 3,000.

(v) Throttle back to +9 lb/sq.in. boost and test each magneto in turn. The drop should not exceed 150 rpm.

(vi) Before taxying check brake pressure (100 lb/sq.in. minm.) and pneumatic supply pressure (220 lb/sq.in.).

8.   CHECK LIST BEFORE TAKE-OFF

T - Trimming tabs	- Rudder: Fully right Elevator: Neutral
P - Propeller control	- Fully forward
F - Fuel	- Check contents of main tanks.
	- MAIN TANKS ON
	- Aux. tank cock or pumps - OFF
	- Pressurising cock - ATMOSPHERE
F - Flaps	- UP (28° down - two divs. on indicator - for shortest take-off run).
Supercharger control	- MODERATE
Radiator shutter	- Fully OPEN

9.   TAKE-OFF

(i) Open the throttle slowly to the gate, or fully if full take-off boost is necessary.

    (ii) Any tendency to swing can be counteracted by the
rudder. When fitted with 2 x 500 lb. bombs the
tendency to swing left is slightly more pronounced.

   (iii) After raising the undercarriage return the selector
lever to neutral, and retrim nose heavy.

   (iv) Do not start to climb before a speed of 140 mph IAS
is attained.

10.   CLIMBING

    (i) The speeds for maximum rate of climb are as follows:

Up to 16,000 feet:	140 mph IAS
At 21,000 feet:	135 mph IAS
At 26,000 feet:	130 mph IAS
At 31,000 feet:	125 mph IAS

       Change to S ratio when the boost has fallen by
5 lb/sq.in.
At full load 155 mph IAS is the most comfortable
climbing speed.
Considerable surging may be experienced above
8,000 feet on aircraft on which the air intake
duct has been removed.

    (ii) When fitted with 2 x 90-gallon drop tanks the
aircraft are longitudinally unstable on the climb.

   (iii) When fitted with 2 x 500 lb. bombs there is a
similar tendency to pitch if the rudder is not
held steady.

    (iv) The fuel tank pressure control should normally be
kept to ATMOSPHERE (except when required to supply
fuel from the drop tanks), but should be turned on
(PRESSURE) if the fuel pressure warning light comes
on.

11.   GENERAL FLYING

    (i) <u>Stability</u>: The aircraft are normally just stable
longitudinally, but when carrying 90-gallon drop
tanks, or R.P. and one 90-gallon drop tank, they
become unstable longitudinally and, in the first
case, 190 mph IAS is the minimum comfortable
flying speed. In conditions of absolute calm this
can be reduced to 180 mph IAS. When carrying
bombs, R.P., or containers, longitudinal stability
is unaffected.

(ii) Change of trim:-

       Undercarriage down   -   Nose slightly down
       Flaps down   -   Nose down

(iii) In steep turns there is a tendency to tighten up.

(iv) In bad visibility near the ground, flaps should be lowered to about 40° (2 divisions) and the propeller speed control set to g.ve 2,650 rpm. Speed may then be reduced to about 11(mph IAS. The radiator shutter must be opened to keep the temperature at about 100°C.

(v) When operating in tropical conditions prolonged flying at maximum cruising power should be avoided when top speed is not essential.

12.   MAXIMUM PERFORMANCE

  (i) Climbing

     See Para.10(i).

  (ii) Combat

     Use S ratio if the boost in M ratio is 2 lb/sq.in. below the maximum permitted.

13.   ECONOMICAL FLYING

  (i) Climbing: Climb at 2,850 rpm and +9 lb/sq.in. boost at the speeds recommended for maximum rate of climb (See Para.10).

  (ii) Cruising: For maximum range fly in M ratio and at maximum obtainable boost not exceeding +4 lb/sq.in. and reduce speed by reducing rpm which may be as low as 1,800, but check that the generator is charging. On some early aircraft it will not do so at below 2,000 rpm. If at 1,800 rpm (or 2,000 if necessary) the speed is higher than that recommended, reduce boost.
S ratio should only be used if at 2,600 rpm the recommended speed cannot be obtained in M ratio.

(iii) The recommended speeds (mph IAS) for maximum
range are:

Standard aircraft:	160
When fitted with 2 x 44 or 45 gal. tanks:	160
When fitted with 2 x 90 gal. tanks:	170
	or as near as possible.
When fitted with 2 x 250 lb. bombs:	170
When fitted with 2 x 500 lb. bombs:	180

Below 5,000 feet these speeds should be increased
by about 10 mph.

14.   STALLING

(i) At the stall one wing usually drops sharply, often
over the vertical, with flaps either up or down.

(ii) The average stalling speeds (mph IAS) for the
aircraft at various AUW (from 7,600 lbs to
9,200 lbs.) are:

Undercarriage and flaps UP:	80-90
Undercarriage and flaps DOWN:	60-75

The speeds for individual aircraft may vary by 5 mph.

15.   SPINNING

(i) Spinning of Mk.IID and Mk.IV aircraft is prohibited
at all times.

(ii) On Mark IIA, B and C aircraft spinning is prohibited
when carrying 90-gallon drop tanks, bombs, S.C.I.
or R.P.

(iii) Recovery is normal, but the loss of height
involved in recovery may be very great and the
following limits are to be observed:

(a) Spins are not to be started below 10,000 feet.

(b) Recovery is to be initiated before two turns
are completed.

(iv) A speed of 150 mph IAS should be attained before
starting to ease out of the resultant dive.

16.   AEROBATICS

   (i) The following speeds are recommended:

   Loop: At least 280 mph IAS

   Roll: 220-250 mph IAS

   Half roll off loop: At least 300 mph IAS

   Upward roll: 300 mph IAS.

17.   DIVING

   (i) Speed builds up slowly in the dive and the aircraft
       becomes tail heavy as the speed increases. The
       elevator trimming tabs should be used with care.

   (ii) Care should be taken not to allow the aircraft to
        yaw to the right, as this produces a marked nose-
        down pitching tendency.

   (iii) If fitted with bombs, S.C.I., or containers, the
         aircraft should be eased out of the dive gently. If
         fitted with drop tanks it should not be dived.

18.   CHECK LIST BEFORE LANDING

   (i) Check brake pressure (100 lbs/sq.in. minm.).

   (ii) Reduce speed to 120 mph IAS and check that cockpit
        hood is locked open.

        U - Undercarriage   - DOWN (check green lights)

        P - Propellor control   - Fully forward

            Supercharger control - MODERATE

        F - Flaps   - DOWN

19.   APPROACH AND LANDING

   (i) Approach speeds (mph IAS) at normal load:

                                        (flaps up)
        Engine assisted: 95   (105)
        Glide: 105   (115)

        Note: If carrying drop tanks, bombs, or R.P.,
               the normal engine assisted approach should
               be made at about 110 mph IAS.

(ii) <u>Undercarriage</u>: The lever should have been left in
neutral, but if it has been left in the UP position,
be careful to disengage the thumb catch by easing
the selector lever forward before trying to move it
to the DOWN position, otherwise the lever may
become jammed. Return the lever to neutral as soon
as the undercarriage is down.

(iii) <u>Flaps</u>: If 120 mph IAS is exceeded with the flaps
fully down, they will be partially raised by the
airflow. They will automatically move to the
fully down position when speed is reduced sufficiently,
provided that the selector lever is left at DOWN.

(iv) Landing with R.P. only on one wing should be made at
as high a speed as possible and care must be taken
to counteract dropping of the wing.

20.   MISLANDING

(i) Raise the undercarriage immediately.

(ii) Climb at about 90 mph IAS.

(iii) Raise the flaps at a safe height of about 200-300
feet, at a speed of not less than 120 mph IAS.

(iv) With one 500 lb. bomb stuck up open the throttle
slowly and speed on the initial climb should be
110 mph IAS before raising flaps at 120 mph IAS.

21.   AFTER LANDING

(i) Raise the flaps before taxying.

(ii) To stop the engine, idle for ½ minute at 800-900 rpm,
then pull the slow-running cut-out and hold it out
until the engine stops.

(iii) Turn OFF the fuel cock and switch OFF the ignition.

(iv) Check that the hydraulic selector safety plate is
covering the WHEELS UP position.

(v) <u>Oil dilution</u>.- (See A.P.2095 Pilot's Notes General)
The correct dilution period for these aircraft is:

Atmospheric temperature above -10°C: 1 minute
Atmospheric temperature below -10°C: 2 minutes

22. FUEL CAPACITIES AND CONSUMPTION

(i) Fuel capacities:

    (a) Normal:
        Two Main tanks (33 gals. each):   66 gallons.
        One Reserve tank: 28 gallons.
                        Total: 94 gallons.

    (b) Long-range (totals):

        With 2 fixed under-wing tanks
                (44 gallons each): 182 gallons.
        With 2 x 45 gallon drop tanks: 184 gallons.
        With 2 x 90 gallon drop tanks: 274 gallons.

(ii) The approximate consumptions (gals/hr.) in WEAK mixture are as follows:

Boost lb/sq.in.	M ratio at 8,000 - 20,000 ft.			S ratio at 14,000 - 30,000 ft.		
	R.p.m.			R.p.m.		
	2,650	2,300	2,000	2,650	2,300	2,000
+4	56	50	46	57	51	47
+2	52	46	42	53	47	43
0	47	42	38	48	43	39
-2	42	37	34	43	39	35
-4	37	33	30	38	34	31

(iii) The approximate consumptions in RICH mixture are as follows:

R.p.m.	Boost lb/sq.in.	Galls/hr.
3,000	+12	115
3,000	+ 9	100
2,850	+ 9	95
2,650	+ 7	80

23. BEAM APPROACH

STAGE	Indicated height(feet)*	I.A.S. m.p.h.	R.p.m.	Approx. Boost	Actions	Change of trim and Remarks
PRELIMINARY APPROACH	1,500	120	2,400	-2	Flaps down 30°	Strongly nose down
	1,500	120	2,400	-1	Lower u/c on Q.D.R. over I.M.B.	Slightly nose down
AT OUTER MARKER BEACON	600	95-100	3,000	-4	Flaps down to 60°	Nose down
			3,000	0		Should give level flight
AT INNER MARKER BEACON	100	90-95	3,000			
OVERSHOOT	Up to 400	95-100	3,000	Full throttle	Raise u/c and retrim. Raise flap to 30° and retrim. Raise flaps fully and retrim. Adjust boost and r.p.m. at 1,000 feet	Nose up Nose up Nose up

* Altimeter adjusted for Q.F.E. and touch-down error as follows:
At take-off, with no flap, the altimeter reads -30 feet.
At touch-down, with 60° flap, the altimeter reads -55 feet,
so add two millibars to Q.F.E. to give zero reading at touch-down.

Note: The above speeds should be increased by 5 m.p.h. for Mark IID and IV aircraft.

Air Ministry
March 1944

Amendment List No.42
to
AIR PUBLICATION 1564B
Volume I

HURRICANE IIA, IIB AND IIC AIRCRAFT

MERLIN XX ENGINE

(1.) SECTION 1   Remove existing sheets bearing
                        Paras.1 to 50, together with
                        those bearing Figs.1 to 4 and
                        their corresponding keys, and
                        substitute new sheets supplied
                        herewith.

(2)   SECTION 2   Remove existing sheets bearing
                        Paras.1 to 23 and any amendment
                        list instruction sheets at end
                        of Section, and substitute new
                        sheets supplied herewith.

NOTE: This Amendment List applies to A.P.1564B, Volume I
       only. A corresponding amendment list, P, to
       A.P.1564B, Pilot's Notes, is being distributed
       separately by A.P.F.S., Fulham Road, London.

Section 4: Instructions for ground personnel.

This Section revised by A.L.No.9
August, 1941
This page amended by A.L.No.35
June, 1943

SECTION 4 - INSTRUCTIONS FOR GROUND PERSONNEL

CHAPTER 1 - LOADING AND C.G. DATA

LIST OF CONTENTS

LIST OF ILLUSTRATIONS

CHAPTER 1 - LOADING AND C.G. DATA

Introduction

1.   For the determination of the C.G. position the aircraft is considered standing with the thrust line (or rigging datum line) horizontal and the main wheels down.

2.   The distance of the C.G. aft of the C.G. datum point, which is called the moment arm of the C.G., is given by the expression:-

$$\frac{(\text{Tare Wt.} \times \text{tare C.G. moment arm}) \pm (\text{Wts. of loads} \times \text{respective moment arms})}{\text{Tare weight} + \text{total weight of loads}}$$

$$= \frac{\text{Tare moment} \pm \text{load moments}}{\text{Total weight}}$$

3.   The moment arm (in inches) is positive when the load considered lies aft of a vertical line through the C.G. datum point and is negative when the load considered lies forward of a vertical line through the C.G. datum point.   The weight (in pounds) is in all cases positive.

Datum point

4.   The datum point is the centre of the engine starting handle shaft and is marked on the port side of the aircraft.   The position of this point is based on the assumption that the centre-line of the bracket supporting the starting shaft is 6 in. from the centre-line of joint X measured along strut XZ (see Loading Diagram).

5.   When determining the aircraft C.G. position by weighing, any variation in the position of the C.G. datum point from the nominal should be noted and the necessary correction made.   For example, if the dimension referred to above differs from the nominal by 0.5 in. (i.e., actual measurement gives 5.5 or 6.5 in.), this correction should be made to the calculated dimension of the C.G. aft of the C.G. datum point, the correction being added if the centre-line of the bracket is aft of its nominal position.

C.G. travel limits

6.   Approved limits of C.G. travel are 56 in. to 60.4 in. aft of the C.G. datum point, measured parallel to the thrust line.   The C.G. position must be kept within the specified range, even with the fuel consumed and with ammunition and flare expended.   For example, if the fully-loaded aircraft has a C.G. position 56 in. aft of the C.G. datum point at the commencement of flight, then in a short time the consumption of the fuel load will move the C.G. position beyond the approved forward limits.

Operational notes

7.   The following operational notes must be observed:-

(i)   The radio must not be deleted from the load unless the ballast
box (Sk.4826) with 3 standard ballast weights is carried in
lieu.

(ii)   On a Mk.IIA aircraft Browning guns are not to be removed unless
ballast is subtituted, 24 lb. in lieu of each gun.   The ballast
is to be securely attached to the respective front and rear gun
mountings.

(iii)   Browning guns are not to be removed from a Mk.IIB aircraft if
R.3002 is not carried, unless equivalent ballast is carried
in lieu of either this radio or eight of the guns.

(iv)   20 mm. guns are not to be removed from a Mk.IIC aircraft if
R.3002 is not carried, unless equivalent ballast is carried in
lieu of this radio.

Examples on the determination of the C.G. position

8.   To determine the C.G. position for an aircraft with any particular
load, the total moment for that loading, as shown on the Loading Diagram,
is divided by the corresponding total weight.   The resultant quotient is
the distance of the C.G. behind the C.G. datum point.

9.   **Normal loading.-**

	Weight (lb.)	Moment (lb.in.)
Mk.IIA aircraft (fig.1)	6,998	413,108

C.G. moment arm = $\dfrac{413,108}{6,998}$ = 59.0 in. aft of datum

10.   With main fuel consumed, and ammunition and flare expended.-

	Weight (lb.)	Moment (lb.in.)
Mk.IIA aircraft	6,998	413,108
Deduct main fuel	- 497	-35,290
Deduct ammunition	- 177	-11,860
Deduct flare (not fitted in later.. aircraft)	- 18	- 2,412
Totals	6,306	363,546

C.G. moment arm = $\dfrac{363,546}{6,306}$ = 57.6 in. aft of datum

11.   This paragraph has been deleted.

12.   Embodiment of modifications.- Assume Modifications nos.114,
132, 163, 170, 173, 202, 207, 217, 225 and 245 have been incorporated
and refer to para.14 for the respective weight and moment values.

	Weight (lb.)	Moment (lb.in.)
Mk.IIA aircraft at tare weight	5,440	300,830
Mod.No.114	-13.66	-751
" " 132	5.45	273
" " 163	1.0	92
" " 163 existing fixed equipt.moved	x	- 53
" " 170	1.69	76
" " 173	10.92	1,332
" " 202	1.5	101
" " 207	7.14	200
" " 217	6.77	359
" " 225	2.55	260
" " 245	0.42	16
	5,463.78	302,735

The above totals represent the new tare condition of the aircraft after
the embodiment of the modifications.   To this condition the desired
operational load should be added, including all or part of the change
in load affected by the modifications introduced.

	Weight (lb.)	Moment (lb.in.)
Aircraft at Modified tare wt.	5,463.78	302,735
Total removable load for Mk.IIA aircraft as on loading Diagram (6,998-5,440)	1,558	112,378
Mod.No.114	22.22	1,222
" " 163 existing removable equipment moved	x	-321
" " 173	31.34	4,012
" " 202	39.06	2,617
" " 225	14.56	1,485
" " 245	13.5	500
	7,142.46	424,628

For new all up weight,

$$\text{C.G. moment arm} = \frac{424,628}{7,142.46} = 59.5 \text{ in. aft of Datum}$$

Modifications included

13.   The tare weight and loading shown on the Loading Diagram include
the following modifications:-

(i)   Mk.IIA, Series I aircraft.- Modifications nos.1, 2, 3, 4, 8,
9, 10, 11, 12, 14, 15, 17, 18, 19, 20, 21, 24, 25, 26, 27, 28
32, 33, 37, 38, 39, 40, 42, 44, 45, 47, 48, 49, 50, 52, 55, 57,
58, 60, 62, 63, 66, 67, 69, 71, 72, 74, 78, 82, 83, 84, 85, 86,
88, 92, 95, 98, 99, 100, 101, 102, 103, 104, 105, 106,107, 108,
109, 112, 113, 116, 117, 119, 123, 124, 125, 127, 128, 129, 130
134, 135, 136, 138, 141, 143, 145, 146, 147, 149, 151, 152, 153,
154, 157, 159, 160, 165, 167, 178, 179, 180, 181, 182, 183, 189.
Mk.IIA Series II aircraft are as above with the addition of
modifications Nos.170 and 222.

(ii)   Mk.IIB aircraft.- Modifications nos.1, 2, 3, 4, 8, 9, 10,
11, 12, 14, 15, 17, 18, 19, 20, 21, 24, 25, 26, 27, 28, 32, 33,
37, 38, 39, 40, 42, 44, 45, 47, 48, 49, 50, 52, 55, 57, 58, 60,
62, 63, 66, 67, 69, 71, 72, 74, 78, 82, 83, 84, 85, 86, 88, 92,

95, 98, 99, 100, 101, 102, 103, 104, 105, 106, 107, 108, 109, 112, 113, 114, 116, 117, 119, 123, 124, 125, 127, 128, 129, 130, 134, 135, 136, 138, 139, 140, 141, 143, 145, 146, 147, 149, 151, 152, 153, 154, 157, 159, 160, 163, 164, 165, 167, 170, 172, 173, 176, 177, 178, 179, 180, 181, 182, 183, 185, 186, 187, 189, 190, 191, 192, 194, 195, 201, 204, 206, 207, 214, 215, 216, 217, 220, 222, 223, 235, 254.

(iii) **Mk.IIC** aircraft.- Modifications nos.1, 2, 3, 4, 8, 9, 10, 11, 12, 14, 15, 17, 18, 19, 20, 21, 24, 25, 26, 27, 28, 32, 33, 37, 38, 39, 40, 42, 44, 45, 47, 48, 49, 50, 52, 55, 57, 58, 60, 62, 63, 66, 67, 69, 71, 72, 74, 78, 82, 83, 84, 85, 86, 88, 92, 95, 98, 99, 100, 101, 102, 103, 104, 105, 106, 107, 108, 109, 112, 113, 114, 116, 117, 119, 123, 124, 125, 127, 128, 129, 130, 134, 135, 136, 138, 139, 140, 141, 143, 145, 146, 147, 149, 151, 153, 154, 157, 159, 160, 163, 165, 167, 170, 172, 173, 176, 177, 178, 179, 180, 181, 182, 183, 185, 186, 187, 189, 190, 191, 192, 194, 195, 201, 204, 206, 207, 214, 215, 216, 217, 220, 222, 223, 232, 235, 254.

Any modifications incorporated on aircraft , that are additional to the appropriate list above must be allowed for when calculating the total weight and C.G. position; weight and moment changes due to additional modifications are given in para.14.

Changes of weight and moment due to modifications

14.   Any modifications that are incorporated on the aircraft but are not shown on the appropriate list in para.13, are additional to those included on the Loading Diagram and must be allowed for when calculating the total weight and C.G. position; the following table gives changes of weight and moment due to such additional modifications.

Mod. No.	Description	Tare weight		Removable load	
		Weight (lb.)	Moment (lb.in.)	Weight (lb.)	Moment (lb.in.)
70	Hydraulic pressure gauge introduced	+ 1.0	72	-	-
87	Fixed ballast at rear introduced	+25.5	7,350	-	-
91	Desert equipment (removable) introduced	-	-	+56.8	8,570
114	Martin Baker blast tubes introduced	-13.66	-751	+22.22	1,222
132	Exhaust glare shields introduced	+ 5.45	273	-	-
139	Prevention of excessive oil pressure	+ 0.39	16	-	-

Mod. No.	Description	Tare weight		Removable load	
		Weight (lb.)	Moment (lb.in.)	Weight (lb.)	Moment (lb.in.)
140	Guide for ammunition boxes	+ 0.47	32	–	–
163	(i) Repositioned oxygen bottle	+ 1.0	92	–	–
	(ii) existing equipment moved	x	-53	x	-321
164	12-gun wings introduced	+28.0	1,875	+208.0	13,940
169	Long-range fuel tanks (removable) introduced	+98.0	6,080	+634.0	39,300
170	Shock strut strengthened	+ 1.69	76	–	–
172	Long-range fuel tanks (fixed) introduced	+ 1.19	91	–	–
173	R.3002 wireless introduced	+10.92	1,332	+ 31.34	4,012

(Contd. on the next page)

Mod. No.	Description	Tare Weight		Removable Load	
		Weight (lb.)	Moment (lb.in.)	Weight (lb.)	Moment (lb.in.)
174	Fuel pressure indicator alternative to gauge	-0.13	-9	-	-
176	Windscreen de-icing introduced	+8.61	+534	-	-
177	G.22 camera removed	-0.89	+48	-	-
185	Heywood compressor introduced	+0.75	+29	-	-
186	Starter countershaft bracket improved	+0.45	+6	-	-
188	Armour forward of header tank	+8.08	+226	-	-
190	2-position foot pedal introduced	+2.58	+147	-	-
191	Push for camera gun introduced	+0.44	+32	-	-
192	Bulkhead sealing improved	+0.25	+10	-	-
193	Upward firing signal discharger	+14.19	+2,180	+2.15	+331
194	Rad. flap control stop introduced	+0.05	+5	-	-
197	Inhibitor in main fuel tanks	+0.44	+38	-	-
199	20 amp. accumulator in lieu of 14 amp. (T.R.9)	-	-	+1.61	+187
201	Sutton harness strengthened	+0.05	+5	-	-
202	Ammn. boxes, capacity increased	+1.50	+101	+39.06	+2,617
204	New air intake	-1.92	-62	-	-
206	Automatic boost control cut-out introduced	+0.58	+36	-	-
207	Armour forward of header tank introduced	+7.14	+200	-	-
208	Rudder bias gear introduced	+3.19	+850	-	-
209	Elevator tab chord increased	+0.25	+78	-	-
210	Crash pylon strengthened	+3.31	+391	-	-
214	Emergency crowbar introduced	+0.13	+12	+0.94	+88
215	Throttle-propeller interconnection deleted	-0.42	-32	-	-
216	Battery for R.3002 deleted	-	-	-0.50	-65
217	Fireproof screen for deck tank introduced	+6.77	+359	-	-

Mod. No.	Description	Tare Weight		Removable Load	
		Weight (lb.)	Moment (lb.in.)	Weight (lb.)	Moment (lb.in.)
218	New tail wheel and shock-absorber unit	+5.88	+1,620	-	-
220	Fuel tanks, internal pressure	+2.53	+235	-	-
222	Fuselage strengthened	+4.75	+945	-	-
223	Improved oil cooler introduced	+1.56	+156	-	-
224	Oxygen economiser introduced	+3.50	+287	-	-
225	Additional oxygen cylinder	+2.55	+260	+14.56	+1,485
228	Fuel tank pressure control introduced	+1.06	+86	-	-
229	Computor, Mk.IIID introduced	+0.11	+10	+1.50	+137
230	Air-intake cover modified	-	-	+0.25	+18
232	Four 20 mm. gun wings introduced	+137.00	+7,980	+169.00	+11,750
235	Oil tank, internal pressure	+0.73	+27	-	-
236	Sutton harness extension introduced	+0.06	+6	-	-
237	Signal discharger, colour selection introduced	+3.75	+570	-	-
241	Pneumatic charging connection repositioned	+0.16	+8	-	-
245	Oil tank capacity increased	+0.42	+16	+13.50	+500
246	Sliding hood, provision for jettisoning	+0.72	+76	-	-
249	Electrical wiring improved	-7.25	-638	-	-
251	Engine couplings at header tank improved	+0.13	+3	-	-
254	Pneumatic system modified	+1.75	+128	-	-
255	Fuel tank sealing, revised method	+1.63	+148	-	-
257	Centre-section ribs redesigned	-0.44	-49	-	-
259	Fuel pressure system vent improved	-0.06	-3	-	-
261	Port fires introduced	+0.09	+9	-	-
262	Tropical cooling introduced	-0.02	-2	-	-
263	Cockpit air conditioning introduced	+17.00	+1,275	-	-
264	Air cleaner for air intake introduced	+28.92	+347	-	-

Mod. No.	Description	Tare Weight		Removable Load	
		Weight (lb.)	Moment (lb.in.)	Weight (lb.)	Moment (lb.in.)
267	Reinforced oxygen bottle introduced	+0.06	+6	+3.00	+279
268	Booster coil in lieu of starter magneto	-3.58	-32	-	-
271	Computor, Mk.IIID, deleted	-0.11	-10	-1.50	-137
273	Formation keeping lamps deleted	-2.75	-325	-	-
275	Throttle mixture control interconnection modified	-1.58	-71	-	-
277	Ammn. counter, Mk.I, introduced	+1.00	+73	-	-
278	Worth oil dilution introduced	+2.25	+86	-	-
282	12v 40A accumulator, type 'D', introduced	-4.00	-460	-	-
284	Combatable long-range fuel tank (Mk.IIC)	+153.00	+10,050	+576.0	+36,050
286	Combatable long-range fuel tank (Mk.IIA & B)	+146.25	+8,850	+577.5	+36,150
289	Flame damping exhausts, introduced	+6.5	+0	-	-
292	Socket for clothing-heating introduced	+0.34	+28	-	-
293	Improved cockpit ventilation	+0.52	+35	-	-
296	Removal of Nos.5 & 6 guns improved	-	-	-0.25	-16
297	Rear guard for hood jettison-cable	+0.27	+29	-	-
303	Filters in oxygen pipe-line	+0.16	+13	-	-
304	Two-250 lb. G.P. bombs introduced	+51.75	+2,950	+500.0	+28,500
306	45-gallon drop tanks - removable (Mk.IIA & B)	-	-	+751.0	+46,800
307	45-gallon drop tanks - removable (Mk.IIC)	-	-	+751.0	+46,800
308	Mod. to W/T wiring to avoid compass deviation	+0.52	+27	-	-
309	Pneumatic installation improved	+2.61	+103	-	-

Mod. No.	Description	Tare Weight		Removable Load	
		Weight (lb.)	Moment (lb.in.)	Weight (lb.)	Moment (lb.in.)
311	Removal of T.R.1133 wiring facilitated	+0.13	+12	-	-
314	Drop tanks, fixed parts in fuselage	+11.00	+83	-	-
316	Drop tanks, fixed parts in wings (Mk. IIA & B)	+9.50	+670	-	-
317	Drop tanks, fixed parts in wings (Mk. IIC)	+13.50	+938	-	-
319	Wiring from camera gun to W/T installation deleted	-0.34	-34	-	-
322	Heavier main wheel tyres introduced	+16.00	+690	-	-
323	Heavier tail wheel tyre introduced	+1.13	+311	-	-
327	Master valve in oxygen system	+1.98	+147	-	-
328	Breather pipe at rear end modified	+0.50	+144	-	-
329	Breather system of improved type	+1.5	+127	-	-
331	G.45 camera gun in lieu of G.42B	-	-	+1.50	+74
333	Downward extension of rear armour	+15.63	+1,425	-	-
336	750-watt generator introduced	+4.88	+52	-	-
339	Two-250 lb. bombs, fixed parts in wings (Mk. IIA & B)	+6.19	+418	-	-
340	Two-250 lb. bombs, fixed parts in wings (Mk. IIC)	+1.41	+111	-	-
341	Two-500 lb. bombs introduced	-	-	+1,048.0	+59,500
342	Radiator flap indicator deleted	-0.75	-66	-	-
346	Air cleaner, rear portion strengthened	+0.41	+11	-	-
351	Exhaust glare shields deleted	-5.19	-259	-	-
358	Auxiliary oil system and sanitary equipment	+19.36	+1,940	+36.0	+4,045

This page amended by A.L.No.35
June, 1943
This page amended by A.L.No.36
July, 1943
para. 14 (contd.)

A.P.1564B, Vol.I, Sect.4, Chap.1

Mod. No.	Description	Tare Weight		Removable Load	
		Weight (lb.)	Moment (lb.in.)	Weight (lb.)	Moment (lb.in.)
359	Two-250 lb. bombs, removable parts in wings (Mk. IIA & B)	-	-	+542.63	+30,950
361	Two-250 lb. bombs, removable parts in wings (Mk. IIC)	-	-	+540.63	+30,850
362	Two-250 lb. bombs, fixed parts in fuselage	+3.00	+267	-	-
364	Port flare tube and control deleted	-2.99	+295	-	-
365	Army type radio - introduced	+14.5	+1,827	-34	-3,944
366	A.1271 radio introduced	+ 9.50	+1,070	+4.41	+590
369	Rear view mirror, type 'B' introduced	+0.25	+20	-	-
370	Header tank, engine coupling improved	-0.55	-14	-	-
372	Power failure warning light introduced	+0.53	+40	-	-
373	New material for walkways introduced	-1.00	-80	-	-
374	Spring-loaded relief valve on header tank	-0.67	-18	-	-
377	90 gal. drop tanks - removable parts	-	-	+1,435.25	+88,100
378	Hurricane with hook Mk. IIB & C conversion	+30.25	+6,201	-	-
379	Incendiary bomb stowage introduced	+0.25	+24	+1.31	+128
381	S.B.C. and S.C.I. fixed parts in fuselage	+0.3	+22	-	-
383	(i) S.B.C. removable parts	-	-	+737.75	+41,000
	(ii) S.C.I. removable parts	-	-	+655.75	+38,300
386	S.B.C. and S.C.I. provision on 500 lb. carriers	-	-	+0.27	+11
387	(i) R.3067 Mk.III and type 90 aerial - introduced	+2.75	+390	+2.75	+390
	(ii) Existing equipment moved	-	-	x	-314

This page amended by A.L.No.36
July, 1943
This page amended by A.L.No.37
October, 1943

Mod. No.	Description	Tare Weight		Removable Load	
		Weight (lb.)	Moment (lb.in.)	Weight (lb.)	Moment (lb.in.)
388	Self-sealing fuel pipes	+1.43	+111	-	-
397	Special equipment - fixed parts in fuselage introduced	+6.75	+859	-	-
399	Special equipment, removable parts - introduced	-	-	+1,217	+62,676
400	U/c wheel, type A.H.8213 as an alternative to A.H.10019	+21.75	+941	-	-
403	Air intake modified	-3.25	-111	-	-
407	Guard for rear oxygen cylinder - introduced	+0.25	+24	-	-
408	(i) Downward ident. lamp, three colour, introduced	+2.5	+348	-	-
	(ii) Existing equipment moved	✗	-25	-	-
409	Ring and bead sight - introduced	+1.0	+45	-	-
411	R.3067 and type 90 aerial, provision for, introduced	+4.5	+608	+2.5 ✗	+326 + 39
412	T.R.1196A, removable parts introduced	-0.75	-81	-44	-5,016
416	R.10A installation - introduced	+0.5	+51	-	-
417	(i) R.10A installation - introduced	-	-	+4.0	+456
	(ii) Existing equipment moved	-	-	✗	+109
418	Incendiary bomb stowage introduced	+.5	+72	-	-
419	Throttle lever, improved type, introduced	+0.5	+59	-	-

Mod. No.	Description	Tare Weight		Removable Load	
		Weight (lb.)	Moment (lb. in.)	Weight (lb.)	Moment (lb. in.)
421	Conversion from Rotol to D.H. c/s propeller	+25·0	—865	—	—
426	(i) Tropical air cleaner of modified type introduced	+1·75	+ 5	—	—
	(ii) Existing parts moved	*	— 99	—	—
428	Signal pistol No. 4, Mk. I and stowage substituted	*	— 10	*	—158
429	U/C switches Pye type introduced	+0·5	+ 24	—	—
433	R.P.M. indicator drive shortened type, introduced	—0·25	— 7	—	—
434	(i) Mk. II L gun sight introduced	—	—	+ 0·5	+ 36
	(ii) Existing parts moved	—	—	*	+ 22
439	Starboard landing lamp deleted	—3·75	—165	—	—
441	Sun screen for gun sight deleted	—2·5	—163	—	—
443	S.C.I. jettisoning provision for	+0·25	+ 14	—	—
452	(i) T.R.1196A radio introduced	—	—	—42·75	—4788
	(ii) Existing parts moved	—	—	*	— 167
453	Master and remote contactors deleted	—3·0	—302	—6·63	— 666

The following modifications have been omitted from the above table because their effect on the C.G. position and weight is negligible:—

Nos. 187, 195, 219, 227, 231, 233, 239, 244, 252, 253, 258, 265, 288, 291, 298, 301, 302, 305, 310, 312, 325, 326, 332, 338, 344, 347, 352, 355, 363, 368, 371, 382, 384, 398, 401, 402, 424, 430, 431, 432, 438, 444, 447, 451.

* = Weight figure not quoted because moving existing equipment involves no change in weight.

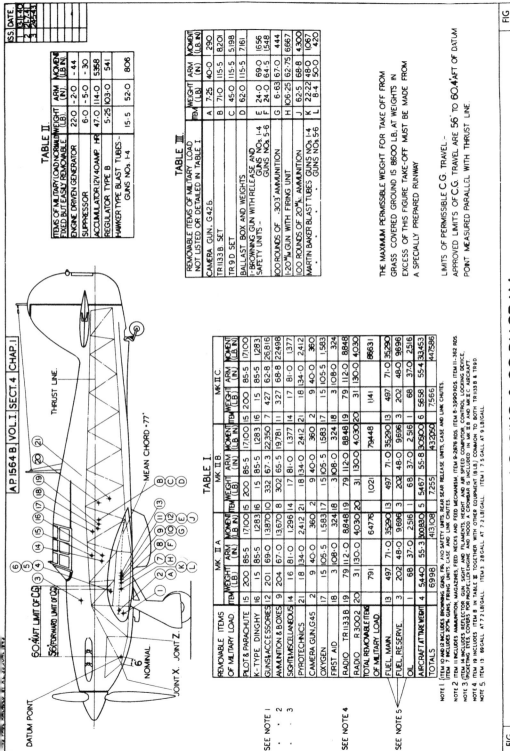

LOADING & C.G. DIAGRAM.

CHAPTER 2 — HANDLING AND GENERAL PREPARATION

LIST OF CONTENTS

LIST OF ILLUSTRATIONS

F.S./1

CHAPTER 2

HANDLING AND GENERAL PREPARATION

General

1. This Chapter contains information on handling the aeroplane on the ground and preparing it for flight; a list of the ancillary equipment is given in the relevant M leaflet of Vol.II of this Air Publication.

Towing

2. No provision is made for attaching towing ropes to the aeroplane as it is normally handled by man-power. Provided, however, that care is taken to avoid damaging the undercarriage, towing ropes may be passed round the inboard branches of the forked upper ends of the shock-absorber struts or round the lugs on the struts to which the side stays are attached. The aeroplane must not be towed by a rope attached to the tail wheel unit.

Tail wheel steering arm

3. A tail wheel steering arm is provided to assist in handling the aeroplane; it consists of twin tubes fitted with hooks at their lower ends for attachment to the axle of the tail wheel. When attached, the hooks are retained in position by spring-loaded catches operated by bowden cable from a toggle on the cross-handle of the steering arm. The arm is shaped to clear the rudder, elevator, and tail plane.

Flying controls locking gear

4. This gear is kept in a canvas bag which is clipped to a fuselage strut on the starboard side of the wireless bay. The locking gear comprises a hinged bracket for attachment to the control column, a pair of tubes for locking the rudder bar to the bracket, and a telescopic interference tube connected to the bracket and adapted to be passed through a slot in the back of the seat. To lock the controls, the bracket should be clamped round the top of the lower portion of the column with its projecting lugs embracing the aileron-actuating tie-rods and in contact with the tie-rod fork-end nuts; movement of the hinged upper portion of the column, and hence the ailerons, is thereby prevented. The rudder bar locking tubes, which are pinned to the bracket, have quick-attachment ends for connection to spigot bolts clipped to the rudder bar. The interference tube prevents occupation of the seat whilst the controls are locked.

Picketing

5.   A pair of picketing rings are stowed in a pocket in the canvas bag
containing the flying controls locking gear.   They screw into sockets in
the underside of the outer planes, sockets being provided at both the
leading and trailing edges of the planes, near the tips.   The engine must not
be run up unless the tail is anchored to a strong ground picket; the picket
should have a long screwed portion and should be screwed into the earth at
such an angle that the force produced by the tendency of the tail to lift
does not act axially on the picket.   Observance of this precaution is
particularly important when the ground is wet or loose as there is then a
risk of the picket being dislodged and the aeroplane tipping over on to its
nose.

Chocks

6.   When chocks are being removed from the wheels, they should be
withdrawn forwards as they would foul and damage the shock-absorber strut
fairing if withdrawn sideways in the usual manner.

Weatherproof covers

7.   A weatherproof cover may be obtained for the cockpit; it fastens
over the hood by means of tapes which tie under the fuselage, one pair
passing in front of, and another behind, the main plane; the cover should
be stowed in the radio bay.   An engine cover fits over the top of the
cowling and has two cords at the rear end which hook on to a lipped angle
on the cover plate of the wheel housing; another cord passes beneath the
engine and hooks on to a ferrule half way along the cover on each side.
At the front, the cover extends slightly over the top of the propeller
boss; it is secured round the top blade, which should be vertical, by
cords which pass round the spinner, behind the remaining blades of the
propeller and hook to the cover again.   Each blade of the propeller has a
separate cover.   An air intake cover may be secured in position by means of
the extra elastic cord bound to the engine cover port rear cord.

Loading parachute flare

8.   Before a flare can be placed in the launching tube fitted on early
aeroplanes, the suspension lug and safety pin must be removed from the
central part of the flare casing; the lug is about a foot from the bottom
of the casing and the safety pin is adjacent the lug.   Release the door
in the front underfairing of the rear fuselage by pushing forward the
projecting pin at the side of the door; the door should then fall open.
Pass the flare into the chute with the large end uppermost and the looped
end of the static cord lying on the top of the flare, then close and fasten
the door.   Remove the appropriate access door in the side of the fuselage
and draw the looped end of the static cord through the top ring of the
chute; attach it to the forked bolt on the fuselage joint near the top of
the chute by means of the toggle pin provided.   Stow any surplus cord in
the canvas pocket on the flare and replace the access door.

.303 in. guns

9.   **Installation.-** The guns and accessories are numbered 1 to 6 in each
plane, the innermost gun on either side being No.1.   If the guns are not
fitted when the aeroplane is delivered, the magazines are mounted in position
but the case chutes, feed necks and blast tubes are stowed in the gun
compartment; the case chute apertures are sealed with cover plates.   The
following procedure should be used when installing each group of guns:-

(i)   Remove the gun and magazine access doors in the top surface
        of the plane.

(ii)   Undo the screws holding the blast tube doors and remove the
        doors.

(iii)   Remove the cover plates over the case chute apertures and, using
        the same nuts and bolts, fit the case chutes.

(iv)   Remove the gun pins from the front and rear mounting and unlock
        the adjusting nuts on the rear mountings.

(v)   Remove the nozzles from guns Nos. 1 to 4, and, in the case of
        No.4 gun only, remove the rear end.

(vi)   Remove the collars from the front ends of the guns and
        substitute the special adaptors supplied.

(vii)   Place the guns in position, Nos. 1 to 4 from above with a
        forwards and sideways movement, and Nos. 5 and 6 by passing
        them on their sides backwards through the holes in the front
        spar in way of the blast tube door.

(viii) Replace the nozzles and the rear end of No.4 gun. (for Nos. 5
        and 6 guns, see para.10).

(ix)   Insert the front and rear mounting pins and replace the
        locknuts on them.

(x)   Attach the link chutes; it is most important that their lips go
        under the channel-section front cartridge stops.   Link chutes
        Nos. 1 to 3 and Nos. 5 to 6 lead into the corresponding case
        chutes, whilst No.4 leads to a separate aperture in the
        underside of the plane.

(xi)   Attach the feed necks and see that the magazine rollers are
        free.

(xii)   Replace the blast tube doors, and insert the blast tubes,
        taking care to see that the catches at their forward ends
        engage properly.

(xiii) Remove the blanking caps from the pneumatic piping and make
        the firing connections to the guns; a flexible pipe should
        connect the underside of each gun to the horizontal branch
        of the corresponding pipe connection and another flexible pipe
        should connect one side of each gun to the vertical branch of
        the connection.

(xiv)   Replace the gun and magazine access doors.

Instructions for loading ammunition are given in A.P.1641C, Vol.I.   If an ammunition counter is fitted in the cockpit, it should be set to the average number of rounds loaded.

10.   **Removal of outboard guns.-** Removal of the guns Nos. 5 and 6 is facilitated by adherence to the following procedure.   To replace the guns, the procedure should be reversed.

(i)   Remove the blast tube, gun, and magazine access doors.

(ii)   Remove the blast tubes, link chutes and feed necks (the case chutes need not be removed).

(iii)   Disconnect the flexible pipes to the rear sear releases and the fire-and-safe units and remove the fire-and-safe units from the guns.

(iv)   Slacken off the locking nuts on the adjusting bolt of No.6 gun, taking care not to disturb the adjustment; remove the rear fixing pins.

(v)   Remove the front fixing pins, working from the front through the blast tube door opening.

(vi)   Push the guns about 2 in. aft and turn them over sideways. Withdraw each gun through the forward opening, taking care not to damage the flexible pipe on the rear sear release.

11.   **Alignment.-** The rear mounting forks of the guns are adjustable vertically and laterally;   the front forks can pivot to permit lateral movement of the rear forks but are normally clamped by slotted nuts locked by split pins.   To align a gun, first release the front fork by slackening the slotted nut and release the rear fork by slackening the lock-nuts at the side of the mounting bracket.   Lateral adjustment of the gun can then be effected by turning the knurled knob at the side of the bracket and vertical adjustment can be made by means of the knurled knob at the bottom of the mounting fork.   It will usually be possible to rotate the knobs by the fingers but, should they be stiff, a 5/32 in. dia. tommy bar may be inserted in the holes in the rims of the knobs.   After adjustment, the inner nut at the side of the rear bracket should be tightened, but not excessively, and locked by the outer nut;   this effects locking both of · the vertical and the lateral adjustments.   Finally, the slotted nut on the front fork should be tightened and the split pin replaced.

20 mm. guns

12.   **Installation.-** The 20 mm. guns and accessories are referred to as inboard and outboard, respectively, in each outer plane.   If the guns are not fitted when the aeroplane is delivered the ammunition boxes and the case and link chutes are assembled in position, and the feed necks and front mountings are stowed in the gun compartments of the outer planes.   Cover plates may be fitted to the case and link chute apertures.

The following procedure should be followed when installing the guns:-

(i) Remove the main gun access doors (see Chap.3, fig.1), in the top skin of each outer plane; each door is held down by tucking the leading edge into the torsion sub-spar of the plane and securing it at the trailing edge by three fasteners.

(ii) Remove the leading-edge door by unfastening the two fixing screws on the leading edge of the outer plane, and draw the door forward.

(iii) Remove the gun access doors on the underside of each outer plane. Each door is attached by eight special fasteners.

(iv) Remove the breech block access doors (see Chap.3, fig.1), on the top and bottom skins of the outer planes. Each door is held down by tucking the leading edge into a recess aft of the rear spar and securing the sides and trailing edge by special fasteners.

(v) Remove the recoil spring from the gun and assemble the front gun mounting (see Sect.11, fig.5), as follows:-
Attach the bearing block (A) to the main casting with screws and assemble the casting on the front end of the gun. Fit the muzzle bearing cylinder (B) to the gun and screw the retaining ring (C) loosely into position. Re-assemble the recoil spring.

(vi) Attach the channel for the gun slide anchorage to the front mounting and attach the anchorage strut to the channel. Connect the other end of the anchorage strut to the shackle and bolt the shackle to the gun slide.

(vii) Swing the rear mounting assembly in the outer plane in a forward direction; assemble the gun, complete with front mounting etc. into position, inserting it through the leading edge of the outer plane. (A tray is incorporated between the front spar and the torsion sub-spar on which the gun may be rested during assembly or removal).

(viii) Attach the gun to the rear mounting. The gun is attached by bolts securing the shoulder on the unit to the rear mounting adaptor.

(ix) Secure the front mounting to the casting on the front spar by special nuts.

(x) Align the gun, (see para.13) and tighten the retaining ring (C) on the front mounting, utilizing the special spanners provided. If the locking tab slots are not in alignment with each other, slacken off the retaining ring to the nearest locking position and lock with tab.

(xi)   Adjust the anchorage strut so that the relative position
of the gun slide to the body will be correct when the
V-notches indicated on these parts are in alignment when
the gun is at rest.

(xii)   Attach the upper feed neck to the magazine by inserting
two pins, one in each side, and turning them so that they
are locked in position by the spring clip attached to the
magazine.

(xiii)   Assemble the lower feed neck, roller and guides together.
The method of attachment is similar to that stated in
sub-para. (xii).

(xiv)   Slide the upper feed neck inside the lower one and attach
the assembly to the feed inlet by means of a special clip.

(xv)   Connect the flexible pipe lines of the pneumatic system to
the firing and cocking connections on the gun.

(xvi)   Re-assemble the breech block access doors, the gun access
doors and the leading edge doors.

Instructions for loading ammunition are given in A.P.1641F, Vol.I.

13.   _Alignment_.- The rear mountings of the guns are adjustable
vertically and laterally, the front mounting bearings being spherically
shaped to permit alignment.   To align the gun, proceed as follows:-

(i)   Slacken the retaining ring on the front mounting, utilising
the special spanner provided.

(ii)   At the rear mounting, slacken the locknut and unscrew the
adjustable barrel.   Vertical adjustment may now be
carried out by inserting a 9/32 in. B.S.F. box spanner in
the barrel and adjusting the vertical spindle.

(iii)   Tighten the adjusting barrel and lock with a locknut when
vertical adjustment is completed.

(iv)   For lateral adjustment, slacken off the locknuts and carry
out the adjustment by turning the horizontal spindle.
Tighten the locknuts when the operation is completed.

(v)   Tighten the retaining ring on the front mounting.

Bomb loading

14.   A box spanner (A.Std.1219) for adjustment of the crutches on the
bomb racks is stowed in the bag containing the flying controls locking
gear.

Fixed long-range fuel tanks

15.   Installation.- Some aeroplanes are adapted to carry fixed non-operational long-range fuel tanks, as shown in the illustration in Sect.8; bolt holes for their attachment are provided through the lower spar booms and the undersurface of the outer planes.   To fit long-range tanks, proceed as follows:-

    (i)   Drain the centre section fuel tanks (see Chap.3).

   (ii)   Remove the gap fairings and gun doors and take out all ammunition and guns.

  (iii)   Stow the feed necks and case and link chutes in the magazines with the exception of the link chute for No.1 gun and the case chute for No.4 gun, which must be wrapped up and tied to the structure in the gun bay.

  (iv)   Fit covers over the holes for the case and link chutes for Nos.1, 3 and 4 guns.

   (v)   Secure the brackets provided to the front and rear spars together with the stay.   Offer up the tank to the brackets with pipe connections on top and in line with the link and case chute hole for No.2 gun, as shown in Sect.8.   To ensure that the tanks are assembled with the pump vertical, and that they are accessible through the door in the outer plane, a red line should be painted across the bracket and the tank.   Tighten straps with the securing bolts centrally disposed on the attachment brackets.

  (vi)   Remove the sealing plate from the end rib and replace the fixing screws in the rib.   Stow the plate in one of the magazines.

 (vii)   Remove the two plugs from the handhole cover on the outboard side of the centre section tank.   Assemble the union bodies, existing washers and supply and return pipes to the centre section and long-range tanks.   Stow the plugs in one of the magazines.

(viii)   Fit switches, fuse boxes and wiring.

  (ix)   Fit the fairing between the undersurface of the main plane and the tank.

Note.- The procedure for installing the fixed operational long-range tanks is similar to that given above but the tanks are fitted with all the guns in position and the special case chutes, existing feed necks and special link chutes should be fitted for the No.2 guns.

16.   Removal.- To restore the aeroplane to normal, remove the operational or non-operational long-range tanks as follows:-

    (i)   Drain the centre section and long-range fuel tanks (<u>see</u> Chap.3).

   (ii)   Remove the fairing between the outer planes and the long-range tanks.

  (iii)   Uncouple the fuel pipes at the connections on the long-range tanks.

   (iv)   Disconnect the electrical lead at the connection on each long-range tank.

    (v)   Release the tank straps and remove the tanks.

   (vi)   Remove the gun doors and unscrew the bolts in the spar booms securing the bracket; remove the nut plates from inside the booms, and the brackets and packing blocks.

  (vii)   Remove the main plane gap fairing and uncouple the fuel pipes at the unions on the outboard side of the centre section tank. Remove the union bodies from the handhole cover; fit the plugs stowed in the magazine, using the existing washers, and lock with wire.

 (viii)   Remove the switches, fuse boxes and wiring, taking care not to disturb any of the other electrical services.

   (ix)   Fit the cover disc, stowed in the magazine, to the access hole in the end rib and secure with the existing screws in the reinforcing ring. Replace the gap fairing.

    (x)   When removing the non-operational tanks, remove the covers from the case and link chute holes, and install the guns and accessories (<u>see</u> para.9).

Jettisonable long-range fuel tanks.

17.   <u>Installation</u>.- On aeroplanes provided with the fixed parts for either 45 or 90-gallon jettisonable long-range tanks, the tanks should be fitted as follows:-

    (i)   Turn the main fuel cock to OFF.

   (ii)   Remove the side fairing panels.

  (iii)   Unlock the jettison lever in the cockpit by moving the screw and nut securing the jettison lever gate at the front end from the inboard hole to the outboard hole.

   (iv)   Remove and retain the plugs from the access doors on the underside of the outer planes.

    (v)   Offer up the tanks to the hooks on the outer planes; secure them in position by closing the release pawl on the rear hooks and assemble according to the instructions given in fig.2, except for the final fitting of the side fairing panels.

(vi)   Before connecting up the rubber pipes to the tanks, test the
        functioning of the jettison gear by trestling up suitably
        padded boards to within about 2 in. of the tanks and releasing
        the tanks.   Care should be taken that no damage is caused
        to the tanks or fairings.

(vii)   Remove the trestles and refit the tanks as before.

(viii) Connect up the rubber fuel and air pressure pipes to the tanks,
        care being taken not to damage the glass break-tubes.

(ix)   Fill the tanks (see para.21) and run the engine on the
        jettisonable tank fuel system to test for accuracy of function
        and absence of leaks.

(x)   Ensure that the indicator streamers attached to the tail fairings
        hang free of obstructions and extend about 18 in. aft of the
        trailing edges.

Note.- The procedure for replacing tanks which have been jettisoned with
        new tanks is similar to that described above, but the stub ends of
        the broken glass tubes should be removed and new glass break-tubes
        fitted.   If an aeroplane, having jettisoned the tanks, is flown
        prior to replacement of the tanks, the plugs removed from the access
        doors on the underside of the outer planes must be refitted and the
        jettison lever in the cockpit locked in the JETTISON position by
        moving the screw and nut securing the front end of jettison lever gate
        from the outboard to the inboard hole.

Filling fuel and oil tanks

18.   Normal tanks.- The points of access to the filler necks of the fuel
and oil tanks are shown in Chap.3, fig.1.   The earthing plug on the hose must
be inserted into the earthing socket adjacent to the filler neck before
filling a tank.   The fuel tanks must be filled separately since fuel cannot
flow from the reserve tank to the main tanks owing to the presence of non-
return valves in the pipes connecting the main tanks to the fuel cock.   The
oil tank should be filled to the top of the filler neck, except when used
in conjunction with the auxiliary oil tank, when the instructions given in
para.22 should be followed.

19.   Fixed non-operational long-range tanks.- The nose fairing of each
tank should be removed to give access to the plug at the forward end of
the tank;   the plug should be removed and held in readiness for immediate
replacement.   Each tank should be filled through the filler neck of the
appropriate centre-section tank until fuel runs out of the plug hole, when
the plug should immediately be replaced and filling of the main tank continued in the normal manner.

20.   Fixed operational long-range tanks.- The filling procedure is
the same as that described in para.19 but the plug is replaced by a cock.
The cock should be unlocked and opened before filling and shut off and
relocked immediately fuel starts to run out, in order to prevent damage
to the protective covering of the tank.

21.   *Jettisonable long-range tanks.*- The tanks should be filled
separately through the filler at the forward end of each tank; a bonding
socket is provided. After filling, care should be taken to screw the
filler cap down tightly as the functioning of the system will be affected
by an air leak at this point.

22.   *Auxiliary oil tank.*- The auxiliary oil tank, which is fitted when
90-gallon jettisonable fuel tanks are carried, is situated in the decking
behind the pilot's seat. Before filling, the cock control on the left-
hand side of the seat must be turned off. The cock control incorporates
a ratchet mechanism which does not allow the cock to be turned off in
flight and therefore a tommy bar must be inserted in the hole in the spindle
below the mounting bracket and the spindle turned until the pointer on the
control indicates OFF. The filler neck is accessible through an access door
in the decking and the tank should be filled up to the base of the neck.
As the oil tank is under pressure during flight, care must be taken that the
filler cap has a well-fitting washer and is securely replaced.

Note.- If this tank is in use the main oil tank should be filled with
        8 gallons of oil only, giving a total oil capacity of 12 gallons.

Exhaust glare shields

23.   To prevent the pilot from being dazzled by exhaust glare at night,
removable shields can be fitted, on early aeroplanes only, to the port and
starboard sides of the tank cowl.

Cold weather fittings for oil cooler

24.   When the aeroplane is flown under extremely cold conditions, the oil
in the earlier - type cooler, which has not central by-pass, becomes so
viscous that the viscosity valve continually by-passes the oil.   To correct
this, blanking boards may be made and these boards secured by tie-rods
passing through the cooler (see fig.3.)

Lifting a crashed aeroplane

25.   In addition to using the normal lifting points, a crashed aeroplane
may be lifted at the pin-joints between the outer planes and centre section,
after first removing the outer planes.

Radio heating element

26.   The master contactor, fitted on the starboard side of the radio bay,
is provided with a heating element which is controlled by a switch adjacent
to the contactor; this switch must be set to "ON" before flight.

Filling windscreen de-icing tank

27.   The de-icing tank may be filled by unscrewing and removing the
filler cap, access to which is obtained by detaching the starboard intermediate side panel (see Sect.4, Chap.3, fig.1).

Loading cartridges - recognition device

28.   Access to the cartridge discharger drum is through the desert
equipment door (see Sect.4, Chap.3, fig.1), the cartridges being inserted
into the drum through an opening in the bottom surface, normally covered
by a flap.   When loading, rotate the drum as far as possible to
automatically render the firing mechanism inoperative.

Oil dilution system

29.   To facilitate re-starting the engine in cold weather, depress the
pushbutton of the oil dilution system, on the port decking shelf, in
accordance with the instructions on the label; full particulars are
given in A.P.2095 and A.P.1464B, Vols.I.

Note.- Two different sizes of jet are fitted and the injection
          period varies according to jet size.

Heater cover

30.   A special shelter-type cover is obtainable for use when the
aeroplane is parked out in cold weather.   When parking overnight,
catalytic heating may be employed, the heater and container being attached
to the cover.   When it is required to start the engine quickly after
it has been stationary for a considerable period, paraffin heating is
employed, a chimney being attached to the heater cone to direct hot air
into the cover.

Accumulator connections

31.   On those aeroplanes fitted with the type-D accumulator, care must
be taken to ensure that the bare ends of the leads are properly insulated
from the fuselage structure and from each other, if the engine is run up
with the accumulator removed.

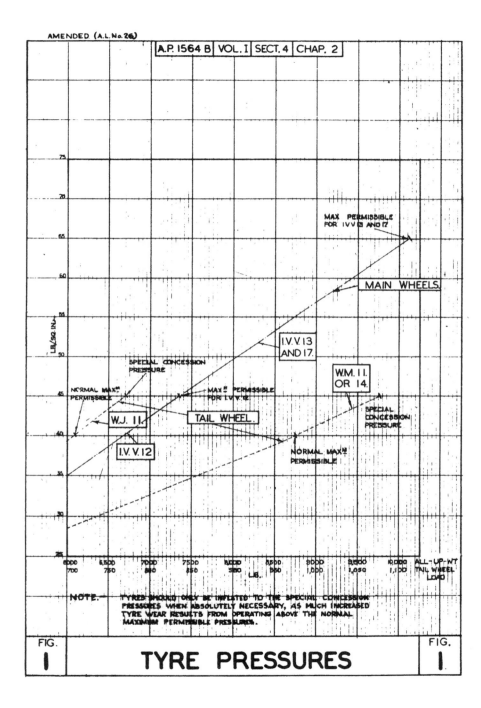

A.P. 1564 B | VOL. I | SECT. 4 | CHAP. 2

MAX PERMISSIBLE
FOR I.V.V 13 AND 17

MAIN WHEELS.

I.V.V.13
AND 17.

W.M. 11.
OR 14.

SPECIAL CONCESSION
PRESSURE

NORMAL MAX^M
PERMISSIBLE

MAX^M PERMISSIBLE
FOR I.V.V. 12

SPECIAL
CONCESSION
PRESSURE

W.J. 11.

TAIL WHEEL.

NORMAL MAX^M
PERMISSIBLE

I.V.V. 12

LB/SQ. IN.

75
70
65
60
55
50
45
40
35
30
25

6000   6500   7000   7500   8000   8500   9000   9500   10,000   ALL-UP-WT
700   750   800   850   900   950   1,000   1,050   1,100   TAIL WHEEL
                                    LB.   LOAD

NOTE.— TYRES SHOULD ONLY BE INFLATED TO THE SPECIAL CONCESSION
         PRESSURES WHEN ABSOLUTELY NECESSARY, AS MUCH INCREASED
         TYRE WEAR RESULTS FROM OPERATING ABOVE THE NORMAL
         MAXIMUM PERMISSIBLE PRESSURES.

FIG.
1

TYRE PRESSURES

FIG.
1

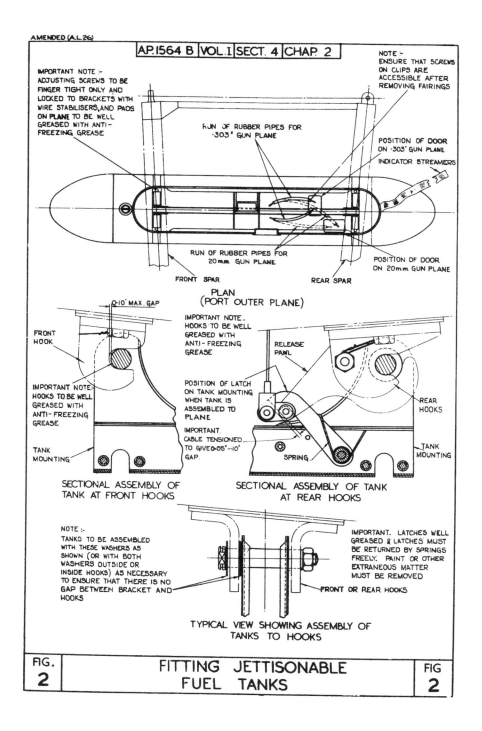

IMPORTANT NOTE :-
ADJUSTING SCREWS TO BE
FINGER TIGHT ONLY AND
LOCKED TO BRACKETS WITH
WIRE STABILISERS, AND PADS
ON PLANE TO BE WELL
GREASED WITH ANTI-
FREEZING GREASE

NOTE -
ENSURE THAT SCREWS
ON CLIPS ARE
ACCESSIBLE AFTER
REMOVING FAIRINGS

RUN OF RUBBER PIPES FOR
·303" GUN PLANE

POSITION OF DOOR
ON ·303" GUN PLANE

INDICATOR STREAMERS

RUN OF RUBBER PIPES FOR
20 m.m. GUN PLANE

POSITION OF DOOR
ON 20m.m. GUN PLANE

FRONT SPAR

REAR SPAR

PLAN
(PORT OUTER PLANE)

0·10" MAX. GAP

FRONT
HOOK

IMPORTANT NOTE.
HOOKS TO BE WELL
GREASED WITH
ANTI-FREEZING
GREASE

RELEASE
PAWL

IMPORTANT NOTE:
HOOKS TO BE WELL
GREASED WITH
ANTI-FREEZING
GREASE

POSITION OF LATCH
ON TANK MOUNTING
WHEN TANK IS
ASSEMBLED TO
PLANE

REAR
HOOKS

IMPORTANT.
CABLE TENSIONED
TO GIVE 0·05"-·10"
GAP.

TANK
MOUNTING

SPRING

TANK
MOUNTING

TANK
MOUNTING

SECTIONAL ASSEMBLY OF
TANK AT FRONT HOOKS

SECTIONAL ASSEMBLY OF TANK
AT REAR HOOKS

NOTE :-
TANKS TO BE ASSEMBLED
WITH THESE WASHERS AS
SHOWN (OR WITH BOTH
WASHERS OUTSIDE OR
INSIDE HOOKS) AS NECESSARY
TO ENSURE THAT THERE IS NO
GAP BETWEEN BRACKET AND
HOOKS

IMPORTANT. LATCHES WELL
GREASED & LATCHES MUST
BE RETURNED BY SPRINGS
FREELY. PAINT OR OTHER
EXTRANEOUS MATTER
MUST BE REMOVED

FRONT OR REAR HOOKS

TYPICAL VIEW SHOWING ASSEMBLY OF
TANKS TO HOOKS

FIG.
2

FITTING JETTISONABLE
FUEL TANKS

FIG
2

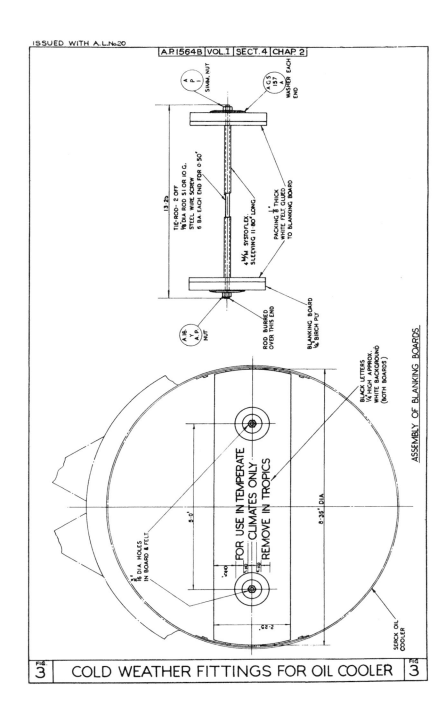

ASSEMBLY OF BLANKING BOARDS

| FIG. 3 | COLD WEATHER FITTINGS FOR OIL COOLER | FIG 3 |

SECTION 4—INSTRUCTIONS TO GROUND PERSONNEL

CHAPTER 3—GENERAL SERVICING

LIST OF CONTENTS

Main wheel units

Tail wheel unit—Spring type

Tail wheel unit—Dowty oleo-pneumatic type

Continued on next leaf

PNEUMATIC SYSTEM

MISCELLANEOUS

LIST OF ILLUSTRATIONS

GENERAL

Introduction

1. The information given in this Chapter implements the Inspection Schedule, Vol. II, Part 2 of this publication, and therefore does not cover all the operations that may be required for the servicing of the aircraft. A list of special tools and equipment necessary for servicing is contained in Vol. III of this publication, and in the relevant M leaflet of Vol. II. For notes on the servicing of equipment not dealt with in this Chapter reference should be made to the Volumes I of the Air Publications listed below.

Electrical equipment manual	A.P.1095
Instrument manual	A.P.1275A
Radio equipment	A.P.2276
Brake system	A.P.1464B
Air pump units	A.P.1519
Propellers	A.P.1538E
Engine	A.P.1590G
Engine starting system	A.P.1181
Guns, ·303 in. Browning	A.P.1641C
Guns, 20 m.m. Hispano	A.P.1641F
Gun-firing control mechanism	A.P.1641E
Camera gun	A.P.1749

Jacking and lifting points

2. The jacking and lifting points are indicated in fig. 1. At the front end the fuselage may be lifted on the jacking pads incorporated in the engine mounting and the centre section may be jacked beneath the front and rear spar pin joints. The rear end of the fuselage may be trestled beneath the handling bar after the latter has been passed through the tube incorporated in the fuselage joints (lower) just forward of the tail wheel; the bar can be introduced from

either the port or starboard side through corresponding holes in the fairing. An emergency jacking point is provided at the lower end of each main wheel shock-absorber strut.

3. Should the aircraft, with engine installed, be raised into the flying position on the wheels or on the emergency jacking points at the lower end of each shock-absorber strut, the rear end of the fuselage must be anchored to a ground ring or a weight of approximately 2 cwt. as a precaution against the fuselage over-balancing on to its nose. A rope may conveniently be attached around the bottom of the tail wheel shock-absorber strut but, when carrying out rigging operations, care must be taken that the tying-down does not distort the fuselage.

4. For handling the wings, the lifting brackets should be screwed into the sockets provided in the undersurfaces of the wings at the root ends and at the tips (*see* fig. 1), the lifting handles then being bolted to the brackets; the handles are of such a length that they project beyond the leading and trailing edges of the wings.

RIGGING

General

5. Since the main plane, tail plane, and fin are fixed, rigging of the aircraft is limited to a general check of the angularity of the main plane and the tail plane relative to the fuselage, of the verticality of the fin and the checking of the ranges of movement of the control surfaces. On similar port and starboard diagonal dimensions, a tolerance of 2 in. is allowed, the measurements being taken from the tips of the wings to suitable points at the nose and tail of the aircraft; the tolerances given are not hard and fast but when they are exceeded, the structure as a whole should be examined to determine the cause of the distortion. The rigging of the wings may be checked by placing the incidence and dihedral boards in the positions shown in fig. 8, after first placing the aircraft in the rigging position as described in para. 6. The ranges of movement of the control surfaces are given in the Leading Particulars.

Rigging position

6. The fuselage should be supported on adjustable trestles beneath the jacking points on the engine mounting and rear fuselage (*see* para. 2) and raised until the undercarriage and tail wheel are clear of the ground; the trestles should then be adjusted until the fuselage is level both longitudinally and transversely. Longitudinal level is checked by placing a straightedge and an inclinometer across the levelling clips on port struts EH and GH (*see* fig. 8), transverse level being checked by placing a straightedge and inclinometer (or spirit level if no inclinometer is available) across the levelling clips on side struts GH, port and starboard.

> *Note.*—A spirit level is not sufficiently accurate for checking longitudinal level and an inclinometer should always be used.

Checking and adjusting rear fuselage

7. The rear fuselage may be checked and adjusted for alignment and freedom from twist as follows; for the designation of the fuselage joints, refer to Sect. 7, Chap. 1.

    (i) Place the fuselage in the rigging position as described in para. 6.

(ii)   Check the rear fuselage for freedom from twist by means of a straight-edge and spirit level laid across joints M and across the plug ends at joints R.

(iii)   Make any necessary corrections for twist by adjusting the bracing in the transverse panels.

(iv)   Drop plumblines from the centre of joint U and the midpoint of cross strut HH; stretch a cord between two weights or other supports a few inches above the ground and directly under the plumblines.

(v)   Drop further plumblines from the midpoints of suitable struts, such as PP, OO, and JJ; if the fuselage is true about the plan centre line, these plumblines will align on the ground cord.

(vi)   Make any necessary corrections to the bracing of the top and bottom panels until all the plumblines align on the ground cord. The adjustments should be spread over as many panels as possible so that the tension of the wires in adjacent panels is not greatly different and equal adjustments should be made in corresponding top and bottom panels.

(vii)   Check all bracing wires to see that they are taut and, at each wire fork-end, verify that a sufficient length of thread is in engagement by inspecting the threads through the safety holes in the fork-end. Ensure that all nuts are locked and split pins fitted where required and see that fibre rubbing blocks are fitted at the crossing points of the wires.

(viii)   Finally, repeat the checks described in sub-paras. (ii) and (v) to ensure that the adjustments are correct.

Checking control surfaces

8.   With the aircraft in the rigging position (*see* para. 6), set the rudder bar at right angles to the fuselage centre line (*see* para. 13), the upper end of the control column in line with the lower portion, and the control column as a whole $7\frac{1}{2}°$ aft of the vertical. Check that the trailing edges of the ailerons have nil to $\frac{1}{4}$ in. droop at the inboard end, measured against the trailing edge of the main plane, that the rudder is in line with the centre line of the fuselage (not the fin centre line), and that the elevator is in line with the tail plane. Also check that the trailing edges of the trimming tabs are in line with the trailing edge of the elevator and rudder when the cockpit indicators are at zero.

Adjusting control surfaces

9.   *Ailerons.*—Secure the trailing edges of the ailerons in line with the trailing edge of the main plane (no droop is intended) and the upper portion of the control column in line with the lower portion; for this latter operation, the lugged bracket of the flying controls locking gear can usually be employed but care should be taken to ascertain that the gear is effectively maintaining the spade grip in its neutral position. Connect the cables to the tie-rods, setting the cables symmetrically about the pulleys in the outer planes and the cable drum in the fuselage; tighten the cable turnbuckles to suit.

     Note.—When adjusting the control rods at the differential gear, the end link of the chain must be held with a spanner whilst tightening the locknut.

10. During flight trials of new aircraft, or tests subsequent to the fitment of new ailerons, the following conditions of aileron trim may be experienced:—

(i) *Aircraft in trim but ailerons overbalanced in both directions.*—Correction may be made by rigging ailerons to give a slight positive droop. The maximum permissible positive droop is ¼ in. on both ailerons.

(ii) *Aircraft out of trim due to over-balance in one direction only.*—Correction may be made by attaching a suitable length of $\frac{3}{16}$ in. manilla cord to the upper side of the trailing edge of the aileron which tends to rise. The length of cord attached should not exceed 24 in.

(iii) *Ailerons too heavy.*—Check aileron to ensure that there is no positive droop, and ensure that the balance cable is tight. If, however, the cable is tight or tightening does not have the desired effect, the ailerons should be rigged with a slight *negative* droop. The maximum permissible negative droop is ⅛ in. on both ailerons.

10A. In the past, some aircraft have been rigged with cord on both ailerons, but this practice is not now permitted; *all trimming by means of cord must be carried out on one aileron only.*

11. Upon fitting a new aileron, it will be necessary to remove any cord already fitted to the other aileron before checking the trim by flying the aircraft "hands off". If the trial flight reveals that the ailerons are out of balance, the length of cord to be applied to the "up-going" aileron must be determined by trial. When the correct length has been found by further flights, the cord should be attached to the upper side of, and mid-way along, the trailing edge of the aileron. The cord should be secured by means of a serrated-edged fabric strip, 2¼ in. wide, doped to the undersurface, around the edge, and to the upper surface.

12. *Elevator.*—Place the aircraft in the rigging position (*see* para. 6) and secure the elevator in its neutral position, i.e. in line with the tail plane; adjust the lengths of the elevator cables by means of the turnbuckles at their forward ends until the control column is

7½ deg. aft of the vertical.

13. *Rudder.*—Place the rudder in line with the fuselage centre line (*not* the fin centre line) and secure the rudder bar at right-angles to the fuselage centre line; for this latter purpose, the flying controls locking gear may conveniently be employed, but care should be taken to ensure that the gear is effective in preventing movement of the rudder bar from the correct position. Adjust the cables to the correct tension by means of the turnbuckles beneath the fuselage cross·strut JJ (*see* Sect. 7, Chap. 1).

14. *Rudder tab.*—The tab cables should be fitted in the inner holes in the arms on each side of the tab, the cable lengths being adjusted so that the tab is in line with the trailing edge of the rudder when the rudder is in line with the fuselage centre line. The cables to the cockpit should be adjusted to the correct tension after setting the cockpit control in the neutral position, the rudder and tab in line with the fuselage centre line and the screw jack in its mid position.

15. *Elevator trimming tabs.*—Rotate the control handwheel in the cockpit until the indicator is at zero, then adjust the turnbuckles in the control cables until the trailing edges of the tabs come into line with the trailing edge of the elevator; one turnbuckle will require slackening to allow the other to be tightened without altering the tension of the cable. With the indicator at zero, the chain round the sprocket of the control handwheel should be symmetrically disposed. The chain round the worm wheel sprocket in each half of the elevator should be disposed so that the ends are approximately 9½ in. from the centres of the guide sprockets. The nipples joining the control cables and the cables attached to the chains round the worm wheel sprockets should be disposed 9 in. forward of the ends of the bowden casing passing under the elevator spar. The connector in the balance cable should be positioned not more than ⅛ in. on either side of the aircraft centre line.

16. The control should be operated to move the tabs to their extreme positions; should the cable connectors foul the fairleads, the position of the chain on the handwheel sprocket should be altered. It should be noted that, from the fairlead clipped to the fuselage cross strut NN, the upper control cable passes to starboard and the lower one to port.

16A. *General.*—After fitting a new or replacement propeller, engine, constant-speed unit or cockpit propeller control, it is necessary to re-adjust the setting of the constant-speed propeller control in the cockpit. The minimum speed setting is governed by the rear stop, which should be set at 1,800 r.p.m.; the maximum speed setting is controlled by the front stop and this should be set at 3,000 r.p.m. The procedure for setting these stops is described in paras. 16B and 16C.

16B. *Setting rear stop.*—To set this stop, proceed as follows after the boost setting and maximum r.p.m. on the ground, have been made satisfactory:—

   (i) Run up the engine and advance the throttle to the gate position. Move the lever on the propeller control so that it is opposite the 2,600 r.p.m. mark on the stop plate and check from the engine speed indicator that 2,600 r.p.m. are being obtained.

(ii) If the engine speed shown is not correct, stop the engine, dismantle the propeller control unit A (without removing it) and reposition the lever on the control. To carry out this operation (*see* fig. 15) first take out the locking D-ring F, and remove the knurled damper thumb wheel E from the spindle L, together with the washers G and H. Next unlock the main hexagonal nut K and slacken it off sufficiently to allow plate J and lever D to be lifted, to disengage the locating teeth B and C, and moved a couple of notches (forward if the r.p.m. were too high and back if they were too low) *without moving the internal gear plate* M. When the lever is repositioned, tighten up and lock the hexagonal nut and replace the thumb wheel and locking D-ring.

Note.—If the internal gear plate is moved when the lever is being repositioned, it will be necessary to re-assemble the control and repeat the whole process from sub-para. (i).

(iii) Run up the engine, check the speed again as described in sub-para. (i) and, if necessary, make further adjustments as detailed in sub-para. (ii).

(iv) When the correct speed of 2,600 r.p.m. is shown on the indicator move the propeller control lever back, with the engine still running, until 1,800 r.p.m. is shown on the indicator. The back stop should then be moved up until it is in contact with the control lever and set in this position.

16C. *Setting front stop.*—The front stop should be set after the test flight. Just before landing, the pilot should advance the lever of the constant-speed propeller control until the engine-speed indicator shows 3,000 r.p.m. and should leave it in this position. When the aircraft has landed, the following procedure should be carried out:—

(i) On the top edge of the stop plate mark the exact position of the control lever so that if this is moved it can be correctly repositioned.

(ii) Remove the locking wire on the constant-speed unit which is attached to the engine, remove the domed cap, unlock the tab washer and slacken off the lock nut.

(iii) Check that the lever on the cockpit control is still in the correct position, adjust the centre screw on the engine unit until it comes into contact with the internal gears and then turn the screw back approximately a quarter of a turn. Move the lever in the cockpit right back, then push it forward and check to see that it comes back to the mark made on the stop plate under sub-para. (i); if not, further slight adjustment of the adjusting screw should be made until the lever does come back to the mark. When a satisfactory adjustment of the screw has been made, tighten up the lock nut, lock with the tab washer, replace the domed cap and lock in place.

(iv) Finally, set the front stop on the constant-speed cockpit control approximately $\frac{1}{16}$ in. forward of the lever, in order to allow a $\frac{1}{16}$ in. spring on the lever.

Note.—The adjustment of the constant-speed unit described in sub-para. (ii) and (iii) ensures that even if the front stop on the cockpit control should slip, the engine cannot be over-revved.

FUSELAGE AND MAIN PLANE

Engine controls

17. *Adjusting for length.*—The lengths of both the throttle and mixture controls may be altered by screwing the fork-ends along the sliding rods at each end of each control in the desired direction; the fork-ends are locked by nuts.

18. *Adjusting control stops.*—The stops are situated at the front ends of the throttle and mixture lever slots in the quadrant plate. Slacken off the two screws in each stop and slide the stop forward or rearward as required to increase or decrease, respectively, the maximum degree of throttle opening or weakness of mixture.

19. *Inspection of inner cable.*—The cable may be inspected by removing the locking barrel from the screwed terminal rod, sliding the inspection tubelet back and then, in turn, moving each olive and tubelet along the cable until it has been examined throughout its length.

20. *Adjustment of inner linkage.*—A linkage is satisfactorily adjusted when there is no end play between the olives and the tubelets; increasing the tension beyond this point makes the control heavy in operation. The adjustment is made by screwing the locking barrel up to the appropriate point on the screwed terminal rod and then screwing the sliding rod along the terminal rod until it is hard against the locking barrel.

Hand starting gear

21. *Adjusting chain from handle shaft sprocket.*—Slacken the nuts attaching the bearing brackets of the handle shaft to engine mounting struts XZ, port and starboard (*see* Sect. 7, Chap. 1), and slide the bearing brackets forward to tighten the chain or rearward to slacken it.

22. *Adjusting chain driving magneto.*—Remove packing washers from under the magneto feet to tighten the chain or add washers to slacken it.

23. *Adjusting chain driving engine.*—Slacken the nuts attaching the bearing bracket to engine mounting strut XY, starboard (*see* Sect. 7, Chap. 1) and slide the bearing with its double sprocket forward to tighten the chain or rearward to slacken it; this adjustment will necessitate adjustment of the two other chains as described in paras. 21 and 22. When tightening the bearing brackets on the struts after adjustment of the chains, care should be taken to ensure that the sprockets are parallel to one another in order to avoid twist in the chains.

Pressure head

24. *Position of Mark VIIIC pressure head.*—This pressure head, which is of the electrically-heated type, is situated below the port outer plane, the tube being parallel to the chord line with a tolerance of $\pm$ 2 deg. The tip of the tube is 9·9 in. from the underside of the plane and 41·65 in. from the leading edge, the latter dimension being measured parallel to the chord line; on both measurements there is a tolerance of $\pm$ ½ in.

Continued on next leaf

Cockpit hood

25. <u>Adjusting buffers</u>.- The rubber buffers, which limit rearward movement of the hood, should be positioned so that, when the hood is fully open, the locking plunger can just engage the ratchet stop at the forward end of the port side of the hood. The buffers are located in the channel-sectioned hood rails by bolts which can be inserted through selected holes in the rails.

26. <u>Adjusting catch plate</u>.- When the hood is moved to the open position, the catch plate at its starboard forward end should engage and withdraw the bolt locking the exit panel. The packing block on the catch plate must be adjusted in thickness so that when the hood is fully open and the locking plunger is in engagement with the ratchet stop, the bolt is completely withdrawn.

Radiator flap

27. <u>Adjusting control</u>.- When the control lever in the cockpit is in the CLOSED position, the gap between the trailing edge of the flap and the fuselage underfairing should be $5\frac{1}{2}$ in; if this dimension is not obtained, the length of the control rods should be adjusted. Adjustment is effected by slackening the locknuts at the upper ends of the rods, disconnecting the fork-ends, and screwing them on or off as required.

Barrel-type fairleads

28. <u>Fitting</u>.- When fitting a new barrel-type fibre fairlead, care should be taken to ensure that the split-line of the fairlead makes an angle of at least 30° with the edges of the channel bracket in which it is mounted (<u>see</u> fig.10). The fairlead should be filed or drilled for the clamping bolt in such a manner that this requirement is satisfied.

Fuel tank covers

29. <u>Fitting</u>.- New covers are drilled with a certain number of location holes only, therefore the remaining holes must be drilled on assembly; there are eight attachment points on the upper cover and seven on the lower. The method of determining the position of the holes for the attachment screws is as follows:-

      (i)   Into the plug and cap fittings on the face of the tank, screw the special marking studs provided in the ground equipment.

(ii)   Apply the cover to the centre section and secure the edges to the fairing strips by a sufficient number of screws to hold it in place.   Note.- On the starboard side only, the holes along the front edges of the top cover must be drilled on assembly; the positions of these holes may be determined by scribing from below, or by adaptation of the method outlined in this paragraph.

(iii)   With a mallet, strike the covering at places above the special studs so that the points of the latter will mark the inner surface of the cover.

(iv)   Remove the cover and, at the points marked by the studs, drill $\frac{3}{8}$ in. diameter holes.

(v)   Replace and secure the cover with 2 B.A. screws to the fairing formers, and with 2 B.A. countersunk screws and drawsunk washers to the tank plug-and-cap fittings.

MAIN WHEEL UNITS

Single units

30.   Retraction.- By disconnecting the latch-operating cable of one unit, it is possible to retract the other unit separately, but this practice is undesirable as damage to the gear may result if the latch should slip. When it is required to retract a single unit, the other unit should be held down by external means, e.g. a weight or a picket.

Latch gear

31.   Adjusting.- Remove the bolt at the outboard end of the latch arm, screw the adjustable end inwards or outwards the required number of complete turns, and replace the bolt and nut.

31a.   Fore-and-aft adjustment at shock-absorber strut attachment.- To take up fore-and-aft movement of the sleeve block on the centre-section outer girder to which the shock-absorber strut is attached, the sleeve on the girder joint behind the sleeve block is drilled with three sets of staggered holes. If fore-and-aft movement is discovered at this point, the three bolts at the joint should be removed and the sleeve rotated until a set of holes is found which, on replacement of the bolts, takes up the end play.

Shock-absorber struts

32.   Warning.- It is extremely important to note that the air pressure must be released before attempting any dismantling operations; failure to observe this precaution may result in a serious accident.

33.   General.- Each oleo-pneumatic shock-absorber strut contains $3\frac{1}{4}$ pints of fluid (see Leading Particulars) and air at the necessary pressure to suit the loading of the aeroplane.

Graphs of air pressure against all-up weight for struts to two different Ft. Nos. are given in fig.11; this diagram is not to be taken as authorizing weights in excess of those laid down in Chap.1. When checking the air pressure or the oil level, the aeroplane should be supported with the appropriate strut clear of the ground. Care should be taken to note that both struts have the same Fart No., i.e. that the aeroplane is fitted with a pair to Fart No.90274 or a pair to Fart No.91205.

34. <u>Storing</u>.- The shock-absorber struts are supplied as spares with the correct quantity of oil, but with the air at atmospheric pressure; they should be stored in this condition with the fork end uppermost. Before use, it is advisable to check the oil level (<u>see</u> para.37); the oil level should also be checked whenever the air has been released.

35. <u>Location of faults</u>.- Once the shock-absorber struts are charged with oil and air as required, it is not advisable to interfere with them unless there is evidence of air or oil leakage. The following notes will assist in the diagnosis of faults:-

   (i) With the oil level correct, <u>the air pressure is too low</u> if less than $3\frac{1}{2}$ in. of the sliding portion of the piston tube is exposed with wheel on ground.

   (ii) With the oil level correct, <u>the air pressure is too high</u> if more than $4\frac{1}{2}$ in. of the sliding portion of the piston tube is exposed with wheel on ground.

   (iii) With the air pressure correct, <u>the oil level is too low</u> if the piston travel is excessive and the aeroplane rolls laterally on a turn.

   (iv) With the air pressure correct, <u>the oil level is too high</u> if the strut is harsh in action.

   (v) An excessive quantity of oil on the piston and attachment fittings usually denotes that the <u>gland packings are worn</u> and need replacement. A leakage from this source can be temporarily remedied by tightening the gland nut but new packings should be fitted (<u>see</u> para.42) at the earliest opportunity.

36. <u>Checking air pressure</u>.- Jack up the aeroplane until the undercarriage wheels are clear of the ground and connect the pipe-line from the Vickers pump to the air valve; charge the line to the pressure required in the strut (<u>see</u> fig.11), open the air valve two turns and read the pressure on the gauge incorporated in the pump.

Alternatively, a cylinder may be used for charging purposes, in which case an air pressure gauge should be incorporated in the pipeline from the cylinder to the air valve.

37. <u>Checking oil level</u>.- If the aeroplane has just landed or taxied, the oil will be in an aerated condition and it is therefore advisable to wait about a quarter of an hour before checking the oil level. Jack up the aeroplane until the undercarriage wheel is clear of the ground. Unscrew the air valve slightly and, when the air pressure inside the strut is 50 lb./sq.in., close the air valve. Allow the oil to settle for a few minutes and then open the oil level valve three or four turns. If the air escaping through the oil valve is free from oil, the oil level is too low but if large quantities of oil are ejected with the air, the oil level is too high; if the escaping air carries only a small amount of oil mist, the level may be taken as correct.

38. <u>Lowering oil level</u>.- Jack up the aeroplane until the under-carriage wheels are clear of the ground. Unscrew the oil valve slightly and pass air through the air valve from a pump or cylinder until the air escaping from the oil valve no longer carries any oil; if the air is passed through the strut too rapidly, it may lower the oil level more than required. Shut off the air supply and wait two or three minutes for the oil to settle to a common level both inside and outside the piston tube; repeat the process until the escaping air carries only a small amount of oil mist.

39. <u>Raising oil level</u>.- After jacking up the aeroplane until the undercarriage wheels are clear of the ground, pump in an excess of oil and lower the oil level as described in para.38.

40. <u>Lubrication</u>.- When lubricating the gland at the lower end of the cylinder tube, it is important that the gland should receive only sufficient oil for its proper lubrication; if large quantities of oil are forced into the gland, some may find its way into the cylinder tube and increase the oil content of the strut.

41. <u>Checking gland packings</u>.- It may be found that a strut which has been standing in one position for a long period is sluggish in action due to the oil attacking the packing rings and causing temporary adhesion to the piston. This should rectify itself after a short period of taxying, but if it persists the gland should be removed and cleaned.

42. <u>Fitting new gland packings</u>.- The new packing rings should be soaked in type A anti-freezing oil (Stores Ref. 34A/43 and 46) for at least twelve hours before they are required for fitting. Remove the strut from the aeroplane (<u>see</u> Sect.5) and proceed as follows:-

    (i)   Remove the wheel and axle from the strut

(ii)   Release the air from the strut by unscrewing the oil level valve, at the same time pumping in oil through the air valve; when oil only is expelled, screw down the oil valve.

(iii)   Remove the oil seal cap, the oil retaining ring, and the gland nut.

(iv)   Continue pumping oil into the cylinder tube until the tubular capping ring and the gland packings are forced out.

(v)   Unscrew and remove the stop ring (use Tool No.7/90287).

(vi)   Remove the six screws in the cylinder tube midway between the gland and the lugged collar to which the radius rod and side stay are connected; this will permit the splined guide ring within the cylinder tube to be withdrawn with the piston tube when the latter is removed.

(vii)   Withdraw the piston tube, together with the splined ring.

(viii)   After draining the cylinder tube, invert it and, with the air and oil valves closed, pour in $3\frac{1}{4}$ pints of type A anti-freezing oil (Stores Ref.34A/43 and 46).

(ix)   Insert the piston tube but do not displace the oil; when replacing the six screws which secure the splined guide ring, the copper washers must be annealed immediately before use.

(x)   Slip the stop ring over the piston tube and screw it into the cylinder tube (use Tool No. 7/90287).

(xi)   Slip the new packing ring over the piston tube with its feather edge inwards and follow it with the tubular capping ring; tap them into place, using a wooden drift on the outer end of the capping ring.

(xii)   Screw the gland nut down on to the capping ring and tighten it to ensure that the packing is in its correct position; slacken the gland about one turn to permit the packing to expand and work automatically.

(xiii)   Slide the oil retaining ring and the oil seal cap over the piston tube; screw on the cap and lock it with wire.

Note.- Paragraphs 43 to 48 have been cancelled.

TAIL WHEEL UNIT - SPRING TYPE

49.   Adjusting friction band.-   In the event of excessive wheel shimmy when taxying, the friction band should be tightened.   Such tightening however should not be sufficient to impair the normal functioning of the strut or to prevent the correct working of the self-centring device.   To adjust the band, proceed as follows:-

(i)   Remove the nut, bolt and distance pieces from the friction clip.

(ii)   If both distance pieces are assembled between the lugs of the clip, shorten either one of them.   If one distance piece is fitted under the nut outside the lug, shorten the other fitted between the lugs.

(iii)   If it is desired to slacken the band, assemble a washer between the lugs and the distance pieces.

(iv)   Replace and tighten the bolt.

50.   Adjusting spring.-   The main spring in the strut should have an initial compression of $\frac{1}{4}$ in.   If the procedure described in para.49 does not reduce tyre wear, the spring may require adjustment; proceed as follows:-

(i)   Remove the strut from the aeroplane.

(ii)   Remove the bolt through the top attachment fitting and withdraw the fitting.

(iii)   Slacken the friction clip and slide the outer tube towards the wheel end of the strut to obtain access to the grubscrew in the end fitting.

(iv)   To adjust the main spring, slacken the grubscrew and unscrew the end fitting until the spring is fully extended; measure the amount by which the end fitting has been unscrewed.   If this is less than $\frac{1}{4}$ in., remove the cap and assemble a washer of the required thickness on top of the spring.

(v)   If further adjustment is required, to reduce tyre wear, insert an additional steel washer (1.95 in. o/d x 1.25 in. i/d x $\frac{1}{4}$ in. thick) on top of the spring.

(vi)   Replace the end fitting and attachment fitting.

51.   Dismantling.-   The following procedure should be followed if it is necessary to dismantle the strut for inspection on the renewal of defective parts.   Instructions are given for complete dismantling but, in any particular case, partial dismantling may be sufficient.   The procedure for assembly is similar to that for dismantling but in the reverse order; all parts must be well greased before assembly.

(i)   Remove the bolt securing the top attachment fitting and withdraw the fitting.

(ii)   Slacken the friction clip bolt and compress the strut until the grubscrew in the end fitting is accessible; slacken the grubscrew and unscrew and remove the end fitting.

(iii)   Withdraw the outer tube from the inner tube; the main spring and
        the upper friction cones can then be withdrawn from the inner
        tube assembly end.   After removing the attachment screws, the
        end fitting and the friction clip can be withdrawn from the outer
        tube.

(iv)   Remove the rivets securing the wheel fork in the inner tube and
        withdraw the fork; the centre tube assembly can then be withdrawn
        from the lower end of the inner tube.

(v)   Remove the rivets securing the plug in the upper end of the
        centre tube and withdraw the plug.

(vi)   Remove the pin passing through the cone and the centre tube;
        the cone can then be withdrawn from the tube and the pin
        carrying the inner spring can be withdrawn from the upper end of
        the tube.

(vii)   To remove the wheel, withdraw the bolts passing through the ends of
        the wheel fork, support the wheel and tap out the axle, using a
        suitable drift.

The number and position of any shims fitted on the axle should be noted so
that they can be replaced when assembling the wheel.   If a new wheel is
being fitted, a sufficient number of shims should be fitted to take up end
play.

    51a. Lubrication.- No greasing nipple or other means is provided
for lubricating the sliding parts of the strut.   The friction clip
should be slackened off completely by removing the bolt.   Grease should
then be smeared on the exposed portion of the inner tube when the
strut is fully extended and the strut compressed and released several
times to carry the grease into the inaccessible parts of the strut, more
grease being applied when necessary.   The friction clip bolt should
then be replaced.

                TAIL WHEEL UNIT - DOWTY OLEO-PNEUMATIC TYPE

General

    52.   The shock-absorber unit contains 0.10 pints of type A anti-freezing
oil (Stores Ref. 34A/43 and 46) and is inflated to an air pressure of
630 lb./sq.in. with the wheel clear of the ground.

Storage

    52a. The tail wheel unit (see Sect.7, Chap.5, fig.5) is supplied with
the correct quantity of oil, but with air at atmospheric pressure; it should
be stored in this condition and with the air cylinder uppermost.   It is
advisable, however, to check the oil level (see para.52k) before charging with
air to the pressure given in para.52; the oil level should also be checked
whenever the air has been released to permit easy compression of the strut.
It may be found that a unit that has not been exercised for some time is
sluggish in action, due to the oil having affected the composition of the
gland rings and causing temporary adhesion to the cylinder walls.   This

should rectify itself after a little taxying, but if it persists, the gland
should be removed and cleaned.

Adaptor

52b. General.- This unit (see fig.12) provides a means of connecting a
gauge to the Schrader-type air valve for pressure checking during inflation
or deflation of the shock-absorber.   It consists of a body E which can be
turned in a block D when being screwed to the shock-absorber inflation valve;
when fitted, it is clamped in any convenient position by the knurled nut B.
The boss M on the block D carries the pressure gauge and a ball valve
(for deflating) controlled by the stud G; its outer end provides a connection
C for a line from an air pump.   The inflation valve is opened by screwing
down the rod F by means of the knob A.

52c. Operation.- Attachment of the adaptor to the inflation valve is
effected by slackening the nut B and screwing the body E on to the inflation
valve; do not overtighten or the washer K may spread, causing subsequent
restriction of the airflow past the rod F.   Position the gauge and block D
as required and tighten nut.B.

52d. Leakages.- (i) At sealing washers H, J, K, L and Q.- Tighten
        the part concerned; if this is ineffective dismantle as necessary
        (see para.52e) and renew the washer.

(ii)   At gland washer C.- Dismantle as described in para.52e and renew
        the washer.

(iii) At ball valve.- Dismantle as described in para.52e and examine for
        dirt or damage; renew damaged parts, clean and reassemble.

52e. Dismantling.- To dismantle the adaptor unit proceed as follows:-

(i)   Unscrew the pressure gauge.

(ii)   Remove the burred-over locking screw P and withdraw knob A from
        rod F.

(iii) Unscrew the nut C to free the spring and sealing washer H.

(iv)   Withdraw the body E from the block D and unscrew the rod F.

(v)   Attempt to force the pin out of the head of stud G; if
        unsuccessful, saw off the pin flush with the head, unscrew the
        stud and drive out the remainder of the pin with a punch.   Unscrew
        the stud and remove the ball.

52f. Assembly.- Assembly of the adaptor unit is the reverse of the
dismantling process described in para.52e, but the pin in the head of
stud G should be fitted so that it will contact the peg in block D when
unscrewed $\frac{1}{2}$ to 1 turn; the pin is of steel, of 1/16 in. diameter and
7/32 in. long.

Shock absorber

52g. <u>Warning</u>.- The air pressure must be released <u>before</u> attempting any dismantling operations; failure to observe this precaution may result in a serious accident.

52h. <u>Checking and correcting air pressure</u>.-

<u>Note</u>.- Correct air pressure is dependent on the oil level being correct; if there is any doubt about the latter, either through visible signs of leakage or because no recent check has been made, the level should be checked (<u>see</u> para.52k) and, if necessary, corrected, <u>before</u> correcting the air pressure.

The air pressure may be corrected, with the aid of the inflation valve adaptor illustrated in fig.12 and described in para.52b, as follows:-

   (i)   Jack the tail of the aeroplane so that the tail wheel is well clear of the ground (i.e. full extension - no load).

  (ii)   Attach the adaptor to the shock-absorber, as described in para.52c.

 (iii)   Screw down the knob A to unseat the inflation valve via the rod F; read the pressure on the gauge.

  (iv)   If the pressure is low, unscrew the knob A to close the inflation valve, remove the dust cap N and attach a line from an air pump to the body D; screw down the knob A and operate the pump until a pressure of 630 lb./sq.in. is obtained. Close the inflation valve by unscrewing knob A, disconnect the air line and replace the washer L and dust cap N.

   (v)   If the pressure is too high open the inflation valve and rotate the stud G half a turn to allow the excess air to escape to atmosphere. When the pressure is correct, screw back the stud G and unscrew the knob A to close the inflation valve.

  (vi)   Remove the adaptor from the inflation valve and replace the dust cap.

52j. <u>Deflating</u>.- The shock-absorber must be deflated by means of the adaptor unit (<u>see</u> paras.52b to 52f) and <u>not</u> by unscrewing the inflation valve.

  52k. <u>Checking and correcting oil level</u>.- (i) With the shock-absorber deflated, remove the plug P and compress the unit; if the oil is level with the plug hole replace plug P and re-inflate as described in (iv).

  (ii) If the oil is not level with the plug hole extend the shock-absorber a short distance and fill the cylinder with oil.

 (iii) Compress the shock-absorber and replace plug P.

  (iv) Re-inflate with air through the inflation valve W to a pressure of 630 lb./sq.in., allowing the unit to extend fully.

52m. <u>Removal from tail wheel unit</u>.-   This operation may be accomplished without removing the tail wheel unit (<u>see</u> Sect.7, Chap.5, fig.5).

(i)   Jack up the tail of the aeroplane and deflate the unit (<u>see</u> para.52j).

(ii)   Remove the split pin, withdraw the hinge pin J1 and swing the wheel fork assembly clear.

(iii)   Unlock and remove the bolts A1 and withdraw the shock-absorber unit.

(iv)   Remove the shims X1 and set aside until require for re-assembly. (Note the number of shims fitted).

52n. <u>Leakages</u>.-   Leakage may occur at the following points on the shock-absorber (<u>see</u> Sect.7, Chap.5, fig.5,, and they should be remedied as stated.   When the leakage has been rectified the oil level must be topped up and the unit re-inflated and tested (<u>see</u> paras. 52h and 52q).

(i)   <u>At sealing washers under plug P and inflation valve W</u>.- In either case, fit a new washer. If a new washer fails to remedy the leakage from the inflation valve, the valve itself is probably unsatisfactory and a new one must be fitted.

(ii)   <u>At rings S and Q1</u>.- Remove the inner cylinder assembly V from the outer cylinder Q.   Cut away the existing rings S or Q1 and expand a new one into the groove provided.

(iii)   <u>At the sealing ring Y or gland rings Z</u>.-   Remove the diaphragm R from the inner tube assembly and inspect the ring Y.   If it shows signs of deterioration, renew the ring.   Withdraw the piston assembly T from the cylinder and inspect the gland ring Z.   If found torn or frayed, rings must be renewed.

52p. <u>Removal of gland rings</u>.-   (i) Remove the shock-absorber unit from the tail wheel unit (<u>see</u> para.52m).

(ii)   Remove plug P together with its washer, and drain the cylinder.

(iii)   Remove the inflation valve W and washer.

(iv)   Detach the wire circlip and unscrew and remove the stop nut U, using the spanner S.T.625.   The inner cylinder V may now be withdrawn from the outer cylinder Q.

(v)   Detach the wire circlip and unscrew and remove the diaphragm R, using the spanner S.T.624, to release the sealing ring Y.

(vi)   Remove the floating piston T from the inner cylinder V.

(vii)   Remove the gland rings Z, by detaching the circlip and withdrawing the retaining ring in each case.

(viii)   The damping valve R1 may be dismantled by removing the split pin, unscrewing the nut, and withdrawing the bolt X.

52q. __Testing__.- In the event of loss of oil or air-pressure, or after assembly and before it is re-fitted to the aeroplane, the following tests should be applied to the shock-absorber unit: faults should be rectified as described in para.52n.

(i)   Substitute a $\frac{1}{4}$ in. B.S.P. union for the filler plug P and attach a line (including a gauge) from a hand pump. Remove the inflation valve.

(ii)   Pump in oil up to 1,500 lb./sq.in. and maintain this pressure for a period of 1 minute, during which time unit should hold this pressure. Loss of pressure (if the union sealing washer is sound) will result in the appearance of oil from the washer at the base of the inflation valve or at the point where the inner cylinder enters stop nut U. In the first case, failure of the innermost floating piston ring Z will be denoted. In the second case the sealing ring S is at fault and either ring Y or ring Q1, in addition.

(iii)   With the shock-absorber unit fully extended, attach the adaptor to the inflation valve and pump in air to a pressure of 1,500 lb./sq.in.

(iv)   If this pressure is not held for at least one minute, the ring Z on the air side of the floating piston, or the washer under the inflation valve, or the valve itself, is unsatisfactory.

52r. __Filling and inflating__.- Before the shock-absorber is assembled to the strut and wheel fork, fill and inflate as follows:-

(i)   Fit a $\frac{1}{4}$ in. B.S.P. union in the filler plug hole, after removing plug P.

(ii)   Remove the dust cap from the inflation valve and fit the adaptor (__see__ para.52b).

(iii)   With the unit fully extended and the union uppermost, inflate with air through the adaptor to a pressure of approximately 50 lb./sq.in. then close the valve.

(iv)   Pour in oil through the union in the filler hole to fill end of cylinder and then connect an oil pump to the union.

(v)   Pump in oil to a pressure of approximately 300 lb./sq.in. then release this pressure by operating the control valve on the test rig to allow trapped air and oil to escape. Repeat this operation three or four times to ensure that all air is expelled.

(vi)   Operate the adaptor to release the air pressure then, keeping the inflation valve and bleeder screw in the adaptor open, pump in oil through the union to a pressure of approximately 200 lb./sq.in.

(vii)   Release the fluid pressure and fully compress the unit to permit all surplus fluid to escape.

Shock-absorber - type-C.7941

52s. . An alternative shock-absorber type-C.7941 may be fitted in the Dowty tail wheel unit in place of the shock-absorber type-C.6595 for which maintenance operations are described in paras.52g - 52r.   Maintenance operations for both components are the same with the exception of the points noted below in paras.52 s - 52z.   The alternative shock-absorber is illustrated in Sect.7, Chap.5, fig.5A.

52t.   Leakage past sealing rings or washers.- In each case leakage at these points will necessitate renewal of the ring or rings concerned and, where the rings are in contact with a sliding surface, this surface should be examined for scoring.   Slight scoring may be remedied by polishing, but serious damage will necessitate renewal of the item concerned.   If the leakage is not apparent externally the tests described in paras.52y and 52z will assist in locating the cause of the trouble.

52u.   Failure of damping valve.- Failure of this valve may be caused by dirt between the valve and diaphragm, damage to either face, or to binding of the valve on bolt F .   After thorough cleaning and examination renew any parts that are damaged and re-assemble the unit.

52w.   Dismantling.- Remove the shock-absorber as described in para.52m. Remove the plug A and drain out all the fluid.   Then continue as follows :-

(i)   Remove the circlip and unscrew the bearing nut R, using spanner S.T.625.   This will free the inner cylinder from the fluid cylinder.

(ii)   Unscrew the diaphragm V from the end of the inner cylinder and remove the nut U and bolt F to free the damping valve E.

(iii)   If it is necessary to renew the ring K, unscrew the locking screw L and then unscrew the end fitting O from the cylinder P.

52y.   Fluid test.- Substitute a 1/4 B.S.P. union for the filler plug A and attach a line (including a gauge) from the handpump.   Remove the inflation valve M.   Pump in fluid to a pressure of 1,500 lb./sq.in. Over a period of 1 minute this pressure should be held.   Any loss of pressure (if the union sealing washer is sound) will result in the appearance of fluid from the inflation valve tapping or at the point where the inner cylinder emerges from stop nut R.   In the first case, failure of the floating piston ring T on the fluid side will be indicated.   In the second case, either ring H or ring J is at fault.

52z.   Air test.- With the shock-absorber unit fully assembled, attach the special adaptor to the inflation valve M and pump in air to 1,500 lb./sq.in.   If this pressure is not held for 1 minute the ring T on the air side of the floating piston or the sealing ring K or N is unsatisfactory.

Failure of ring N will cause air to emerge round the outside of the
inflation valve, failure of ring K will cause air to emerge at the
junction of end-fitting O and cylinder P and failure of the air ring
T on the floating piston will cause air to enter the fluid side of the unit

Removal of wheel fork and wheel, etc.

52aa. This operation may be accomplished without removing the tail
wheel unit (see Sect.7, Chap.5, fig.5) from the aeroplane.   The procedure
is as follows :-

    (i)   Remove the split pin and washer and withdraw the pin K1.

   (ii)   Remove the locking screw and unscrew the end plug O, using
          spanner S.T.626.

 (iii)   Remove the bolt F1 and remove the hinge pin N1 by tapping it
          out with a suitable drift.   The wheel fork and wheel may now be
          separated from the pivot bracket.

   (iv)   Remove the locking plate over the axle plug M and unscrew the
          plug.

   (v)   Remove the nuts and bolts affixing the axle blocks M1 in
          position and remove the blocks.   The complete wheel and axle
          may then be withdrawn free of the fork.   The towing bracket
          N under the locking plate may be slipped off the axle end;
          removal of the opposite bracket will first necessitate withdrawal
          of the axle.

Removal of self-centring mechanism

52ab. In order to carry out this operation, a special tool (S.T.627)
is required.   Failure to use such a tool may result in a serious
accident.   The procedure is as follows :-

    (i)   Withdraw bolt B1 and remove the outer tube assembly from the
          strut.

   (ii)   Extract the screwed pins which secure the lower cam F to the
          pivot bracket.   The complete self-centring mechanism may now
          be withdrawn from the pivot bracket.

 (iii)   Detach the wire circlip which retains the bolt E;   the bolt will
          then drop out, together with the rollers D1.

   (i)   Assemble the special clamping tool (S.T.627) to the self-
          centring mechanism, as illustrated in fig.14.

   (v)   Release the spring stop C, as instructed on the diagram.
          All the remaining parts may then be withdrawn from the torque
          fitting D.

Bearing inspection

52ac. When the strut (see Sect.7, Chap.5, fig.5) is dismantled, the following surfaces must be examined and any part showing signs of wear renewed :-

(i)   The inner surface of bearing H1.

(ii)   The inner surfaces of bearings O1.

(iii)   The contact surfaces of cams E1 and F.

(iv)   The outer surface of top end of the pivot bracket I.

(v)   The inner surface of stop nut U in the shock-absorber.

(vi)   The inner surface of the bush in the end plug A.

Assembly

52ad. The assembly procedure is mainly a reversal of the dismantling operations and providing the following points are noted carefully, no difficulty should be experienced in carrying out this operation.

(i)   All parts must be clean before assembly and internal parts should be well greased.   The broad groove formed round the cam E1 should be packed with grease.

(ii)   When assembling the self-centring mechanism refer to fig.14 regarding the use of the special clamping tool (S.T.627). After assembly remove the tool and fit bolt E and rollers D1; replace the wire circlip to retain them.   The mechanism must be assembled before the lower cam F is re-attached to the pivot bracket.

(iii)   The screw pins which secure the cam F in the pivot bracket should be locked by means of a punch.

(iv)   The floating piston T should be assembled in the cylinder V with the aid of a special steel sleeve S.T.622 to avoid damage to the outer lips of the gland rings Z.   The inner cylinder, complete with diaphragm R should be inserted in the outer cylinder Q with sleeve S.T.623 (see fig.13).

(v)   The inflation valve W and the filler plug P should be securely locked with wire, the former to the inner cylinder and the latter to the outer cylinder.

(vi)   Ensure that the shims between the pivot bracket and lugs on the wheel fork are replaced, one either side of the bracket.

(vii)   When re-assembling plug O and stop nut U, tighten as far as possible, then slacken back to nearest locking position.

(viii) When re-assembling the wheel and axle in the fork, tighten axle plug M firmly before replacing the locking plate. Care must be

taken to assemble the towing brackets N so that the distance
piece under the nut for locking plate and the setscrew in the
opposite fork arm prevent any downward movement of the brackets.

(ix) The shock-absorber unit must be filled and inflated before it is
reassembled to the fork and pivot bracket. Care to be taken that
original number of shims X1 are replaced.

(x) After the strut has been fitted in the aeroplane, the four-bolts
which secure the cap of bracket H should be locked to one another
with 20 s.w.g. wire.

(xi) New gland rings should be soaked in type A anti-freezing oil
(Stores Ref. 34A/43 and 46) for at least twelve hours before they
are required for fitting.

TAIL WHEEL UNIT - LOCKHEED OLEO-PNEUMATIC TYPE

General

53.   The shock-absorber unit contains approximately 1/4 pint of fluid
(Stores Ref. 34A/82 and 83) and is inflated to an air pressure of 385 lb./
sq.in. with the wheel clear of the ground.

Storage

53a. The tail wheel unit is illustrated in Sect.7, Chap.5, fig.6 to
which the references in the following paragraphs refer. It is supplied
with the correct quantity of oil, but with air at atmospheric pressure
and should be stored in this condition and with the air cylinder uppermost.
It is advisable, however, to check the oil level (see para.53b) before
inflating the strut to the pressure given in para.53.

Checking air pressure and oil level

53b. The inflation pressure is checked by using the pressure gauge
(ADS.110) together with the adaptor (AIR.13820) which are obtainable for
this purpose. No check can be made of the oil level other than by
carrying out the filling instructions given in para.53t.

Inflating and deflating

53c. To inflate the strut, proceed as follows:-

(i) Jack up the tail of the aeroplane so that the tail wheel is clear
of the ground and the strut is fully extended.

(ii) Remove the air valve cap (5) and screw the hose connection of the
air pump (Part No.AIR.10278) to the air valve.

   (iii) Inflate to a pressure of 385 lb./sq.in. and check the
       pressure with a pressure gauge (ADS.110), using an
       adaptor (AIR.13820).

   (iv) If it is necessary to deflate the strut, reverse the
      air valve cap (5).

    (v) Unscrew the pump connection and replace the air valve cap.

   (vi) Check the air valve for leaks.

Lubrication

53d. Anti-freezing grease (Stores Ref.34A/49) must be applied at
the lubricating nipples which are located on the air head and in the
forward side of the wheel fork (see appropriate lubrication diagram).

Leakages

53e. Leakages of oil or air may occur at any one of the following
points (see Sect.7, Chap.5, fig.6) and they should be remedied as
stated. When the leakage has been rectified the unit must be re-
filled (if necessary) and re-inflated.

   (i) Leakage at air head seal (4).
      Deflate the strut (see para.53f) and remove the air valve
      (5) and the grease nipple (30) from the plunger tube
      assembly. Remove the circlip (65) and withdraw the bolt
      (29) to release the wheel fork from the plunger tube and
      withdraw the bush (59) from the plunger tube. Remove one
      of the fluid plugs (39) and pump sufficient oil into the
      strut to force the air head partially out of the end of
      the plunger tube. Cease pumping and withdraw the air
      head. Collect the distance piece (18). Inspect the seal
      (4); if worn or damaged a new one must be fitted.

   (ii) Leakage at the separator seals (17).
      Proceed according to instructions in para.53u (i) and
      remove the air head. Continue pumping until fluid
      appears out of the air valve hole and then lever the
      separator (16) downwards by inserting a blunt tool
      through the air valve hole, until the separator can be
      withdrawn from the end of the plunger tube. Inspect
      the seals (17); if found worn or damaged, new seals must
      be fitted.

   (iii) Leakage at fluid head seal (40) and/or piston seals (10).
      Remove the fluid head (37) and/or the piston (6) from the
      strut (see paras. 53m and n). Examine the rubber seals;
      if they are torn or frayed, they must be renewed.

Dismantling and inspection

53f. Warning.- The air pressure must be released before attempting

any dismantling operations; failure to observe this precaution may
result in a serious accident.

53g. <u>Removal of wheel and axle</u>.- (i) Deflate the unit (<u>see</u> para.53f)

(ii) Remove the bolts (62) from the fork bosses.

(iii) Withdraw one of the spools (69) together with the hook (54) from
the fork boss and axle tube (52).

(iv) Withdraw the second spool and hook together with the axle from
the wheel fork and tap the spool off the axle. During the
operation support the wheel in a true position.

53h. <u>Removal of wheel fork assembly</u>.- (i) Deflate the unit
(<u>see</u> para.53f).

(ii) Remove the split pin, nut, and washer and withdraw the bolt (28)
from the hinge fitting (19). The two bushes (61) in the wheel
fork are a press fit and should not be removed unless worn.

(iii) Remove the circlip (65) and supporting the wheel fork, withdraw
the bolt (29). The wheel fork may now be removed.

53j. <u>Removal of the self-centring assembly</u>.- (i) Remove the clip
(43) from the top end of the unit, and, using a screwed rod,
withdraw the four dowels (42).

(ii) Withdraw the self-centring mechanism from the top end of the
strut.

53k. <u>Dismantling self-centring components</u>.- (i) Cut the legs from
the split taper pin (51) and secure the assembly between the jaws
of a clamp.

(ii) Remove the split pin and gently release the clamp, which is taking
the tension of the spring (49). until the tension is released.

(iii) Remove the assembly from the clamp and withdraw the spring retainer
(50) together with the spring.

(iv) Remove the roller (48) from the pin (47).

(v) Slide the sleeve (46) together with the pin to the bottom of the
slots incorporated in the top attachment fitting (45), turn the pin
until the flats correspond with the slots, and remove it from its
housing.

(vi) Withdraw the sleeve and the cam (41), together with its bush (44),
from the top attachment (45).

<u>Note</u>.- The bush is a press fit in the bore of the cam and should not
be removed unless worn.

53m.   **Removal of fluid head and plunger-tube assembly.-** (i) Remove the wheel fork assembly (**see** para.53h).

(ii)   Remove the locking wire and unscrew the air valve assembly (5).

(iii) Drive the bush (59) from the air valve head (3) and remove the greaser (30) at that point.

(iv)   Remove the self-centring mechanism (**see** para.53j).

(v)   With the strut in an upright position, remove the filler plugs (39) and drain the strut of oil.

(vi)   File the riveting from the two taper pins (38) and remove the pins from the cylinder tube (2).

(vii) Push the plunger tube (1) into the cylinder tube until it reaches the fluid head and, using a wooden rod in contact with the air head (3), push the fluid head and plunger-tube assembly out of the cylinder tube.

        NOTE:- During the above operation, the rubber seals on the fluid head and piston must be eased carefully past the holes in the cylinder tube.

53n.   **Removal of piston and plunger-tube components.-** (i) Remove the plunger-tube assembly (1) from the cylinder tube (2) (**see** para.53m).

(ii)   Unscrew the countersunk screw (9), which secures the dowel retaining ring (8) to one of the dowels, and tap the ring back to expose the dowels.

(iii) Using a screwed-rod, withdraw the four dowels (7), and the piston, from the plunger tube. Remove the dowel retaining ring.

(iv)   Using a wooden rod in contact with the separator (16), push the air head, distance piece (18) and the separator, out of the plunger tube.

(v)   Extract the circlip (15) out of its recess in the piston and remove the piston cap (14), flutter plate (13) and spring (12).

(vi)   The rubber seals may now be inspected and removed, if necessary, by easing them out of their respective grooves.

53p.   **Removal of attachment bracket, end fitting, etc.**

(i)   Remove the plunger-tube assembly (**see** para.53m).

(ii)   Remove the clip (36) from the retaining ring (33) and withdraw the four dowels (34) by means of a screwed-rod. The stop ring (35), inside the cylinder tube, is now free to be removed.

(iii)   Slide the attachment bracket (31), complete with its bushes (32),
        and the retaining ring, off the cylinder tube.   The bushes (32)
        are a press fit in the attachment bracket and should not be
        removed, unless worn.

(iv)   Remove the 1/8 in. dia. plug (22) by means of a 1/16 in. dia.
        shallow drill, tap 8 B.A., and a screwed rod.   Care to be
        taken not to drill right through.   (See Sect.CC, Sect.7, Chap.5,
        fig.6).   Slide the retaining ring (21) off the cylinder tube,
        extract the four dowels (20), and withdraw the hinge fitting
        from the cylinder tube.

(v)   Extract the circlip (26) from its groove in the hinge fitting and
        remove the retaining ring (25), split block (23) and rubber
        seal (24).

53q. Bearing inspection.- Periodical inspection should be made of
bearing surfaces for signs of wear particulars of which are given in
Vol.II, Part 2.

Assembly

53r. General.- With the exception of the detail assembly of the self-
centring mechanism, instructions for which are given in para.53s, no
difficulty should be experienced in assembling the parts as the procedure
is mainly a reversal of the dismantling operations.   The following points,
however, should be noted:-

(i)   Ensure that all parts are free from dirt or any foreign matter
        before assembly.

(ii)   After fitting the dowels (7) and (20), they should be filed flush
        with the respective tube.

(iii)   The plug (22) should be locked, using a centre punch, and then filed
        flush.

(iv)   The countersunk screw (9) is locked by punching the retaining ring
        metal (8) into the screwdriver slot.

(v)   When assembling the bush (59), ensure that it protrudes an equal
        amount on each side of the plunger tube.

(vi)   The two taper pins are locked by riveting them over.

(vii)   After assembly, the wheel fork should be checked for movement.

(viii) Ensure that the hooks (54) face aft when the axle is assembled.

(ix)   Ensure that all setscrews, etc. are securely locked with wire.

Note.- The filler plugs (39) must not be locked until after the strut
        is filled with oil.

53s. *Self-centring mechanism.*—

(i) Insert the top attachment fitting (45) through the bush (44) in the cam (41).

(ii) Slide the sleeve (46), pin hole foremost, over the top attachment tube, so that the holes in the former are in line with the slots in the latter.

(iii) Fit the pin (47) through the holes in the sleeve and the slots in the tube and slide the pin and sleeve along the tube so that one end of the pin enters the bore of the cam. Fit the roller (48) on the pin and slide the sleeve down the tube until the roller is in contact with the bottom of the cam.

(iv) Place the spring (49) in position on the sleeve and assemble the spring retainer (50) on the outer end of the spring.

(v) Using a clamp, compress the spring so that the inner portion of the spring retainer enters the bore of the top attachment fitting ensuring that the taper pin holes are in line.

(vi) Fit the split taper pin (51) and secure the latter by bending the legs against the outer diameter of the top attachment fitting. Ensure that the head and legs of the taper pin cannot foul the coils of the spring. Remove the clamp.

(vii) Insert the self-centring mechanism assembly in the bore of the cylinder tube and line up the dowel holes. The locating hole in the cam (41) must be on the centre-line of the strut, as indicated in Sect. 7, Chap. 5, fig. 6. Fit the four dowels (42) and secure with the clip (43).

Note.—It is important to remember that the alternative shock-absorber type C.7941 requires an air pressure of 990 lb./sq. in. while type C.6595 only requires a pressure of 630 lb./sq. in. To enable the two shock-absorbers to be recognised, the sliding cylinder on type C.7941 has been stamped with the figure II between the inflation valve and the lubricator.

Filling

53t. *First method.*—It is essential that the correct amount of fluid be maintained in the strut; too little or too much fluid, even with the correct air pressure, may result in failure of the strut. A special fluid gun (Part No. AIR.10280) is necessary for attachment to the strut. To fill the strut with the full weight of the aircraft on the tail wheel, proceed as follows:—

(i) Open the inflation valve (5) and remove one of the filler plugs (39); ensure that the strut is fully compressed and that the inflation valve remains open during the complete operation.

(ii) Charge the fluid gun with oil to Spec. D.T.D.388, taking care not to draw in air.

(iii) Screw the fluid gun extension piece into the orifice and force the fluid into the strut. This will require a considerable effort and will ensure that the separator (16) is forced down to the limit of its travel.

(iv) Remove the other fluid plug and gently force fluid from the gun until a stream, free from air bubbles, emerges from the orifice.

(v) Unscrew the fluid gun and extension piece, replace both filler plugs and lock with wire.

53u. *Second method.*—To fill the strut when it has been removed from the aircraft, proceed as follows:—

(i) Open the inflation valve (5) and charge the fluid gun (*see* para. 53t (ii)).

(ii) With the strut in a vertical position, remove one of the fluid plugs, screw the fluid gun extension piece into the orifice and force fluid into the strut until no more will enter. This operation, which will require considerable effort, ensures that the separator is forced down to the limit of its travel and will also extend the strut.

(iii) Unscrew the fluid gun and extension piece, and fully compress the strut in order to discharge all surplus fluid; replace the fluid filler plug (39) and lock both plugs with wire.

FUEL SYSTEM

Filter

54. *Cleaning.*—Turn the fuel-distributing cock to the OFF position and remove the filter unit. To do this, hold up the locking spring and unscrew the wing nut securing the stirrup; swing the stirrup clear of the bottom casing and withdraw the latter together with the filter and spring. Wash the filter in petrol and re-assemble the filter unit; do not use rag for cleaning the filter.

Main tanks

55. *Draining.*—Turn the fuel-distributing cock to the OFF position, remove the drain plug from the four-way piece situated at the centre of the rear wall of the undercarriage wheel housing, and drain the fuel into a suitable receptacle.

56. *Draining one tank.*—Turn the fuel-distributing cock to the OFF position. Remove the door at the inboard edge of the tank bottom covering and remove the locking wire from the isolating cock in the tank sump; turn the cock to the OFF position. Uncouple the fuel delivery pipe at the cock and loosen the coupling at the other end of the pipe; this coupling is at the four-way piece on

Continued on next leaf

the centre of the rear wall of the undercarriage wheel housing.
Fit a length of hose to the cock, open the cock, and drain the
fuel into a suitable receptacle.

Reserve tank

57. Draining.- Remove the split pin which locks the sleeve
of the drain valve situated at the bottom of the sump. Fit a
suitable piece of hose to the nozzle of the drain valve, unscrew
the sleeve a few turns and drain the fuel through the hose into a
convenient receptacle. When the fuel has ceased to flow,
retighten the sleeve and lock it with a split pin.

Long-range tanks

58. Draining.- If fixed long-range tanks are fitted, they may be
drained through the main tanks as follows. Drain the main tanks as
directed in para. 55, then switch on the electric fuel pumps; this
will cause the fuel to be pumped from each long-range tank to the
corresponding main tank. Any small amount of fuel left in the bottom
of the tank when the electric pump ceases to function can only be
removed by removing the tank, or by syphoning. To drain only one
tank, proceed as directed in para. 56, and only switch on the pump of
the tank to be drained. The jettisonable long-range tanks should be
removed in the normal way for draining (see Sect.4, Chap.2).

OIL SYSTEM

Draining

59. General.- The oil system should be drained when the oil is hot to ensure adequate draining and in order that the viscosity valve shall not close the oil cooler circuit; the system is drained by separately draining the oil tank and the oil cooler as described in paras.60 and 61 respectively. For particulars of flushing the oil system and cleaning the oil tanks see A.P.1464A, Vol.I.

60. Draining oil tank.- Remove the under-fairing strip at the bottom rear edge of the oil tank and then the wire locking the drain valve situated at the bottom rear corner of the tank about midway along its length. Unscrew the valve a few turns and drain the oil through a funnel into a suitable receptacle.

61. Draining oil cooler.- Lower the radiator flap to its lowest possible position, and remove the wire locking the drain plug in the bottom of the cylindrical cooler. Remove the drain plug and drain the oil cooler with the aid of a funnel and a hose leading to a suitable receptacle; when the oil has ceased to flow, replace the drain plug and lock it with wire. If the oil does not flow freely, uncouple either the oil inlet or oil outlet connection at the top of the oil cooler; access to these connections may be obtained by removing the door in the fuselage fairing above the flap.

Filter

62. Cleaning.- Remove the locking wire and release the adjusting screw at the top of the filter. Unscrew the top cap and remove the inner sealing cap, the spring, and the gauze filter. Wash the filter in petrol and dry it in an airblast; do not use rag for cleaning the gauze. When reassembling, the filter should be filled with oil before replacing the top cap and care must be taken to ensure that an airtight joint is made.

Viscosity valve

63. Cleaning filter.- Remove the large screwed plug at the rear end of the valve; the nut which locks the centre screwed plug to this large screwed plug must not be unscrewed or removed under any circumstances as it is sweated in position after the valve has been calibrated. Without removing the filter from the valve head, clean the gauze in petrol and dry it by means of an air-blast. The screwed plug at the front end of the valve may be removed, if necessary, for inspection of the valve at that end.

COOLING SYSTEM

General

64. Attention is drawn to the general instructions on the maintenance of cooling systems given in A.P.1464A. Vol.I.

Draining

65. Remove the door in the bottom of the radiator fairing and the wire locking the drain plug. Remove the drain plug and drain the radiator with the aid of a funnel and a hose leading to a suitable receptacle; when the coolant has ceased to flow replace the drain plug and lock it with wire.

Filling

66. With the tail wheel of the aeroplane on the ground, provide vents as follows:-

   (i) Remove the radiator drain plug.

   (ii) Remove the plug on top of the return pipe from the radiator
        to the engine, about 12 in. aft of the centre section
        front spar.

   (iii) Remove the two vent plugs on the engine outlet pipes
         at the front.

   (iv) Open one cock on the base of the engine-driven pump.

67. Remove the filler cap from the header tank and pour in slowly, through a fine-mesh strainer, sufficient coolant to obtain a flow from the radiator drain hole; screw in the drain plug and lock it with wire.

68. Continue to pour in coolant as above, and as the coolant content of the system is increased, it will flow in turn from each of the above-mentioned vents. Close and lock each vent as soon as coolant flows from it; coolant flowing from the vents should be caught in suitable receptacles so that the total quantity remaining in the system may be checked. When the coolant is level with the rim of the filler neck of the header tank, replace the filler cap and run the engine as for warming up; this will disperse any trapped air. Stop the engine and check the level of the coolant; top up if the level has dropped. Run the engine again until the coolant temperature reaches 60°C, when the engine should be stopped and the header tank topped up if necessary. The system should require 18 gallons of coolant.

HYDRAULIC SYSTEM

General

69. Absolute cleanliness is essential for the satisfactory operation of the system. The fluid must be maintained at the correct level in the handpump reservoir, otherwise air will probably be pumped

into the system; the reservoir should be full when the aeroplane is
in the flying position. When replenishing the fluid, the filter must
be left in the filler neck and only clean fluid should be used;
care should be taken not to spill the fluid as it may remove the
protective coating from parts with which it comes in contact. After
replenishing the fluid, the filter in the filler neck should be
cleaned. When it is necessary to drain any part of the system and
retain the fluid for further use, the receptacle used must be
scrupulously clean as grease or other types of oil will injure the gland
and jointing compositions employed in the system. When pipelines are
disconnected, their ends must be protected against the entry of dirt
and all parts must be thoroughly examined before reassembly to ensure
freedom from foreign matter. If it is necessary to wash foreign matter
from a component, only the fluid employed in the system (see para. 70)
may be used.

Filling

70. General.- The fluid used in the hydraulic system is anti-
freezing oil, type A (Stores Ref. 34A/43 and 46). Two methods of
filling the system are given ; the first method will usually be
satisfactory and is of value when time is an important factor; the
second method is more thorough and should be followed whenever time
allows. A procedure similar to the second method should be adopted if
it is necessary to bleed air from a system already-filled.

71. First method.- Trestle the aeroplane in the flying position
with the undercarriage wheels clear of the ground and proceed as
follows:-

(i)   Fill the handpump reservoir with fluid and set the
        selector lever to WHEELS UP.

(ii)   Operate the handpump until the fluid level in the
        reservoir ceases to fall, pausing and topping up when
        necessary.

(iii)   Repeat the operations given in sub-para. (ii) with the
        selector lever in the WHEELS DOWN, FLAPS DOWN and
        FLAPS UP positions, successively.

(iv)   Repeat the operations detailed in sub-paras. (ii) and
        (iii) two or three times to expel air from the
        handpump system, finishing with the undercarriage down.

(v)   Lower the aeroplane to the ground and chock the wheels;
        anchor the tail to prevent it lifting when the engine
        is run.

(vi)   Set the selector lever at NEUTRAL and run the engine at a
        fairly high speed so as to expel air from the engine-
        driven pump circuit.

72. <u>Second method</u>.- Trestle the aeroplane in the flying position with the undercarriage wheels clear of the ground and proceed as follows :-

Note.- During the whole of the operations detailed below the oil level in the handpump reservoir must be maintained to prevent air entering the system.

(i)　　Fill the reservoir with fluid, move the selector lever to WHEELS DOWN and operate the handpump to ensure that the undercarriage is fully down. Slacken the unions at the anchored ends of the undercarriage jacks and operate the hand pump; tighten the unions immediately the fluid escapes freely and air bubbles cease to appear. Slacken the connection at the catch gear jack and operate the hand pump; tighten the connection immediately the fluid escapes freely and air bubbles cease to appear. Slacken the connection at the pressure gauge and operate the hand pump; tighten the connection immediately the fluid escapes freely and air bubbles cease to appear.

(ii)　　Move the selector lever to the WHEELS UP position and remove each piston rod eyebolt pin. Operate the handpump to retract the jacks. Swing the jacks upwards until the piston rod ends are above the level of the anchored ends. Slacken the pipe unions at the piston rod ends of the jacks to produce vents. Operate the handpump; tighten the unions immediately fluid flows freely and air bubbles cease to appear. Swing the jacks downwards until the piston rod ends are slightly below the level of the anchored ends. Move the selector lever to the WHEELS DOWN position and operate the hand pump to extend the jacks. Refit the piston rod eyebolt pins.

(iii)　　Move the selector lever to the FLAPS DOWN position and operate the handpump to ensure that the flaps are fully down. Slacken the union at the anchored end of the flap jack and operate the hand pump; tighten the union immediately fluid flows freely and air bubbles cease to appear. At the T-piece near the control box return connection, slacken the connection of the pipe from the pressure relief valve. Operate the hand pump; tighten the connection immediately fluid flows freely and air bubbles cease to appear.

(iv) Move the selector lever to the FLAPS UP position.   Remove the
      piston rod eyebolt pin.   Operate the handpump and retract the jack.
      Swing the jack upwards until the piston rod end is above the level
      of the anchored end.   Slacken the pipe union at the piston rod end
      of the jack to provide a vent.   Operate the handpump and tighten the
      unions immediately the fluid flows freely and air bubbles cease to
      appear.   Swing the jack downwards until the piston rod end is
      slightly below the level of the anchored end.   Move the selector
      lever to FLAPS DOWN position and operate the handpump to extend the
      jack.   Refit the piston rod eyebolt pin.

(v)   The supply pipe leading from the engine-driven pump to the system
      must now be filled;   the pipe should be disconnected at the
      automatic cut-out valve and fluid poured in slowly through a funnel
      and filter until the pipe is full.

(vi) Lower the aeroplane to the ground, chock the undercarriage wheels,
      and anchor the tail to prevent its lifting when the engine is run.
      Set the selector lever at NEUTRAL and run the engine at a fairly
      high speed in order to expel air that may still be present in
      the system.

Testing system

73.   When testing the operation of the undercarriage and flaps, the
blow-off pressures of the various relief valves in the system should be
checked by comparing the pressure registered on the gauge fitted in the
cockpit at the termination of each operation with the value given in the
table below.   The component incorporating the relevant relief valve is
indicated in brackets by one of the following abbreviations:-

      C.B. = Control box   A.C.O. = Automatic cut-out
      P.R.V. = Pressure relief valve.   valve

Position of selector lever	lb./sq.in.
Using handpump -	
WHEELS UP and DOWN	* 1,650 minimum (C.B.)
FLAPS UP	* 1,650 minimum (C.B.)
FLAPS DOWN	370 ± 15 (P.R.V.)
Using engine-driven pump - WHEELS DOWN	1,200 $^{+50}_{-0}$ (A.C.O.)

      * In aeroplanes having the alternative rotary control valve (Part
         No.C.6165) in place of the control box, no pressures for these
         positions are obtainable, as relief valves are not incorporated.

Fault finding

74.   The following table may help in locating faults in the system.
In addition, the tests described in the preceding paragraph will
disclose faulty settings of the relief valves in the system.

Symptom	Possible causes	Remedies
Jack can be operated by hand-pump but not by engine-driven pump.	Faulty engine-driven pump. Faulty cut-out valve.	Substitute new pump. See paras.93 to 102.
Jack fails to operate or operates slowly.	Insufficient fluid. Air in system. Faulty ½ in. B.S.P. non-return valve. Faulty control box or rotary control valve. Faulty jack. Faulty cut-out valve.	Top up reservoir. See paras.70 and 72. See paras.138 to 141. See paras.103 to 114 or 114a to 114k. See paras.115 to 127. See paras.93 to 102.
Jack operates slowly and returns to original position.	Leakage past jack piston. Faulty control box or rotary control valve.	See paras.121 to 127. See paras.103 to 114, or 114a to 114k.
Flaps fail to lower.	Faulty pressure relief valve.	See paras.132 to 137.
Undercarriage fails to lower.	Faulty catch gear jack.	See paras.128 to 131.
Cut-out valve cuts in and out repeatedly.	Leakage in control box or rotary control valve.	See paras.103 to 114, or 114a to 114k.
Cut-out valve fails to cut-out at end of jack stroke. Note.- It is normal for the cut-out not to operate when the selector lever is at FLAPS DOWN.	Dirty filter causing high back-pressure.	See paras.90 and 92.

Testing components

75. <u>Test rig.</u>- For testing the hydraulic components, a test rig is required consisting essentially of a handpump and reservoir and a pressure gauge capable of reading up to 1,800 lb./sq.in. In addition, testing will be greatly facilitated if a control valve is connected between the handpump and the component under test. Preferably, the control valve should be of a type having four pipe connections, two for connection to the handpump and the reservoir, respectively, and two more for connection to the component under test; also, it should be possible, by an appropriate setting of the control handle of the valve, to put either test connection into communication with the handpump and the other with the reservoir, or to put both test connections into communication with the reservoir. The pressure gauge should be connected in the pipe-line leading from the handpump. In subsequent paragraphs dealing with testing components, it is assumed that such a control valve is being used but the tests can be carried out without a control valve by slackening the pipe connection between the handpump and the component when it is desired to release the pressure. For testing the handpump of the hydraulic system, an air pressure gauge and an air pump or other source of air supply, capable of producing a pressure of 5 lb./sq.in., is required.

76. <u>Blanking off components.</u>- It is necessary, during the tests, to blank off various pipe connections in the components. This may be done by inserting a fibre or metal washer into an ordinary A.G.S. union nut or alternatively, by placing a steel ball in the end of the union body and holding it in place by a nut.

Handpump

77. <u>Leakage at joint between casing and cover.</u>- Remove the cover (<u>see</u> para.84) and fit a new paper joint; a coat of gold-size must be applied to the new joint. The test given in para. 89 should be made after assembly.

78. <u>Leakage at gland.</u>- The gland packing should be removed as follows:-

    (i)   Remove the cover from the casing (<u>see</u> para.84).

    (ii)   Remove the old packing from the cover.

    (iii)   Apply a coat of goldsize to the paper joint and replace the cover.

    (iv)   Insert the new packing; about $\frac{3}{4}$ in. should be cut off the packing otherwise it will not be possible to screw in the gland nut far enough for the locking plate to engage it.

(v)   The test described in para.89 should then be applied.

(vi)   If the test shows that the gland is satisfactory, the gland nut should be locked by means of its locking plate.

79.   Leakage at pipe connections.- To obtain access to the pipe connection locking nuts inside the casing, the cover must be removed (see para.84); in the case of the connection at the bottom of the casing, the pump must also be removed (see para.85). The connections should then be made fluid-tight as follows:-

(i)   Slacken the locknuts on the leaky connections. A special spanner (Part No. S.T.237) is provided for the locknuts on the connections at the rear top and bottom of the casing.

(ii)   Tighten the connections and re-tighten the locknuts.

(iii)   Test the connections as described in paras. 88 and 89.

(iv)   If the connections still leak, remove the locknuts from the connections and remove the connections from the casing. In the case of the pipe connection at the front top of the casing, the delivery pipe between the pump and the connection must be first removed. Clean the faces on the casing and connections and apply a coat of Duralac (Stores Ref. No.33B/214). Screw the connections into the casing and replace and tighten the locknuts.

(v)   Repeat the tests described in paras. 88 and 89.

80.   Leakage between valve bodies and pump body.- Leakage past the sealing washers between the suction and delivery valves and the pump body can often be remedied by tightening the valve bodies on to the sealing washers. If this does not stop the leak, new sealing washers should be fitted. The pump must be removed from the casing (see para. 85) to enable these operations to be performed and the tests described in paras. 86 to 89 should be applied after completing the operations.

81.   Leaky valves.- If a suction or delivery valve does not close correctly, proceed as follows:-

(i)   Remove the pump from the casing (see para.85).

(ii)   Remove the faulty valve from the pump body.

(iii)   If foreign matter is present, carefully wash the valve and seat. If the steel ball is not seating correctly,

remove the pin holding it to the valve body and give
the ball a sharp tap on to its seat; replace the pin.

(iv)   Screw the valve body into the pump body and perform the
tests described in paras. 86 to 89. If the valve still
does not close correctly, fit a new steel ball and
repeat the tests.

82. Leakage past pistons.- After removing the pump from the
casing (see para.85), proceed as follows:-

(i)   Disconnect the piston links from the shaft by removing
the coupling pins.

(ii)   Withdraw the pistons from the cylinders.

(iii)   Inspect the piston rings. If they appear to be in good
condition, tighten the piston nut slightly and re-lock by
means of a centre-punch. If the rings are damaged, fit
new ones.

(iv)   Assemble the pump and perform the test described in
para.87.

(v)   Replace the pump in the casing, connect the delivery pipe,
and test as described in paras. 88 and 89.

83. Leakage past cylinder liner.- Should leakage occur between a
cylinder liner and the cylinder, a new cylinder block must be
substituted since the block is supplied with the liners in position.

84. Removing cover from casing.- To obtain access to the interior
of the casing, the cover should be removed as follows:-

(i)   Remove the locking plate from the gland nut and remove
the gland nut.

(ii)   Remove the bolts attaching the cover to the casing and
withdraw the cover, taking care not to damage the gland
packing as the cover is being drawn off the shaft.

Note.- When replacing the cover, a coat of goldsize must be applied
to the paper joint.

85. Removing pump from casing.- Remove the cover as described in
the preceding paragraph and proceed as follows:-

(i)   Disconnect the delivery pipe at the pump and at the
connection in the casing wall and withdraw the pipe.

(ii)   Remove the screws attaching the pump to the casing and
withdraw the pump.

86. Testing delivery valves.- This test is carried out with the pump removed from the casing and the pistons removed from the cylinders.

     (i)   Connect the test rig to the delivery connection on the pump.

     (ii)   Set the control valve on the test rig to feed fluid to the pump body and operate the handpump until the gauge shows a pressure of 1,600 lb./sq.in. This pressure should hold indefinitely. Leakage past a delivery valve will be shown by fluid appearing at the bottom of the cylinder bore with which the leaky valve is associated.

87. Testing pistons, cylinder liners, and suction valves.- For this test the pump must be completely assembled and mounted in the casing; the outlet connection at the bottom of the casing must be blanked off and instead of the normal cover, a special half cover (Part No. S.T. 238) must be attached to the casing.

     (i)   Pour fluid into the casing until the suction valves are completely submerged.

     (ii)   Operate the pump to ensure that fluid is flowing freely and to eject any foreign matter from the pump.

     (iii)   Set the handle so that one piston is at the top of its stroke.

     (iv)   Blank off the delivery connection on the pump.

     (v)   Apply pressure to the handle; if the piston, cylinder liner, and suction valve are in good condition it will be impossible to move the handle. If leakage is taking place past the piston, fluid will appear on the top of the piston; if leakage is taking place between the cylinder and liner, fluid will appear at the top of the cylinder block; if there is no sign of leakage at either of these points but the pump handle can be moved, the suction valve is faulty.

     (vi)   Remove the blank from the delivery connection and repeat the operations described in sub-paras. (ii) to (v) to test the other cylinder.

88. Testing delivery pipe.- This test is most conveniently performed immediately after the test described in preceding paragraph. In the following instructions, it is assumed that the preceding test has just been completed.

     (i)   Connect the delivery pipe to the pump and to the

connection in the casing wall; blank off the
connection outside the casing.

(ii)   Apply pressure to the pump handle. If it is possible
to move the handle, inspect the connections at each
end of the delivery pipe for leakage.

89. Blanking test.- For this test an air pump, or other source of
air supply, and a pressure gauge are required. The test is carried out
with the handpump and casing completely assembled.

(i)   Blank off the three pipe connections.

(ii)   Connect the air pump to the filler neck of the pump
casing. For this purpose a special air adaptor (Part
No. S.T.107/A) and sealing washer (Part No. S.T.107/B)
are provided. One end of the adaptor screws into the
filler neck and the other is made to receive a $\frac{3}{8}$ in.
i/d rubber pipe carrying the air supply.

(iii)   Operate the air pump to produce a pressure of 5 lb./sq.
in.

(iv)   Submerge the casing in water and watch carefully for
signs of leakage at the joint between the casing and
cover, at the gland, and at the pipe connections.

Filter

90. Cleaning.- Remove the plug in the bottom of the filter; remove
the filter element and wash it; the element should be dried in an air
blast before replacement. When assembling the filter, care should be
taken to ensure that the washer above the element is placed with its lip
downwards. A special spanner (Part No. S.T.245) is provided for
the plug.

91. Leakage.- Leakage past the sealing washers under the pipe
connections or the plug in the bottom of the filter can often be
remedied by tightening the connections or plug. If this fails to stop
the leakage, a new sealing washer should be fitted. The test
described in para.92 should then be applied.

92. Testing.- The following test checks the filter for leakage
at the connections and plug.

(i)   Connect the test rig to the inlet connection.

(ii)   Operate the handpump and see that fluid flows freely
from the outlet connection.

(iii)   Blank off the outlet connection.

(iv)   Operate the handpump to produce a pressure of 20 lb./
         sq.in. and inspect the filter for leakage.

Automatic cut-out valve

93.   **Leakage at pipe connections or caps.-** If leakage occurs past
the sealing washers at the pipe connections or caps, an attempt should
be made to stop the leak by tightening them. If this has no effect,
the sealing washers should be renewed. The test described in para. 97
should then be applied.

94.   **Leakage past piston.-** In the event of leakage taking place
past the piston, the gland ring should be renewed as follows:-

    (i)   Remove the cap at that end of the cut-out remote from
            the pipe connections.

    (ii)   Withdraw the piston assembly.

    (iii)   Slacken the grubscrew and remove the cap from the piston.
            (The distance piece, washers, and spring in the hollow
            end of the piston are now free; care should be taken to
            replace them when assembling the piston).

    (iv)   Withdraw the spacer ring and the gland ring.

    (v)   Place a new gland ring in position and assemble the
            piston.

    (vi)   After assembly, the tests described in paras. 97 and 98
            should be applied.

95. **Leakage past non-return valve.-** If the non-return valve in the
outlet connection leading to the control box is faulty, proceed as
follows:-

    (i)   Remove the pipe connection.

    (ii)   Withdraw the cruciform spring abutment, the spring, and
            the valve.

    (iii)   Inspect the valve and the seat; any foreign matter presen
            should be carefully washed off. If the valve or seat is
            damaged, a new one should be substituted. If the valve
            and seat appear to be in good condition, leakage may be
            taking place past the sealing washer under the seat; this
            should be remedied by tightening the seat or fitting a
            new sealing washer. A special spanner (Part No.S.T.240)
            is provided for tightening or removing the seat.

(iv) Assemble the valve and perform the test described in para.98.

96.   Leakage past by-pass valve.- If the by-pass valve does not close correctly, proceed as follows:-

(i)   Remove the cap at that end of the cut-out nearest the pipe connections.

(ii) Withdraw the valve and spring.

(iii) Wash off any foreign matter from the valve or seat; at the same time examine for signs of damage such as scoring. If this is slight the valve and seat may be re-lapped together with fine emery paste. Extensive damage will necessitate the renewal of the faulty members.

(iv) Re-assemble and test as described in para. 99. If the leakage persists, it may be due to a fault in the washer which is fitted, in the later cut-outs, under the valve seating. If there is no washer present or if the fitting of a new one proves ineffective, a new by-pass valve complete with seat must be fitted.

97.   Blanking test.- This test checks the pipe connections and caps for leakage past the sealing washers.

(i)   Blank off the two outlet connections.

(ii) Connect the test rig to the inlet connection.

(iii) Operate the handpump until the gauge reads 1,800 lb./sq.in. Inspect the cut-out for signs of leakage.

98.   Testing piston and non-return valve.- The following test will discover leakage past the gland ring on the piston or past the non-return valve in the outlet connection leading to the control box.

(i)   Connect the test rig to the outlet connection leading to the control box.

(ii) Operate the handpump until a pressure of 700 lb./sq.in. is attained. This pressure should hold indefinitely. Leakage past the piston will be indicated by fluid appearing at the outlet connection adjacent to the inlet connection. Fluid appearing at the inlet connection would indicate a faulty non-return valve. Increase pressure gradually, until 1,250 lb./sq.in. is indicated. The same conditions should be fulfilled.

99.   Testing by-pass valve.- To test the by-pass valve for correct closing, proceed as described in para.100 but use a test pressure of only 1,000 lb./sq.in. At this pressure the by-pass valve will remain closed and fluid dripping from the outlet connection would indicate leakage past the valve.

NOTE.- A non-return valve should be fitted in the handpump delivery line to the cut-out to ensure that there is no difference between the pressure applied to the by-pass valve and that behind the piston, such as might be

F.S./17

occasioned by a fall of pressure in the delivery line, which would tend to operate the cut-out and so negative the test.

100.   Checking cut-out pressure.- This test checks the pressure at which the by-pass valve opens.   The correct pressure is 1,200 lb./sq.in. + 50-0.

  (i)   Blank off the outlet connection leading to the control box.

 (ii)   Connect the test rig to the inlet connection.

(iii)   Operate the handpump and note the pressure at which the fluid is diverted to the outlet adjacent to the inlet.   In order to obtain an accurate reading, the handpump must be operated by slow and steady strokes;   when the cut-out pressure is nearly reached, the pump handle should be returned to the beginning of its stroke and then operated smoothly to obtain the cut-out pressure.   If the pressure is incorrect, adjust the valve as described in para.101.

101.   Adjusting cut-out pressure.- The method of adjusting the cut-out pressure is as follows:-

  (i)   Remove the cap at the opposite end of the cut-out to the pipe connections.

 (ii)   Withdraw the piston assembly.

(iii)   Slacken the locknut and remove the pin locking the adjusting cap to the plunger protruding from the piston.

 (iv)   Screw the cap further on to the plunger to increase the cut-out pressure or unscrew it to decrease the pressure.

  (v)   Tighten the locknut, assemble the cut-out, and perform the test described in para. 100.

 (vi)   Alternately,   adjust and test until the correct cut-out pressure is obtained.

(vii)   Fit a new locking pin;   this will involve drilling another hole through the cap and plunger, and a new plunger must be fitted; it is not permissible to drill a second hole in the existing plunger.

(viii)   Assemble the cut-out and test as described in para. 97.

102.   Adjusting spring in piston.- The spring housed in the end of the piston assembly should have an initial compression of 0.1 in + 0.02.   The following is the procedure for checking and adjusting the spring:-

  (i)   Remove the cap at the end of the cut-out remote from the pipe connections.

 (ii)   Withdraw the piston assembly.

(iii)   Slacken the grubscrew and remove the cap from the end of the piston.   Removal of the cap allows the spring to expand completely and force the distance piece partly out of the spring housing.

(iv) Measure the amount by which the distance piece has been pushed
out, i.e., measure the gap between the end of the housing and the
flange on the distance piece. If this measurement is not within
the limits set out above, it should be corrected by altering the
number of washers assembled between the end of the spring and the
distance piece.

(v) When the correct measurement has been obtained, assemble the piston
in the reverse order to the dismantling described in sub-paras. (i)
to (iii) and apply the tests described in paras. 97, 98 and 100.

Control box

103.   Leakage at caps or pipe connections.- Leakage past valve caps
or pipe connections can often be cured by tightening them but, if this is
ineffective, new sealing washers should be fitted.

104.   Leakage past non-return valves.- A faulty non-return valve should
be dismantled and the rubber washer on the valve inspected. Foreign
matter adhering to the washer can usually be washed off without damaging
the washer. If, however, the washer is damaged, a new valve should be
substituted. Replacement valves are supplied with the nut not locked and
with a number of distance washers of various thicknesses under the rubber
washer. In the case of a cam-operated valve, it is very important that
the new valves shall be identical with the old one as regards the distance
between the rubber washer and the tip engaged by the cam. The nuts and
rubber washers should be removed from both the old and the new valves and
selected distance washers assembled on the stem of the new valve until,
when compared by means of a pair of calipers, it is identical with the old
valve; the rubber washer and nut should then be replaced and the end of
the stem riveted over the nut. During the riveting operation, the tip of
the valve should rest on a block of wood to obviate damaging the part
engaged by the cam. The purpose of this accurate adjustment of the height
of the rubber washer above the tip of the valve is to ensure that the valves
open in the correct order when the camshaft is turned from the neutral
position to an operative position; it is essential for the valve in the
return circuit to open before the valve in the supply circuit. In the
case of the non-return valves which are opened by the fluid and not by the
camshaft, the height of the rubber washer above the tip is not important.
After assembling the valves, the tests described in paras. 110 and 111
should be performed.

105.   Leakage past camshaft packings.- Slight leakage past the gland
rings at the ends of a camshaft can often be remedied by tightening the
gland nuts slightly; this is ineffective if the unit is one which
incorporates gland rings of U-type section, in which case new rings must
definitely be fitted. In cases where the nuts are of the slotted type,
use the special spanner ST.102. Overtightening will damage the rings and
render the operating lever more difficult to actuate. If further tightening is ineffective, or if leakage is occuring past the sealing rings
between the cams (where such rings are fitted) the camshaft should
be removed, as follows, and the rings renewed where necessary (see
paras. 106 and 107).

for the method of inserting the camshaft and gland rings).

(i)   Remove the actuating arm from the camshaft.

(ii)   Remove the six non-return valves associated with the
        camshaft. Careful note should be made of the positions
        of the valves as it is of the utmost importance that
        they should be replaced in their original positions.

(iii)   Remove the plates or grubscrews locking the gland nuts
        and remove the nuts. Withdraw the camshaft; one gland
        ring will be withdrawn with the camshaft and the other
        can then be removed from the control box.

106. <u>Inserting camshaft</u>.- A special tool is required for inserting
the camshaft into the control box. The tool (Part No. S.T.209) is in
the form of a sleeve which fits in the position normally occupied by
one of the gland nuts; the sleeve has a tapered bore so that, when the
camshaft is pushed through the sleeve, the sealing rings are compressed
and guided into the plain bore of the control box beyond the threads.
When the camshaft is in position, the six non-return valves may be
assembled.

107. <u>Fitting camshaft gland rings</u>.- Two special sleeves (Part Nos.
S.T.209 and 218) are provided to facilitate insertion of the gland rings.
One sleeve fits over the end of the camshaft to guide the gland ring
on to the larger diameter of the shaft and the other sleeve fits in the
threaded portion of the bore of the control box to cover the threads and
to guide the gland ring into the plain bore beyond the threads. After
inserting the gland rings and removing the sleeves, the spacer rings and
gland nuts should be inserted. The nuts should be screwed down tight
and then slackened back about a quarter of a turn. The tests described
in paras. 110 and 112 should then be applied and if the control box
passes these tests, the gland nuts should be locked by means of the
locking plates or grubscrews.

108. <u>Leakage past removable relief valve seat</u>.- To obtain access to
the seat, remove the appropriate relief valve cap. It may be possible
to stop the leak by tightening the seat by means of the special tool
(Part No. S.T. 211) and tommy bar (Part No. S.T.111/13); if this does not
effect a cure, the sealing washer under the seat should be renewed. After
replacing the sealing washer and valve cap, the test described in para.
110 should be performed to ensure that the joint between the cap and the
body is fluid-tight. The blow-off pressure of the relief valve should
then be checked as described in para.113 to ascertain whether it has
been affected by tightening the seat.

109. <u>Faulty relief valves</u>.- If faults develop in the relief valves,
they may be dismantled as follows:-

(i)   Unscrew and remove the relief valve caps; remove the
        sealing washers.

(ii)   Unscrew and remove the valve seats by means of the
        special tool (Part No. S.T.211) and tommy bar (Part No.
        S.T.111/13).

(iii)   Invert the control box; the upper ball valves and the
        capsules containing the springs will then fall out.

(iv)   Slacken the adjusting screw locknuts, using the special
        spanner (Part No. S.T.210) and remove the adjusting
        screws. The bottom capsules and balls will then fall
        out.

The defective parts should be renewed and the valves assembled; the
procedure for assembly is similar to that for dismantling but in
the reverse order. Care should be taken to ensure that the parts are
assembled in their original positions and, in particular, it should
be noted whether any of the capsules had shims under the springs; these
are sometimes necessary to enable the correct blow-off pressure to be
obtained and it is important that they should not be omitted during
assembly. The test described in para.110 should then be applied.

110. Blanking test.- This is a test of the effectiveness of the
glands and the sealing washers in the pipe connections and the non-return
and the relief valve caps. For this test, the relief valves must be
assembled; the valve caps and the locknuts on the adjusting pins must
be screwed down tight to prevent leakage at these points. The test should
be carried out as follows:-

(i)   Blank off the undercarriage and flaps "up" and "down"
        connections and the main return connection.

(ii)   Connect the test rig to the main supply connection.

(iii)   Set the control valve on the test rig to feed fluid to
        the control box and move both camshafts to the UP
        position.

(iv)   Operate the handpump until a pressure of 1,750 lb./sq.in.
        is shown on the gauge. Watch for any signs of leakage;
        the control box should hold this pressure indefinitely.

(v)   Release and re-apply the pressure several times.

(vi)   Release the pressure, set the camshafts to the DOWN
        position, and perform the operations described in sub-
        paras. (iv) and (v). During the test, the control box
        should be examined for leakage at the pipe connections,
        valve caps and glands.

111. **Testing non-return valves.**- The following procedure tests the non-return valves for correct seating.

    (i)   Connect the test rig to one of the four jack connections on the control box and blank off the remaining jack connections.

    (ii)   Set the control valve on the test rig to feed fluid to the control box and set both camshafts to NEUTRAL.

    (iii)   Operate the handpump to produce a pressure of 1,600 lb./sq.in. This pressure should hold indefinitely. A fall in pressure indicates that one or both of the non-return valves communicating with the connection into which fluid is being fed is faulty.

Note.- If the relief valves are not known to be in good order, the possibility of leakage past them should be borne in mind. This may be due to a damaged ball or seat or to a poor joint between the removable seat and the body.

    (iv)   Repeat the above procedure on each of the three other jack connections.

    (v)   Connect the test rig to the main supply connection on the control box; none of the other connections need be blanked off.

    (vi)   Set the control valve on the test rig to feed fluid to the control box, leaving the camshafts at NEUTRAL.

    (vii)   Operate the handpump to produce a pressure of 1,600 lb./sq.in. If this pressure does not hold, one or more of the non-return valves set obliquely in the control box is faulty.

112. **Testing shaft packings.**- This test will disclose leakage along the camshafts between the cams. It is assumed that the control box has passed the tests described in paras. 110 and 111.

Each camshaft is tested separately as follows:-

    (i)   Blank off the flaps and undercarriage "up" and "down" connections.

    (ii)   Connect the test rig to the main supply connection.

(iii)   Set the control valve on the test rig to feed fluid to the control box and turn the camshaft under test to the UP position and the other camshaft to NEUTRAL.

(iv)   Operate the handpump until the gauge shows a pressure of 300 lb./sq.in. This pressure should hold, though leakage past the gland ring at lower pressures is permissible.

(v)   Increase the pressure to 1,600 lb./sq.in. If there is no leakage at the gland and the relief valves are known to be in good condition, loss of pressure will indicate leakage along the camshaft between the cam at the opposite end of the control box to the pipe connections and the central cam. If the relief valves are not known to be in good condition, loss of pressure may be caused by a faulty relief valve or by leakage past the sealing washer under the removable relief valve seat. When applying the test pressure, watch carefully for longitudinal movement of the camshaft. If movement is observed, the gland nuts should be tightened until no movement takes place when the pressure is released and re-applied.

(vi)   Turn the camshaft under test to the DOWN position and apply a pressure of 1,600 lb./sq.in. If the operations described in sub-paras. (iv) and (v) have not disclosed any leakage, a fall of pressure will indicate leakage along the camshaft between the central cam and the cam at the end of the shaft nearest the pipe connections or, if the relief valves are not known to be in good condition, loss of pressure may be due to a faulty relief valve.

(vii)   Test the other camshaft by repeating the operations described in sub-paras. (iii) to (vi).

113. <u>Testing relief valves</u>.- The following procedure checks the relief valves for correct blow-off pressure:-

(i)   Connect the test rig to the flaps "up" and "down" connections. Turn the camshafts to NEUTRAL.

(ii)   Set the control valve on the test rig to feed fluid to each connection in turn and operate the handpump; read the blow-off pressure of the relief valve associated with each connection. The correct pressure is 1,700 lb./sq.in. $\pm \frac{100}{50}$.

(iii)   Connect the test rig to the undercarriage "up" and "down" connections and repeat the operations described in sub-para. (ii). The correct blow-off pressure is 1,700 lb./sq.in. $\frac{+\ 100}{-\ 50}$.

114.   Assembly and adjustment of relief valves.- The four relief valves
in the control box are adjusted by means of two threaded pins which project
through that end of the control box in which the pipe connections are
situated.   The pins can be rotated by means of a screwdriver, and locked
by means of nuts under which sealing washers are placed to make a fluid-tight
joint.   A special box spanner (Part No.S.T.21Q) is provided for the locknut;   the spanner is made so that a screwdriver can be inserted through it
to turn the adjusting pin whilst the locknut is held by spanner.   The inner
end of each pin, on which the spring capsules of the valve bear, is in the
form of a concentric cone;   these pins are to be screwed down as far as
possible and, under this condition, no leakage must occur past relief valves
under 1,650 lb./sq.in. minimum.

Rotary control valve

114a.   Leakage at external sealing washers.- If leakage occurs at the
external sealing washers, tighten the part concerned; if this is
ineffective, fit a new sealing washer and test as described in para.114g.

114b.   Leakage at valve joint washers.-   To cure, proceed as follows:-

   (i)   Remove the four jack connections A, C, E and G, from the
         base block (see Sect.9, fig.6A).

  (ii)   Remove the split pins and nuts from the four securing bolts D
         and withdraw the bolts.

 (iii)   Carefully separate the valve housing J and base block N.

  (iv)   Fit a new sealing washer T round each boss.

   (v)   Ensure that the contact faces of the housing and block are
         clean and undamaged and that the disc valves are correctly
         located relative to their shafts and the base block;   the
         radial slot in the underside of the valve disc should point
         in the same direction as the arrow on the outer end of the
         shaft.

  (vi)   Refit the base block to the housing and re-insert the four
         securing bolts.   Tighten the nuts fully but do not replace the
         split pins until the test (see para.114g) has been satisfactorily
         completed.

114c.   Leakage at face of disc valves.-   To cure, proceed as follows:-

   (i)   Disconnect the valve housing J from the base block N (see para.
         114b (i), (ii) and (iii)).

  (ii)   Remove the disc valves and examine the springs for damage or
         fatigue and, if necessary, fit a new spring.

 (iii)   Examine the valve and base block for signs of damage, wear,
         scoring etc., and relap the two parts.   If damage is
         extensive renew one or both components.

(iv)   Reassemble the unit (see para.114b (v) and (vi)) and test as described in para.114k.

114d. Leakage at gland ring.- To cure, proceed as follows:-

(i)   Disconnect the valve housing from the base block (see para.114b (i), (ii) and (iii)).

(ii) Remove the operating lever from the shaft concerned and withdraw the shaft from the housing.

(iii) With the ball race K and spacer ring W in position on the shaft, expand a new gland ring Q over the shaft but not right up to the spacer ring.

(iv) Re-insert the shaft in the housing, reassemble and test the unit as described in para.114g.

114e. Leakage at sealing washer under head of bolts.- To cure, proceed as follows:-

(i)   Remove the split pin and tighten the nut on the bolt concerned.

(ii) If this is ineffective remove the union, split pin, nut and bolt D and fit a new sealing washer under the bolt head.

(iii) Refit the bolt and union and test the unit (see para.114g) before replacing the split pin.

114f. Leakage at non-return valves.-

(i)   Remove the valve cap U and withdraw the spring and valve.

(ii) Examine the spring, valve and valve seat for signs of damage, wear or the presence of foreign matter. If necessary, fit a new valve or valve spring.

(iii) Reassemble valves and test as described in para.114j.

114g. Pressure test.-

(i)   Connect the unit by union B to an external oil pump and blank off the flaps "down" and undercarriage "down" connections. Move both control handles to the "down" position and build up a pressure of 1,800 lb./sq.in.

(ii) The unit should hold this pressure. Failure to do so indicates leakage at any of the following points:-

(a) External sealing washers.
(b) Contact faces of disc valve and body.
(c) Operating shaft, indicating faulty gland ring Q.

For remedy refer to paras. 114a to 114e.

(iii)   Release the pressure at the two "down" connections before
        moving the control handles, then blank off the two "up"
        connections and move the control handles to the "up" position.

(iv)   Repeat the above test as for the "down" connections and remedy
        any leakage that occurs.

114h.   Flow test.-

(i)   Connect the unit by union B to the external pump and leave
        all other unions open.

(ii)   Select, in turn, the flaps "up", flaps "down", undercarriage
        "up" and undercarriage "down" and see that fluid flows from the
        correct unions.

(iii)   Fluid flowing from the wrong connections indicates incorrect
        location of the disc valve concerned.

114j.   Non-return valve test.-

(i)   Connect union A to the external pump and blank off all re-
        maining unions except union B.

(ii)   Move the undercarriage control lever to the UP position and
        build up a pressure of 1,800 lb./sq.in.

(iii)   Examine the valve for leakages at the joints and unions. Any
        fluid escaping from the union B indicates a faulty non-
        return valve S.

(iv)   Disconnect the unit from the pump and blank off the union A;
        remove the blank from the union E and connect this to the
        pump.

(v)   Repeat the above test and inspect for leakages.

114k.   Disc valve test.-

(i)   With both levers within 7° on either side of the central or
        neutral position, connect union B to the external pump.

(ii)   Leave all other unions open and build up a pressure of
        1,800 lb./sq.in.

(iii)   Escape of fluid from either of the flap unions indicates a
        faulty flap disc valve, or from either undercarriage union a
        faulty undercarriage disc valve. Leakage from union F may
        occur if either valve is at fault.

(iv)   With a pressure of 1,800 lb./sq.in. in the box, the effort
        required to move either lever must not exceed 39 lb./sq.in.

Note.- The levers must not be moved with a pressure in excess of
        1,800 lb./sq.in. in any part of the valve.

Undercarriage and flap jacks

115.   Storing.- Jacks are supplied as spares with a small quantity of fluid on each side of the piston.   To prevent adhesion of the packing rings to the piston rod and cylinder wall, each jack should be extended and retracted at intervals of about fourteen days.   It is necessary to remove the sealing caps from the pipe connections to enable the jacks to be operated;   care should be taken to ensure that the caps are afterwards replaced.   Any jack withdrawn from service should be treated in this way.

116.   Checking positions of undercarriage jacks.- The length of each undercarriage jack and its position relative to the undercarriage may be checked by removing the bolt coupling the piston rod to the triangulated lever.   The length of the piston rod must be such that, when the jack is fully extended and the undercarriage locked down, the eye of the piston rod can be placed outboard of the fork on the triangulated lever and not more than 3/32 in. from it.

117.   Adjusting for length.-   The length of the piston rod of a jack can be adjusted as follows:-

(i)   Slacken the locknut on the eyebolt screwed into the end of the piston rod and remove the eyebolt.

(ii)   Fit a new tabwasher, screw the eyebolt into the desired position, tighten the locknut and lock it with the tabwasher.

118.   Leakage at pipe connections.- If leakage occurs at the pipe connections, the connections should be tightened;   if this fails to stop the leak, the sealing washers should be renewed.   The test described in paras. 126 and 127 should then be applied.

119.   Leakage at locking ring.- The undercarriage jacks have an end fitting at the anchored end of the jack and the flap jack has an end fitting at the gland end.   The end fitting is screwed on to the jack cylinder and locked by a ring which, in turn, is locked by wire; a sealing ring is gripped between the end fitting and the locking ring.   If leakage occurs past the sealing ring, proceed as follows:-

(i)   Break the locking wire and unscrew the locking ring; the
       sealing ring can then be inspected. A special spanner
       (Part No. S.T.151) is provided for the locking rings on
       the undercarriage jack and another special spanner (Part
       No. S.T.189), for that on the flap jack.

(ii)   If the sealing ring requires renewing, remove the end
       fitting; the sealing ring can then be withdrawn. In the
       case of the flap jack, refer to para: 123 for the method
       of removing the end fitting; the complete piston assembly
       will be withdrawn with it.

(iii) Place a new sealing ring in position on the cylinder and
       replace the end fitting. See para.124 for the method of
       inserting the piston into the cylinder when replacing
       the flap jack end fitting.

(iv)   Screw the locking ring on to the end fitting and lock
       with wire

(v)   Test as described in para. 126 or 127.

120.   **Leakage at gland.**- Leakage at the gland can be remedied as
follows:-

(i)   Measure the distance between the centre of the eyebolt
       and the end of the piston rod. Slacken the locknut and
       remove the eyebolt.

(ii)   Remove the gland nut by means of the special spanner (Part
       No. S.T.149 for an undercarriage jack ; Part No. S.T.188
       for the flap jack).

(iii) With tne jack retracted, blank off the pipe connection at
       the gland end of the jack. Slowly extend the jack;
       the air pressure thus produced in the cylinder will blow
       out the gland rings. An alternative method of blowing
       out the gland rings is to pump air into the pipe connection
       at the gland end of the jack.

(iv)   Inspect the rings; renew them if they are damaged or
       replace them if they are in good condition. The fit of
       the rings on the piston rod and in the gland should be
       checked.

(v)   Tighten and lock the gland nut. Care should be taken
       not to over-tighten the nut as this might cause the rings
       to bind on the piston rod

(vi)   Test the gland as described in paras.126 and 127.

(vii) Replace and lock the eyebolt in its original position;
       a new tabwasher should be fitted to lock the nut.

121. <u>Leakage past piston of undercarriage jack.</u>- If leakage
occurs past the piston of an undercarriage jack, proceed as follows:-

(i)   Dismantle the gland assembly (<u>see</u> para.120, sub-paras.
        (i) to (iii)).

(ii)   Break the locking wire and unscrew the locking ring from
        the end fitting, using the special spanner S.T.151.

(iii)   Unscrew the end fitting from the cylinder.

(iv)   Withdraw the piston from the cylinder.

(v)   Remove the split pin and unscrew the nut from the
        piston; one cup ring can then be withdrawn from the
        piston.

(vi)   Remove the circlip and locking pin and unscrew the piston
        from the piston rod; the support ring and the other cup
        ring can then be withdrawn from the piston.

(vii)   Place a new cup ring in position on the piston, replace
        the support ring, and screw the piston into the piston
        rod: replace the locking pin and circlip.

(viii) Place another new cup ring on the piston and screw on the
        nut; lock it with a split pin.

(ix)   Insert the piston into the cylinder as described in
        para.124.

(x)   Complete the assembly of the jack and apply the tests
        described in paras. 125 and 126.

122. <u>Leakage past piston of flap jack.</u>- If leakage occurs past the
piston of the flap jack, remove the end fitting complete with piston
assembly (<u>see</u> para. 123) and proceed as follows:-

(i)   Withdraw the end fitting from the piston rod.

(ii)   Remove the circlips locking the piston nuts and remove
        the nuts.

(iii)   Substitute new cup rings, screw on the piston nuts and
        lock them with circlips.

(iv)   Assemble the jack (<u>see</u> para.124 for the method of
        inserting the piston into the cylinder).

(v)   Perform the tests described in paras. 125 and 127.

123. **Removing end fitting** and piston from flap jack.- When dismantling the flap jack to obtain access to the piston rings or to the sealing ring under the end fitting, it is most convenient to remove the end fitting and piston assembly together as follows:-

  (i)   Remove the pipe connection in the end fitting and remove the bush thus disclosed. (The bush passes through the end fitting and into the cylinder wall).

  (ii)   Break the locking wire and unscrew the locking ring using the special spanner (Part No. S.T.189).

  (iii)   Unscrew the end fitting from the cylinder and withdraw the end fitting together with the piston assembly.

124. **Inserting piston.**- To facilitate the insertion of the pistons into the cylinder, two special tools are provided, the one for the flap jack being Part No. S.T.191 and the other for the undercarriage jacks being Part No. S.T.192. Each tool is in the form of a tube which fits on the end of the jack in the position normally occupied by the end fitting. The bore of the tube is tapered in order to compress the piston rings to enable them to enter the cylinder bore when the piston is pushed through the tube.

125. **Testing jacks for free movement.**- This test checks a jack for smooth movement of the piston. The test pressure is 25 lb./sq.in. for an undercarriage jack and 50 lb./sq.in. for the flap jack.

  (i)   Connect the test rig to one of the pipe connections.

  (ii)   Operate the handpump to produce the test pressure given above. The piston should travel smoothly to the opposite end of the jack. If a higher pressure is needed to move the piston, binding may be taking place between the gland packings and the piston rod.

  (iii)   Connect the test rig to the other pipe connection and repeat the operation described in sub-para. (ii).

126. **Testing undercarriage jacks for leakage.**- The following test checks an undercarriage jack for leakage; the test pressure is 1,600 lb. sq.in.

  (i)   Connect the test rig to the pipe connection in the end fitting.

  (ii)   Operate the handpump to produce the test pressure. Inspect for leakage at the following points:-

           (a) Pipe connection to which test rig is connected.

           (b) Locking ring.

(c) Piston: this will be indicated by fluid dripping from the pipe connection at the gland end of the jack.

(iii) Disconnect the test rig and re-connect it to the pipe connection at the gland end of the jack.

(iv) Operate the handpump to produce the test pressure. Inspect for leakage at the following points:-

(a) Pipe connection to which the test rig is connected.

(b) Gland.

(c) Piston: this will be indicated by fluid dripping out of the pipe connection in the end fitting.

127. **Testing flap jack for leakage**.- The following test checks the flap jack for leakage:-

(i) Connect the test rig to the pipe connection at the anchorage end of the jack.

(ii) Operate the handpump until the gauge reads 700 lb./sq.in. Inspect for leakage at the following points:-

(a) Pipe connection to which test rig is connected.

(b) Pistons: this will be indicated by fluid dripping out of the pipe connection at the gland end of the jack.

(iii) Disconnect the test rig and re-connect it to the pipe connection at the gland end of the jack.

(iv) Operate the handpump to produce a pressure of 1,800 lb./sq.in. Inspect for leakage at the following points:-

(a) Pipe connection to which test rig is connected.

(b) Piston: this will be indicated by fluid dripping out of the pipe connection at the anchorage end of the jack.

(c) Locking ring.

(d) Gland.

Catch gear jack

128. **Leakage at pipe connection**.- Leakage at the banjo connection

can often be remedied by tightening the banjo bolt. If this does not stop the leak, the sealing washers should be renewed.

129. **Leakage past piston.**- This can be remedied by renewing the gland ring on the piston as follows:-

    (i)   Remove the end plug from the jack body.

    (ii)   Withdraw the spring and the piston.

    (iii)   Unscrew and remove the nut on the piston, using the special spanner (Part No. S.T.165).

    (iv)   Substitute a new gland ring for the old one, replace the nut and lock it with a split pin.

    (v)   Assemble the jack and test as described in para.131.

130. **Adjustment of travel.**- The travel of the piston rod can be adjusted by screwing the end plug in the jack inwards or outwards as required.

131. **Testing.**- The test is for discovering leakage at the banjo connection or past the piston.

    (i)   Connect the test rig to the jack.

    (ii)   Operate the handpump until a pressure of 1,800 lb./sq.in. is attained. This pressure should hold. There should be no leakage past the sealing rings at the banjo connection or past the piston; leakage past the piston would be disclosed by fluid escaping through the end plug in the jack.

Pressure relief valve

132. **Leakage at pipe connections.**- If leakage occurs where the reducing unions screw into the **valve** body, the reducing unions should be tightened; if this has no effect, the sealing washers should be renewed.

133. **Leakage between spring housing and body.**- Remove the locking plate; if the leak cannot be stopped by tightening the joint, a new sealing washer should be fitted. The locking plate should be replaced and its locking screw inserted.

134. **Leakage at gland.**- Remove the wire locking the gland nut and stop the leak by tightening the nut or renewing the packing; relock the gland nut with wire.

135. **Leakage past valve.**- Leakage when the valve is closed may be due to a faulty valve or seat or to a poor joint between the seat and the body. The valve should be dismantled by unscrewing the spring housing from the body. If either the valve or seat is damaged, a new valve and seat must be fitted as follows:-

(i) Withdraw the valve spindle from the spring housing and remove the valve.

(ii) Remove the reducing union from the inlet connection of the valve body.

(iii) Slacken the grubscrew in the interior of the body by means of a screwdriver inserted through the inlet connection.

(iv) Using the special spanner (Part No. S.T.174) and tommy bar (Part No. S.T.111/12), remove the valve seat and insert the new one; a new sealing washer should also be fitted.

(v) Tighten the grubscrew and assemble the valve.

(vi) Apply the tests described in paras. 136 and 137.

If neither the valve nor seat show signs of wear, leakage is probably taking place past the sealing washer between the seat and the body. This may be remedied by tightening the seat or renewing the sealing washer. The procedure is similar to that given in sub-paras. (iii) to (vi). above.

136. **Testing.**- The following procedure should be adopted when testing the relief valve for leakage.

(i) Connect the test rig to the outlet connection.

(ii) Operate the handpump until a pressure of 1,000 lb./sq.in. is attained. Inspect the valve for leakage at the following points:-

(a) Joint between the valve body and the reducing union.

(b) Joint between the valve body and the spring housing.

(c) Gland.

(d) Leakage past the valve; this would be shown by fluid dripping from the inlet connection.

(iii) Blank off the outlet and connect the test rig to the inlet connection.

(iv)   Operate the handpump to produce a pressure of 1,000 lb./
sq.in. Inspect the inlet connection for leakage.

137. **Checking and adjusting blow-off pressure.-** The valve should
blow-off at 370 lb./sq.in. ± 15. The method of adjusting the valve to
blow-off at this pressure is as follows:-

    (i)   Remove the wire locking the adjusting stud to the gland
nut.

    (ii)   Connect the test rig to the inlet connection.

    (iii)   Operate the handpump and note the pressure at which the
valve blows off. If the pressure is too high, screw
the adjusting stud outwards; if the pressure is too low,
screw it inwards.

    (iv)   When the correct blow-off pressure has been obtained.
re-wire the adjusting stud to the gland nut.

Non-return valves

138. **Leakage at joint in body.-** Leakage at the joint between the
two parts of the valve body can be stopped by tightening the joint,
or, if this has no effect, by renewing the sealing washer. The test
described in para. 141 should then be applied.

139. **Leakage past valve.-** Leakage past the valve can be remedied
as follows:-

    (i)   Dismantle the valve by unscrewing the two parts of the
body.

    (ii)   Inspect the valve and seat. If foreign matter is present,
carefully wash the valve and seat. If the rubber
valve washer is damaged, fit a new one. The valve
washer in the $\frac{1}{2}$ in. B.S.P. non-return valve is attached
to the cruciform valve by a special screw whilst the
washer in the $\frac{3}{8}$ in. B.S.P. non-return valve is attached
to the valve by being sprung over a protuberance on
the valve.

    (iii)   Assemble the valve and test as described in paras. 140
and 141.

140. **Flow test.-** This test checks the valve for freedom of flow.

    (i)   Connect the test rig to the inlet connection.

    (ii)   Operate the handpump; the flow of fluid through the
valve should be free and steady. If there is resistance
to free flow, the valve should be dismantled and

inspected to find the cause.

141.   Testing for leakage.-   This test discovers leakage past the
valve and at the joint in the body.

(i)   Connect the test rig to the outlet connection.

(ii) Operate the handpump until a pressure of 1,400 lb./
sq.in. is indicated by the gauge.   Inspect the joint
in the body for signs of leakage.   Leakage past the
valve will be shown by fluid dripping out of the inlet
connection.

Variable flow valve

142.   General.-   This component is similar to the $\frac{3}{8}$ in. B.S.P.
non-return valve, the only difference being that a small hole passes
through the centre of the cruciform valve;   the remedies for leakage
are the same as those given in paras. 138 and 139.

143.   Testing.-   This test checks the joint in the valve body for
leakage and the valve washer for correct functioning.

(i)   Connect the test rig to the connection above the valve.

(ii)   Blank off the other connection.

(iii) Operate the handpump to produce a pressure of 1,400 lb./
sq.in.   Inspect the joint in the valve body for leakage.

(iv)   Remove the blank from the connection.

(v)   Operate the handpump and inspect the valve;   fluid should
flow through the central hole only;   there should be no
leakage past the valve washer.

PNEUMATIC SYSTEM

Charging

144.   If the pressure in the system is less than 150 lb./sq.in.
(as shown on the "supply" scale of the pressure gauge in the cockpit),
it should be increased to not more than 300 lb./sq.in. by means of
a handpump or compressed air cylinder.   The charging connection is
mounted either on the port side of the firewall or on the starboard
side of the air bottle sealing cover.   Access to the former is via
the intermediate side panel of the engine cowling and, to the latter,
through the undercarriage well.

Oil trap

145. <u>Draining</u>.- Slacken off the locknut and unscrew the drain
plug in the bottom of the trap; after two or three turns, the oil
should flow through the small hole in the side of the drain connection
and may be caught in a suitable receptacle. If necessary, the
drain plug may be removed completely.

146. <u>Cleaning</u>.- Detach the inlet and outlet pipes by unscrewing
the union nuts, and, with a C-spanner, unscrew the top half of the
trap. Slacken the clamping bolts in the supporting bracket and withdraw the trap downwards; lift out the cap embodying the outlet
connection. Clean the trap with a dry rag and make sure that the
inlet, outlet and drain connections are free from foreign matter.

Oil reservoir

147. <u>Draining</u>.- Slacken off the locknut and unscrew the plug in the
overflow connection two or three turns, detach the air pipe from the
bottom connection and allow the oil to drain away through a funnel and
tube into a suitable receptacle.

148. <u>Replenishing</u>.- Slacken off the locknut and unscrew the plug
in the overflow connection. Remove the filler cap and insert a filter
funnel in the filler neck; pour in treated castor oil to Specification
D.T.D.72 (Stores Ref. 34A/5 and 45) until the oil commences to flow
through the small hole in the underside of the overflow connection.
Tighten the overflow plug and the locknut; replace the filler cap.

Air cylinder

149. <u>Draining</u>.- Detach the air pipe at each end of the cylinder
by unscrewing the union nuts; release the cylinder by removing the
bolts from the securing straps. Swing the straps clear and withdraw
the cylinder downwards and to starboard; unscrew the union from one
end of the cylinder and drain any condensed moisture.

Air filter

150. <u>Draining</u>.- Slacken off the locknut and unscrew the drain
plug in the bottom of the filter; after two or three turns, the oil
should flow through the small hole in the side of the drain connection
and may be caught in a suitable receptacle. If necessary, the drain
plug may be completely removed.

151. <u>Cleaning</u>.- Detach the inlet and outlet pipes by unscrewing
each union nut and, with a C-spanner, unscrew the top half of the
filter. Slacken the clamping bolt in the supporting bracket and withdraw the filter downwards; lift out the cap embodying the outlet

connection and remove the felt filter element.   Wash the element in
petrol and dry it in an air blast.   Clean the internal surfaces of the
filter with a dry rag, and see that all the connections are free from
foreign matter.   Assemble the filter and replace it in its mounting
bracket.

Pressure reducing valve

152.   Adjusting.- To adjust the delivery pressure, remove the split pin
securing the screwed plug in the end of the valve casing and screw the plug
in to increase the pressure or out to decrease the pressure;   replace the
split pin.   The correct delivery pressure is 150 lb./sq.in.

Oil/water trap

153.   On some aeroplanes an oil/water trap is incorporated in place of the
oil trap; for maintenance operations, reference should be made to A.P.1519,
Vol.I.

Minimum bend of compressor-to-oil-trap pipe

154.   If the flexible pipe between the B.T.H. air compressor and the oil
trap is to Part No.A.120183 care should be taken to ensure that a
minimum bend radius of 3.25 in. is maintained.

Pipe connections

155.   On certain aeroplanes the low pressure pipes have been painted
yellow near each end to enable satisfactory joints to be made;   the pipe
should be pushed into the rubber joint until no unpainted portion extends
beyond the joint thus ensuring that the pipe is properly gripped when
the joint is tightened.

Vacuum system

156.   A test adaptor is fitted in the suction pipe-line just forward of
the instrument panel; the adaptor has two branches, one for a suction
gauge and the other for an external pump to enable the instruments to be
tested when the engine is not running.   Access to the adaptor is obtained
by removing the tank cowl.   Maintenance of the engine-driven vacuum pump
and adjustment of the relief valve are described in A.P.1519, Vol.I.

MISCELLANEOUS

Bonding

157.   The complete bonding of the aeroplane is shown in fig.9.

Draining reservoir of oil drain collector

158.   To drain the oil collector reservoir remove the access door on the underside of the port leading edge fillet and open the drain cock at the rear of the reservoir allowing the oil to flow out of the drain pipe into a suitable receptacle.   Close the drain cock and replace the access door.

Oil dilution valve

159.   No attempt should be made to service or repair this unit; if faults develop, a new valve must be fitted and the faulty valve returned for maintenance.

Ammunition counter

160.   If it should be necessary to check the operation of this unit, set the counter at "300", and with all the guns unloaded and uncocked, press the firing button on the control column and time the counter, which should return to "0" in 15 seconds approximately.

Lubrication

161.   Lubrication diagrams are given in figs. 2 to 7; a key to the lubricant symbols is given in fig.3.   Before applying the high-altitude control lubricant (D.T.D.539) to a bearing which has previously been lubricated with other oil or grease, the bearing should be washed through with paraffin; a special oil can or gun should be reserved for each lubricant.   Where D.T.D.539 is used, it must be applied more frequently than D.T.D.417A.

A.P. 1564. B | VOL I | SECT. 4. | CHAP. 3.

REF	DESCRIPTION
1	TOP ENGINE PANEL
2	TANK COWL
3	EMERGENCY EXIT PANEL
4	FOOTSTEP DOORS (PORT SIDE)
5	ACCESS DOOR IN SIDE FAIRING (STARBOARD)
6	ACCESS DOOR IN SIDE FAIRING (PORT)
7	REMOVABLE PORTION OF NOSE COWLING
8	FRONT SIDE PANEL (PORT & STARBOARD)
9	JACKING POINT
10	EMERGENCY JACKING POINT (UNDER STUB AXLE)
11	INTERMEDIATE SIDE PANEL (PORT & STARBOARD)
12	REAR SIDE PANEL (PORT)
13	PANEL FOR RADIATOR & COOLER DRAIN PLUGS.
14	REAR SIDE PANEL (STARBOARD)
15	DOOR FOR TRAINING FLARE (PORT)
16	ACCESS DOOR IN UNDERFAIRING.
17	TUBE FOR HANDLING BAR
18	ACCESS DOOR IN TAIL BAY FAIRING (PORT)
19	ACCESS DOOR TO ELECTRIC STARTER PLUG.
20	ACCESS DOOR FOR GREASING FLAP JACK. (PORT)
21	RADIATOR FAIRING PANEL
22	WOODS FRAME ELEVATOR FLAP CABLES
23	INTERMEDIATE UNDER PANEL
24	ACCESS DOOR FOR FUEL TANK SUMP (BOTTOM SKIN)
25	GAP FAIRING
26	DOOR FOR FUEL CONTS GAUGE TERMINAL BLOCK (TOP SKIN)
27	WALKWAYS
28	LIFTING HANDLE SOCKET
29	ACCESS DOOR TO G42 B CAMERA CONNECTIONS (STARB)
30	ACCESS DOOR FOR INBOARD 20m GUN
31	ACCESS DOOR FOR G.42 B CINE-CAMERA (STARB)
32	ACCESS DOOR FOR INBOARD 20m GUN FRONT MOUNTING
33	ACCESS DOOR FOR OUTBOARD 20mm GUN
34	ACCESS DOOR FOR OUTBOARD 20mm GUN FRONT MOUNTING
35	LANDING LAMP WINDOW
36	INSPECTION DOOR (BOTTOM SKIN)
37	PICKETING RING SOCKET
38	NAVIGATION LAMP WINDOW
39	HAND HOLES FOR TIP REMOVAL
40	ACCESS DOORS FOR COCKING LEVERS (BOTTOM SKIN)
41	ACCESS DOORS FOR BREECH BLOCKS (TOP SKIN)
42	ACCESS DOORS INCORPORATING LINK CHUTES (BTM SKIN)
43	ACCESS DOOR FOR LANDING LAMP PULLEY (BTM SKIN)
44	ACCESS DOOR FOR AILERON CABLES (BOTTOM SKIN)
45	ACCESS DOOR FOR AILERON CONTROL LEVER (BTM SKIN)
46	ACCESS DOOR FOR AILERON CONTROL GEAR (TOP SKIN)
47	OUTER PLANE REMOVABLE TIP
48	BLAST TUBE DOOR (GUNS Nº 1 TO 4)
49	ACCESS DOOR FOR MAGAZINES (GUNS Nº 5 & 6)
50	BLAST TUBE DOOR (GUNS Nº 5 & 6)
51	ACCESS DOOR FOR GUNS Nº 5 & 6
52	ACCESS DOOR FOR GUNS (INNER)
53	ACCESS DOOR FOR GUNS (CENTRE)
54	ACCESS DOOR FOR GUNS (REAR)
55	ACCESS DOOR FOR GUNS OUTER
56	HOLES FOR GUN COCKING HANDLES
57	ACCESS DOOR FOR DESERT EQUIPMENT ETC
58	ACCESS DOOR FOR L.R TANK FUEL PUMP

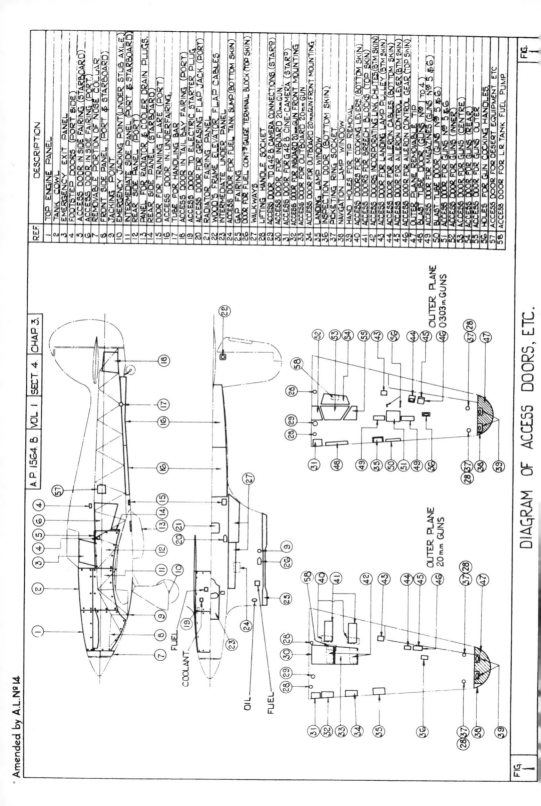

DIAGRAM OF ACCESS DOORS, ETC.

FIG. 1

+ LUBRICATE HOOD ROLLERS WITH ☒ IF THEY HAVE PLAIN BEARINGS INSTEAD OF BALL BEARINGS.

FOR KEY TO SYMBOLS SEE FIG. 3

(P) - PORT
(S) - STARBOARD

ALL BOWDEN CONTROLS TO BE WELL LUBRICATED WITH GRAPHITED WAX, STORES REF 34A/94.

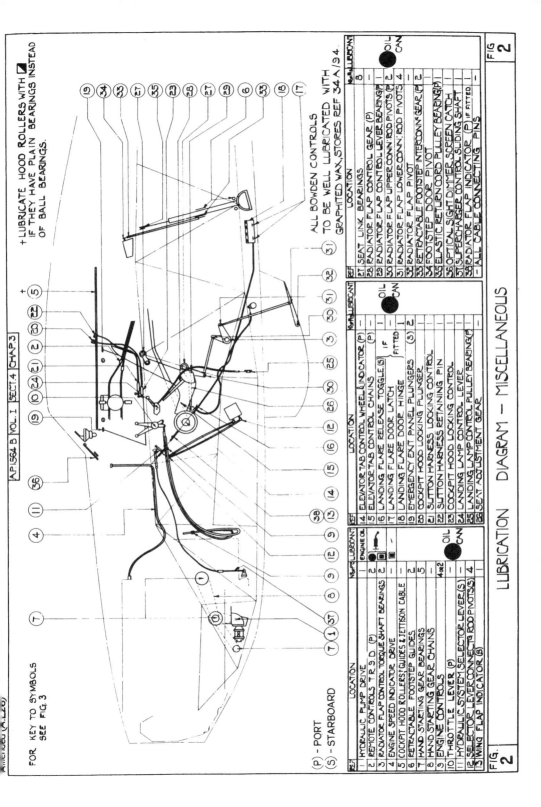

REF	LOCATION	No.off	LUBRICANT
1	HYDRAULIC PUMP DRIVE	-	
2	REMOTE CONTROLS T.R.9.D. (P)	2	ENGINE OIL
3	RADIATOR FLAP CONTROL TORQUE SHAFT BEARINGS	2	ENGINE OIL
4	ENGINE SPEED INDICATOR DRIVE	-	
5	COCKPIT HOOD ROLLERS; GUIDES & JETTISON CABLE	-	
6	RETRACTABLE FOOTSTEP GUIDES	2	
7	HAND STARTING GEAR BEARINGS	5	
8	HAND STARTING GEAR CHAINS	-	
9	ENGINE CONTROLS	4 or 2	
10	THROTTLE LEVER (P)	-	
11	HYDRAULIC SYSTEM SELECTOR LEVER(S)	-	
12	SELECTOR LEVER CONNECTG ROD PIVOTS(S)	4	
13	WING FLAP INDICATOR (S)	-	

REF	LOCATION	No.off	LUBRICANT
14	ELEVATOR TAB CONTROL WHEEL & INDICATOR (P)	-	
15	ELEVATOR TAB CONTROL CHAINS	-	
16	LANDING FLARE RELEASE TOGGLE (S)	-	IF FITTED
17	LANDING FLARE DOOR LATCH	1	
18	LANDING FLARE DOOR HINGE	-	
19	EMERGENCY EXIT PANEL PLUNGERS	(3) 2	OIL CAN
20	COCKPIT HOOD LOCKING PLUNGER	-	
21	SUTTON HARNESS LOCKING CONTROL	-	
22	SUTTON HARNESS RETAINING PIN	-	
23	COCKPIT HOOD LOCKING CONTROL	-	
24	LANDING LAMP CONTROL LEVER	-	
25	LANDING LAMP CONTROL PULLEY BEARINGS(P)	-	
26	SEAT ADJUSTMENT GEAR	-	

REF	LOCATION	No.off	LUBRICANT
27	SEAT LINK BEARINGS	8	OIL CAN
28	RADIATOR FLAP CONTROL GEAR (P)	-	
29	RADIATOR FLAP CONTROL LEVER BEARINGS(P)	-	
30	RADIATOR FLAP UPPER CONN' ROD PIVOTS (P)	2	
31	RADIATOR FLAP LOWER CONN' ROD PIVOTS	4	
32	RADIATOR FLAP PIVOT	-	
33	RETRACTABLE FOOTSTEP INTERCONN'G GEAR (P)	2	
34	FOOTSTEP DOOR PIVOT	-	
35	ELASTIC RETURN CORD PULLEY BEARING(P)	-	
36	OPTICAL SIGHT DIMMER SCREEN CATCH	-	
37	SUPERCHARGER CONTROL SLIDING SHAFT	-	
38	RADIATOR FLAP INDICATOR (P) IF FITTED	-	
-	ALL CABLE CONNECTING PINS	-	

LUBRICATION DIAGRAM - MISCELLANEOUS

FIG. 2

| AP.1564B | VOL.I | SECT.4 | CHAP.3 |

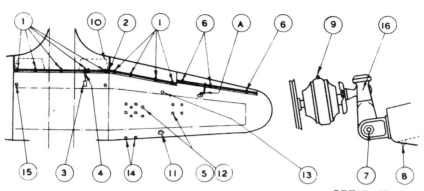

DETAIL AT A

KEY TO LUBRICANTS

● OIL, LUBRICATING, ANTI-FREEZING, TYPE 417 A
(D.T.D 417 A) (STORES REF. 34/A/86 AND 87.)

▣ GREASE, ANTI-FREEZING (D.T.D 143) (STORES REF. 34A/49)

◪ OIL, LUBRICATING, HIGH ALTITUDE CONTROLS
(D.T.D 539) (STORES REF. 34 A/134.)

ALL CABLE CONNECTING PINS TO BE WELL
LUBRICATED WITH ● EXCEPT IN AILERON
CIRCUIT WHERE ▣ SHOULD BE USED

REF.	LOCATION	Nº OF PTS.	LUBRICANT
1	FLAP HINGES	13	
2	FLAP SPAR UNIVERSAL JOINTS	2	
3	FLAP JACK PIVOT	1	
4	FLAP LEVER JACK PIVOT	1	●
5	REAR 20 MM. GUN MOUNTINGS	8	
6	AILERON HINGE BOLTS	6	
7	AILERON LEVER LINK PIVOT	2	◪
8	AILERON LEVER SWIVEL FORK	2	
9	DIFFERENTIAL GEAR BALL BEARINGS	2	
10	FLAP GAP PANEL HINGE	2	
11	LANDING LAMP PIVOTS	4	●
12	·303" GUN MOUNTINGS	24	
13	LANDING LAMP CONTROL WIRE PULLEY	2	OIL CAN
14	FRONT 20 MM. GUN MOUNTINGS	4	
15	AILERON CABLE PULLEYS	4	◪
16	AILERON LEVER LINK BALL UNIVERSAL	2	OIL CAN

FIG.
3

LUBRICATION DIAGRAM-OUTER PLANES

FIG.
3

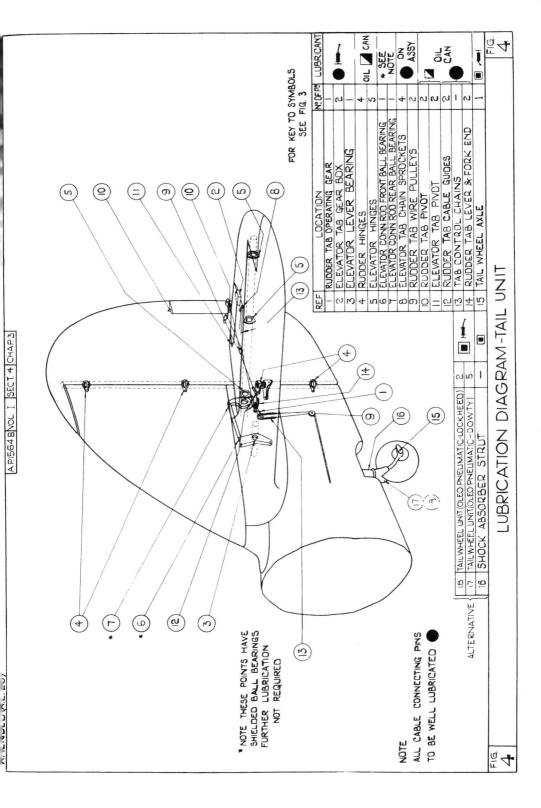

FOR KEY TO SYMBOLS
SEE FIG. 3

REF	LOCATION	Nº OF P.TS	LUBRICANT
I	RUDDER TAB OPERATING GEAR	I	●
2	ELEVATOR TAB GEAR BOX	2	●
3	ELEVATOR LEVER BEARING	I	OIL ◣ CAN
4	RUDDER HINGES	4	OIL ◣ CAN
5	ELEVATOR HINGES	5	* SEE NOTE
6	ELEVATOR CONN ROD FRONT BALL BEARING	I	* SEE NOTE
7	ELEVATOR CONN ROD REAR BALL BEARING	I	* SEE NOTE
8	ELEVATOR TAB CHAIN SPROCKETS	4	● ON ASSY
9	RUDDER TAB WIRE PULLEYS	2	● ON ASSY
10	RUDDER TAB PIVOT	2	◪
II	ELEVATOR TAB PIVOT	2	OIL CAN
12	RUDDER TAB CABLE GUIDES	2	●
13	TAB CONTROL CHAINS	I	OIL CAN
14	RUDDER TAB LEVER & FORK END	2	●
15	TAIL WHEEL AXLE	I	■

ALTERNATIVE	18	TAILWHEEL UNIT (OLEO PNEUMATIC-LOCKHEED)	2	■
	17	TAILWHEEL UNIT (OLEO PNEUMATIC-DOWTY)	5	❚
	16	SHOCK ABSORBER STRUT	I	■

LUBRICATION DIAGRAM-TAIL UNIT

NOTE
* THESE POINTS HAVE
SHIELDED BALL BEARINGS
FURTHER LUBRICATION
NOT REQUIRED

NOTE
ALL CABLE CONNECTING PINS
TO BE WELL LUBRICATED. ●

FIG. 4

FIG. 4

| A.P.1564 B | VOL. I | SECT. 4 | CHAP. 3 |

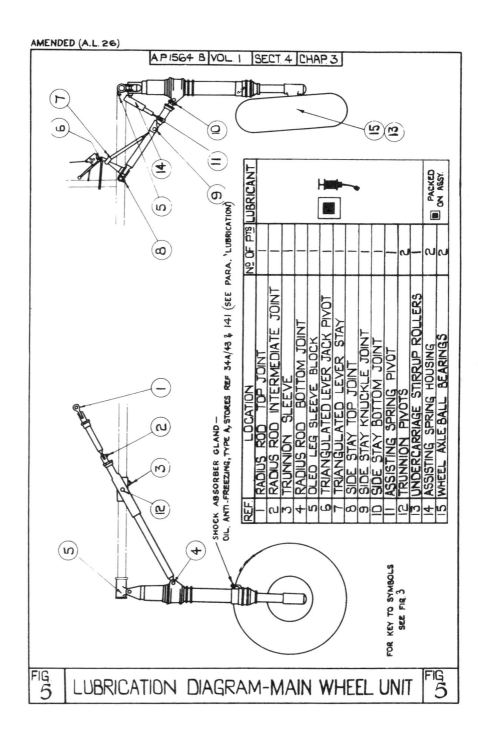

SHOCK ABSORBER GLAND—
OIL, ANTI-FREEZING, TYPE A, STORES REF 34A/43 & 141 (SEE PARA. 'LUBRICATION')

REF	LOCATION	Nᵒ OF PTS	LUBRICANT		
1	RADIUS ROD TOP JOINT				
2	RADIUS ROD INTERMEDIATE JOINT				
3	TRUNNION SLEEVE				
4	RADIUS ROD BOTTOM JOINT				
5	OLEO LEG SLEEVE BLOCK				
6	TRIANGULATED LEVER JACK PIVOT				
7	TRIANGULATED LEVER STAY				
8	SIDE STAY TOP JOINT				
9	SIDE STAY KNUCKLE JOINT				
10	SIDE STAY BOTTOM JOINT				
11	ASSISTING SPRING PIVOT	1			
12	TRUNNION PIVOTS	2			
13	UNDERCARRIAGE STIRRUP ROLLERS				
14	ASSISTING SPRING HOUSING	2			
15	WHEEL AXLE BALL BEARINGS	2	PACKED ON ASSY.		

FOR KEY TO SYMBOLS
SEE FIG. 3

| FIG 5 | LUBRICATION DIAGRAM—MAIN WHEEL UNIT | FIG 5 |

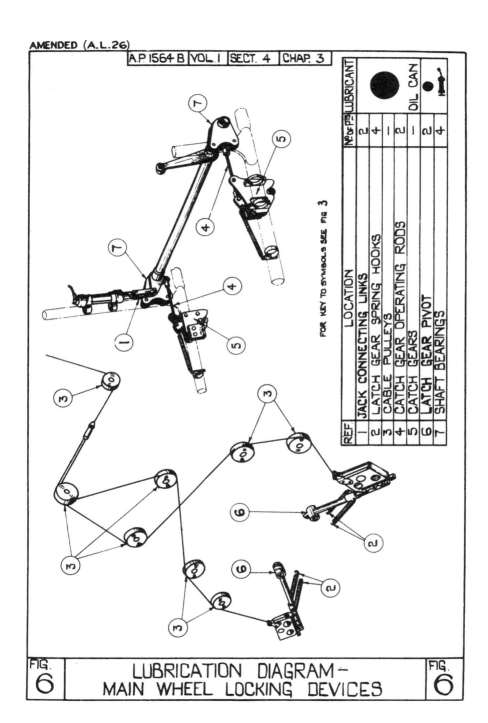

N° OF PTS	LUBRICANT
2	●
4	
1	
2	
1	OIL CAN
2	●
4	

FOR KEY TO SYMBOLS SEE FIG 3

REF.	LOCATION	N° OF PTS
1	JACK CONNECTING LINKS	2
2	LATCH GEAR SPRING HOOKS	4
3	CABLE PULLEYS	1
4	CATCH GEAR OPERATING RODS	2
5	CATCH GEARS	1
6	LATCH GEAR PIVOT	2
7	SHAFT BEARINGS	4

FIG. 6

LUBRICATION DIAGRAM —
MAIN WHEEL LOCKING DEVICES

FIG. 6

| A.P. 1564 B | VOL. I | SECT. 4 | CHAP. 3 |

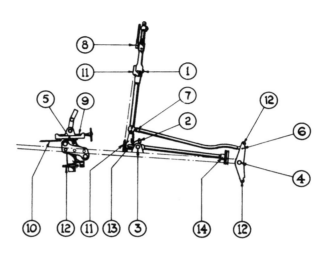

FOR KEY TO SYMBOLS SEE FIG. 3

REF	LOCATION	Nº OF PTS	LUBRICANT
1	CONTROL COLUMN TOP JOINT	1	
2	UNIVERSAL JOINT	1	
3	CRANK BEARINGS	2	
4	ELEVATOR LEVER BEARING	1	
5	RUDDER BAR PEDESTAL	1	
6	CONNECTING ROD REAR END	1	
7	CONNECTING ROD FRONT END	1	
8	BRAKE LEVER & PARKING CATCH PIVOTS	2	
9	RUDDER BAR ADJUSTING GEAR	SLIDE & SCREW	
10	RELAY VALVE CONTROL CONNECTING ROD ENDS	2	OIL-CAN
11	CHAINS & SPROCKETS	—	
12	CONTROL CABLE CONNECTING PINS	4	
13	CONTROL COLUMN BALL BEARINGS	2	
14	TORQUE TUBE BALL BEARING	1	

FIG 7 — LUBRICATION DIAGRAM—FLYING CONTROLS — FIG 7

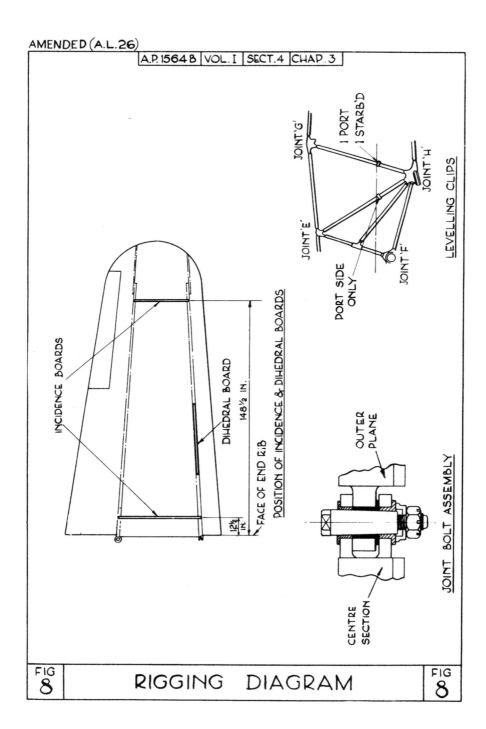

INCIDENCE BOARDS

DIHEDRAL BOARD

148½ IN.

FACE OF END RIB

12½ IN.

POSITION OF INCIDENCE & DIHEDRAL BOARDS

JOINT 'G'

1 PORT
1 STARB'D

JOINT 'H'

JOINT 'E'

PORT SIDE
ONLY

JOINT 'F'

LEVELLING CLIPS

OUTER PLANE

CENTRE SECTION

JOINT BOLT ASSEMBLY

| FIG 8 | RIGGING DIAGRAM | FIG 8 |

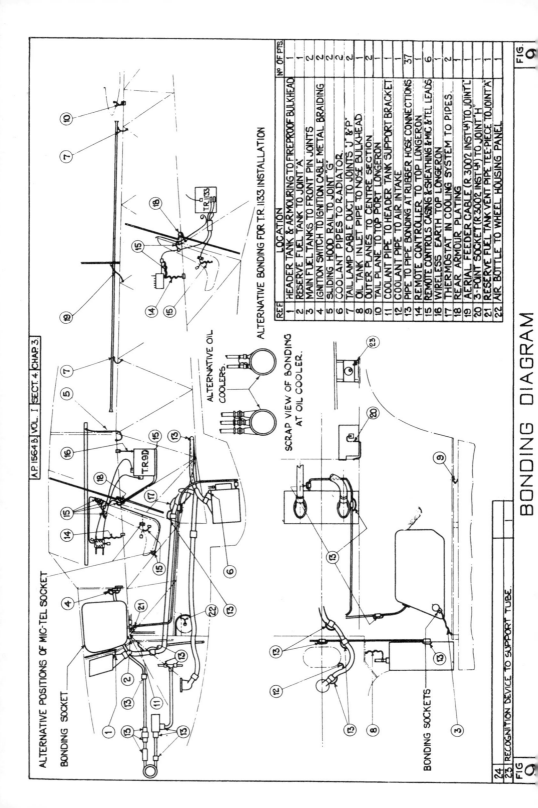

AP.1564B | VOL. I | SECT. 4. | CHAP. 3.

ALTERNATIVE POSITIONS OF MIC-TEL SOCKET

BONDING SOCKET

ALTERNATIVE OIL COOLERS.

ALTERNATIVE BONDING FOR T.R. 1133 INSTALLATION

SCRAP VIEW OF BONDING AT OIL COOLER.

BONDING SOCKETS

REF	LOCATION	N° OF PTS
1	HEADER TANK & ARMOURING TO FIREPROOF BULKHEAD	1
2	RESERVE FUEL TANK TO JOINT 'A'	1
3	MAIN FUEL TANKS TO FRONT PIN JOINTS	2
4	IGNITION SWITCH TO IGNITION CABLE METAL BRAIDING	2
5	SLIDING HOOD RAIL TO JOINT 'G'	2
6	COOLANT PIPES TO RADIATOR.	2
7	TAIL LAMP CABLE DUCT TO JOINTS 'J' & 'P'	2
8	OIL TANK INLET PIPE TO NOSE BULKHEAD	2
9	OUTER PLANES TO CENTRE SECTION	2
10	TAIL PLANE TO TOP PORT LONGERON	2
11	COOLANT PIPE TO HEADER TANK SUPPORT BRACKET	1
12	COOLANT PIPE TO AIR INTAKE	1
13	PIPE TO PIPE BONDING AT RUBBER HOSE CONNECTIONS	37
14	REMOTE CONTROLLER TO TOP LONGERON	1
15	REMOTE CONTROLS CASING & SHEATHING & MIC & TEL LEADS	6
16	WIRELESS EARTH TOP LONGERON	1
17	THERMOSTAT IN COOLING SYSTEM TO PIPES.	2
18	REAR ARMOUR PLATING	1
19	AERIAL FEEDER CABLE (R 3002 INST 'L") TO JOINT 'C'	1
20	3-POINT SOCKET (R3002 INST 'L") TO JOINT 'H'	1
21	RESERVE FUEL TANK VENT PIPE TEE-PIECE TO JOINT 'A'	1
22	AIR BOTTLE TO WHEEL HOUSING PANEL	1

BONDING DIAGRAM

24		
23	RECOGNITION DEVICE TO SUPPORT TUBE.	
FIG		FIG.
9		9

The cockpit of the RAF Museum's Hurricane IIc is incomplete with many instruments missing. The Museum's Hurricane I has a more complete cockpit, which differs only slightly from that of the IIc, and the photographs reproduced here are of that earlier aircraft. The cables attached to the control column are used to hold the control surfaces steady, and would not appear in a service aircraft. The leather seat cushion and the cable crossing it are not used in the original aircraft.

The instrument panel

The cockpit floor and rudder pedals

The seat and port side of the cockpit. The thick cable looped under the canopy is part of the Museum's display lighting.

The seat and starboard side of the cockpit. The pilot's parachute would fit into the bottom of the seat pan, and the wooden cover seen here normally supports a pilot figure.

Wing Commander Ian Gleed, Officer Commanding No. 87
Squadron, photographed by Charles E Brown

Another view of the same

A Hurricane of No. 87 Squadron being prepared for a sortie, photographed by Charles E. Brown

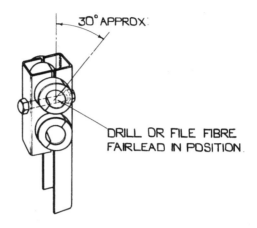

30° APPROX.

DRILL OR FILE FIBRE
FAIRLEAD IN POSITION.

VIEW OF FAIRLEAD AFTER DRILLING.

FIG. 10   TYPICAL MTG. OF BARREL TYPE FAIRLEAD.   FIG. 10

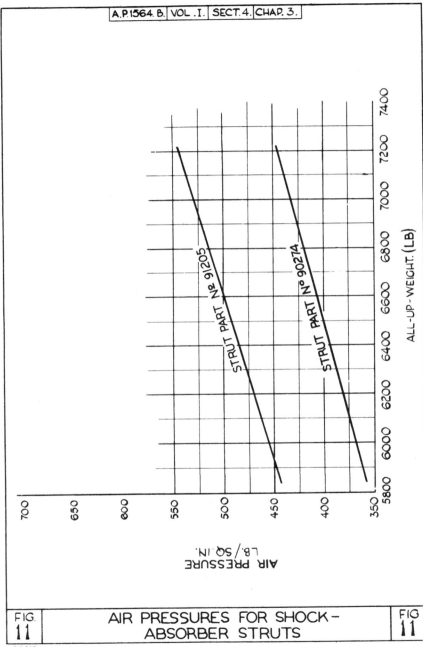

FIG.
11

AIR PRESSURES FOR SHOCK –
ABSORBER STRUTS

FIG
11

F.S./32.

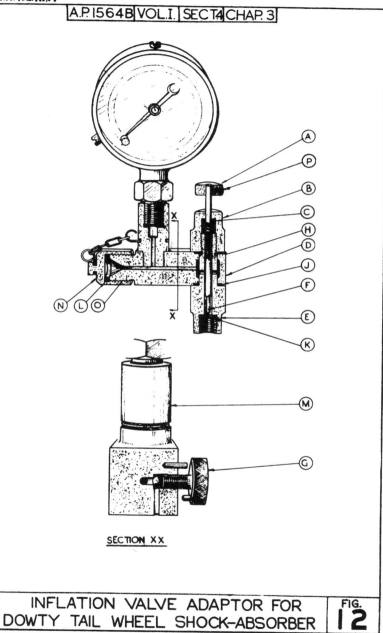

SECTION XX

FIG.
12

INFLATION VALVE ADAPTOR FOR
DOWTY TAIL WHEEL SHOCK-ABSORBER

FIG.
12

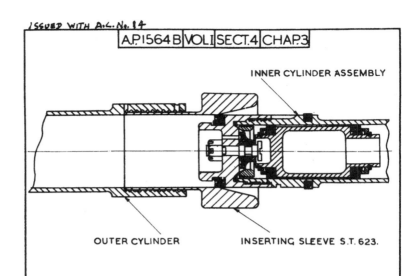

INNER CYLINDER ASSEMBLY

OUTER CYLINDER

INSERTING SLEEVE S.T. 623.

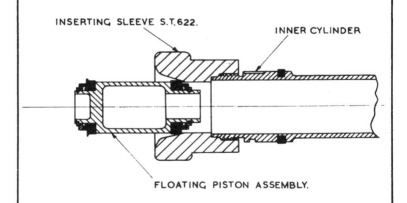

INSERTING SLEEVE S.T.622.

INNER CYLINDER

FLOATING PISTON ASSEMBLY.

FIG. 13 | METHOD OF USING INSERTING SLEEVES FOR DOWTY TAIL WHEEL SHOCK-ABSORBER. | FIG. 13

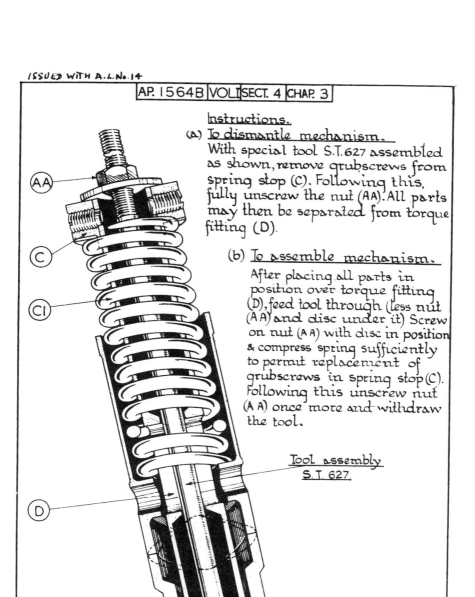

Instructions.

(a) To dismantle mechanism.

With special tool S.T.627 assembled as shown, remove grubscrews from spring stop (C). Following this, fully unscrew the nut (AA). All parts may then be separated from torque fitting (D).

(b) To assemble mechanism.

After placing all parts in position over torque fitting (D), feed tool through (less nut (AA) and disc under it) Screw on nut (AA) with disc in position & compress spring sufficiently to permit replacement of grubscrews in spring stop (C). Following this unscrew nut (AA) once more and withdraw the tool.

Tool assembly
S.T.627.

FIG. 14 — METHOD OF USING COMPRESSION TOOL FOR DOWTY TAIL WHEEL SHOCK-ABSORBER — FIG. 14

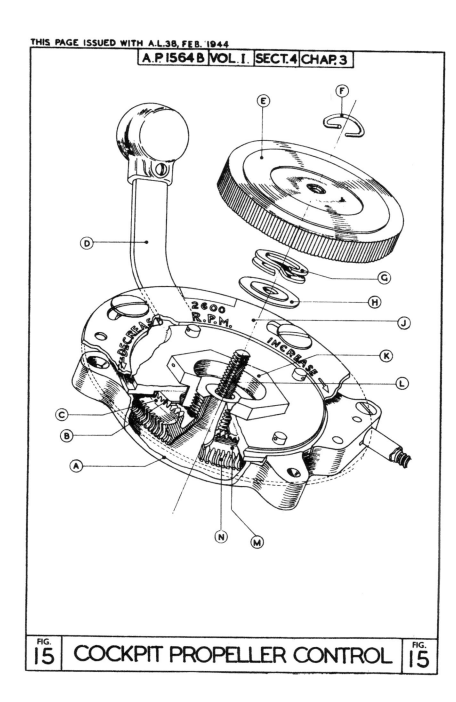

FIG. 15

COCKPIT PROPELLER CONTROL

FIG. 15

Section 5: Removal and assembly operations.

SECTION 5

REMOVAL AND ASSEMBLY OPERATIONS

LIST OF CONTENTS

GENERAL

ALIGHTING GEAR

FLYING CONTROLS

FUEL SYSTEM

OIL SYSTEM

COOLING SYSTEM

HYDRAULIC SYSTEM

PNEUMATIC SYSTEM

VACUUM SYSTEM

WINDSCREEN DE-ICING

REMOVAL AND ASSEMBLY OPERATIONS

GENERAL

Introduction

1. Of the following paragraphs dealing with the removal and assembly of components, the majority refer to the removal of components and, providing additional or contrary instructions for assembly are not given, the procedure for assembly may be assumed to be the same as that for removal but in the reverse order. For the designation of fuselage joints, refer to the relevant figure in Sect.7, Chap.1.

Division for transport

2. For transport purposes, Hurricane II aeroplanes are packed in cases measuring internally 29 ft. 6 in. long x 9 ft. 6 in. wide x 8 ft. 3 in. high, each case containing one complete aeroplane with engine installed; the aeroplane is divided into the following units before being packed:-

    (a)   Airscrew

    (b)   Port outer plane

    (c)   Starboard outer plane

    (d)   Rudder

    (e)   Fin

    (f)   Tail plane and elevator

    (g)   Engine, fuselage, and centre section

Instructions for assembling the aeroplane from these units will be found in the following paragraphs.

FUSELAGE

Engine, with or without mounting

3. Removal.- The operations described in this paragraph should be performed when removing the engine alone or when removing the engine

together with its mounting.   Care should be taken to disconnect bonding
wires, where necessary, before removing or disconnecting each item.

    (i)   By raising the tail, set the aeroplane approximately in
          flying position and chock the undercarriage wheels to
          prevent fore-and-aft movement.

   (ii)   Turn the fuel distributing cock to the OFF position.

  (iii)   Drain the oil tank (see Sect.4, Chap.3).

   (iv)   Drain the cooling system (see Sect.4, Chap.3).

    (v)   Remove airscrew and hub (see para.8 for removal of spinner
          and refer to A.P.1538, Vol.I for removal of airscrew).

   (vi)   Remove the following cowlings:-

         (a)   Engine and tank cowls.

         (b)   Front and intermediate side panels.

         (c)   Front and intermediate bottom panels.

         (d)   Leading-edge fillets.

  (vii)   Remove stays supporting arch cowl rail over engine.

 (viii)   Remove the exhaust manifolds.

   (ix)   Disconnect the flexible pipe from the pneumatic system air
          compressor.

    (x)   Remove the oil breather pipe between the engine connection
          and the oil tank vent pipe.

   (xi)   Remove the large flexible pipe between the engine oil pump and
          the oil filter; also remove the flexible portion of the oil
          outlet pipe leading from the engine to the viscosity valve.

  (xii)   Remove the coolant pipe between the engine-driven pump and the
          joint just forward of the centre-section front spar, and
          disconnect the couplings between the engine and the header tank.

 (xiii)   Disconnect the pressure gauge banjo fitting at the engine fuel
          pump; tie the banjo fitting to the nearest structural member,
          taking care not to produce sharp bends in the capillary tube.

(xiv) Disconnect the priming pipe at the engine end, and the flexible
pipe of the oil dilution system from the engine fuel pump.

(xv) Disconnect the oil thermometer bottle and the oil pressure gauge
banjo at the oil relief valve on the starboard side of the engine
and tie them to the adjacent structure, taking care not to produce
sharp bends in the capillary tubes.

(xvi) Disconnect the two leads at the accumulator in the fuselage and
stow them at once on the dummy terminal block below the accumulator;
access to the leads is obtained by removing the detachable panel
on the starboard side of the fuselage.

Note.- It is important that this disconnection is effected before any
other electrical leads are disturbed.

(xvii) Disconnect the ignition leads from the magneto and the leads from
the front end of the generator; tie the ignition leads to the
engine mounting. Stow the generator leads on the dummy terminal
block on the engine mounting if only the engine is being removed
or tie them to the fireproof bulkhead if the mounting is also
being removed.

(xviii) Disconnect the throttle and mixture control rods at the levers
on the engine; move the throttle control lever in the cockpit
to the CLOSED position.

(xix) At the rear of the engine, disconnect the engine speed indicator
drive and the cable from the supercharger control; tie the cable
to the adjacent structure.

For the subsequent procedure, see para. 4 if only the engine is being
removed or see para.5 if it is desired to remove the engine together
with its mounting.

4   When removing the engine without its mounting, the following
operations should also be performed:-

(i) Remove the arch cowl rail.

(ii) Remove the bolts attaching the vertical cowl rail to the
horizontal top cowl rail and then remove the latter.

(iii) Remove the bolts attaching the lower cowl rail, at each
end and those attaching the nose collar diaphragm to the
spigots on the engine mounting; remove the nose collar and
lower cowl rail.

(iv)   Remove the starter chains and the starter sprockets from
the countershaft above the electric starter; also, remove
the sprocket on the electric starter and its housing.

(v)   Remove the air-intake at the flange at the rear of the engine.

(vi)   Remove the fuel pump cooling duct.

(vii)   Remove the cooling pipes from the electric generator.

(viii)   Remove the drain pipes from the fuel pump, hydraulic pump and
supercharger; disconnect the pipe from the breather to the
connection adjacent to the firewall.

(ix)   At the fuel pump, disconnect the flexible pipe leading from
the filter.

(x)   Remove the drain plug in the engine-driven pump of the
hydraulic system and drain the fluid into a suitable
receptacle; disconnect the flexible pipes at the pump.

(xi)   Disconnect the boost gauge pipe at the engine end.

(xii)   Disconnect the two leads from the electric starter motor;
push down the rubber sleeves to uncover the connections.

(xiii)   Attach the engine hoisting sling to the engine (as detailed
in A.P.1590G, Vol.1) and to the hoist hook, adjusting the
hoist so that it just takes the weight; remove the engine
holding-down bolts.

(xiv)   Hoist and swing the engine forward to clear, making sure
that no fittings, cables, pipes etc. are left in such a
position that they impede the removal of the engine; lower
the engine into a suitable cradle.

5.   When removing the engine together with the engine mounting, the
following disconnections and removals should be made in addition to those
enumerated in para.3.

(i)   Remove the two fore-and-aft rails which support the
intermediate bottom panel.

(ii)   Remove the oil tank (see para.49).

(iii)   Remove the flexible pipe between the filter and the fuel pump.

(iv)   Remove the pipes of the hydraulic system which run between
the engine-driven pump and the firewall.

(v)   Remove the boost gauge pipe between the engine and the
       fuel trap.

(vi)   From the engine mounting, remove the clips attaching
       the capillary tubes for the fuel pressure gauge, the
       oil pressure gauge, and the oil temperature gauge.

(vii) From the engine mounting, remove the clips attaching
       the ignition leads and those attaching the electric
       generator leads.

(viii) Remove the cover plates on the fireproof bulkhead at
       fuselage joints A.

(ix)   At their joints on the fireproof bulkhead, disconnect
       the horizontal top cowl rail and the fillet rail.

(x)   At the starboard bottom rear strut of the engine
       mounting, disconnect the leads from the electric
       starter to the terminal block and the magnetic relay.
       Remove the clips securing the accumulator and push-
       button leads and disconnect the leads from the terminal
       block, starter socket and magnetic relay respectively;
       tie them back clear of the engine mounting.

(xi)   Attach the engine hoisting sling to the engine (as
       detailed in A.P. 1590G, Vol. I) and to the hoist hook,
       adjusting the hoist so that it just takes the weight;
       remove the engine mounting attachment bolts at joints
       A, port and starboard.

(xii) At the lower boom of the front centre section spar,
       remove the bolts attaching the lower rear struts of the
       engine mounting and the pins attaching the engine
       mounting bracing wires to the shackles; tie the bracing
       wires to the lower rear struts of the engine mounting.

(xiii) Swing the engine and mounting forward and hoist it away
       from the centre section, making sure that no fittings,
       cables, pipes etc. are left in such a position that they
       impede removal of the engine and mounting; lower the
       engine and mounting into a suitable cradle.

6. Installation of engine.- The installation of the engine is the
same as the removal procedure given in paras. 3 and 4, but in the
reverse order; reference should also be made to the installation notes
in A.P.1590G, Vol.I. The engine holding down bolts should be assembled
in the following manner:-

(1)   Place a piece of packing (supplied with the engine)
       between each engine bearer and engine foot; the rubber
       packings should be placed beneath the rear feet and

the Ferebestos packings beneath the front feet (see illustration in Sect. 7, Chap. 1).

(ii)   At each of the front feet, first insert the rear bolt, with a washer in place under its head; screw it downwards into the engine bearers and pass the locking strip over the bolt head. Then fit a washer over each front bolt and pass each bolt upwards through the engine bearer, the packing, the engine foot, another washer, the rear bolt locking strip and finally through a third washer; screw a slotted nut on to each bolt and lock it with a split pin.

(iii)   At the rear feet, the two bolts for the port foot are $6\frac{1}{2}$ in. long under the head and those for the starboard foot are $5\frac{1}{2}$ in. long. Each of the four bolts should be fitted with a washer and passed up through the engine bearer, the lower packing, the engine foot, the upper packing, the capping strip and finally through a second washer; a slotted nut should then be screwed over each bolt and locked with a split pin.

7.   **Installation of engine and mounting.**- The installation of the engine mounting complete with engine is the same as the removal procedure described in paragraphs 3 and 5, but in the reverse order and with the following additions:-

(i)   Set the fuselage in the rigging position (see Sect.4, Chap.3), using the jacking points at the lower ends of the shock-absorber struts.

(ii)   Drop plumblines from the centre of the airscrew boss, the centre of joint U, and the mid-point of the centre section front spar.

(iii)   Adjust the bracing wires in engine mounting bay ZB until the three plumblines are in the fore-and-aft alignment.

Variable-pitch airscrew spinner

8.   **Removal of spinner (Rotol type).**- The spinner shell is secured by six lock pins to the back plate and may be removed by turning the six lock pins to the unlocked position and withdrawing the spinner forwards. The flexible ring may be removed from the back plate by unlocking and removing six nuts.

9.   **Assembly of spinner (Rotol type).**- To assemble the spinner, proceed as follows:-

(i)   Locate the flexible ring channel on the spinner back plate at the front of the airscrew hub and secure it

in position with the six nuts. The ring must be positioned
so that the red arrow on the ring is in line with the red painted
guide pin on the back plate. Screw the securing nuts hard up and
lock with tab washers.

(ii)   Fit the flexible ring into the channel and ensure that it is well
home all round.

(iii) Check that the six lock pins in the shell are turned to the unlocked
position and locate it so that the guide pin housing marked with red
paint is in line with the paint-marked guide pin on the back plate.

(iv)   Push the shell home and at the same time draw the back plate forward
until all the guide pins and lock pegs are engaged and the front
support ring has entered the flexible ring.

(v)   Turn all the six lock pins to the locked position and check again
that all the lock pegs are engaged.

Radiator flap

10.   Removal.- The following is the procedure for removing the
radiator flap; when assembling the flap, the hinge pin attachment bolts
should be locked with 18 s.w.g. iron wire.

(i)   Disconnect the radiator flap control rods at the flap and operate
the control lever in the cockpit until the indicator is in the
NORMAL position; this latter operation will lift the control rods
out of the way.

(ii)   Cut the locking wires and remove the two bolts attaching each of
the hinge pins at the forward end; withdraw the flap downwards
and rearwards.

Radiator fairing

11.   Removal.- Disconnect the two bracing struts at the rear end of
the radiator fairing and the control rods to the radiator flap at the port
and starboard sides of the flap. Remove the cover plates in the rear wall
of the undercarriage wheel housing; reach through the holes thus disclosed
and disconnect the link on the centre stiffener of the radiator fairing
from the fork bolt on the lower boom of the centre section rear spar.
Support the fairing, remove all the attachment bolts and screws around its
upper flange, and lower the fairing away from the fuselage.

12. Assembly.- During assembly, the length of the rear bracing struts may be adjusted, if necessary, by slackening the lock-nuts and screwing the fork ends in or out as required.

Radiator

13. Removal.- To remove the radiator proceed as follows:-

(i)   Remove the oil cooler as described in para. 51.

(ii)   Drain the cooling system (see Sect.4, Chap.3).

(iii   Disconnect the pipe couplings at the top rear of the radiator (See para. 56).

(iv)   Disconnect the bonding wires at the rear edge of the radiator, port and starboard.

(v)   Support the radiator, remove the four attachment bolts and withdraw the radiator downwards.

Engine controls inner linkage

14. Removal.- At the engine end, uncouple the throttle and mixture controls at the ball joints and unscrew and remove the sliding rods. Disconnect the throttle control at the cockpit end by removing the split pin, nut, washer, and roller from the bolt attaching the fork-end to the throttle lever; disconnect the mixture control by removing the split pin and tabwasher from the headed pin coupling the fork-end to the mixture lever. After removing the bolt from the throttle lever, and the header pin from the mixture lever, withdraw each inner linkage with its olives and tabelets from their respective casing tubes by pulling on the rear sliding rods.

15. Assembly.- Insert the linkage into the casing tube. If the fork-end has been removed from the rear end of the linkage, care must be taken to insert the linkage so that the fixed end is at the front and the adjustable end at the rear; the fixed end of each sliding rod and casing tube is marked with an F, while the adjustable ends are marked with an A. Screw the non-adjustable sliding rod on to the front terminal rod; open the inspection hole by moving the spring clip and check that the sliding rod has been screwed fully home. Close the inspection hole and connect up the control at each end.

Aerial mast

16. Removal.- To remove the aerial mast, proceed as follows:-

(i)   Remove the rear detachable panel of the fuselage underfairing.

F.S./6

  (ii) If an aerial is fitted to the mast, detach the aerial lead from
the terminal on the side of the mast and detach the aerial from the
mast. If no aerial is fitted, detach the feeder from the base of
the mast (inside the fuselage).

 (iii) Slacken the nuts on the U-bolt clamping the base of the mast.

  (iv) Remove the four screws in the corners of the insulation panel
surrounding the mast where it emerges from the fuselage.

   (v) Withdraw the mast complete with the insulation panel.

Cockpit hood

17. <u>Removal.-</u> To remove the sliding cockpit hood, remove the
aerial mast as described in para.16 and then proceed as follows:-

   (i) Detach the handles from inside the hood by removing the screws
attaching them to the front frame of the hood.

  (ii) Detach the stiffener at the front end of the hood by removing
the screws attaching it to the front frame.

 (iii) Detach the catch plate, which operates the bolt locking the exit
panel, by removing the screws attaching it to the starboard side
of the front frame.

  (iv) Detach the ratchet stop from the port side of the hood by removing
the screws attaching it to the front end of the lower frame of the
hood.

   (v) Remove the buffers from the rear ends of the port and starboard
rails.

  (vi) Slide off the hood.

17A. <u>Assembly.-</u> If jettison gear is fitted, care must be taken to
eliminate movement between the port detachable hood rail and the decking.
Insert extra packing pieces (Pt.No.A.113022) as required and after fitting
operate the jettison lever and check that the cable is not binding.

Cockpit seat

18. <u>Removal.-</u> To remove the seat, proceed as follows:-

   (i) At the lower end of the rear strap of the pilot's harness, remove
the pin attaching the shackle to the bracket at the rear of the
seat; the strap stop should be re-attached to the shackle by means
of the pin.

(ii)   Remove the nuts attaching the harness strap links to
       the spigots on the sides of the seat and pull the
       rear harness strap up through the hole in the back of
       the seat; stow the harness out of the way.

(iii) Remove the split pins locking the quadrant bolts to the
       bosses on the seat and remove the bolts, quadrants,
       and distance tubes.

Note.- The seat should not be supporting any load when the
quadrant bolts are removed.

(iv)   Remove the split pins locking the spigots to the bosses
       on the seat and remove the bosses; the latter may be
       unscrewed by means of the flats provided on the outer
       flanges for a 9/16 in. spanner.

(v)   Support the seat and remove the bolts attaching it at
       the upper brackets; lift the seat out of the cockpit.

Barrel-type fairleads

19. Assembly.- One half of each fibre fairlead has a groove
engaged by the clamping bolt to prevent rotation of the fairlead (see
Sect.4, Chap.3). When assembling a fairlead, care should be taken
to replace it in its original position to ensure that the control cable
does not bear on the split-line of the fairlead.

MAIN PLANE

Gap fairing

20. Removal.-

(i)   With the flaps down (or removed), remove the locknut
       and fixing bolt attaching the upper main panel of the
       fairing to the upper rear panel; this bolt is situated
       on the inner side of the upper fairing above the
       universal joint between the flap spars.

(ii)   Remove the corresponding bolt in the lower main and
       rear panels.

(iii) Remove the three screws at the leading-edge and with-
       draw the upper and lower main panels.

(iv)   Remove the washer-head bolts attaching the upper and
       lower rear panels and withdraw these panels.

21. **Assembly.-**

    (i)   Attach the upper main panel to the lower main panel by means of three screws at the leading-edges and secure the lower rear panel in position by means of the washer-head bolts.

    (ii)   Place the main fairing in position and bolt it to the lower rear panel with the fixing bolt, leaving approximately $\frac{3}{4}$ in. gap between the brackets.

    (iii)   Secure the upper rear panel in position by means of the washer-head bolts and bolt it to the main fairing with the fixing bolt.

    (iv)   Tighten the upper fixing bolt, and adjust the lower fixing bolt to suit, until the fairing is in contact with the skin of the outer plane and centre section at all points; lock the fixing bolts by means of the locknuts.

Leading edge fairing

22. **Removal.-**

    (i)   Remove the cover over the starboard main fuel tank.

    (ii)   Remove the screw attaching the top edge of the fairing and the screws at the inboard lower corner.

    (iii)   Remove the four nuts, on the rear faces of the spar booms, which attach the two intermediate formers to the spar.

    (iv)   From each end former, remove the two bolts which attach these formers to the spar shear plates: withdraw the fairing forwards.

Flaps

23. **Removal.-**

    (i)   Lower the flaps and disconnect the flap jack at its attachment to the flap lever.

    (ii)   Uncouple the universal joints and disconnect the flap indicator cable at its attachment to the eyebolt on the centre section flap spar.

    (iii)   Remove the radiator fairing (see para.11).

    (iv)   Remove the bolts attaching the centre bearing of the flap spar to the bracket mounted on the fuselage bracing struts.

(v)   Remove the bolts attaching the remaining flap spar
        bearings to the centre section and outer plane ribs;
        withdraw the flaps.

24.   Assembly.- The procedure for assembly is the reverse of that
for removal, but in addition the following points should be noted. To
ensure accurate alignment with the flap spar, the bearings should be
adjusted during assembly by means of the shims provided. The shims
should be introduced between the bearings and the ribs of the centre
section, any shims not so required being used as packing beneath the
head of the corresponding bolt of the bearing. When inserting the bolt,
care should be taken not to use undue force lest the fibre locking
device in the nut be dislodged; it is advisable to see that the end of
the bolt has a small amount of taper at the tip.

Centre section

25.   Removal.-

    (i)   First remove the engine mounting complete with engine as
            described in paras. 3 and 5 and then remove the following
            cowling:-

        (a)   Rear side panels

        (b)   Front and rear walkways

        (σ)   Trailing-edge fillet

        (d)   Covering under trailing-edge

        (e)   Cover strip at rear of wheel housing

    (ii)   Remove the fireproof bulkhead inboard of the oil tank
            by removing the fibre blocks at the oil pipes, the
            diagonal strut and the bolts holding the two portions
            of the bulkhead together.

    (iii)   Fit a hoisting bar through the fuselage in the angles
            formed by struts AB and AD; attach the fuselage
            slinging gear and hook it to the hoist.

    (iv)   Fit the handling bar through the tube between fuselage
            joints Q and jack up the rear fuselage with an
            adjustable trestle.

    (v)   Close the isolating cock at the reserve fuel tank in the
            fuselage and drain the main fuel tanks in the centre
            section (see Sect.4, Chap.3).

(vi)   Remove the outer planes (see para. 28).

(vii)   Remove the bolts attaching the rear walkway support to
        the innermost trailing-edge rib of the centre section;
        the support should be left attached to the cross tube.

(viii) At the electric fuel contents gauge on each main fuel tank,
        lift the wire clip and remove the socket which houses the
        leads to the indicator in the cockpit.

(ix)   Remove the main fuel tanks (see para.43).

(x)   Remove the flying controls from the cockpit (see
        paras. 38 to 42).

(xi)   Remove the pipes between the main fuel tanks and the
        T-piece on the rear wall of the wheel housing.

(xii)   Remove the fuel pipe between the T-piece on the rear wall
        of the wheel housing and the 3-way fuel-distributing cock
        on the port longeron at joint B.

(xiii) Remove the fuel pipe between the 3-way cock and the fuel
        filter connection at the front spar.

(xiv)   Remove the underfairing and the radiator fairing (see
        para.11).

(xv)   Remove the two pipes between the oil cooler and the
        viscosity valve; on aeroplanes fitted with the later type
        cooler, disconnect the third pipe between the cooler and the
        firewall.

(xvi)   Remove the coolant pipes between the radiator and the joint
        just forward of the centre-section rear spar; disconnect
        the remaining coolant pipe at the radiator.

(xvii) Remove the radiator (see para.13).

(xviii) From the port longeron, just aft of joint F, remove the
        clip attaching the pipes from the flap jack.

(xix)   Remove the pipes from each end of the air cylinder; the
        port pipe may be disconnected at the union near to the
        cylinder and the starboard pipe may be disconnected at the
        union to the rear of the mid-point of fuselage starboard
        strut AB.

(xx)   At joint F1, remove the bolt through the tubular rigst
        attaching the bracket which supports the T-piece in the
        gun-firing circuit of the pneumatic system.

(xxi)   Remove the clips attaching the brake-operating pipes of the
        pneumatic system to the lower longeron just aft of

joints B, port and starboard.

(xxii)   At the latches locking the undercarriage in the "down" position, disconnect the leads from the micro-switches and remove the pin attaching the two springs to the pivot arm; remove the bolts attaching the pivot tube and push out the tube, leaving the cables attached to the latch.

(xxiii)   From the pulleys on the centre section, free the cables operating the undercarriage latch gear.

(xxiv)   Remove all clips attaching cablé ducts to the centre section structure.

(xxv)   At the outer ribs, remove the fibre fairleads for the landing lamp control cables; withdraw the cables inboard, coil them, and stow them out of the way.

(xxvi)   Remove the bolts attaching the fireproof bulkhead to the front spar.

(xxvii)   Support joint F1 by means of a cable or cord attached to any convenient point of the fuselage and remove the bolts attaching the joint to the rear spar.

(xxviii)   Disconnect the pipes leading to the undercarriage jacks at the T-piece situated on the starboard side, just above and to the rear of the centre section front spar.

(xxix)   At the control box of the hydraulic system, disconnect the pipes leading to the flap jack, and the rods from the cockpit control.

(xxx)   Disconnect the air-speed indicator tubes at the unions just outboard of joint F, port.

(xxxi)   Disconnect the cables from the terminal blocks on the top boom of the centre section outer girder and draw them back through the duct on the front face of the rear spar; remove the duct, coil the cables and stow them out of the way.

(xxxii)   Disconnect the cable of the flap indicator at its attachment to the eyebolt on the centre section flap spar.

(xxxiii)   Remove the bolts attaching the rear heelboard support
           to the lower longeron; remove the rear heelboard
           support.

(xxxiv)   Remove the undercarriage (see para.35).

(xxxv)   Support the centre section by means of adjustable trestles
           placed as close to the outer girders as practicable and
           slacken off the wires in bays BD and DF.

(xxxvi)   Disconnect the struts in the inner bay of the centre
           section at joints B and F; swing the freed ends clear.

(xxxvii)   Remove the strut between the rear spar lower boom
           and joint H.

(xxxviii) Remove the bolts securing the top booms of the spars to
           the fuselage at joints B and F.

(xxxix)   Lower the trestles on which the centre section is now
           resting and hoist the fuselage until it clears, making
           sure that no fittings, cables, pipes, etc., are left in
           such a position that they impede the removal of the
           centre section.

(xl)   Withdraw the centre section.

26. Assembly.- The procedure for assembly is the reverse of that
given for removal but with the following additions:-

(i)   Drop the plumblines as when checking the rear
           fuselage (see Sect.4, Chap.3).

(ii)   Drop the plumblines from the mid-points of the front
           and rear spars.

(iii)   Adjust the wires in bays BD and DF until the lines
           dropped from the spars are in fore-and-aft alignment
           with the other plumblines.

(iv)   Adjust all control cables to the proper tautness;
           fit new split-pins and locking wires as required.

Centre section front spar

27. Removal.-

(i)   Remove the engine mounting complete with engine (see
           paras. 3 and 5).

(ii)   Sling the aeroplane from joints A (see para.25,
           sub-para. (iii), or alternatively, place a trestle under

a wooden beam supporting the fuselage across joints D.

(iii)   Remove the outer planes (see para.28).

(iv)   Remove the rear side panels and the front walkways.

(v)   Remove the leading edge fairing (see para.22) and the
        oil tank (see para.49).

(vi)   Remove the oil filter from the front face of the front
        spar opposite joint B, starboard.

(vii)   Remove the main fuel tanks (see para. 43).

(viii) Remove the starboard top fairing angle.

(ix)   Remove the fuel filter from the front face of the centre
        section front spar.

(x)   Disconnect each end of the coolant pipe elbow which passes
        through the front centre section spar and remove the
        bolts attaching the flanges on the elbow of the spar.

(xi)   Remove the undercarriage (see para.35).

(xii)   From the undersurface of each spar, remove the two screws
        securing each end of the lower boom of each outer girder;
        at the web bracing joints with the lower boom, remove the
        three bolts at the front joint and, at the rear joint,
        the three bolts and eye bolt.

(xiii) Remove the undercarriage latch gear from the channel
        section at the front end of each inner girder and disconnect
        the electrical leads from the micro-switches on the latch
        gear.

(xiv)   Remove the pulleys (which carry the latch gear operating
        cables) from the brackets mounted on the spar stiffeners
        above the latches; stow the latch gears, cables and
        pulleys out of the way.

(xv)   Remove the air cylinder (see para.73).

(xvi)   Remove the web plate of the channel fitting attaching the
        inner girder to the front spar.

(xvii) Disconnect the port side fairing angle from the brackets
        on the front spar top boom.

(xviii)   Slide the lower boom of the outer girder forwards out of the rear spar; should the boom be tightly held in place, it will be necessary to remove the outer trailing edge rib and tap the boom until it clears, using a mallet and a block of wood.

(xix)   Dismantle the joint of the outer girder with the top boom of the front spar.

(xx)   Dismantle the joint of the inner girder with the large channel fitting on the front spar.

(xxi)   Support the front spar and remove the three bolts attaching the top boom at joints B, port and starboard.

(xxii)   Lower the front spar to clear the spool fittings at joints B and withdraw forwards.

Outer plane

28.   **Removal.-**

(i)   Trestle the aeroplane until it is approximately in its flying position.

(ii)   Remove the gap fairing between the centre section and the outer plane (see para.20) and, if the flaps have not been removed, uncouple the outer plane flap spar from the centre section flap spar.

(iii)   Disconnect the two aileron cables and the landing lamp control cable at the gap between the outer plane and the centre section, immediately aft of the rear spar.

(iv)   Disconnect the navigation and landing lamp leads at the terminal block on the centre section end rib; access may be obtained through the door in the upper surface of the centre section.

(v)   When removing the port outer plane, disconnect the tubes to the pressure head and, if the outer planes are of the stressed-skin type, disconnect the pressure head heater lead at the terminal block on the centre section end rib.

(vi)   Disconnect the pipe in the pneumatic gun-firing circuit at the joint on the trailing edge portion of the inner end rib. In the cannon planes there are two pipes to be disconnected.

(vii)   Disconnect the gun heating pipes and the electrical bonding wires at their joints just aft of the rear spars.

(viii) Screw the lifting brackets into the sockets provided in the undersurface of the outer plane (see Sect.4, Chap.3, para.4) and bolt the lifting handles in place; place trestles under both outer planes to take the load off the pin-joints and to maintain the stability of the aeroplane when one outer plane has been removed.

(ix) Remove the split pin, nut and recessed washer from each main plane joint pin. Withdraw the ⅜ in. bolt from the special extractor and screw it into the head of the joint pin to ensure that the pin threads are free from dirt. Remove the bolt and re-assemble it to the extractor. Note.- Ensure that the hexagon sleeve is screwed down to the base of the extractor. (The threads are left hand).

(x) Place the extractor on the joint pin and screw the centre bolt tightly into the top of the pin. Tighten the hexagon sleeve of the extractor until it bears on the underside of the centre bolt and then tap the top of the bolt. Again tighten the sleeve and tap the bolt. Repeat this operation until the pin has been loosened sufficiently for it to be withdrawn easily.

(xi) Perform the operation described in 28 (x) on the remaining joint pins.

(xii) Ease the plane away by means of the lifting handles and, after withdrawing the trestles, lower the plane on to a suitably padded support.

NOTE.- When the outer plane to be removed has fitting for jettisonable fuel tanks, the following additional operations must be carried out before the plane can be removed. Unlock the jettison lever in the cockpit and move it to the forward position. Disconnect the jettison control cables from the release pawls and remove the cables from the plane, leaving the retaining clips on the plane. Coil the cables and lash them to the centre-section structure; lash the release pawls to the plane. Disconnect the fuel and air pressure pipes at the root of the plane, ensuring that the coupling hoses and clips remain on the fuel pipes in the fuselage, and suitably blank off the pipes to prevent the ingress of dirt. Finally, lock the jettison lever in the JETTISON position.

29.   Assembly.-

(i) Trestle the aeroplane until it is in the rigging position (see Sect.4, Chap.3).

(ii) Support the outer plane on adjustable trestles so that the plug-ends at the root end of the outer plane are close to and just below the fork-ends of the centre section.

(iii) Using the lifting brackets and lifting handles, raise the outer plane up to the centre section.

(iv) Grease the taper pins and bushes and insert the pins into the bushes, if necessary using a wooden mallet.

(v) Assemble the recessed washers and nuts on the joint pins and tighten the nuts until there is no slackness in the joint; split-pin the nuts.

NOTE.- On no account must spanners with a leverage greater than 8 in. be used.

   (vi) With the aid of the dihedral and incidence boards, check the rigging of the main plane in accordance with the rigging diagram (see Sect.4, Chap.3).

  (vii) Couple up the outer plane services which were uncoupled when the outer plane was removed (see para.28); remove the lifting handles and brackets.

 (viii) Replace the gap fairing between the centre section and the outer plane (see para.21).

Aileron

30. Removal.-

    (i) At the aileron lever, uncouple the connecting rod between the aileron control gear and the aileron.

   (ii) Remove the nuts from the aileron hinge bolts that pass through the aileron spar.

  (iii) Withdraw the aileron, leaving the bolts attached to the outer plane.

TAIL UNIT

Rudder

31. Removal.-

    (i) Disconnect the rudder control cables at the lever on the rud spar and the tab cables at the connections on the lever forw of the finpost.

   (ii) Disconnect the radio aerial (if fitted) at the rear insulator.

  (iii) Remove the access door in the port side of the tail bay and disconnect the cable to the tail navigation lamp at the terminal block on fuselage strut TU, port.

   (iv) Detach each hinge by removing the two bolts holding it to the hinge bracket on the rear finpost.

    (v) Withdraw the rudder, taking care not to damage the tail lamp cable and tab cables.

Elevator

32. Removal.- This is most conveniently effected by removing the half-elevators separately as follows:-

    (i) Remove the access door in the port side of the tail bay.

   (ii) Loosen the fairing around the elevator spar at each side of the fuselage; the bottom portion of the fairing need not be unfastened.

  (iii) Uncouple the elevator connecting rod at the lever on the elevator spar.

   (iv) Open the Woods frames in the upper surface of the tail plane at the rear inner corners and disconnect the cables leading to the elevator trimming tabs; remove the fairleads from these cables from the front face of the tail plane rear spar.

    (v) Uncouple the trimming tabs cable running behind the elevator spar at the connector between the half-elevators.

(vi)   Uncouple the half-elevators by removing the bolt through the coupling sleeve on the elevator spar.

(vii)   Detach each hinge by removing the bolts holding it to the tail plane rear spar and withdraw the half-elevators. The port half-elevator can be easily withdrawn by moving it to port until the end of the spar is clear of the fairing and then moving it rearwards, taking care that the connector on the trimming tabs cable does not foul the tail plane rear spar as it passes through it. To withdraw the starboard half-elevator, first pull the trimming tabs cable through the tail plane rear spar and then lower the outboard end of the half-elevator, at the same time springing the fairing away from the fuselage; this will allow the lever on the elevator spar to clear the fairing.

Note.- If the rudder and fin have been removed, the elevator can be removed complete, i.e. without separating the halves.

Fin

33. Removal.- After removing the rudder, proceed as follows:-

(i)   Remove the fairing between the tail plane, fin. and fuselage.

(ii)   Disconnect the elevator control cables at the lever in the tail plane. Remove the pulleys from the bracket on the rear face of the tail plane front spar and pull the cables through the spar from the front; replace the pulleys.

(iii)   Remove the four bolts attaching the lower end of the front finpost to fuselage joint SI; also remove the packing washers.

(iv)   Detach the front finpost from fuselage cross-strut RR by withdrawing the two bolts sufficiently to clear the packing block on the strut and to permit removal of the shims (if any); the bolts should be left in the finpost to keep the distance tubes in place.

(v)   Detach the rear finpost from the rear end of the top longerons by withdrawing the four attachment bolts and removing the shims (if any); the bolts should only be withdrawn sufficiently to clear the fittings on the fuselage.

(vi)   Remove the four bolts attaching the bottom end of the
rear finpost and withdraw the fin vertically.

(vii)   Push home the two bolts left in the front finpost
and the four left in the rear finpost and replace the
nuts.

Tail plane

34. **Removal**.- After removing the rudder, fin, and elevator, proceed
as follows:-

(i)   Remove the fairleads for the trimming tabs cables from
the web of the tail plane front spar and pull the cables
through from the front; replace the fairleads.

(ii)   Remove the four bolts attaching the tail plane to the
fuselage at joints R and T, port and starboard, and lift
the tail plane clear of the fuselage.

Note.- When re-connecting the trimming tab control cables, care
must be taken to couple them correctly; to the rear of the
fairlead on cross-strut NN, the upper cable passes to starboard
and the lower cable to port.

ALIGHTING GEAR

Undercarriage

35. **Removal**.- Jack up the aeroplane until the wheels are just clear
of the ground, and remove each undercarriage unit as follows:-

(i)   Disconnect the hydraulic jack from the undercarriage unit
by removing the bolt attaching the piston rod to the
triangulated lever on the sidestay; replace the bolt, nut,
and washer in the lever and tie the free end of the jack
to the channel fitting on the centre section spar.

(ii)   Disconnect the assisting spring gear at its attachment to
the shackle on the sidestay; care should be taken to
hold the lower portion of the gear and allow it to ease
off to its full extension gradually.

(iii)   Disconnect the side-stay at the shock-absorber strut by
removing either the bolt connecting the sidestay to the
shackle or that connecting the shackle to the shock-
absorber strut.

(iv)   Remove the shock-absorber strut fairing by withdrawing
the bolts attaching the fairing clips and removing the
clips.

(v)   Disconnect the radius rod from the strut by removing the bolt; swing the free end upwards and tie it to any convenient part of the centre section structure.

(vi)   Release the pressure in the pneumatic system by depressing the valve at the charging connection and, at the upper end of the shock-absorber strut, uncouple the lower end of the flexible tube from the pipeline running down to the brake unit; remove the clip attaching the end of the flexible tube to the air valve on the shock-absorber strut.

(vii)   Remove the split-pin locking the special nut for the assisting spring on the shock-absorber strut pivot bolt.

(viii) Whilst supporting the shock-absorber strut and assisting spring gear, unscrew and withdraw the pivot bolt; remove the strut and the assisting spring gear.

(ix)   At the joint of the sidestay with the inner girder, remove the split-pin and the slotted nut at the rear end of the pivot bolt and withdraw the bolt; the head of the bolt is on the front face of the front spar lower boom.

(x)   Whilst supporting the sidestay, wedge the end of a piece of wood into the bore of the pivot distance piece and withdraw the distance piece rearwards; remove the sidestay.

Note.- If required, the sidestay may be disconnected at the elbow joint.

36. Assembly.- When assembling the undercarriage, care must be taken to ensure full freedom of movement without undue slackness in the joints.

(i)   Assemble the two portions of the sidestay if they have been disconnected at the elbow joint. Test for freedom of movement by holding the lower portion upwards and allowing the upper portion to fall; the upper portion should be just capable of swinging downwards under its own weight.

(ii)   Connect the upper end of the sidestay to the fitting at the joint between the inner girder and the front spar; note that the thin washer should be placed under the bolt head on the front face of the spar boom.

(iii)   Test the sidestay assembly for freedom of movement; when raised and allowed to fall, it should fall freely under its own weight but there should be no side play.

(iv)   Lift up the shock-absorber strut (axle inboard) to the forked sleeve at the front end of the centre section outer girder and insert the pivot bolt from the outboard side.

Note.- On no account may an aeroplane be fitted with one old-type strut to Pt.No.90274 and the other strut to Pt.No.91205. Therefore, if one strut is damaged, it must be replaced by another of the same part number; if this is not available, both struts must be replaced.

(v) Remove the locking plate on the inboard side of the forked upper end of the strut and place the large washer over the end of the pivot bolt.

(vi) Screw the special ball nut for the assisting spring gear on to the end of the pivot bolt; tighten the nut and lock it in place with a split pin.(It is unnecessary to separate the assisting spring gear from the ball nut).

(vii) Replace the locking plate, turning the pivot bolt by its head (if necessary) to ensure that the ball nut fits inside the locking plate with the ball uppermost.

(viii) Swing the shock-absorber strut fore-and-aft and sideways to test for freedom of movement; should there be too much play in the universal sleeve on the outer girder boom, the sleeve must be renewed. Fore-and-aft movement can be taken up as described in Sect.4, Chap.3.

(ix) Attach the radius rod to the strut; the bolt head should be on the inboard side.

(x) Raise the latch assembly and tie it back clear of the sidestay triangulated lever to avoid damage.

(xi) Attach the sidestay to the shock-absorber strut.

(xii) Attach the lower end of the assisting spring gear to the shackle on the sidestay.

(xiii) At the upper attachment of the assisting spring gear, set the ball on the ball nut aft to the limit allowed by the locking plate, i.e. 3° approximately; this may be done by turning the pivot bolt.

(xiv) With the main wheels retracted, ensure that a small clearance exists between the upper end of the assisting spring gear and the spar plate; lock the locking plate attachment bolt.

(xv) Couple the jack piston rod to the fork at the top of the sidestay triangulated lever, making sure that the flat faces of the fork are inboard.

(xvi) Lower the latch assembly into position. There should be a clearance of 0.03 in. between the end of the latch gear tube and the face of the fork; in plan view, the centre line of the latch gear tube should line up with the centre of the front cheek of the fork. (See Sect.4, Chap.3, for adjustment of latch gear).

(xvii) Attach the fairing to the shock-absorber strut.

(xviii) Test the undercarriage for freedom of movement. Raise the undercarriage by selecting WHEELS UP and operating the handpump. Set the selector lever to WHEELS DOWN; the undercarriage should fall under its own weight. (See Sect. 4, Chap.3 for the method of retracting the undercarriage units separately).

Tail wheel unit

37. Removal.-

(i) Trestle the aeroplane until the tail wheel is clear of the ground.

(ii) Remove the access panel in the port side of the tail bay fairing and disconnect the tail wheel shock-absorber strut at its upper attachment point by removing the securing bolt.

(iii) At the lower attachment point, remove the wire locking the four bolts for the securing cap; remove the four bolts and withdraw the tail wheel unit downwards.

(iv) Unless the tail wheel unit is to be replaced immediately, it will be advisable to remove the V-strut assembly that provides the upper attachment point for the shock-absorber strut; this is effected by removing a bolt at fuselage joints R, port and starboard.

FLYING CONTROLS

Control column

38. Removal.-

(i) Remove the intermediate and rear side panels of the cowling.

(ii) Remove the cockpit seat (see para.18).

(iii) From the heelboards, remove the screws attaching the pipe connections of the pneumatic system; the nuts are fixed in the brackets so detached.

(iv)   Remove the heelboards; whilst the attachment screws are
being removed, the 4 B.A. nuts may be held against rotation
by inserting a box spanner through the holes in the underside
of the heelboard support tubes.

 (v)   Disconnect the elevator connecting rod at both ends and
remove it.

(vi)   Disconnect the bowden cable at the brakes control lever on the
spade grip; hold the lever forward and, with a suitable
instrument inserted in the slot at its base, lift the cable
nipple clear and slide the cable out through the slot.

(vii) Remove the clips attaching the bowden cable and the rubber tubes
of the pneumatic system to the control column; coil the cable
and stow where convenient.

(viii) Disconnect the rubber tubes at their upper ends and tie them
to the mounting tube of the control column.

(ix)   Disconnect the aileron torque tube at the universal joint at
the bottom of the control column.

 (x)   From the control column mounting tubes, remove the bolts
attaching the crank bearing brackets.

(xi)   Remove the control column together with the bearing brackets.
As soon as the bearing brackets are clear, slip them off the
cranks and replace them on the mounting tubes; replace the
attachment bolts, screwing on the nuts finger-tight only.
Care should be taken to prevent the distance tubes within the
mounting tubes from falling out of position.

39.   Installation.- The installation procedure is the reverse of that
for removal but the following points should be observed.   When re-
assembling the cranks in the bearings, brass shims (1¼ in. o/d x 13/16 in.
i/d) should be fitted between the inner faces of the bearings and the shoulders
of the cranks, if necessary, to take up end play.   If the pivot pin removed
from the front of the elevator connecting rod has a knurled head it is an
oversize pin fitted to correct for slack (see A.P.1564B, Vol.II, Pt.3);
care should be taken not to replace it with a standard size pin.

Cockpit aileron controls

40.   Removal.-   After carrying out the operations described in para.38,
sub-paras. (i) to (iv), proceed as follows:-

 (i)   At the rear end of the aileron torque tube, disconnect
the aileron cables at the turnbuckles immediately outboard
of the cable drum.

(ii)   Remove the three bolts attaching the housing for the torque
tube bearing to the support bracket on the centre section
rear spar.

(iii)   Disconnect the torque tube at the universal joint at the bottom of the control column.

(iv)   Remove the torque tube, complete with cable drum; replace the bolts removed under (ii) above to retain the cable guard.

Cockpit elevator controls

41. Removal.- After carrying out the operations described in para.38, sub-paras. (i) to (iv) proceed as follows:-

(i)   At the ends of the elevator lever countershaft, remove the caps of the rudder cable fairleads; remove the cables and replace the fairleads and caps.

(ii)   Disconnect the elevator cables at each end of the elevator lever and stow the freed ends out of the way.

(iii)   At the rear end of the flying controls mounting tubes, remove the bolts attaching the supporting plug-ends for the elevator lever countershaft.

(iv)   Remove the complete countershaft assembly by withdrawing it rearwards.

Rudder bar

42. Removal.- After carrying out the operations described in para.38, sub-paras. (i) to (iv) proceed as follows:-

(i)   At the rudder lever, disconnect the rudder cables and uncouple the connecting rod to the brakes relay valve of the pneumatic system; the shackle should remain with the connecting rod.

(ii)   Remove the bolts attaching the front heelboard support tubes to the bottom longeron; remove the support tubes.

(iii)   Remove the bolts attaching the rudder pedestal support tubes to the pedestal and those attaching the tubes to the brackets on the flying controls mounting tubes.

(iv)   Remove the pedestal support tubes, taking care to avoid damage should it be found necessary to drive them with a hammer.

(v)   Turn the rudder bar fore-and-aft as far as possible and lift out the complete assembly.

FUEL SYSTEM

Main fuel tank

43. Removal.-

   (i)   Remove the upper and lower tank covers and drain the
           tank (see Sect. 4, Chap.3).

   (ii)   At the electric fuel gauge, lift the wire clip and with-
           draw the socket which houses the leads to the indicator
           in the cockpit.

   (iii)   Disconnect the fuel pipe from the cock situated in the
           inboard lower edge of the tank.

   (iv)   Disconnect the vent pipe at the connection in the front
           upper edge of the tank, holding the pipe connection at
           the tank against rotation by a $\frac{1}{2}$ in. spanner fitted
           over the flats provided.

   (v)   Disconnect the bonding wire from the socket fitting at
           the filler cap seating by removing the attaching screw.

   (vi)   Remove the bolts by which the two struts that pass
           through the tank are attached to the joints on the centre
           section structure.

   (vii)   Remove the locking wire, bolt, washer, and rubber pad
           from each of the four tank feet.

   (viii) Lift the tank out vertically, taking care to see that
           the struts through the tank do not foul the centre
           section structure or damage the tank.

   (ix)   Remove the struts and, to avoid loss, replace the rubber
           pad, washer, and bolt.

44. Installation.- The installation procedure is the reverse of that
for removal but the following point should be noted. The rubber pads
should be arranged so that one is under each tank foot, and one between
the tank foot and the washer under the bolthead; the bolts should be
locked with wire.

Reserve fuel tank

45. Removal.-

   (i)   Remove the tank cowl and the intermediate side panels.

   (ii)   Remove the bolts attaching the rearmost portions of the
           horizontal top cowl rails; remove the rails.

(iii) Drain the tank and sump (see Sect. 4, Chap.3).

(iv) On the port side, disconnect the vent pipe in the undersurface of the tank, holding the pipe connection at the tank against rotation by a $\frac{1}{2}$ in. spanner fitted over the flats provided.

(v) Disconnect the priming pipe at the top of the rear face of the tank by removing the nut and sliding off the banjo.

(vi) At the electric fuel gauge, lift the wire clip and withdraw the socket which houses the leads to the indicator in the cockpit.

(vii) Disconnect the bonding wire from the outer web of the port front foot.

(viii) At each of the four tank feet, remove the slotted nuts and bolts holding the four clamps closed; swing the clamps clear and lift out the tank vertically.

Fuel tank gauges

46. Removal.-

(i) Lift the wire clip and withdraw the socket on the leads for the cockpit indicator.

(ii) Remove the twelve bolts round the securing flange; the gauge can then be lifted from the tank. Great care should be taken to avoid bending the float arm.

Corrosion inhibitor

46a. Removal.- When removing the calcium chromate inhibitor for replacement, proceed as follows:-

(i) Drain the main fuel tank (see Sect. 4, Chap.3.)

(ii) Remove the fuel gauges (see para. 46.)

(iii) Reach through the hole to the inhibitor at the bottom of the tank, remove the locking wire securing the lid of the container, and remove the lid.

(iv) Remove the inhibitor.

Fuel filter

47. Removal.- To be issued later.

48. Assembly.- To be issued later.

F.S./16

OIL SYSTEM

Oil tank

49. Removal.-

(i) Remove the front and intermediate side cowling panels, the
leading edge fillet on the port side, and the gap fairing between
the centre section and port outer plane.

(ii) Remove the upper cover over the port main fuel tank and the port
side fairing strip under the centre section front spar.

(iii) Drain the oil tank (see Sect.4, Chap.3).

(iv) Disconnect the vent pipe at its connection in the top of the
rear wall of the tank by removing the jubilee clips and sliding
the rubber hose along the vent pipe.

(v) Disconnect the inlet and outlet pipes in the inboard end
wall of the tank.

(vi) Support the tank and remove the four bolts attaching the tank
feet to the brackets on the centre section front spar.

(vii) Withdraw the tank, replacing the bolts and rubber pads to
prevent their loss.

50.   Installation.- The procedure for installation is the reverse
of that for removal but in addition the following point should be noted.
The rubber pads should be arranged so that one is placed between each
tank foot and bracket, and the other between the tank foot and the
washer under the bolt head; it is important that the tank feet attachment
bolts are locked with wire.

Oil cooler

51. Removal.-

(i) Remove the radiator fairing (see para.11).

(ii) Remove the access door in the underfairing panel aft of
the radiator.

(iii) Drain the oil cooler (see Sect.4, Chap.3).

(iv) Disconnect the two (or in some aeroplanes three), pipes at the top rear end of the cooler.　These connections are the same as the coolant system connections described in para.56 and should be disconnected as described there.

(v) Remove the four bolts attaching the cooler at the front end to the coolant radiator.

(vi) Withdraw the cooler from the rear.

Oil filter

52.　Removal.-

(i) Drain the oil tank (see Sect.4, Chap.3).

(ii) At the bottom of the filter, uncouple the flexible pipe leading to the engine.

(iii) At the top of the filter, uncouple the pipe leading to the tank; disconnect the other end of the pipe at the tank and the pipe leading to the oil dilution valve;　move the filter end of the pipe clear of the filter.

(iv) Support the filter and remove the bolts attaching the bracket cap;　withdraw the filter.

Viscosity valve

53.　Removal.-

(i) Place a suitable receptacle beneath the viscosity valve to catch the oil liberated when the pipes are disconnected.

(ii) Disconnect and remove the two pipes between the oil cooler and the viscosity valve.

(iii) At the viscosity valve, disconnect the pipe or pipes which pass through the firewall.

(iv) Remove the two bolts attaching the viscosity valve to the bracket on fuselage strut FH1.

54.　Installation.- The installation procedure is the reverse of that for removal but to ensure the correct attitude of the valve on the strut, the bolts attaching the valve to the mounting should not be tightened until all four pipes are connected to the valve.

Oil drain collector

55.   Removal.-   To remove the oil drain collector, proceed as follows:-

    (i)   Remove the port intermediate side panel and the intermediate
       under panels.

    (ii)   Drain the reservoir.

    (iii)   Disconnect the pipe at the reservoir from the hydraulic pump,
       the fuel pump and the supercharger bearing drain.

    (iv)   Disconnect the drain cock and pipe.

    (v)   Remove the two bolts in the side plates of the mounting and
       remove the unit.

COOLING SYSTEM

Pipe connections

56.   The majority of the pipe connections in the cooling system are
made by a special non-rigid coupling.   The procedure for disconnecting
pipes at these couplings is as follows:-

    (i)   Slacken off the screw on the outer band and slide the
       band away from the coupling.

    (ii)   Remove the two halves of the channel section clamping ring
       exposing the rubber connection.

    (iii)   Ease the rubber connection off the end of one of the pipes
       and withdraw the pipe.

Header tank

57.   Removal.-

    (i)   Drain the cooling system (see Sect.4, Chap.3).

    (ii)   Slacken the clip at the vent pipe hose connection to the
       relief valve on the tank and ease off the vent pipe.

    (iii)   Disconnect the bonding strips at each of the engine
       connections to the tank and the wire at the connection
       below the tank.

    (iv)   Slacken the clips at the two hose connections on the front
       face of the tank and disconnect the pipe coupling under

the tank (see para. 56).

(v) From the connection in the front face of the tank, remove the thermometer bottle and at the relief valve disconnect the pressure gauge connection; stow the pipes in a safe place, taking care to avoid making sharp bends in the capillary tubing.

(vi) Disconnect the bonding wire at the web of the port rear foot and remove the bolts attaching the four tank feet to their mounting brackets.

(vii) Ease off the hose connections and withdraw the tank.

58. Installation.- When installing the tank, place a rubber packing over each bolt hole in the mounting brackets, thread the washer and another rubber packing on to each bolt, and insert the bolts from below; there should thus be a rubber packing between each tank foot and bracket and between the bracket and the washer under the bolt head.

HYDRAULIC SYSTEM

General

59. Absolute cleanliness is essential for the satisfactory operation of the system. When pipelines are uncoupled, the ends of the pipes must be protected against the entry of dirt. The receptacle into which the fluid is drained must be scrupulously clean if it is desired to retain the fluid for further use; if grease or other oil is allowed to enter the system, it will injure the gland and jointing compositions. Care should be taken not to spill the fluid as it may remove the protective coating from parts with which it comes into contact.

Automatic cut-out valve

60. Removal.- The automatic cut-out valve is mounted between the starboard fuselage struts FC.H and EH. To remove the valve proceed as follows:-

(i) Remove the starboard rear cowling panel and the panel immediately aft of it.

(ii) Uncouple the three pipes entering the valve and drain the fluid into a suitable receptacle.

(iii) Remove the bolt attaching the valve to the support bracket on the strut FC.H.

      (iv)   Support the valve and remove the bolt attaching it to
the channel bracket on strut EH.

Filter

61. <u>Removal</u>.- The filter is mounted on starboard fuselage strut EH.
A special four-way piece is screwed into the filter and a cruciform
four-way piece, with non-return valves fitted at its vertical branches,
is screwed into the upper branch of the special four-way piece. To
remove the filter, proceed as follows:-

      (i)   Remove the starboard rear cowling panel and the fuselage
panel immediately aft of it.

      (ii)   At the non-return valve screwed to the upper branch of the
cruciform four-way piece, uncouple the pipe leading from
the handpump.

      (iii)   Uncouple the two pipes from the horizontal branches of
the cruciform four-way piece.

      (iv)   Uncouple the two pipes from the underside of the special
four-way piece.

      (v)   Unscrew from the special four-way piece, as one unit, the
cruciform four-way piece and the two non-return valves.

      (vi)   Unscrew the special four-way piece from the filter.

      (vii)   Remove the two bolts attaching the filter to the channel
bracket on strut EH.

Handpump

62. <u>Removal</u>.- The handpump is mounted between starboard fuselage struts
EF, EH, and FC.H; to remove it, proceed as follows:-

      (i)   Remove the starboard rear cowling panel and the fuselage
panel immediately aft of it.

      (ii)   Uncouple the three pipes from the handpump casing; a funnel
and hose should be held in readiness to convey the fluid
to a suitable receptacle.

      (iii)   Slacken the bolt clamping the operating lever to the
pump shaft and withdraw the lever.

      (iv)   Support the pump casing and remove the bolts attaching
it to the brackets on the three struts.

Selector gear

63.   Removal.- The selector gear is mounted in the cockpit on starboard fuselage strut CF; to remove the gear, proceed as follows:-

(i)   Remove the starboard rear cowling panel.

(ii) Disconnect the connecting rods which couple the selector gear to the control box.

(iii) Disconnect the cables which operate the undercarriage latch gears.

(iv) Detach the instruction plate by removing the three screws attaching it to struts CF and CF1.

(v)   Remove the two bolts attaching the selector gear to the bracket on strut CF; remove the slow-running cut-out bracket and then tie to the strut.

(vi) Remove the three bolts attaching the selector gear spindle to the bracket; the outer portion of the bracket will then fall away and the selector gear can be withdrawn.

Control box or rotary control valve

64.   Removal.- The control box is mounted in the bottom of the cockpit on a bracket depending from the starboard bottom longeron BF. The following is the procedure for removing the control box.

(i)   Remove the starboard rear cowling panel.

(ii) Uncouple, at their upper ends, the two rods connecting the selector gear to the arms on the camshafts projecting from the front of the control box.

(iii) Uncouple the six pipes entering the rear of the control box; a funnel and hose should be held in readiness to convey the fluid to a suitable receptacle.

(iv) Remove the four screws attaching the control box to the bracket; the control box, together with the connecting rods, can then be withdrawn upwards.

Note.- The same procedure applies to those aeroplanes which have a rotary control valve in place of a control box.

Undercarriage jacks

65.   Removal.- The undercarriage jacks are mounted in the undercarriage wheel housing behind the centre section front spar; to remove a jack, proceed as follows:-

(i)   Set the selector lever in the cockpit to NEUTRAL.

(ii)   Uncouple the two pipes from the jack and drain the fluid into a suitable receptacle.

(iii)   Disconnect the jack piston rod by removing the bolt coupling it to the triangulated lever on the under-carriage side-stay; stow the bolt in the triangulated lever and replace the washer and nut.

(iv)   Disconnect the anchored end of the jack by removing the bolt boupling it to the universal joint mounted on the centre section spar; stow the bolt in the universal joint and replace the nut.

When installing the jack, the nuts should be locked by split pins.

Flap jack

66. Removal.- The flap jack is situated behind the centre section rear spar on the port side of the fuselage. To remove the jack, proceed as follows:-

(i)   Remove the port rear walkway.

(ii)   Uncouple the two pipes from the jack and drain the fluid into a suitable receptacle.

(iii)   Disconnect the jack piston rod from the flap lever by removing the special greaser bolt; replace the bolt and nut in the flap lever.

(iv)   Disconnect the anchored end of the jack by removing the special greaser bolt attaching it to the centre section spar; replace the bolt and nut in the lugs on the spar.

When installing the jack, the nuts should be locked by split pins.

Catch gear jack

67. Removal.- The catch gear jack is mounted on starboard fuselage strut CD and can be removed as follows:-

(i)   Remove the starboard intermediate and rear cowling panels.

(ii)   Uncouple the pipe from the jack and drain the fluid into a suitable receptacle.

(iii)   Uncouple the connecting rod from the jack piston rod.

(iv)   Remove the two bolts attaching the cap of each clip clamping the jack to the strut.

Pressure relief valve

68. Removal.- The pressure relief valve is situated on the starboard side of the fuselage just aft of the seat and is mounted on a bracket fixed to the centre section rear spar. The valve may be removed as follows:-

(i)   Remove the starboard rear cowling panel.

(ii)   Uncouple the pipes from the valve and drain the fluid into a suitable receptacle.

(iii)   Remove the two bolts attaching the cap of the clip round the top of the valve body.

(iv)   Support the valve and remove the two U-bolts attaching it to the bracket on the spar.

Variable-flow valve

69. Removal.- The variable-flow valve is inserted in one of the pipelines leading from the control box to the undercarriage jacks; the pipes run on the starboard side of the fuselage immediately under the large coolant pipe. To remove the valve, proceed as follows:-

(i)   Remove the starboard rear cowling panel and the forward walkway.

(ii)   Uncouple the pipes from the valve and drain the fluid into a suitable receptacle; withdraw the valve.

Non-return valves

70. Removal.- Remove the cruciform four-way piece, together with the non-return valves, as described in para.61, sub-paras. (i), (ii), (iii), and (v); the non-return valves can then be unscrewed from the four-way piece.

PNEUMATIC SYSTEM

Oil reservoir

71. Removal.- Remove the starboard front panel and, after draining

the oil reservoir as described in Sect.4, Chap.3, proceed as follows:-

(i)   Uncouple the pipe from the top of the reservoir.

(ii)   On the rear face of the fireproof bulkhead, remove the four nuts and washers from the U-bolts; support the reservoir and withdraw the U-bolts from the front face of the bulkhead. The reservoir, together with the block on which it is mounted, can then be withdrawn.

When replacing the reservoir, it should be filled as described in Sect.4, Chap.3.

Oil trap

72. Removal.- Remove the starboard front panel and, after draining the oil trap as described in Sect.4, Chap.3, proceed as follows:-

(i)   Uncouple the two pipes from the trap.

(ii)   Using a C-spanner, remove the top half of the trap.

(iii)   Slacken the bolt closing the supporting bracket and withdraw the trap downwards.

Air cylinder

73. Removal.- Uncouple the pipes from each end of the cylinder by unscrewing the union nuts; release the cylinder by removing the bolts from the securing straps. Swing the straps clear and withdraw the cylinder downwards and to starboard.

Air filter

74. Removal.- Remove the port intermediate side panel. Uncouple the inlet and outlet pipes by unscrewing the union nuts and, with a C-spanner, unscrew the top half of the filter. Slacken the bolt closing the supporting bracket and withdraw the filter downwards.

Brakes relay valve

75. Removal.-

(i)   Detach the four air pipes from the relay valve and uncouple the connecting rod at the lever on the valve.

(ii)   Pull off the moulded cover from the valve.

(iii)   Remove the small spring clip from the cylindrical fitting
        connecting the bowden inner cable to the operating chain.

(iv)   Raise the cable connector by operating the brakes control lever on
        the spade grip, hold the connector in the raised position, release
        the brakes control lever, and slide the cable and ball end out of
        the connector;   replace the spring clip on the connector.

(v)   Slacken the locknut and unscrew the bowden cable adjusting bush
        from the valve frame; withdraw the bowden cable.

(vi)   Remove the four bolts attaching the valve to its mounting; the
        valve can then be withdrawn.

76.   Installation.- When installing the valve, the cylinders should
project forward and to port, with the starboard cylinder about 10° to
port of a fore-and-aft line; the attachment bolts will then secure the
valve in its correct position.

VACUUM SYSTEM

Pump

77.   Installation.- Before installing a pump, it should be tested for
freedom of rotation by turning the shaft by the fingers; if the shaft
does not rotate freely, the pump should not be installed.   The pump
receives its oil supply through one of four holes in its mounting flange
which aligns with a hole in the engine mounting pad.   Care must be
taken to ensure that the jointing packing has a hole similarly placed,
otherwise the pump will fail due to lack of lubrication.   See also
A.P.1519, Vol.I.

WINDSCREEN DE-ICING

Tank

78.   Removal.- The tank is mounted on the starboard strut AD and CD.

(i)   Remove the starboard intermediate and rear side panels.

(ii)   Disconnect the pipe leading to the pump from the tank.

(iii) Remove the four bolts holding the straps together at the front
       and rear of the tank and remove tank.

Pump

79.   Removal.- The pump is mounted on a bracket attached to the
starboard strut C F.

(i)   Remove the starboard rear side panel.

(ii)   Disconnect the pipe leading to the tank and windscreen, at the
       pump.

(iii) Remove the two bolts attaching the clips of the mounting to
       the strut C F. and remove the pump complete with mounting.

Section 6:
Electrical and radio wiring and servicing.

This leaf issued with A.L. No. 41
February, 1944

SECTION 6

ELECTRICAL AND RADIO WIRING AND SERVICING

LIST OF CONTENTS

LIST OF ILLUSTRATIONS

Early system

SECTION 6

ELECTRICAL AND RADIO WIRING AND SERVICING

Introduction

1. This section contains maintenance notes on items of equipment either peculiar to this aircraft or not yet described in other publications; for maintenance notes on equipment not covered in this section, reference should be made to the appropriate publications detailed in Sect. 10. For a description of the electrical installation, reference should also be made to Sect. 10. On certain aircraft the electrical installation is in accordance with figs. 1 to 12, but some aircraft have a simplified form of wiring as shown in figs. 13 to 25. If wings with the simplified wiring are fitted to a fuselage in which the wiring has not been modified, reference should be made to fig. 26. Certain aircraft have a fuel pressure warning lamp fitted instead of the fuel pressure gauge. Station-keeping lamps may be fitted to aircraft at the discretion of individual units, but provision is no longer made for the wiring of these lamps. The radio installations are similar on all aircraft except that the fuse arrangement differs; both these arrangements are indicated on figs. 27 to 29.

Interpretation of diagrams

2. The location diagram (fig. 1 or 13) shows the approximate position of all the terminal blocks and of some of the electrical equipment. Figs. 2 and 14 illustrate the manner in which the fuses are connected to the power supply, and figs. 3 to 12 and 15 to 25 show the connections for those circuits fed from the generator circuit; each illustration comprises a wiring and theoretical circuit. Figs. 27 to 29 cover the radio installation and comprise wiring diagrams only, and should be used in conjunction with fig. 29A, which shows the junction box connections for later aircraft.

3. The fuses and terminal blocks have been numbered in sequence and, in the case of the fuses, the method adopted can be seen by referring to figs. 2 and 14. The terminal blocks are prefixed by the letters T.B., and where the same terminal block occurs on more than one diagram it bears the same number throughout the relative set of diagrams, but the numbering of the terminal blocks on figs. 1 to 12 bears no relation to the numbering of those on figs. 13 to 25.

4. As an example of how the circuits may be traced, reference is made to the heated pressure head circuit, fig. 4. From fuse 9, which supplies the circuit, two lengths of Unicel 7 cable feed T.B.8 through a switchbox, type B, the second terminal on T.B.8 being connected by Unicel 7 to the main negative on T.B.2. From T.B.8, the feed is taken by a length of Ducel 7 to T.B.19, across which the pressure head is connected by another length of Ducel 7.

TESTING AND MAINTENANCE

Undercarriage indicator

5. *Testing circuit.*—Switch on the indicator circuit at the ON–OFF switch; the green lamps should light for both the port and starboard undercarriage units. Operate the change-over switch and note that the green lamps in the alternative circuit light for each undercarriage unit.

6. *Testing micro-switches.*—Some aircraft are fitted with Burgess standard micro-switches but others incorporate Burgess Mk. II type switches, and these latter may be recognised by the fact that they are 1⅛ in. high and that the cable connections at the base are covered. The plungers for the standard type of micro-switches, which are in circuit with the undercarriage indicators, should operate under a load of 1 lb. ± 4 oz.; the load required to operate the Mk. II type is 1¼ lb. ± 4 oz.

Undercarriage horn

7. *Testing.*—With the throttle lever in the CLOSED position, raise by hand the latch locking one of the undercarriage side stays until the lever operating the micro-switch is just engaged; the warning horn should then sound. Repeat the operation on the other latch. Move the throttle lever forward to slightly more than one-third of its travel and raise each latch as before; this time the horn should not sound. When a latch is lifted, the corresponding green lamp on the visual indicator should go out.

8. *Adjusting throttle switch.*—The position of the throttle control lever at which the switch in the warning horn circuit closes, can be adjusted by slackening the pivot screw of the cam plate on the throttle micro-switch, moving the cam plate in the required direction, and re-tightening the screw. Access to the cam plate is obtained by removing the appropriate fuselage panel.

9. *Cleaning contacts.*—Remove the five screws round the outside of the instrument and gently pull the horn from its case. Disconnect the wires from the terminals outside the case and remove the gauze cover by taking out the two countersunk screws on the top. Unscrew the six countersunk screws from the back of the unit and remove the diaphragm assembly. Clean the contacts by passing a slip of fine emery cloth between them, or, if they are very dirty, remove the adjusting screws and clean the contacts with a magneto file.

10. *Adjusting contacts.*—Apply the working voltage to the leads and adjust the contact screw to produce the correct note; re-lock the contact adjusting screw with the locknut provided. Replace the gauze cover and re-check the horn for the correct note before replacing the unit in its case.

Fuel pressure warning lamps

11. *Testing and adjusting.*—Before installing the fuel pressure warning lamp, the following tests and adjustments should be made.

(i)   Connect the pressure unit to a source of pressure (with a
        suitable gauge) and apply the maximum pressure (10 lb./sq.in.)
        for about 10 secs; repeat three times.

(ii)   Connect the lamp unit to a 12-volt battery.

(iii)   Apply a pressure of 6 lb./sq.in. and turn the adjusting screw
        until the lamp goes out.   Check with a pressure below 6 lb./sq.in.
        to ensure that the lamp comes on at the correct pressure.

(iv)   Lock the unit.

Note.- The Smith's type of instrument has a locknut and the adjusting
        screw turns anti-clockwise to increase pressure; when the
        desired setting has been obtained the screw should be locked
        with the locknut and sealed with varnish.   On other types
        of instruments the adjusting screw turns clockwise to increase
        pressure; Negretti and Zambra instruments have a click detent
        and no other locking is necessary.

Access to components (Early system)

12.   The location of, or means of access to, the components (see figs.
2 to 12) in the early circuit is shown in the following table;   the
numbers in brackets refer to the access panel numbering in Sect.4, Chap.3,
fig.1.

GENERATOR CONTROLS CIRCUIT

Generator   Port front cowling panel (8)
Suppressor
T.B.1

T.B.2, 15 and 27
Cut-out   Port rear cowling panel (12)
Main fuse
Ammeter
Voltmeter
Switchbox, type B.

Voltage regulator   Port fairing panel (6)

Accumulator
T.B.14 and 25   Starboard fairing panel (5)

LANDING LAMPS CIRCUIT

Relay   Port rear cowling panel (12)
T.B.15

F.S./2A

Landing lamps T.B.17 and 18	Landing lamp windows (35)
T.B.7 and 16	Access doors (26)
Switch	Port decking shelf, front end

ENGINE STARTING

Motor	Starboard front cowling panel (8)
Pushbutton terminals	Tank cowl (2)
Ground supply socket Relay T.B.20	Starboard nose fillet; to gain access to the terminals of the ground supply socket, remove the three bolts and allow the socket to drop.

STATION-KEEPING LAMPS CIRCUIT

Lamp (starboard) Lamp (port) T.B.29	Starboard fairing panel (5) Port fairing panel (6)
Switchbox, type B	Port decking shelf

REFLECTOR GUN-SIGHT CIRCUIT

Dimmer switch	Starboard decking, front end; to gain access to the back of the switch, remove the three screws holding the switch to its mounting
Switchbox, type B T.B.3 and 4 T.B.28	Tank cowl (2)

INTERIOR LIGHTING CIRCUIT

Lamps Dimmer switches	Cockpit
T.B.3 and 4	Tank cowl (2)
T.B.2	Port rear cowling panel (12)

NAVIGATION LAMPS CIRCUIT

Lamps T.B.6 and 9	Navigation lamp windows (38)
T.B.10	Tail bay fairing (18)
T.B.5,7 and 8	Access doors (26)
Switch terminals T.B.4	Tank cowl (2)

IDENTIFICATION LAMPS CIRCUIT

Upward lamp terminals T.B.11	Starboard fairing panel (5); unscrew the lamp-glass bezel to gain access to terminals
Downward lamp terminals T.B.12	Rear fuselage front underfairing panel (16); unscrew the lamp-glass bezel to gain access to terminals
Identification switchbox	Starboard decking, front end
T.B.3 and 4	Tank cowl (2)

FUEL GAUGES CIRCUIT

Main tank transmitters	Fuel tank cover
Reserve tank transmitter Indicator T.B.4 and 13	Tank cowl (2)
Selector switch	Instrument panel; to gain access to the terminals, remove the four bolts holding the switch to the panel

UNDERCARRIAGE INDICATOR CIRCUIT

Latch gear switches	Undercarriage housing (wheels down)
Catch gear switches	Port and starboard intermediate cowling panels (11)
Horn	Port decking, front end
Terminals of indicator and master switch T.B.4	Tank cowl (2)

Throttle switch   Port rear cowling panel (12)
T.B.2, 26 and 27

HEATED PRESSURE HEAD CIRCUIT

T.B.19   Access door (44)

T.B.8   Access door (26)

Switchbox   Tank cowl (2)

CINE-CAMERA GUN CIRCUIT

Camera gun   Access door (31)
T.B.23 and 24

Pneumatic switch   Starboard inboard gun access door (52)
                                            or cannon access door (30)

Switchbox, type B   Tank cowl (2)

Footage indicator   Port decking, front end

T.B.2, 21, 22 and 27   Port rear cowling panel (12)

FUEL PRESSURE WARNING LAMP CIRCUIT

Resistance unit   Tank cowl (2)
Warning lamp

Pressure unit   Intermediate under panel (23)

OIL DILUTION CIRCUIT

Oil dilution valve   Port intermediate side panel (11)
T.B.31

Pushbutton switch   Port rear cowling panel (12)

Access to components (Simplified system)

    13.   The location of, or means of access to the components (see figs. 13
to 25) in the simplified circuit is shown in the following table; the
numbers in brackets refer to the access panel numbering in Sect.4, Chap.3,
fig.1.

GENERATOR CONTROLS CIRCUIT

Suppressor   Port front cowling panel (8)
Generator

Voltmeter   Port rear cowling panel (12)
Cut-out
Main fuse
T.B.2
Switchbox

Voltage regulator   Port fairing panel (6)

Accumulator   Starboard fairing panel (5)
T.B.14

LANDING LAMPS CIRCUIT

Relays   Port rear cowling panel (12)

Landing lamps   Landing lamp windows (35)
T.B.17 and 18

T.B.7 and 16   Access door (26)

Selector switch   Port decking shelf, front end

ENGINE STARTING CIRCUIT

Motor   Starboard front cowling panel (8)

Pushbutton terminals   Tank cowl (2)

Ground supply socket   Starboard nose fillet; to gain access to the
Rotax relay   terminals of the ground supply socket, re-
                                  move the three bolts and allow the socket
                                  to drop.

T.B.14   Starboard fairing panel (5)

Booster coil (if fitted)   Starboard front cowling panel (8)

REFLECTOR GUN-SIGHT CIRCUIT

Dimmer switch   Starboard decking, front end; to gain access
                                  to the back of the switch, remove the three
                                  screws holding the switch to its mounting.

Switchbox, type B   Tank cowl (2)
T.B.13

T.B.4   Cockpit decking

INSTRUMENT LAMPS CIRCUIT

Lamps   Cockpit
Dimmer switches

T.B.22   Port rear cowling panel (12)

NAVIGATION LAMPS CIRCUIT

Lamps   Navigation lamp windows (38)
T.B.6 and 9

Switch terminals   Tank cowl (2)

T.B.4   Cockpit decking

T.B.17 and 18   Landing lamp windows (35)

T.B.7, 8 and 16   Access door (26)

T.B.10   Fairing panel (18)

IDENTIFICATION LAMPS CIRCUIT

Upward lamp terminals   Starboard fairing panel (5); unscrew
P.B.11   the lamp-glass bezel to gain access to
                                       terminals
Downward lamp terminals   Rear fuselage front underfairing panel
T.B.12   (16); unscrew the lamp-glass bezel to gain
                                       access to terminals.
Identification switchbox   Starboard decking, front end.
T.B.4

FUEL CONTENTS GAUGES CIRCUIT

Main tank transmitters   Fuel tank cover

Reserve tank transmitter   Tank cowl (2)
Indicator
T.B.13

Selector switch   Instrument panel; to gain access to
                                       the terminals, remove the four bolts
                                       holding the switch to the panel.

T.B.4   Cockpit decking

UNDERCARRIAGE INDICATOR CIRCUIT

Latch gear switches   Undercarriage housing (wheels down)

Catch gear switches   Port and starboard intermediate cowling
                                 panels (11)

Horn   Port decking, front end

Terminals of indicator and   Tank cowl (2)
master switch

Throttle switch   Port rear cowling panel (12)

HEATED PRESSURE HEAD CIRCUIT

Switchbox, type B   Tank cowl (2)

T.B.7 and 8   Access door (26)

T.B.19   Access door (44)

CINE-CAMERA GUN CIRCUIT

Camera gun   Access door (31) leading edge of starboard
T.B.23, 24 and 27   outer plane, at inner end.

Pneumatically-operated switch   Starboard inboard gun access door (52)
                                 or cannon access door (30).

Switchbox, type B   Tank cowl (2)

T.B.2, 15 and 21   Port rear cowling panel (12)

Footage indicator   Port decking, front end

FUEL PRESSURE WARNING LAMP CIRCUIT

Resistance unit   Tank cowl (2)
Warning lamp

Pressure unit   Intermediate underpanel (23)

OIL DILUTION CIRCUIT

Oil dilution valve   Port intermediate side panel (11)
T.B.28

Pushbutton switch   Port rear cowling panel (12)

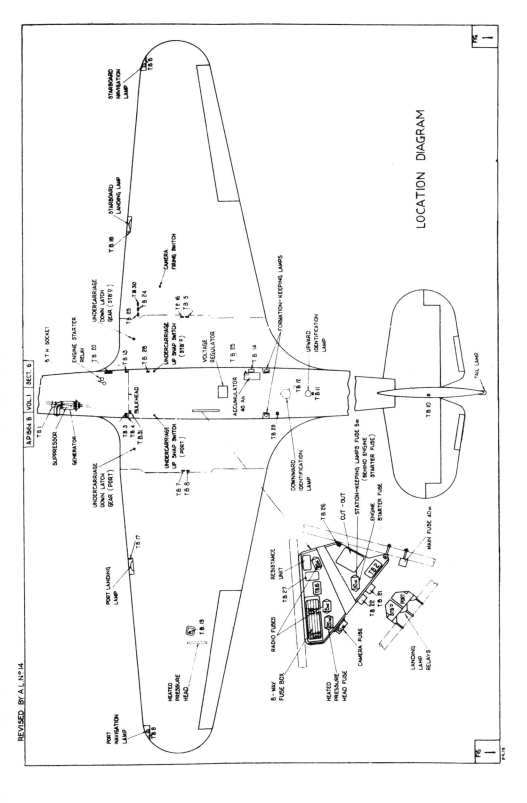

LOCATION DIAGRAM

STARBOARD
NAVIGATION
LAMP

T.B.6

STARBOARD
LANDING LAMP

T.B 18

CAMERA
FIRING SWITCH

UNDERCARRIAGE
DOWN LATCH
GEAR (STB'D)

T.B 30
T.B 24
T.B 25
T.B 16
T.B 5
T.B 20
T.B 13
T.B 28

UNDERCARRIAGE
UP SNAP SWITCH
(STB'D)

VOLTAGE
REGULATOR

T.B 25

T.B 14

FORMATION-KEEPING LAMPS

UPWARD
IDENTIFICATION
LAMP

B.T.H. SOCKET

ENGINE STARTER
RELAY

BULKHEAD

ACCUMULATOR
40 Ah

T.B 12
T.B 11

TAIL LAMP

T.B 10

T.B 1

SUPPRESSOR

GENERATOR

T.B.3
T.B.4
T.B.31

UNDERCARRIAGE
DOWN LATCH
GEAR (PORT)

UNDERCARRIAGE
UP SNAP SWITCH
(PORT)

T.B 7
T.B 8

T.B 29

DOWNWARD
IDENTIFICATION
LAMP

T.B 17

PORT LANDING
LAMP

T.B 26

CUT-OUT

STATION-KEEPING LAMPS FUSE 5≡

ENGINE
STARTER FUSE

(BEHIND ENGINE
STARTER FUSE)

MAIN FUSE 40≡

RESISTANCE
UNIT

T.B 27

RADIO FUSES

T.B 22
T.B 21

T.B.2

LANDING
LAMP
RELAYS

8-WAY
FUSE BOX

HEATED
PRESSURE
HEAD FUSE

CAMERA FUSE

T.B.19

HEATED
PRESSURE
HEAD

PORT
NAVIGATION
LAMP

T.B.6

FIG
1

FIG
1
FL./R

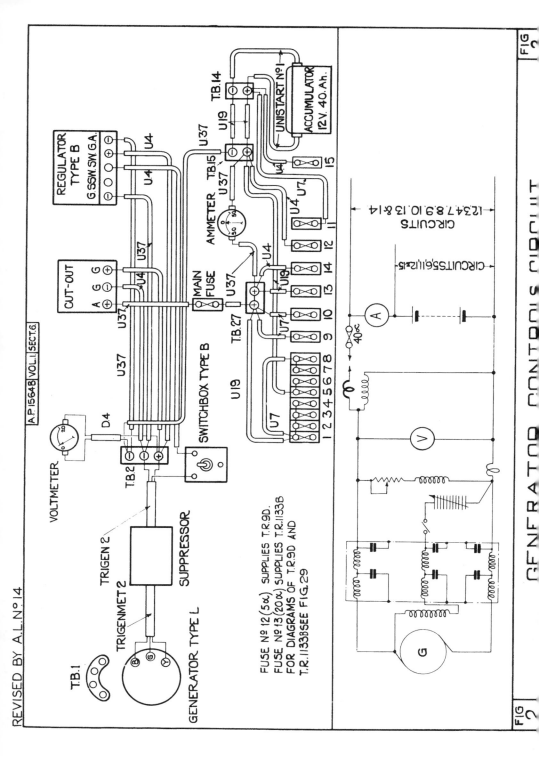

GENERATOR CONTROLS CIRCUIT

FIG 2

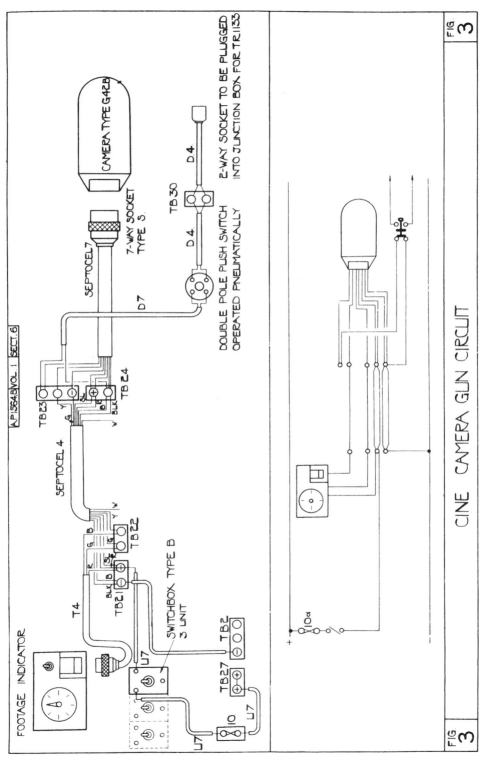

A.P.1564.B.VOL.1 SECT.6

FOOTAGE INDICATOR

CAMERA TYPE G42B

SEPTOCEL 7

7-WAY SOCKET TYPE S.

D7

TB23

TB24

SEPTOCEL 4

T4

TB22

TB21

SWITCHBOX TYPE B
3 UNIT

U7

TB2

TB27

U7

U7

10

TB30

D.4.

D.4.

DOUBLE POLE PUSH SWITCH
OPERATED PNEUMATICALLY

2-WAY SOCKET TO BE PLUGGED
INTO JUNCTION BOX FOR TR.1153

10

CINE CAMERA GUN CIRCUIT

FIG 3

FIG 3

F.S./4

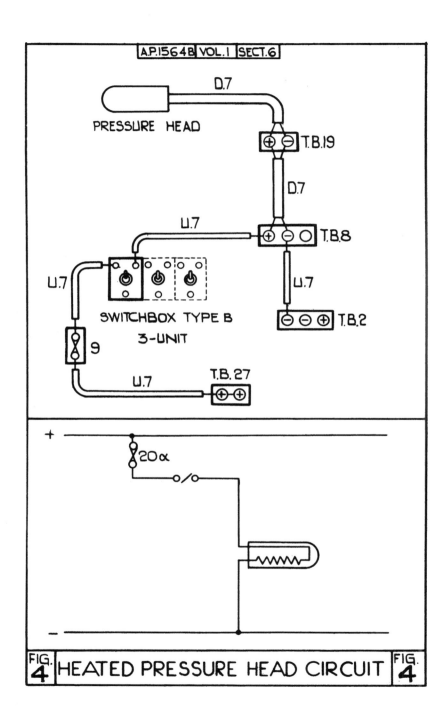

FIG. 4 — HEATED PRESSURE HEAD CIRCUIT — FIG. 4

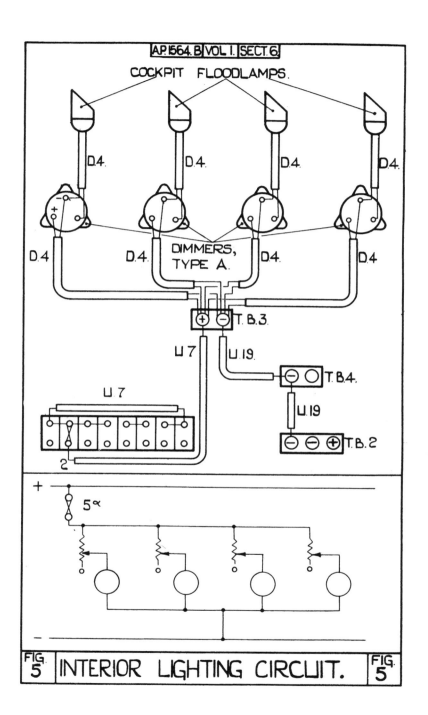

A.P. 1564. B. VOL. I. SECT. 6.

COCKPIT FLOODLAMPS.

D.4.   D.4.   D.4.   D.4.

D.4.   D.4.   DIMMERS,   D.4.   D.4.
TYPE A.

T.B.3.

L.I.7   L.I.19.

T.B.4.

L.I.7   L.I.19.

2   T.B.2.

+

5∝

−

| FIG.
5 | INTERIOR LIGHTING CIRCUIT. | FIG.
5 |

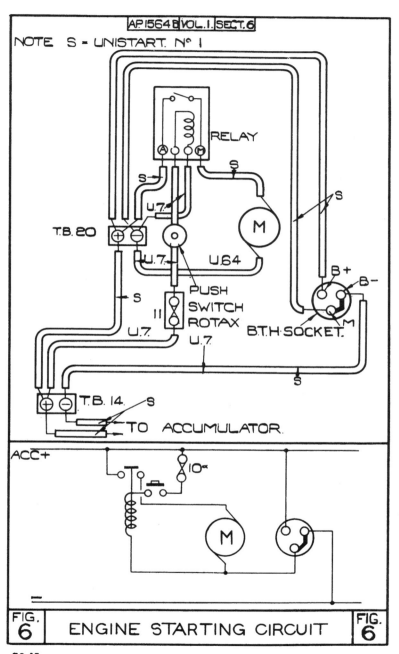

NOTE S - UNISTART. Nº 1

RELAY

S

T.B. 20

U.7.

U.64

PUSH
SWITCH
ROTAX

U.7.

II

U.7.

U.7.

B+

B−

M

B.T.H. SOCKET.

S

T.B. 14.   S

TO ACCUMULATOR.

ACC+

10ᵃ

M

| FIG. 6 | ENGINE STARTING CIRCUIT | FIG. 6 |

F.S./5

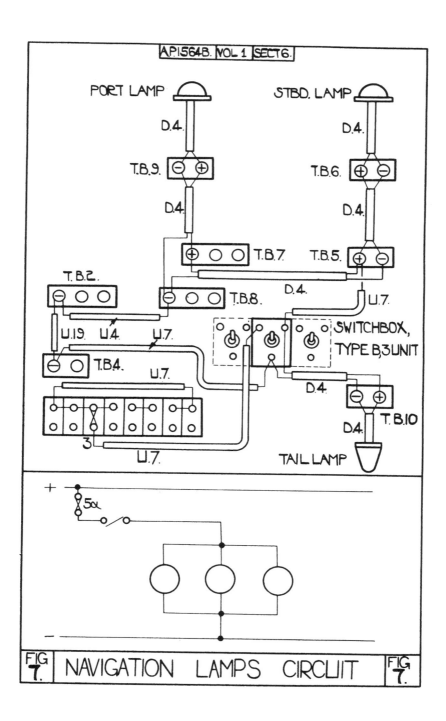

NAVIGATION LAMPS CIRCUIT

FIG 7.

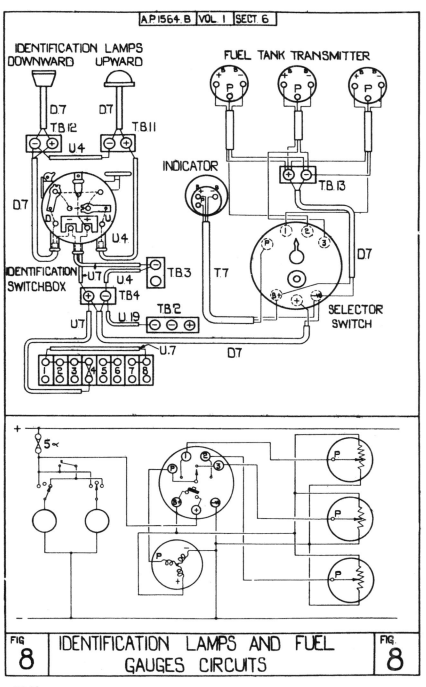

IDENTIFICATION LAMPS
DOWNWARD   UPWARD

FUEL TANK TRANSMITTER

D.7   D.7
TB.12   TB.11
         U4
D.7   U.4

INDICATOR

IDENTIFICATION
SWITCHBOX

U.7   U.4   TB.3
      TB.4
T.7
U.7   U.19   T.B.2

TB.13

D.7

U.7   D.7

SELECTOR
SWITCH

1 2 3 4 5 6 7 8

+
5

FIG 8   IDENTIFICATION LAMPS AND FUEL
        GAUGES CIRCUITS   FIG. 8

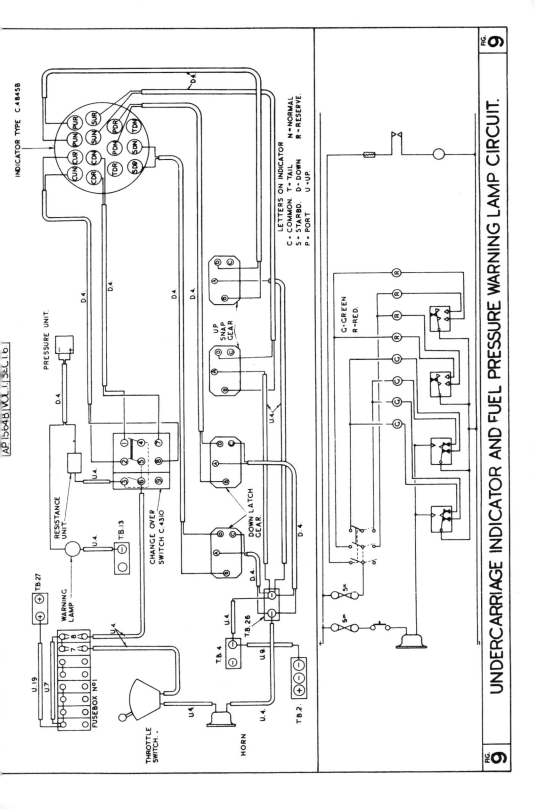

UNDERCARRIAGE INDICATOR AND FUEL PRESSURE WARNING LAMP CIRCUIT.

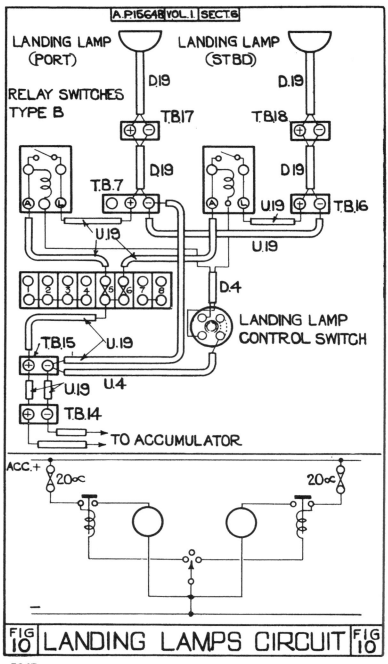

LANDING LAMP
(PORT)

LANDING LAMP
(STBD)

D.19

D.19

RELAY SWITCHES
TYPE B

T.B.17

T.B.18

D.19

D.19

T.B.7

U.19

T.B.16

A L

U.19

A L

U.19

U.19

1 2 3 4 5 6 7 8

D.4

LANDING LAMP
CONTROL SWITCH

T.B.15

U.19

U.19

U.4

T.B.14

TO ACCUMULATOR

ACC.+

20∝

20∝

FIG
10

LANDING LAMPS CIRCUIT

FIG
10

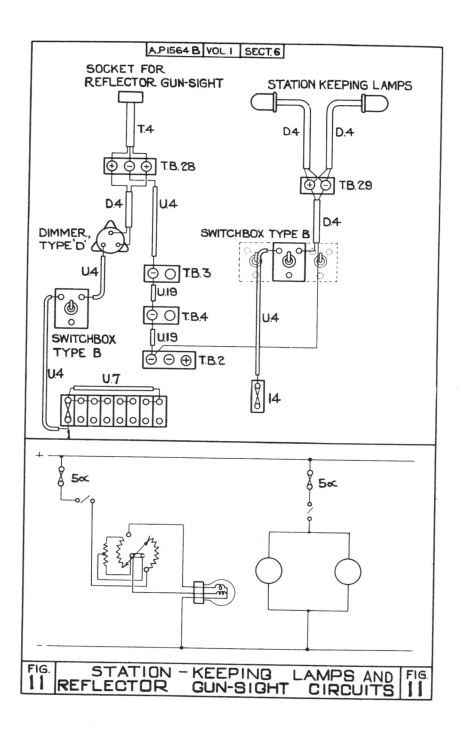

SOCKET FOR
REFLECTOR GUN-SIGHT

STATION KEEPING LAMPS

T.4

D.4   D.4

T.B. 28

T.B. 29

D.4   U.4

D.4

DIMMER,
TYPE 'D'

SWITCHBOX TYPE B

U.4

U.4   T.B. 3

U.19

U.4

SWITCHBOX
TYPE B

T.B. 4

U.19

T.B. 2

U.4

U.7

14

+

5∝

5∝

FIG. 11 | STATION – KEEPING LAMPS AND REFLECTOR GUN-SIGHT CIRCUITS | FIG. 11

AP.1564B VOL. I. SECT. 6

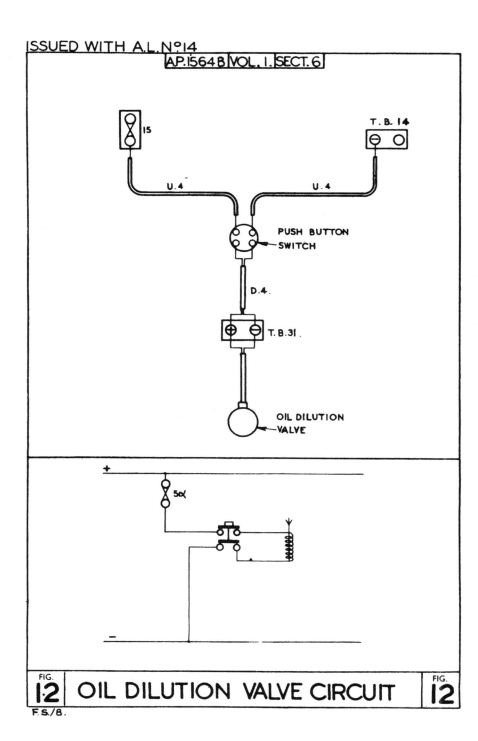

15

T.B. 14

U.4 U.4

PUSH BUTTON
SWITCH

D.4.

T.B.31.

OIL DILUTION
VALVE

+

50χ

−

FIG.
12 OIL DILUTION VALVE CIRCUIT FIG.
12

F.S./8.

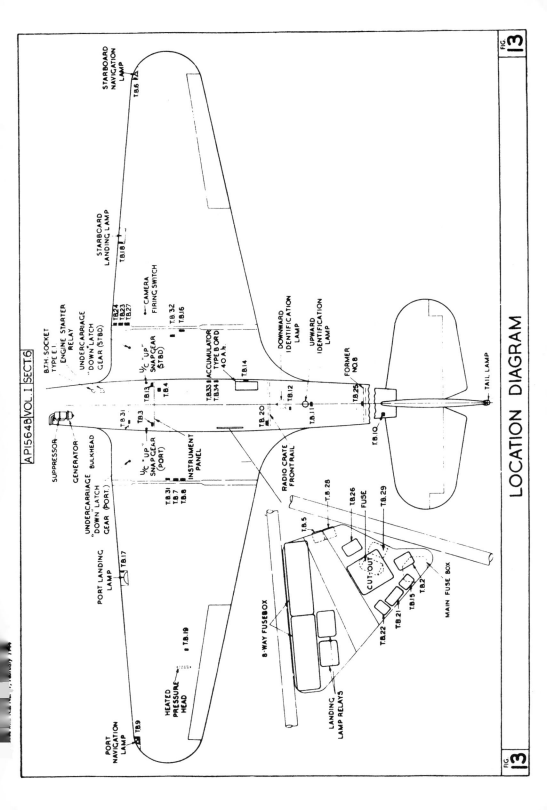

LOCATION DIAGRAM

STARBOARD NAVIGATION LAMP
T.B.6

STARBOARD LANDING LAMP
T.B.18

B.T.H. SOCKET TYPE E 1

ENGINE STARTER RELAY

UNDERCARRIAGE "DOWN" LATCH GEAR (STBD)
T.B.24
T.B.23
T.B.27

CAMERA FIRING SWITCH
T.B.32
T.B.16

U/C "UP" SNAPGEAR (STBD)
T.B.13
T.B.4

ACCUMULATOR TYPE B (ORD) 40 A.h.
T.B.33
T.B.34

DOWNWARD IDENTIFICATION LAMP

UPWARD IDENTIFICATION LAMP

T.B.14

T.B.12

FORMER No.8
T.B.25

TAIL LAMP

T.B.31
T.B.3

T.B.20

T.B.11

T.B.10

SUPPRESSOR

GENERATOR

BULKHEAD

UNDERCARRIAGE "DOWN" LATCH GEAR (PORT.)

U/C "UP" SNAPGEAR (PORT)
T.B.31
T.B.7
T.B.8

INSTRUMENT PANEL

RADIO CRATE FRONT RAIL

T.B.5

T.B.28

T.B.26
FUSE

T.B.29

CUT-OUT

T.B.2

MAIN FUSE BOX

T.B.21
T.B.15

T.B.22

8-WAY FUSEBOX

PORT LANDING LAMP
T.B.17

LANDING LAMP RELAYS

B T.B.19

HEATED PRESSURE HEAD

PORT NAVIGATION LAMP
T.B.9

FIG. 13

FIG. 13

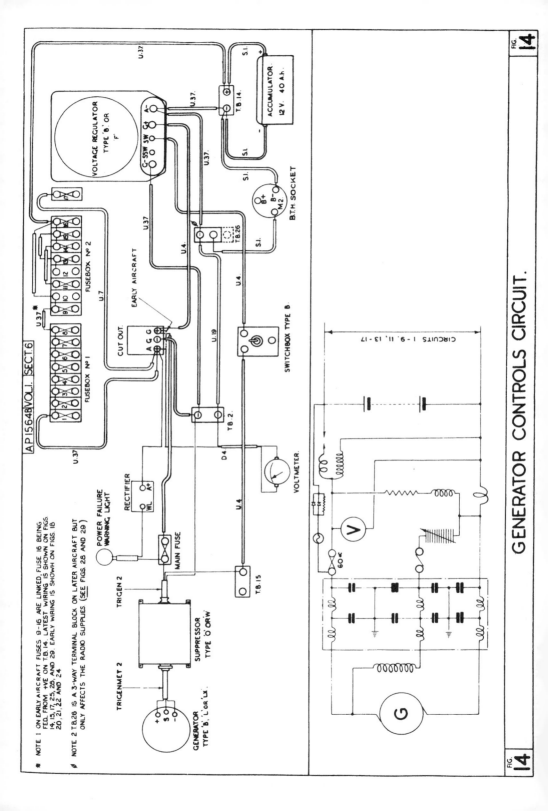

GENERATOR CONTROLS CIRCUIT.

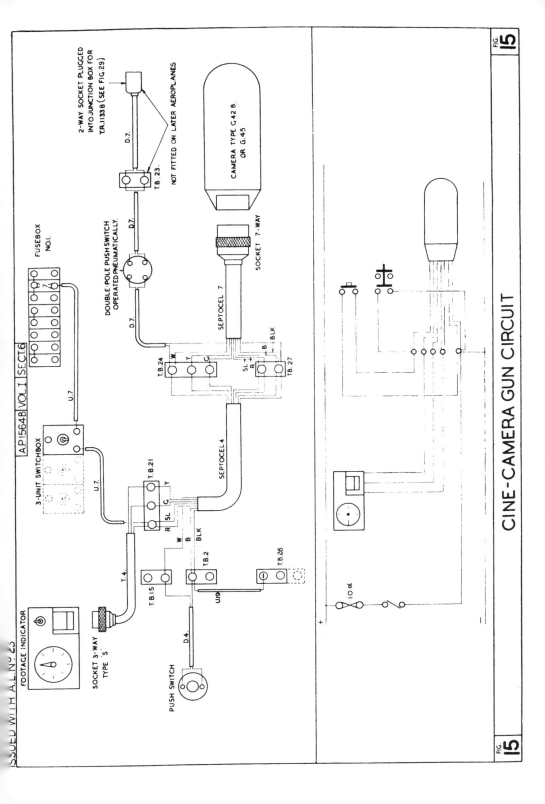

CINE-CAMERA GUN CIRCUIT

AP.1564.B.VOL.I.SECT.6

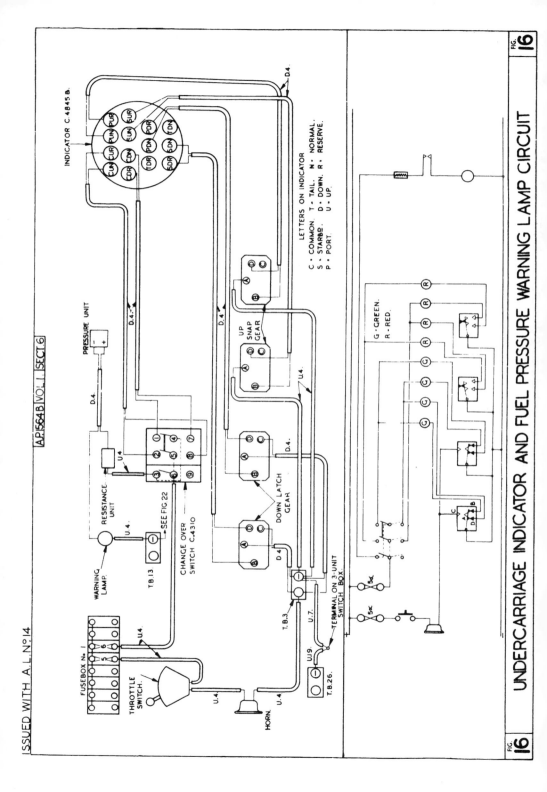

LETTERS ON INDICATOR

C - COMMON.   T - TAIL.   N - NORMAL.
S - STARB?.   D - DOWN.   R - RESERVE.
P - PORT.   U - UP.

G - GREEN.
R - RED.

FIG. 16

UNDERCARRIAGE INDICATOR AND FUEL PRESSURE WARNING LAMP CIRCUIT

AP1564B VOL.1 SECT.6

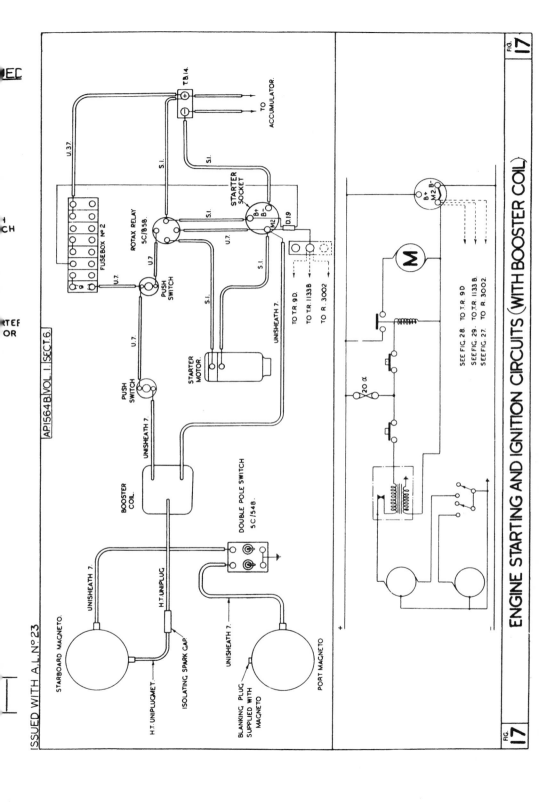

FIG. 17

ENGINE STARTING AND IGNITION CIRCUITS (WITH BOOSTER COIL)

FIG. 17

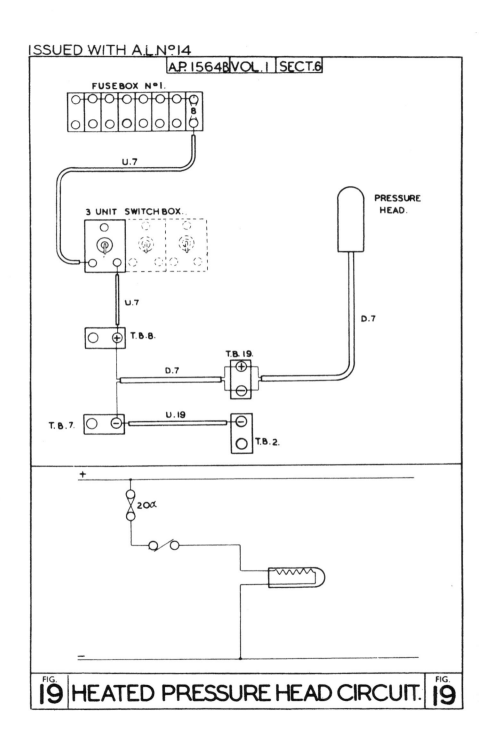

FUSEBOX N°1.

U.7

3 UNIT SWITCH BOX.

PRESSURE
HEAD.

U.7

T.B.B.

D.7

T.B. 19.

D.7

T. B. 7.

U.19

T.B. 2.

+

20α

−

FIG.
19 HEATED PRESSURE HEAD CIRCUIT. FIG.
19

AP.1564B VOL. 1 SECT.6

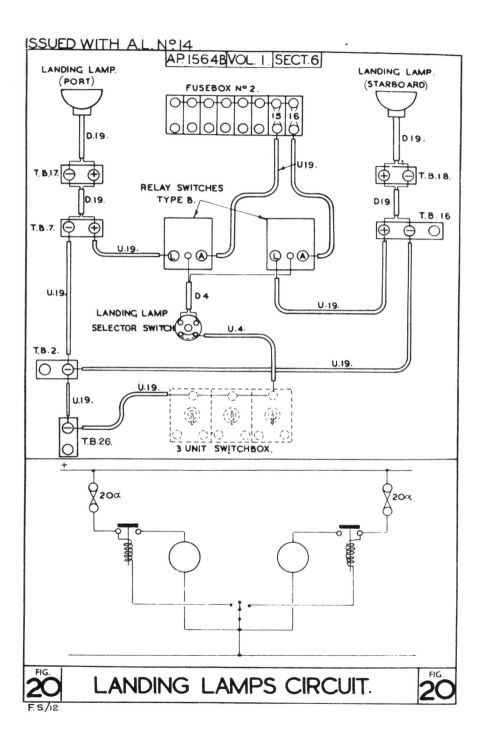

LANDING LAMP.
(PORT)

FUSEBOX N° 2.

LANDING LAMP.
(STARBOARD)

D.19.

15 16

D.19.

T.B.17.

U19.

T.B.18.

D.19.

RELAY SWITCHES
TYPE B.

D19

T.B.16.

T.B.7.

U.19.

L   A

L   A

U.19.

D 4

LANDING LAMP
SELECTOR SWITCH

U.4.

T.B.2.

U.19.

U.19.

U.19.

3 UNIT SWITCHBOX.

T.B.26.

+

20α

20x

FIG.
20

LANDING LAMPS CIRCUIT.

FIG.
20

F.S./12

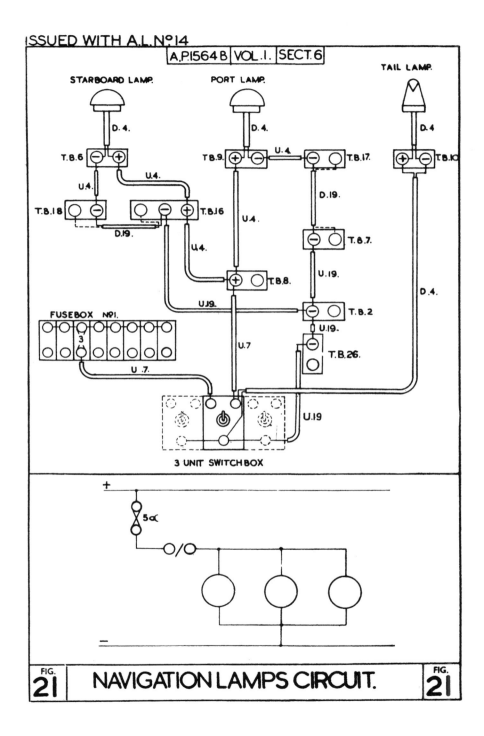

A.P.1564 B | VOL.I. | SECT.6

TAIL LAMP.

STARBOARD LAMP.

PORT LAMP.

FUSEBOX Nº1.

3 UNIT SWITCHBOX

FIG. 21   NAVIGATION LAMPS CIRCUIT.   FIG. 21

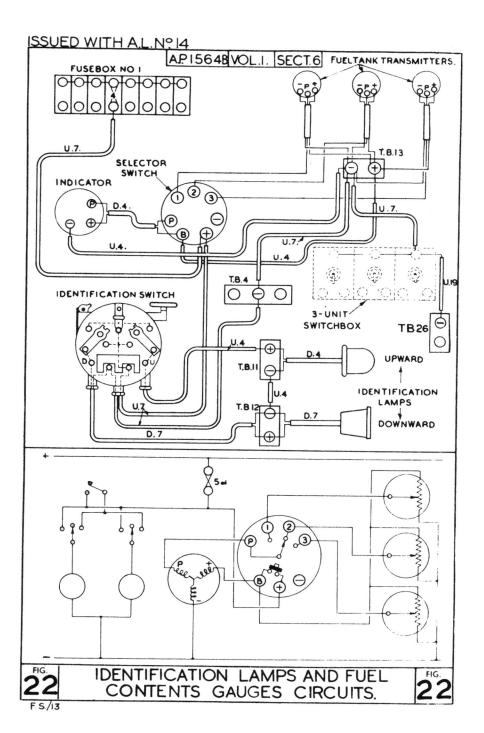

FIG. 22

IDENTIFICATION LAMPS AND FUEL CONTENTS GAUGES CIRCUITS.

FIG. 22

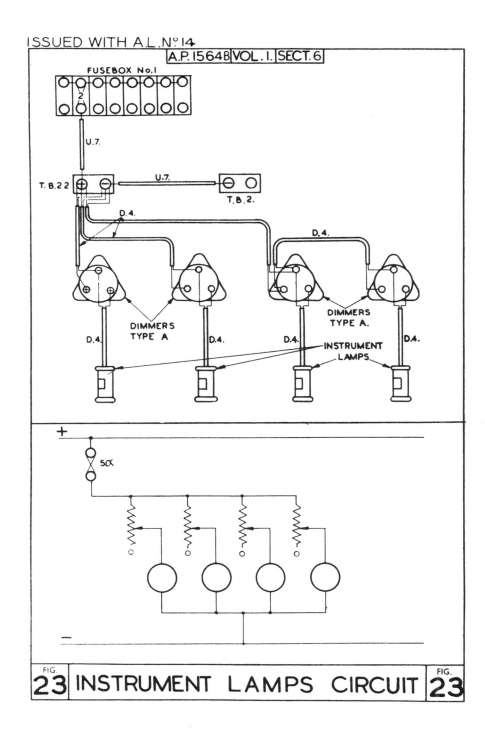

FUSEBOX No.1

U.7.

T.B.22

U.7.

T.B.2.

D.4.

D.4.

DIMMERS
TYPE A.

D.4.

D.4.

DIMMERS
TYPE A.

D.4.

INSTRUMENT
LAMPS

D.4.

+

50α

−

| FIG. 23 | INSTRUMENT LAMPS CIRCUIT | FIG. 23 |

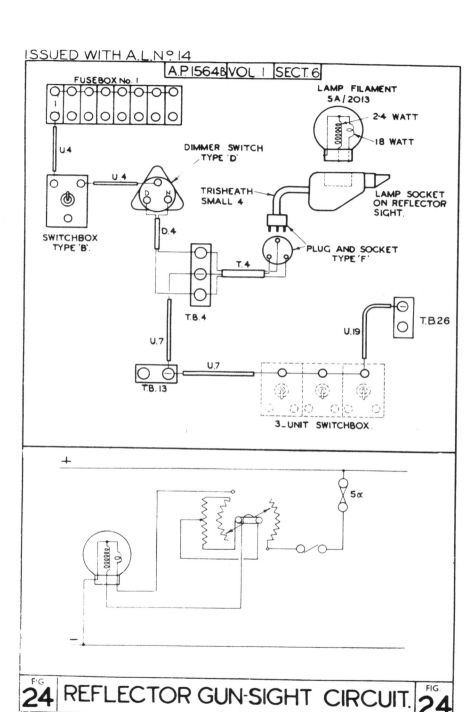

FUSEBOX No. I

LAMP FILAMENT
5A/2013

2·4 WATT

18 WATT

U.4

U.4

DIMMER SWITCH
TYPE 'D'

TRISHEATH
SMALL 4

LAMP SOCKET
ON REFLECTOR
SIGHT.

SWITCHBOX
TYPE 'B'.

D.4

PLUG AND SOCKET
TYPE 'F'

T.4

T.B.4

T.B.26

U.7

U.19

T.B.13

U.7

3-UNIT SWITCHBOX.

+

5α

−

FIG. 24 REFLECTOR GUN-SIGHT CIRCUIT. **FIG. 24**

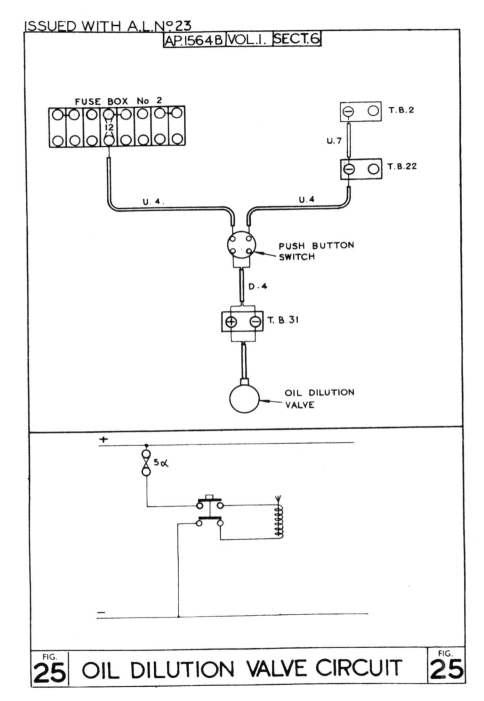

FUSE BOX No 2

T.B.2

U.7

T.B.22

U.4.

U.4

PUSH BUTTON
SWITCH

D.4

T.B.31

OIL DILUTION
VALVE

+

5α

−

FIG.
25 OIL DILUTION VALVE CIRCUIT FIG. **25**

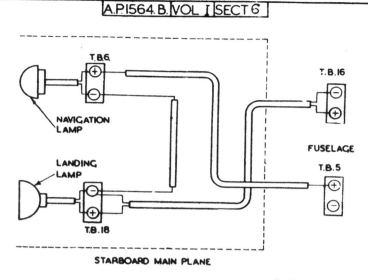

STARBOARD MAIN PLANE

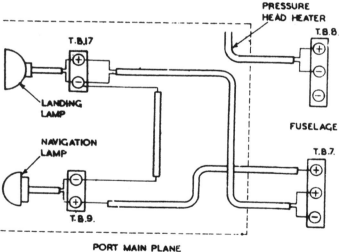

PORT MAIN PLANE

METHOD OF CONNECTING ELECTRICAL CABLES OF MAIN
PLANES WITH MOD. HURR.249. INCORPORATED, TO TERMINAL
BLOCKS ON AEROPLANES WITHOUT MOD.249.INCORPORATED

| FIG. 26 | ALTERATIONS TO MAIN PLANE ELECTRICAL CONNECTIONS | FIG. 26 |

A P I564B VOL.I SECT.6

FUSE NR. 14 · 20 α

FUSEBOX NR 2.

T.B 15
T.B. 26.

SEE FIG
17 OR 18

NOTE.—
THE ALTERNATIVE ARRANGEMENT
OF THE FUSE FOR EARLIER AIRCRAFT
IS SHOWN DOTTED.

RECEIVER

5. PIN PLUG.
TYPE. 172.

SOCKET
TYPE 107.

CABLE
DULOCAPMET NR 3

DUFLEX. 4.

2 - PIN SOCKET
TYPE 185.

7 - POINT SOCKET
TYPE 105.

T.B.25

INSULATOR
TYPE. 18.

AERIAL WIRE.

T.B.20

U.4.

U.4

IMPACT
SWITCH

CABLE
QUINTOCORE

7 PIN PLUG
TYPE 174.

3 - PIN
SOCKET.

U.4.

3 - PIN PLUG
TYPE. 48.

CONTROL UNIT
TYPE. 17.

CABLE
QUINTOSHEATH
SMALL.

5. PIN PLUG
TYPE. 172.

D.7.

SWITCHBOX
TYPE. B.

PUSH SWITCHES.

D.4.

D.19.

A.R.I. 5000 OR A.R.I. 5025 INSTALLATION.

FIG.
27

F S/16

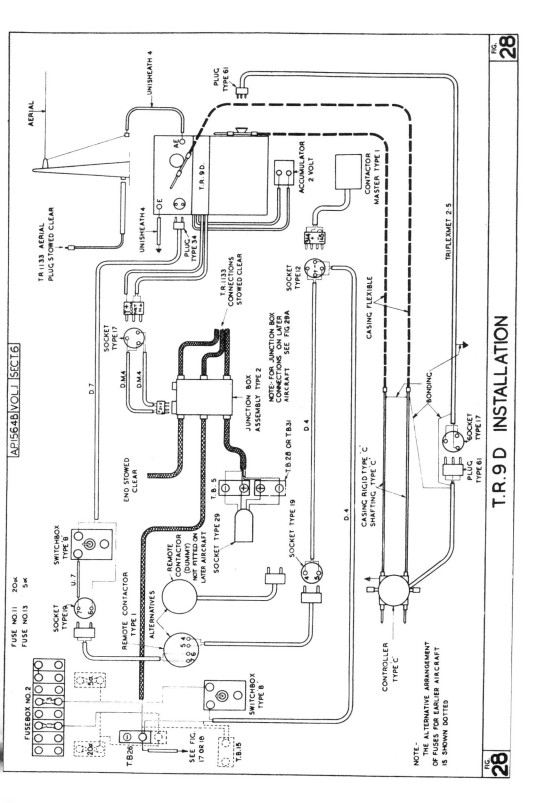

T.R.9 D INSTALLATION

FIG. 28

This leaf issued with A.L. No. 41, February 1944

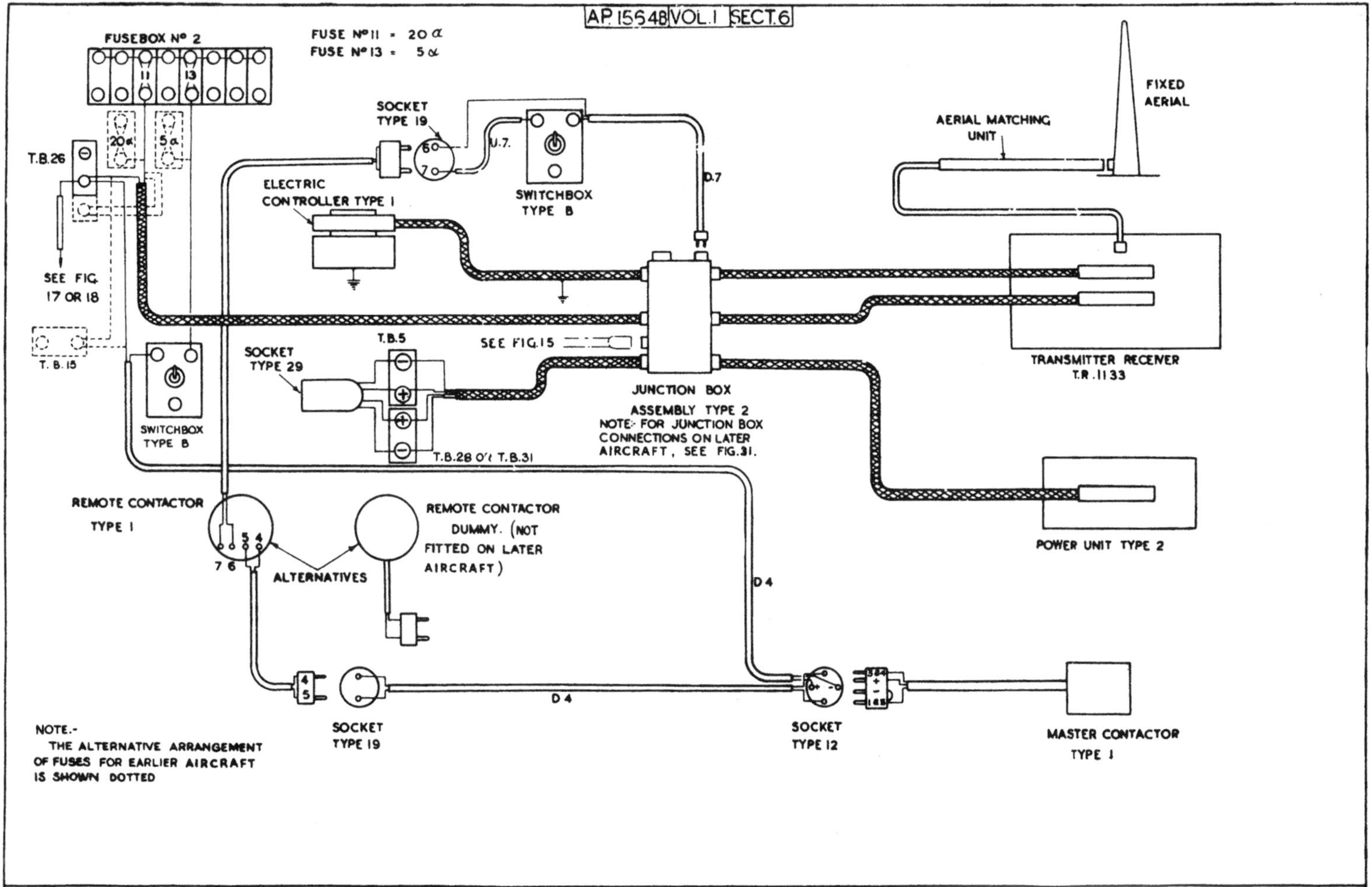

FIXED AERIAL

AERIAL MATCHING UNIT

TRANSMITTER RECEIVER T.R.1133

POWER UNIT TYPE 2

MASTER CONTACTOR TYPE 1

SOCKET TYPE 12

JUNCTION BOX
ASSEMBLY TYPE 2
NOTE: FOR JUNCTION BOX CONNECTIONS ON LATER AIRCRAFT, SEE FIG.31.

D.7

SWITCHBOX TYPE B

U.7.

SOCKET TYPE 19

ELECTRIC CONTROLLER TYPE 1

SEE FIG.15

T.B.5

T.B.28 OR T.B.31

D.4

REMOTE CONTACTOR DUMMY. (NOT FITTED ON LATER AIRCRAFT)

SOCKET TYPE 29

ALTERNATIVES

SOCKET TYPE 19

D.4

FUSE No.11 = 20α
FUSE No.13 = 5α

FUSEBOX No.2

13

5α

20α

11

T.B.26

SEE FIG. 17 OR 18

T.B.15

SWITCHBOX TYPE B

REMOTE CONTACTOR TYPE 1

NOTE:-
THE ALTERNATIVE ARRANGEMENT OF FUSES FOR EARLIER AIRCRAFT IS SHOWN DOTTED

T.R. 1133B or D INSTALLATION

FIG. 29

FIG. 29

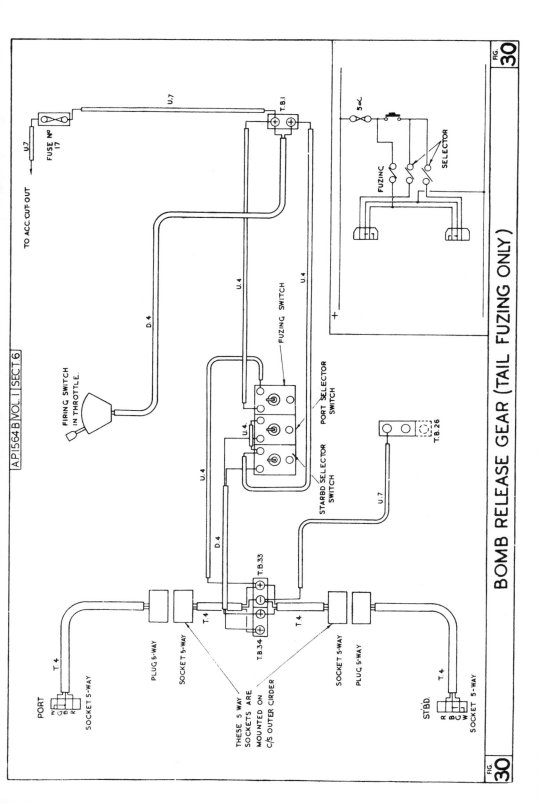

BOMB RELEASE GEAR (TAIL FUZING ONLY)

FIG. 30

A.P. 1564B VOL I SECT 6

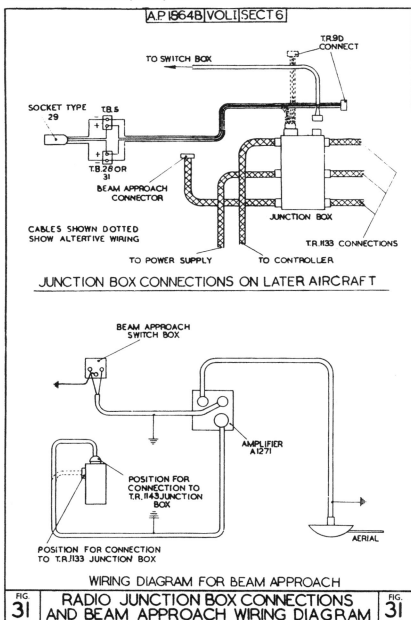

JUNCTION BOX CONNECTIONS ON LATER AIRCRAFT

WIRING DIAGRAM FOR BEAM APPROACH

| FIG.
31 | RADIO JUNCTION BOX CONNECTIONS
AND BEAM APPROACH WIRING DIAGRAM | FIG.
31 |

Section 7: Construction of airframe —Description.

CHAPTER 1

FUSELAGE

LIST OF CONTENTS

LIST OF ILLUSTRATIONS

CHAPTER 1

FUSELAGE

General

1. For descriptive purposes, the fuselage may conveniently be divided into the following four portions:—engine mounting, centre fuselage, rear fuselage and tail bay, the longerons being discontinuous at the joints between these portions. The extent of each of these portions is shown in fig. 1, which also indicates the manner in which the joints are lettered for reference purposes; this nomenclature is the same as that adopted by the makers and used in the Schedule of Spare Parts, Vol. III, Part 1 of this publication.

2. The main members of the fuselage (*see* fig. 1) are of steel and duralumin tube; most of the top, bottom and cross panels are braced with swaged steel wires, the side panels being tubular braced. No welding is employed in the structure, the ends of the tubes being rolled to rectangular sections and bolted or riveted between steel side plates. At the more complicated joints, machined steel stampings take the place of the side plates and some of the tubes are fitted with end plugs instead of being rolled to a rectangular section. The engine mounting and centre fuselage sides are covered with duralumin panels (most of which are detachable), the decking with fabric-covered plywood and the rear fuselage fairing with fabric on wooden formers and stringers.

3. The general construction of the fuselage is such that it cannot be considered as completely dissociated from the centre section of the main plane structure, for the spars and bracing girders of the latter provide means for connecting the engine mounting to the centre fuselage and the centre section to joints H on the rear fuselage. The centre section is described in Chap. 2, paras. 2 to 9.

Engine mounting

4. The engine mounting (*see* fig. 3) is a detachable unit of tubular construction which is pinned to the centre fuselage at joints A and to the bottom boom of the centre section front spar at joints B1. The engine is cradled between two side panels connected at the bottom by two cross tubes; all the panels are tubular braced except the bottom rear panel adjacent to the centre section front spar which is wire braced, the strainers being fitted at the aft end of each wire. Four duralumin blocks support the engine feet, the rear pair being offset inboard from the main structure on two subsidiary struts to joint Z; packing strips are inserted between the duralumin blocks and the engine feet as shown in fig. 2. Joint W includes a spigot which provides an attachment for the cowling nose collar, and joint Z incorporates a wooden jacking pad between the side plates. A shaft for the engine starting handles is carried in bearing brackets at the front ends of tubes XZ; the axis of the shaft provides the arbitrary datum point from which the centre of gravity of the aeroplane is defined. The hand starting magneto is carried on a bracket mounted at the rear end of the starboard strut XZ, and a triple sprocket (which connects the chains from the handle shaft, the magneto and the engine-driven sprocket) is slung from tube XY adjacent to joint Y. The frames which support the cowling are bolted or clipped to the engine mounting struts at various suitable places.

Centre fuselage

5. The centre fuselage extends from joints A and B to joints G and H, between which points the longerons are continuous except at joints F. At these joints and at joint B, the various tubular members are bolted to the flanged U-shaped stampings (*see* fig. 4), which house the upper booms of the centre section spars. Tubular bracing is mainly employed, but wire bracing is used in the top panels in front of and behind the cockpit (i.e. panels AC and EG), the bottom panels BD and DF, and the diagonal panels E.FC and EH.

6. The front panel of the first bay, braced by a single diagonal tube, supports the fireproof bulkhead (*see* para. 12), the brackets for the front feet of the reserve fuel tank being carried on a cross strut AA; the tank rear feet are mounted on brackets around the top longerons approximately midway between joints A and C. The windscreen de-icing tank is attached to the starboard strut AD and CD. The rudder bar, its bearing bracket and the front ends of the supporting tubes and heelboards are located in this bay, the rear ends extending into the next bay. Catches for retaining the undercarriage in the retracted position are clipped round the lower longerons close to joints D.

7. The second bay of the centre fuselage accommodates the pilot in his adjustable seat with all the necessary control gear. The control column is carried on the same support tubes as the rudder bar assembly, these tubes being secured to cross strut DD and at each end to the top boom of the centre section front and rear spars (*see* Chap. 4, fig. 1). The portion of the decking over this bay includes the windscreen, the sliding hood and the emergency exit panel. The instrument panel is bolted and riveted to the front half-loop of the decking and secured to cross strut CC by two of the brackets which support the standard instrument-flying panel. The compass bracket is hung from the mid-point of cross strut CC whilst the hydraulic selector box is hung from the starboard longeron approximately midway between joints D and F. The electrical panel is secured to the port top longeron (between joints C and E) and port side strut EF. The oxygen bottle is mounted in the bottom of this bay, just forward of the rear spar.

8. In the third bay, a wireless tray is secured across the fuselage between side struts EH and GH, and on some aeroplanes station-keeping lamps are mounted on the port and starboard struts GH. In the angle between side struts EF and EH, the upper footstep is secured on the port side, whilst on the starboard side is the hydraulic-system handpump together with the filter, non-return valves and four-way piece. The countershaft of the radiator flap control is carried in bearing brackets on bracing struts F.H1, the oil system viscosity valve being secured to the forward end of the port bracing strut; the centre journal bearing of the torque tube of the trailing edge flaps is hung on a bracket bolted between the rear ends of bracing struts F.H1. The decking above the third bay of the centre fuselage is of robust construction to provide a crash pylon; beneath the bay, the radiator is hung from the bottom boom of the centre section rear spar and from the subsidiary tubes between the bottom boom and joints H.

Rear fuselage

9. The rear fuselage, extending from joints GH to RS, is a simple structure of triangulated side frames connected by cross struts top and bottom through plate-type joints. All the top and bottom panels are wire braced except the bottom rearmost panel which is tubular braced to withstand the loads from the tail wheel leg; wire bracing is also employed in the five cross panels which slope towards the rear at the top. Typical joints in the rear fuselage are shown

in fig. 5. An understructure for two training flare launching chutes is clipped to the bottom longerons between joints H and K, but only the port chute is fitted; immediately aft of this chute is situated the lower retractable footstep. The launching chutes are not fitted on later aircraft.

10. Fibre fairleads for the elevator and rudder duplicate control cables are mounted between two small L-section members which are clipped between side struts LM; other fairleads for these cables are mounted on cross strut PP. The cables for the trimming tabs in the elevators are carried in fairleads at port joints G and J and at the mid-point of cross strut NN. The rear ends of the safety harness anchorage cables are secured to joints J, port and starboard. An open-ended tube is incorporated beneath cross strut QQ for reception of the handling bar, which is used when lifting the rear fuselage.

Tail bay

11. The tail bay carries the tail plane, the fin and the tail wheel shock-absorber strut. The structure is tubular braced except for the wire bracing employed in the top panel. The tail plane is attached to end plugs at joints R and to double-lugged fittings at joint T by means of high-tensile steel bolts. At the top, the front finpost is bolted to cross strut RR at joint R1, whilst at the bottom it is bolted between the side plates at joint S1. The rear finpost is bolted at the top to flanges on the upper and lower plates of joint T and at the bottom to a plate channel at joint U. The upper end of the tail wheel strut is secured by two tubes forming a V which project into the rearmost bay of the rear fuselage from joints R; the upper end of the strut is bolted between the double lugs of a fitting riveted to the apex of the V-shaped strut. The lower end of the strut is clamped to the lower tube of a stirrup-shaped stamping which is itself clamped to cross strut SS at its mid-point; the stirrup-shaped stamping is braced laterally to joints S and longitudinally to joint U.

Fireproof bulkhead

12. The fireproof bulkhead consists of a sheet of asbestos sandwiched between two sheets of duralumin and stiffened by five lengths of duralumin channel section; it is situated on the front face of bay AB and extends from the engine cowling down to the centre section front spar. The bulkhead is secured by two brackets to cross strut AA, by a U-bolt to diagonal strut AB and by bolts to the upper boom of the centre section front spar; it is braced by several cowling support tubes on either side. At the top of the bulkhead, two brackets are fixed to the front face to provide a mounting for the coolant header tank.

Cockpit seat

13. The pilot's seat accommodates a seat-type parachute and is made from duralumin sheet. A hole is cut in the back for the straps of the safety harness and a strip of leather is riveted to the port side of the seat tray to prevent chafing of the parachute rip cord housing.

14. The seat is mounted on two pairs of parallel links to permit adjustment of its height at any time. The upper links are free to rotate about cross strut EE and, at their front ends, are hinged between the sides of the seat and the horizontal seat stiffener. The lower links are secured to cross strut FC. FC, which may rotate as a whole between the side struts EF at joints FC. The front end of the port lower link is hinged to the side of the seat at its bottom rear corner but the starboard link, after being similarly joined to the seat, is extended forward to form the height-adjusting handle. Thus, raising the handle raises the seat. The seat may be locked in one of several positions by means of the ratchet gear incorporated in the handle, depression of the handle knob releasing a stop from engagement with a quadrant fixed to the seat.

Flare installation

15. On early aircraft a launching chute for a single 4 in. training flare is secured to the fuselage underfairing just aft of the wireless tray. The cylindrical chute leans towards the front at the top, and the bottom end is located over a small door in the underfairing; the door is provided for loading the flare on the ground and for launching during flight. The door bolt is spring-loaded to remain in the closed position and must be withdrawn by hand when either opening or closing the doors during loading. In flight, the bolt is withdrawn by pulling upwards on the pilot's toggle which is connected to the bolt by a bowden cable; under the weight of the flare the door opens and the flare is subsequently launched. The installation, secured within the fuselage as described in para. 9, includes a mounting on the centre line of the aeroplane for the downward identification lamp.

Footsteps

16. Of the two footsteps provided (*see* fig. 6), the lower is retractable whilst the upper is fixed. When the retractable footstep is pulled downwards it loads the elastic cable and, at the bottom of its stroke, operates a trigger which trips the catch holding the spring-loaded cover over the hand-hole above. After the pilot has used the footstep and hand-hole (and is standing upon the centre section walkway) the hand-hole cover is pressed back over the hole; this action releases a catch which has retained the footstep in the "down" position and permits the footstep to be returned into the fuselage by the elastic cord. The upper footstep, used for entering the cockpit from the centre section walkway, has a spring-loaded flap which is pushed inwards when inserting the foot and returns flush with the fuselage outer surface as soon as the foot is removed.

Engine cowling

17. Detachable duralumin panels cover most of the engine, and are secured by turnbutton fasteners, the nose collar and front undercowl being the only fixed portions of the cowling. At the bottom of the engine reduction gear casing, the nose collar is provided with a detachable under-portion for access to the vacuum pump. The engine cylinders are cowled with three detachable panels, one over the top and one on each side, the side panels being cut away at the top to take the exhaust manifolds. Three similarly-positioned panels are used to cover the engine auxiliaries, but these latter panels extend beyond the fireproof bulkhead to the front of the decking, thus enclosing the first bay of the centre fuselage. The rear undercowl beneath the engine auxiliaries is divided into front and rear detachable portions, each portion being cut away at its junction with the other to take the air intake scoop. The rear portion has a fairing incorporated to streamline the air intake scoop.

Centre fuselage fairing

18. *Decking—general.*—The decking, of fabric-covered plywood on spruce formers, comprises that portion of the top fairing which covers the cockpit and the wireless bays, i.e. bays CE and EG; it includes the windscreen, sliding hood, emergency exit panel and crash pylon.

19. *Decking—windscreen.*—The centre panel of the windscreen is of thick bullet-proof safety glass but the remainder is of transparent acetate material. An inverted U-shaped tube, fixed at its extremities to the top longerons, supports the rear edge of the screen, the front edge being screwed to the decking. To provide a handgrip for the pilot when leaving the cockpit, another tube is bolted

between the sides of the U-shaped tube and braced at its mid-point to the instrument panel cross tube; the handgrip tube is also used to provide a mounting for the reflector gun sight and an upper fixing for its dimming screen; the lower fixing for the screen is on the instrument panel cross tube. The top of the U-shaped tube is braced by two wires to the top of the instrument panel former. A mirror, to provide the pilot with rearward vision, is attached to the top of the windscreen.

20. *Decking—sliding hood.*—The sliding hood, of transparent acetate panels on a strip duralumin framework, is carried on rollers which run in channels fixed on each side to the decking. A bowden-controlled plunger, operated by a lever on the port side of the cockpit, engages with two ratchet strips fitted to the port bottom edge of the hood, a short length at the front and a longer length at the rear; when the plunger is engaged with the ratchet strip it prevents the hood from moving forward. A handle is fitted inside the hood at each front bottom corner, a single handle for external operation being fitted at the front, half-way up the port side. Provision is made for emergency jettisoning of the pilot's hood, by operating a control (*see* Sect. 1), which disengages the securing pins on the port side by means of a cable acting against a spring; the cable is protected by a guard. After the pins have been withdrawn in this manner the hood is sucked into the airstream.

21. To provide the pilot with a clear view when landing should the windscreen be covered with ice, a knockout panel is incorporated in the sliding hood at its port front bottom corner. The panel is jettisoned by pushing forward a sliding plate, situated along the top edge of the panel, by means of a handle at its rear end and then punching the panel out into the airstream.

22. *Decking—crash pylon.*—The portion of the decking immediately behind and above the pilot's head is strengthened to act as a crash pylon in order that the pilot may not be trapped under the aeroplane should it overturn.

23. *Decking—emergency exit panel.*—On the starboard side of the cockpit, the portion of the decking which extends down to the top longerons is removable to afford an emergency exit. To remove the panel, the sliding hood must first be thrust right back to its rearmost position, which action disengages a bolt on the decking from the top rear corner of the panel. The lever in the top centre of the panel must be pulled backwards and upwards, before the panel can be pushed out into the airstream, top edge first; the operation of the lever disengages two bolts from the decking, one being in the front and one in the rear edge of the panel. It should always be ascertained before flight that the panel is securely fastened, i.e. that the lever is vertical and that the pegs at the bottom are properly engaged with the holes in the decking.

24. *Side panels.*—The sides of the centre fuselage are covered with removable panels secured by turnbutton fasteners, those covering the foremost bay of the centre fuselage having been mentioned in para. 17. A duralumin panel is fitted on either side of the cockpit bay and a fabric-covered panel on either side of the wireless bay; on some aeroplanes the latter panels incorporate a window, through which the formation-keeping lamps throw beams on to the trailing edges of the main planes. Each fabric-covered panel is removed by disengaging the turnbutton fasteners along its lower edge, utilizing the two tabs provided; the lower edge is then swung outwards and the whole panel drawn downwards. When replacing, the two plate dowels along the top edge must be engaged in their sockets before the panel is swung into position and secured by

the turnbutton fasteners. The duralumin panels have L-section edgings and are reinforced where necessary by U-section channels, being entirely secured by turnbutton fasteners.

25. *Underfairing.*—The fuselage front underfairing comprises several fixed duralumin panels, the fairing being recessed at the front to form a well which houses the undercarriage units when retracted; the radiator fairing is bolted to the rear portion. A subsidiary housing for the air cylinder is incorporated at the front of the undercarriage well and a trough for the coolant return pipe from the radiator runs lengthwise down the middle of the well. Two small apertures, covered with transparent acetate material, are provided for observation of the position of the undercarriage units and an access panel is situated around each undercarriage catch gear. The panels facing the centre section flaps are also recessed above the main panels to allow the flaps, when in the "up" position, to lie flush with the undersurface of the centre section door. The panel to the rear of the radiator is provided with a door, secured by five turnbutton fasteners, to permit access to the radiator and oil cooler pipe couplings; two holes on either side of the door accommodate the radiator flap operating levers and gun-heating tubes respectively.

26. *Radiator fairing.*—The radiator fairing is double walled in front of and behind the radiator in order to provide a smooth flow for the air entering and leaving the radiator honeycomb. The fairing is screwed to the fuselage front underfairing (*see* fig. 7) around its upper edge and its rear ends are stabilized by two short struts through the underfairing to joint H1; its top is joined by a short stay to the bottom boom of the centre section rear spar. A flap is hinged to the rear lower edge and may be operated from the cockpit (*see* Sect. 8, fig. 10) to control the volume and velocity of the cooling air through the radiator; immediately beneath the radiator a small removable door is provided for access to the radiator drain plug.

Rear fuselage and tail bay fairing

27. *Top and side fairings.*—The fabric-covered top and sides of the rear fuselage are constructed of spruce and plywood formers and stringers. The top fairing incorporates a mounting for the upward identification lamp and a top fixing for the aerial mast; for access to the tail bay, the port side fairing includes a duralumin detachable panel secured by four turnbutton fasteners. The top and side fairings are clipped to the longerons at each former, the top fairing stringers being tongued and glued into the decking at their front ends.

28. *Bottom fairing.*—At the front end, the bottom surface of the rear fuselage is provided by the flare installation (*see* para. 15), aft of which are two detachable panels secured by turnbutton fasteners. The front detachable panel is fabric covered and constructed with spruce formers and stringers, the sides being of plywood; it extends from just aft of joint K to just forward of joint O. The rear detachable panel is of similar construction to the front detachable panel, except that the central portion is of plywood formed to fair the tail wheel strut and the bottom of the fuselage into the rudder. The bottom surface under the tail bay consists of a non-detachable panel constructed of fabric-covered plywood over spruce formers and stringers; the panel is secured by clips to the bottom longerons.

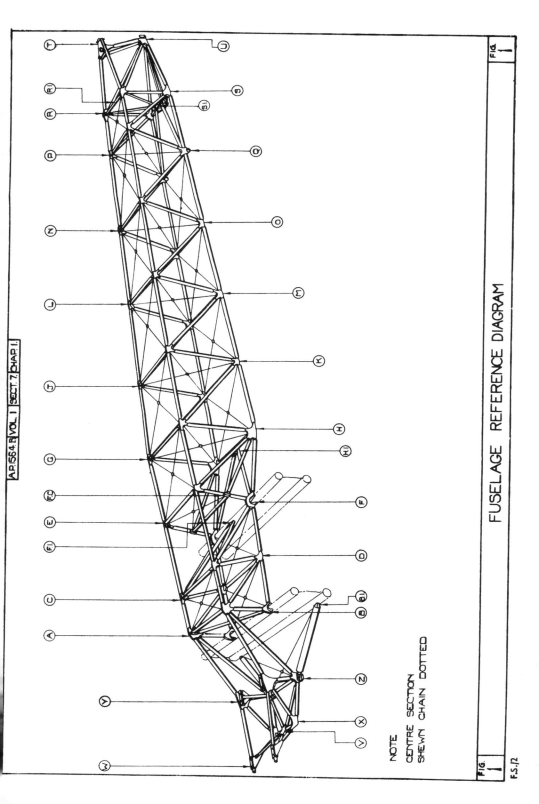

FUSELAGE REFERENCE DIAGRAM

NOTE

CENTRE SECTION
SHEWN CHAIN DOTTED

FIG. 1

FIG. 1

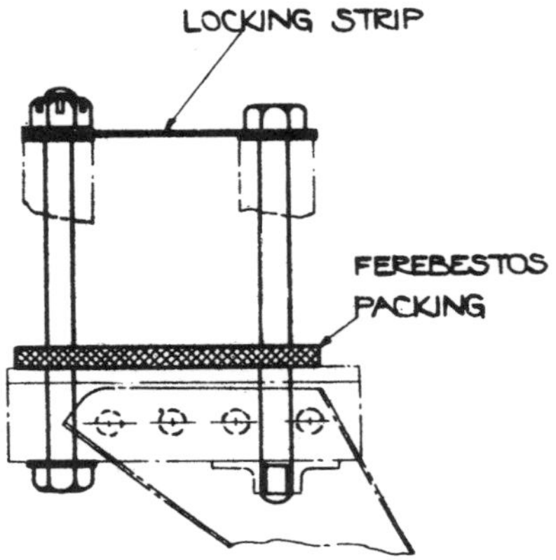

LOCKING STRIP

FEREBESTOS
PACKING

FRONT FOOT ASSEMBLY
AT FUSELAGE JOINT W.

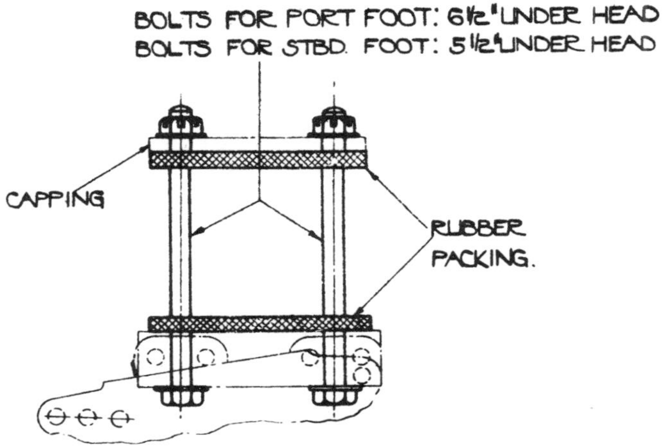

BOLTS FOR PORT FOOT: 6½" UNDER HEAD
BOLTS FOR STBD. FOOT: 5½" UNDER HEAD

CAPPING

RUBBER
PACKING.

REAR FOOT ASSEMBLY
AT FUSELAGE JOINT Y

FIG.
2

ENGINE SUPPORTS.

FIG.
2

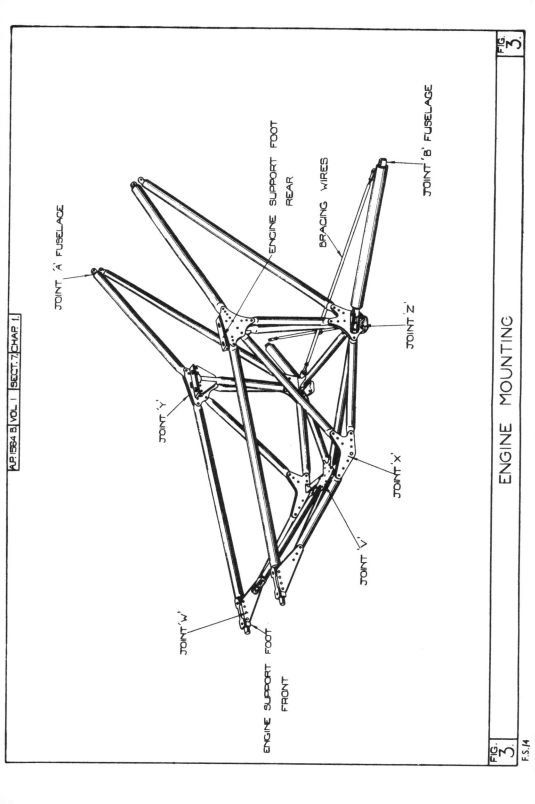

JOINT 'A' FUSELAGE

JOINT 'Y'

ENGINE SUPPORT FOOT REAR

BRACING WIRES

JOINT 'B' FUSELAGE

JOINT 'Z'

JOINT 'X'

JOINT 'V'

JOINT 'W'

ENGINE SUPPORT FOOT FRONT

ENGINE MOUNTING

FIG. 3.   FIG. 3.

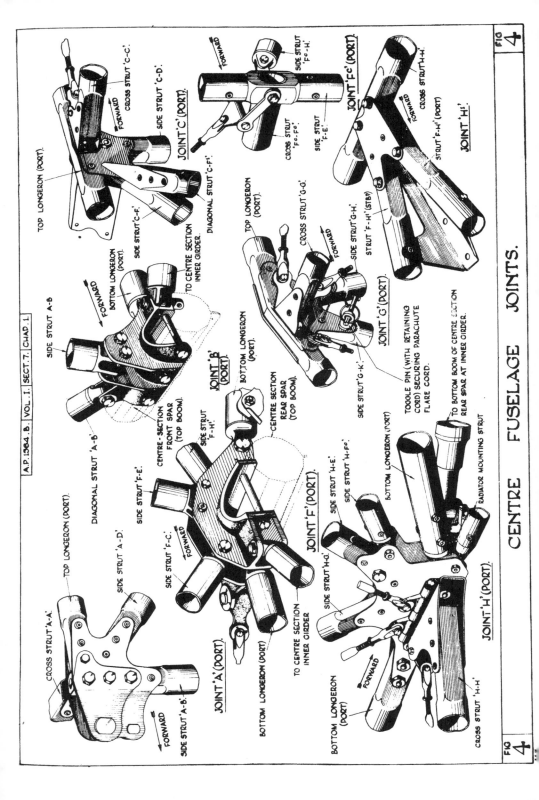

FIG 4

JOINT 'C' (PORT).

CROSS STRUT 'C-C'.

SIDE STRUT 'C-D'.

FORWARD

TOP LONGERON (PORT).

SIDE STRUT 'C-F'.

DIAGONAL STRUT 'C-F'.

FORWARD

SIDE STRUT 'F-G-F₀'.

JOINT 'F₀' (PORT).

CROSS STRUT 'F₀-F₀'.

SIDE STRUT 'F-E'.

CROSS STRUT 'H-H'.

STRUT 'F-H' (PORT).

JOINT 'H'.

SIDE STRUT 'G-H'.

STRUT 'F-H' (STBD).

FORWARD

SIDE STRUT A-B

FORWARD

BOTTOM LONGERON (PORT).

TO CENTRE SECTION INNER GIRDER.

JOINT 'B' (PORT).

BOTTOM LONGERON (PORT).

CENTRE-SECTION FRONT SPAR (TOP BOOM).

TOP LONGERON (PORT).

CROSS STRUT 'G-G'.

FORWARD

SIDE STRUT 'G-H'.

JOINT 'G' (PORT).

SIDE STRUT 'G-K'.

TOOGLE PIN (WITH RETAINING CORD) SECURING PARACHUTE FLARE CORD.

TO BOTTOM BOOM OF CENTRE SECTION REAR SPAR AT INNER GIRDER.

DIAGONAL STRUT 'A-B'.

TOP LONGERON (PORT).

SIDE STRUT 'A-D'.

CENTRE-SECTION REAR SPAR (TOP BOOM).

SIDE STRUT 'F-H'.

SIDE STRUT 'F-E'.

JOINT 'F' (PORT).

SIDE STRUT 'F-C'.

FORWARD

BOTTOM LONGERON (PORT).

TO CENTRE SECTION INNER GIRDER.

SIDE STRUT 'H-E'.

SIDE STRUT 'H-F₀'.

BOTTOM LONGERON (PORT).

RADIATOR MOUNTING STRUT

CROSS STRUT 'A-A'.

SIDE STRUT 'A-B'.

JOINT 'A' (PORT).

SIDE STRUT 'A-B'.

FORWARD

BOTTOM LONGERON (PORT).

SIDE STRUT 'H-G'.

JOINT 'H' (PORT).

BOTTOM LONGERON (PORT).

FORWARD

CROSS STRUT 'H-H'.

CENTRE FUSELAGE JOINTS.

FIG 4

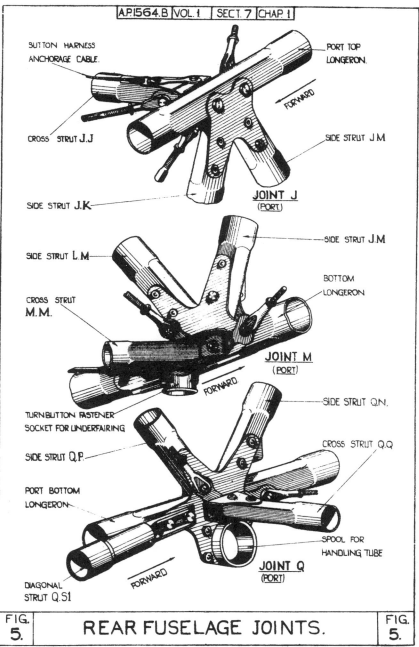

SUTTON HARNESS
ANCHORAGE CABLE.

PORT TOP
LONGERON.

FORWARD

CROSS STRUT J.J

SIDE STRUT J.M

SIDE STRUT J.K

JOINT J
(PORT)

SIDE STRUT L.M

SIDE STRUT J.M

CROSS STRUT
M.M.

BOTTOM
LONGERON

JOINT M
(PORT)

FORWARD

TURN BUTTON FASTENER
SOCKET FOR UNDERFAIRING

SIDE STRUT Q.N.

SIDE STRUT Q.P.

CROSS STRUT Q.Q

PORT BOTTOM
LONGERON

SPOOL FOR
HANDLING TUBE

DIAGONAL
STRUT Q.S1

FORWARD

JOINT Q
(PORT)

| FIG. 5. | REAR FUSELAGE JOINTS. | FIG. 5. |

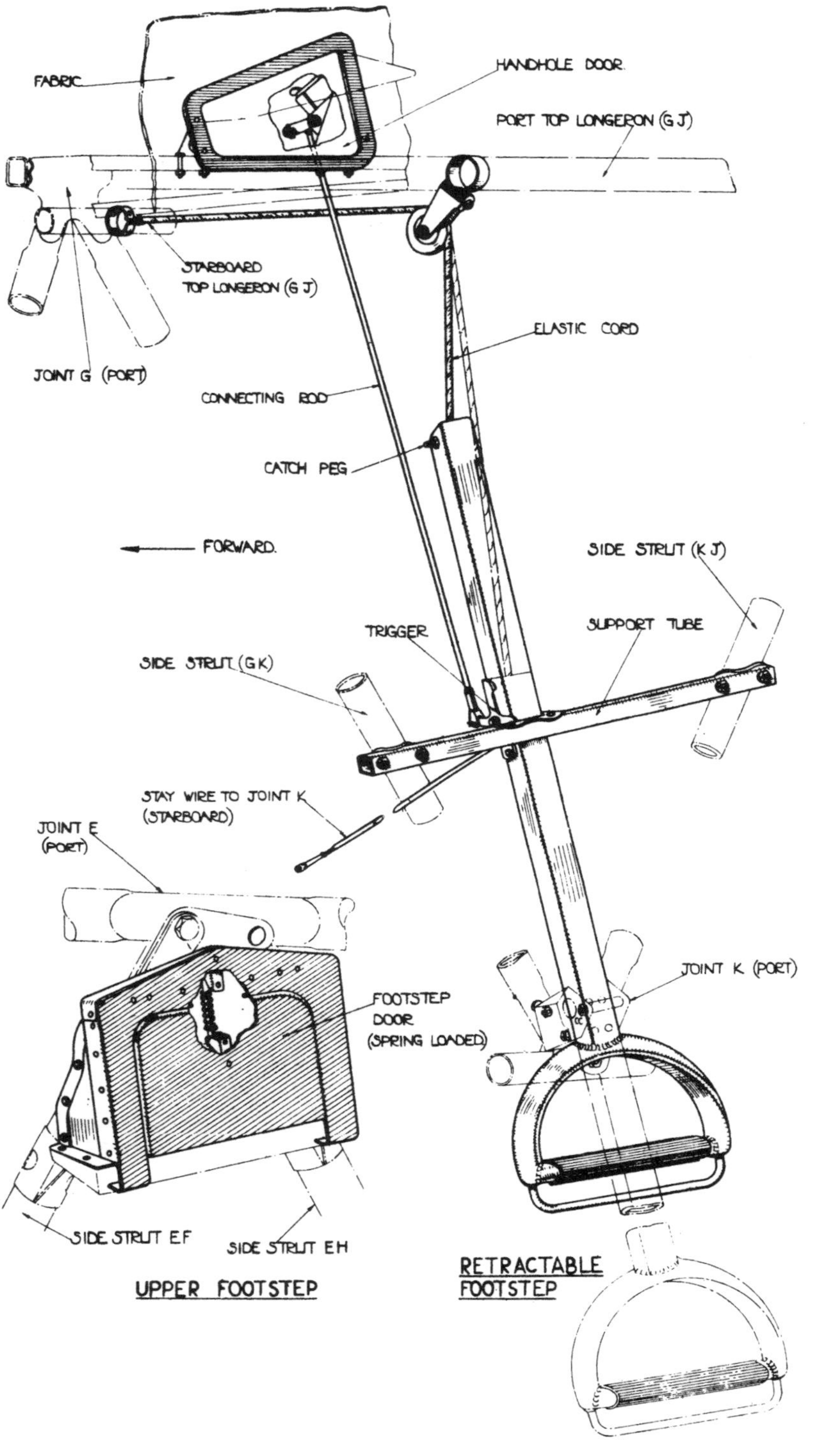

FOOTSTEPS.

RETRACTABLE FOOTSTEP

UPPER FOOTSTEP

JOINT K (PORT)

FOOTSTEP DOOR (SPRING LOADED)

SIDE STRUT EH

SIDE STRUT EF

JOINT E (PORT)

STAY WIRE TO JOINT K (STARBOARD)

SIDE STRUT (G.K)

SIDE STRUT (K.J)

SUPPORT TUBE

TRIGGER

FORWARD.

CATCH PEG

CONNECTING ROD

ELASTIC CORD

JOINT G (PORT)

STARBOARD TOP LONGERON (G.J)

PORT TOP LONGERON (G.J)

HANDHOLE DOOR

FABRIC

FIG. 6

FIG. 6

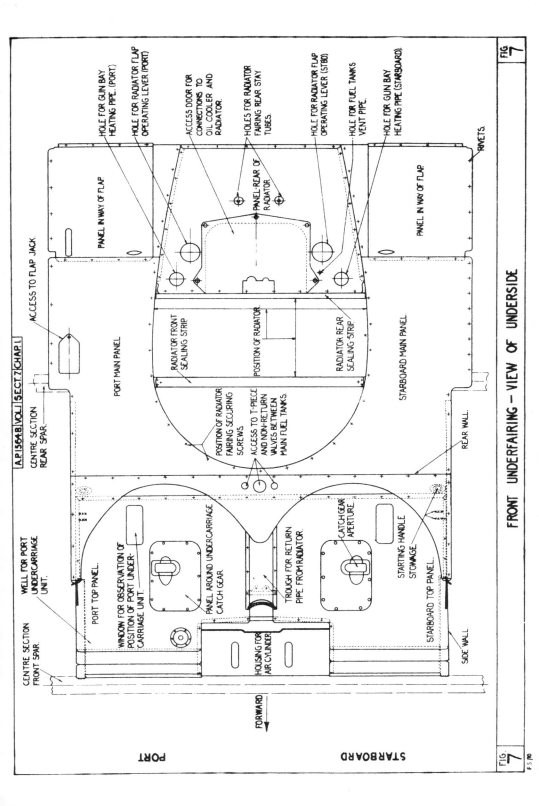

FRONT UNDERFAIRING – VIEW OF UNDERSIDE

FIG. 7

PORT

STARBOARD

FORWARD

January, 1941
Amended by A.L. No. 16

AIR PUBLICATION 1564B
Volume I
SECTION 7

CHAPTER 2

MAIN PLANE

LIST OF CONTENTS

LIST OF ILLUSTRATIONS

Note: Fig. 5—For "Cannon" read "20 mm. gun"

CHAPTER 2

MAIN PLANE

General

1. The non-folding cantilever main plane is built in three portions, centre section and port and starboard outer planes; split trailing edge flaps are fitted between the inner ends of the ailerons. The tapered outer planes are pin-jointed to the parallel centre section and are of stressed-skin construction; the centre section, beneath the fuselage, is recessed to receive the undercarriage when retracted. The main fuel tanks are carried in the centre section, one on either side of the fuselage and the oil tank forms the port leading edge; each outer plane carries four or six Browning ·303 in. guns or two Hispano 20 mm. guns (*see* Sect. 11).

Centre section

2. The centre section basic structure (*see* fig. 1) comprises a pair of parallel high-tensile steel spars, braced by tubular girders and diagonal tubes; it is attached to the centre fuselage by spool fittings at joints B and F and by tubular bracing to joints Z and H. The centre section is metal covered.

3. *Spars.*—The spars are built up from high-tensile steel strip to a dumb-bell section, their booms being parallel throughout the span. The booms are rolled to a 12-sided section and are joined to the plate webs by rivets 1 in. apart. The booms comprise outer and inner booms with a full-length round-section liner fitted inside the latter; the front spar booms have an additional liner extending for 3 ft. on either side of the centre line. For the attachment of the outer planes, the booms are fitted at each end with forked end plugs, the forks being drilled for the tapered joint bolts (*see* fig. 2); the axes of the front bolts are horizontal and the axes of the rear bolts are vertical. The web is reinforced at intervals along each face by small channel sections riveted or bolted in position, larger sections being fitted at the girder and fuselage attachment positions; certain sections are lightened with flanged holes. At the fuselage attachment positions on the rear face of the front spar, the cylinders of the undercarriage hydraulic jacks are anchored through universal joints to U-shaped extrusions bolted through the channel sections and spar web. On the front face of the front spar opposite the port outer and inner girders, four brackets are riveted to the channel sections to provide a mounting for the oil tank, and on the front face of the rear spar, five short lengths of conduit for the electrical wiring are clipped to the channel sections.

4. *Drag bracing.*—The outer (undercarriage) girders are situated at each end of the centre section; each comprises upper and lower booms of round-section tubular steel braced by round-section struts of duralumin, plate type joints being employed. The ends of the lower boom are received in sockets incorporated in the forked end plugs which provide the attachment for the outer planes. At the front end, the lower boom provides a bearing for the shock-absorber strut sleeve block (*see* Chap. 5, para. 3) and, over the middle rear portion of its length, a bearing for the radius rod trunnion sleeve (*see* Chap. 5, para. 3), the boom being fitted with sleeves at these points. The ends of the upper boom are joined to

the front and rear spars through U-plates, the rear plates providing a fixing for the upper end of the radius rod; the mounting brackets for the outer feet of the centre section fuel tank are bolted around the upper booms (*see* fig. 2).

5. For the inner (engine mounting) girders, square-section tubing is used apart from the round-section upper boom. The lower boom comprises two tubes raised at their junction to clear the shock-absorber strut when in the retracted position, a U-shaped fibre block for receiving the strut being bolted between the joint side plates. The mounting brackets for the inner feet of the centre section fuel tank are bolted around the upper booms. The ends of the booms are joined to the spars through U-plates, the front attachments being combined into one large flanged U-plate. The outer face of this U-plate is used for the attachment of the undercarriage side stay and latch gear, the side stay being carried on a bolt in a U-plate at the bottom and the latch gear on a pin in a bracket at the top; the plate is lightened with several holes, one of which is utilized for the passage of the piston rod of the undercarriage jack. On the front face of the front spar opposite the bottom boom of the inner girder (*see* fig. 1 and Chap. 1, fig. 1, joint B1), a U-shaped extrusion is bolted through the spar boom; it provides the attachment for the strut to joint Z and for the shackle of the bracing wire to the other strut Z. On the rear face of the rear spar opposite the bottom booms of the inner girders, other U-shaped extrusions are similarly bolted through the spar boom to receive the front ends of the struts to joints H; the port extrusion also provides an anchorage for the cylinder of the flap hydraulic jack.

6. The inner and outer girders are braced diagonally by four struts symmetrically placed on each side, port and starboard. A strut is taken from each fuselage attachment point (joints B and F, *see* Chap. 1, fig. 1) to the mid-point of the upper boom of each inner girder. From the other side of the inner girder boom, one strut is taken to the mid-point of the outer girder lower boom and another to the rear end joint of the upper boom, these two struts passing through holes incorporated in the main fuel tank (*see* Sect. 8, para. 4).

7. *Ribs and covering.*—The centre section has no inter-spar ribs, the upper aerofoil contour being maintained by the fuel tanks and by channel-section formers mounted on brackets attached to the girder booms; the aerofoil surface consists of a duralumin panel secured to the formers through Simmonds double anchor nuts and to the upper surface of the fuel tanks by special nuts. Beneath the fuel tanks, the aerofoil surface is of duralumin sheet attached to the rear spar and girder lower booms; it incorporates a trough for the undercarriage radius rod when retracted and a removable panel for access to the fuel tank sump. A duralumin sheet bulkhead is fitted between the inter-spar girders in front of the fuel tank, the gap in the lower surface between the bulkhead and the front spar being closed by the shock-absorber strut fairings (*see* Chap. 5, para. 19) when the undercarriage is retracted.

8. Aft of the rear spar, there are four trailing edge ribs on each side, the rear ends of the innermost ribs being joined by a square-section duralumin tube; the lower booms of the ribs are stepped to provide a recess for the centre section flap. These ribs are of varying lengths to fair the trailing edge into the fuselage and, with the exception of the innermost port rib, have duralumin channel booms and tubular bracing struts. The innermost port rib is robustly built of square-section tubes in order to withstand the reaction of the flap hydraulic jack which is located just inboard of the rib. Pulleys for the aileron control cables and a fairlead for the landing lamp control cable are mounted on the

channels attaching the outer ribs to the rear spar, whilst on the innermost rib attachment channels are fairleads for the aileron cables. Clipped to the front bracing struts of the port trailing edge ribs are the pipes which run to and from the pressure head mounted in the lower surface of the port outer plane. The upper surface of the trailing edge ribs and the underside between the centre section spar and the flap wells are covered with duralumin sheet.

9. Forward of the front spar, the leading edge comprises the oil tank (*see* fig. 2) on the port side, and the nosing on the starboard side; the oil tank is attached as described in para. 3 and the nosing by means of its skin to the upper and lower booms of the front spar. The nosing is of duralumin sheet riveted to four flanged formers and a channel-section stiffener; all but the outer former are holed for lightness.

Outer plane (Browning guns)

10. *General.*—The basic structure of the outer planes (*see* fig. 3) comprises a pair of spars braced at the inner end by two diagonal girders and at the outer end by the sheet metal skin in conjunction with two intermediate spars; heavy-gauge reinforcing plates are fitted locally beneath the skin to transfer the loads between the two differently-constructed portions. The distance between the spars decreases from root to tip to give the desired tapered plan form, the spars and girders being all built from steel plate on the warren girder principle. The metal covering is riveted to the spars and ribs and is strengthened by a series of stringers riveted to its inner surface.

11. *Spars.*—The main spars are of box construction at their inner ends (*see* fig. 3, sections DD and CC), over their mid-length their top and bottom sides are open (*see* section BB) whilst their outer ends, extending to the outer ends of the ailerons, comprise a single plate web with T-section flanges (*see* section AA); the webs taper towards their outer ends and, over most of their length, are lightened with triangulated holes forming a warren girder. The two intermediate spars are approximately evenly spaced between the main spars, being of similar constructions to their outer ends. The fittings are shaped and drilled to form eyes suitable for bolting between the centre section forked fittings (*see* para. 3).

12. At their outer ends, the main and intermediate spars are extended to the plane tip by tapered channel sections, the webs being lightened with flanged circular holes. The portion of the plane outboard of the outer end of the aileron is detachable, the eight bolts securing it to the outer rib being accessible through two doors in the under-surface. The window and the mounting for the navigation lamp are incorporated in the leading edge of the detachable tip.

13. The aileron hinge brackets are secured to the rear face of the rear spar, two just outboard of ribs F and H respectively and the third opposite rib L. The brackets are shaped to the contour of the upper surface of the plane and are stabilized sideways by a sub-spar running along the length of the aileron gap; over the nose of the aileron the upper skin is carried on formers attached between the sub-spar and the rear main spar. The aileron control gear is mounted between two square-sectioned tubes which are bolted between the aileron centre hinge bracket and the trailing edge rib but one on the inboard side; the control gear is accessible through doors in both the upper and lower surfaces of the plane (*see* para. 29 (*a*)).

14. *Drag bracing.*—The drag bracing over the portion of the plane occupied by the inner gun compartment is provided by two diagonal girders of similar construction to the intermediate spars. The four inboard guns are mounted between these girders on two tubes and protrude through their webs and through circular holes in the front spar. Outboard of the two diagonal girders the drag stresses are taken by the metal skin riveted to the spars and ribs, a diagonal strut being provided at the outboard gun door frame. The rib bay outboard of the inboard gun compartment is reinforced top and bottom by heavy gauge plates beneath the skin covering; the plates transfer the drag stresses from the diagonal girders to the skin covering.

15. *Ribs.*—The inter-spar ribs are of sheet duralumin lightened with flanged circular holes, and the majority of the nose and trailing edge ribs are built up from duralumin channel section in a similar manner to the trailing edge ribs in the centre section (*see* para. 8). The nose ribs behind the blast tube door are braced transversely by the channels used for securing the door, the landing lamp mounting tube similarly bracing the nose ribs on either side of the landing lamp window. The inter-spar ribs are discontinuous over the diagonal bracing girders, the boundary ribs and spars being solid, thus forming an enclosed compartment for heating the inboard four guns. The rib at the outboard end of the heavy-gauge plates (*see* para. 14) is also a solid rib and forms the outboard end of a torsion box. The ribs on each side of the two outboard guns are in some cases solid ribs, while others have lightening holes blanked off with plates to enclose these guns for heating (*see* fig. 4); the compartments are heated by warm air extracted from the rear of the radiator.

16. *Covering.*—The metal covering is riveted to the spars and ribs, the panels being shaped and disposed as shown in the small views in fig. 3; the ribbed stringers are riveted to the inner surface of the skin.

17. Access for inspection and/or adjustment of the specified parts is provided as follows (*see* Sect. 4, Chap. 3, fig. 1), all the access doors being removable by withdrawing the screws around their edges:—

(a) *Aileron control gear.*—A metal plate door is incorporated in each upper and lower surface aft of the rear spar and just inboard of the centre aileron hinge, a further door being situated in the bottom skin just inboard of these two doors; the door in the upper surface provides access to the sprocket and, in the lower surface, the outboard door provides access to the lever and the inboard door to the cables.

(b) *Landing lamp pulley.*—A metal plate door is fitted in the bottom skin immediately inboard of the aileron.

(c) *Guns and ammunition boxes.*—At the inboard end of each outer plane, four metal doors are situated in the top skin between the front and rear spars to give access to the four inboard guns and outboard of the torsion box three other doors provide access to the two outer guns.

(d) *Interior structure.*—A metal door is incorporated in the bottom skin immediately forward of the aileron centre hinge and approximately at mid chord.

18. *Blast tube doors.*—Each blast tube door consists of a duralumin panel shaped to conform with the nosing contour, the inboard one being pierced with four holes and the outboard door with two, through which the guns fire. On the inner faces of the doors each aperture is fitted with a short belled tube which

fits over the forward end of the blast tube and incorporates a catch to lock the blast tube in position. Each door is held in place by three long screws which screw into anchor nuts secured inside the channel members which span the nose ribs behind the door. The heads of the screws are flush with the outer surface, and a pair of locknuts are fitted to each screw on the inside to provide an adjustable stop: the stops prevent the screws being over-tightened and thereby distorting the door.

Outer planes (20 mm. guns)

19. *General.*—The 20 mm. gun outer planes are interchangeable with and of similar basic construction to the Browning gun outer planes, the only differences occurring in the neighbourhood of the gun bay (*see* fig. 5).

20. *Gun bay.*—The guns are housed at the inboard end of each outer plane between the end rib and rib D. An intermediate stiff rib extends between the front and rear spars approximately mid-way between the end rib and rib D, but the rib is divided by a torsion sub-spar which extends between the end rib and rib D approximately mid-way between the spars. Two small ribs extend between the sub-spar and the front spar. The area bounded by the end rib sub-spar, front spar and rib D is covered with a fixed skin; on the undersurface the skin between the rear spar and the sub-spar is strengthened with channel stiffeners which provide a base for the ammunition boxes and also the framework for the empty link and case chute doors.

21. The nose ribs adjacent to the front gun mountings are of plate construction lightened with flanged holes, the remaining ribs in front of the gun bay being similar to those of the gun outer plane. The ribs between the sub-spar and the front spar are of plate construction with one lightening hole in each.

22. The front and rear spars are of similar construction to the ·303 in. gun outer planes, with the exception that, in way of the 20 mm. gun bay, the webs have three circular flanged holes in each.

23. The intermediate stiff rib comprises a single plate web with T-section booms; the webs are strengthened by two stiffeners and lightened with three flanged holes. The torsion sub-spar is of similar construction to the intermediate stiff rib, the web having four lightening holes but no stiffeners.

24. Access for inspection and/or adjustment of the specified parts is provided as follows (*see* Sect. 4, Chap. 3, fig. 1); the doors mentioned below are in addition or (where stated) replace those in para. 17.

(a) *Gun and ammunition boxes.*—At the inboard end of each outer plane two metal doors are situated in the top skin between the sub-spar and the rear spar. These doors replace those mentioned in para. 17 (*c*).

(b) *Leading edge cannon doors.*—Two doors are situated on the leading edge in way of the gun front mountings.

(c) *Empty link and case chute doors.*—Two doors are situated on the underside of the outer plane between the sub-spar and the rear spar.

(d) *Breech blocks.*—Two doors, in the top skin, are situated aft of the rear spar.

(e) *Cocking levers.*—Two doors in the bottom skin are situated aft of the rear spar.

(f) *Long-range fuel tank pump.*—On certain aeroplanes, a metal-plate door, attached by four screws to the bottom skin of the gun bays forward of the rear spar.

Landing lamp window

25. This window is of acetate sheet moulded on to the contour of the leading edge and is situated at approximately one-third of the length of the outer plane from the inner end rib. The acetate sheet is secured to a light metal frame which lies between two adjacent nose ribs, to both of which it is attached by means of countersunk screws; it is similarly attached along its upper and lower transverse edges between the two nose ribs. The window is detached by removing the screws.

Navigation lamp window

26. This window is situated in the angle formed by the nose portion of the outermost rib and the front spar extension; it is of moulded acetate sheet shaped to conform with the contour of the leading edge. The window is a separate detachable unit fixed to the front spar extension by means of four captive screws, two in each upper and lower face. The window is removed by withdrawing these screws until their heads stand clear when the unit may be slid off in a forward direction.

Screwed sockets for lifting and picketing

27. Four screwed sockets are provided in the lower surface of each outer plane, two at the inner and two at the outer end; the outer sockets are incorporated in the attachment fittings of the extensions to the front and rear spars, and the inner sockets are situated at the front ends of the innermost inter-spar rib and trailing edge rib. These sockets may be used for picketing rings or lifting brackets, which latter are employed in conjunction with the lifting handles described in Sect. 4, Chap. 3, para. 4.

Ailerons

28. The ailerons (see fig. 6) are of normal single spar construction. The leading edge is reinforced with duralumin sheet, the whole aileron being covered with fabric attached to the ribs by channel sections; the ribs align with those in the outer plane. Partial balance is obtained by setting the spar back from the aileron leading edge, the remaining unbalanced mass being neutralized by the nose ribs of steel joined by a steel stringer. The nose ribs and each end rib are of flanged plate construction, the two end ribs being of duralumin; the nose ribs and the innermost rib are lightened with flanged holes. Between each nose rib L-section intermediate stiffeners are cup-riveted to the tubular steel spar. The trailing edge ribs have special channel section booms for the attachment of the fabric covering. The trailing edge tube, of streamline-section duralumin, is secured to each rib through a small U-piece.

29. Each aileron is hinged to three brackets on the outer plane rear spar (see para. 13). Three eyebolts are bolted through the aileron spar, one inboard of rib No. 2, one outboard of rib No. 5, and the other outboard of rib No. 10. The eyes of these bolts are carried on pins between the flanges of the aileron hinge brackets on the outer plane rear spar; the centre hinge is the locating hinge, ample clearance being allowed between the eyebolts and the bracket lugs at the other two hinges. Secured to the spar just inboard of rib No. 5, i.e. close to the locating hinge, is the operating lever of stainless steel channel section; at its outer end the lever incorporates a housing for the forked bolt by which it is attached to the aileron connecting rod, the forked bolt being free to rotate about the axis of the operating lever.

Flaps

30. The split trailing edge flaps (*see* fig. 7) are in three sections, one beneath the centre section and one beneath each outer plane. The centre section flap is cut away in the centre to accommodate the radiator fairing, but the flap spar is continuous; it is connected at its outer ends to the outer plane flap spar by a Hooke type universal joint.

31. *Centre section flap.*—This flap is constructed from single sheets of rib stiffened duralumin mounted on a tubular steel spar. The duralumin sheet is riveted to six ribs on each side of the gap for the radiator fairing, the ribs being riveted to spools sweated to the spar. The leading edge of the sheet is stiffened by beading the edge, whilst the trailing edge is beaded and folded around the ends of the ribs to which it is then riveted. A small triangular-shaped plate is hinged to each outer end of the sheet and is spring loaded to close the gap between the centre section and the outer plane flaps.

32. The centre section flap is hinged on five journal bearings, all but the centre being bolted to the centre section trailing edge ribs (*see* fig. 7); the securing bolts engage with Simmonds nuts on the inner face of the mounting channels on the rib. The centre bearing, on the centre line of the aeroplane, is bolted to a bracket attached to the fuselage plan bracing structure at joint H1 (*see* Chap. 1, fig. 1). The journal bearings are not detachable from the assembled flaps; the port innermost bearing provides the locating hinge. To ensure their easy operation, provision is made for accurately aligning the bearings along the axis of the spar by means of adjusting washers, or shims, assembled either under the head of the securing bolt or between the bearing and mounting channel on the rib (*see* fig. 7). The flaps are operated from a single lever on the port side of the centre section flap between ribs Nos. 4 and 5 just inboard of the locating hinge; the lever is of channel section steel, bolted to a spool which is sweated to the spar. An eyebolt is clipped tangentially to the spar just inboard of the starboard inner rib; it provides an anchorage for the flexible control of the flap position indicator (*see* Chap. 4, para. 13).

33. *Outer plane flaps.*—The outer flaps are of similar construction to the centre section flap except that the small triangular gap-closing plates are not fitted to the centre section flap. Each outer plane flap is carried on four journal bearings mounted on the trailing edge ribs in a similar manner to that adopted for the centre section flap bearings.

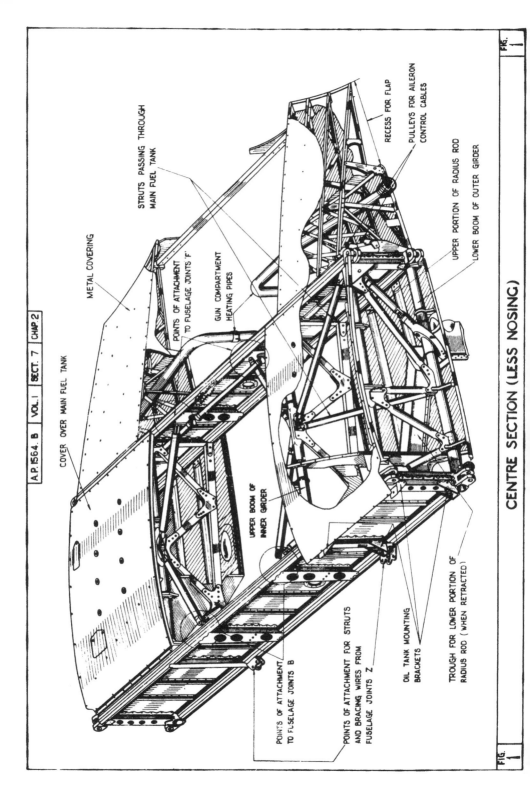

STRUTS PASSING THROUGH MAIN FUEL TANK

RECESS FOR FLAP

PULLEYS FOR AILERON CONTROL CABLES

METAL COVERING

POINTS OF ATTACHMENT TO FUSELAGE JOINTS 'F'

GUN COMPARTMENT HEATING PIPES

UPPER PORTION OF RADIUS ROD

LOWER BOOM OF OUTER GIRDER

COVER OVER MAIN FUEL TANK

UPPER BOOM OF INNER GIRDER

POINTS OF ATTACHMENT TO FUSELAGE JOINTS B

POINTS OF ATTACHMENT FOR STRUTS AND BRACING WIRES FROM FUSELAGE JOINTS Z

OIL TANK MOUNTING BRACKETS

TROUGH FOR LOWER PORTION OF RADIUS ROD (WHEN RETRACTED)

CENTRE SECTION (LESS NOSING)

FIG. 1

FIG. 1

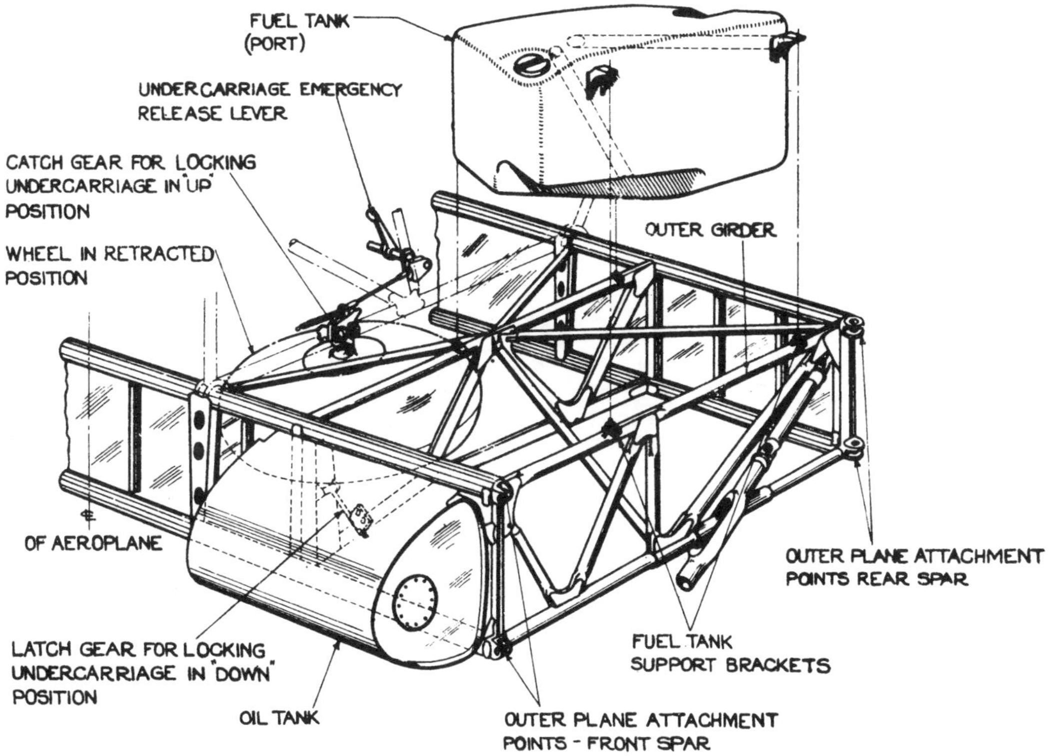

FUEL TANK (PORT)

UNDERCARRIAGE EMERGENCY RELEASE LEVER

CATCH GEAR FOR LOCKING UNDERCARRIAGE IN UP POSITION

WHEEL IN RETRACTED POSITION

OF AEROPLANE

LATCH GEAR FOR LOCKING UNDERCARRIAGE IN DOWN POSITION

OIL TANK

OUTER PLANE ATTACHMENT POINTS - FRONT SPAR

FUEL TANK SUPPORT BRACKETS

OUTER PLANE ATTACHMENT POINTS REAR SPAR

OUTER GIRDER

FIG. 2

CENTRE SECTION (PORT END) SHOWING OIL TANK & PORT FUEL TANK

FIG. 2

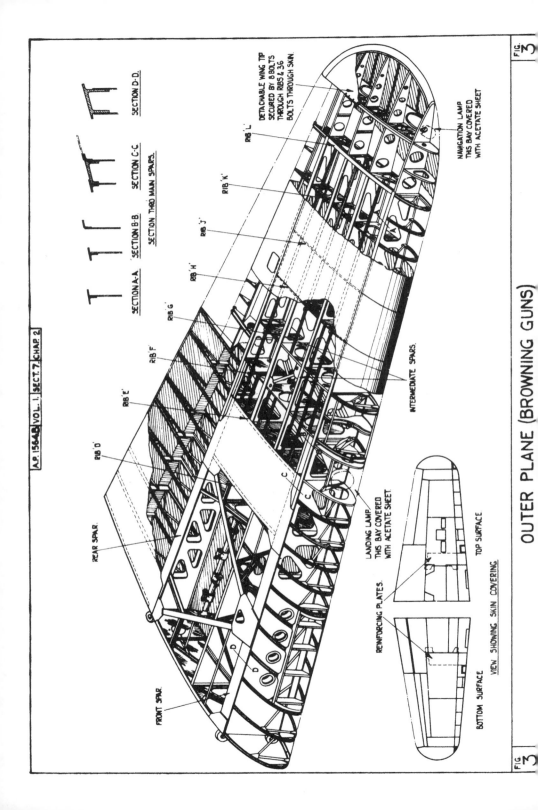

SECTION A-A   SECTION B-B   SECTION C-C   SECTION D-D.

SECTION THRO MAIN SPARS.

REAR SPAR.

RIB 'D'

RIB 'E'

RIB 'F'

RIB 'G'

RIB 'H'

RIB 'J'

RIB 'K'

RIB 'L'

FRONT SPAR.

LANDING LAMP
THIS BAY COVERED
WITH ACETATE SHEET

INTERMEDIATE SPARS.

DETACHABLE WING TIP
SECURED BY 8 BOLTS
THROUGH RIBS & 36
BOLTS THROUGH SKIN.

NAVIGATION LAMP
THIS BAY COVERED
WITH ACETATE SHEET

REINFORCING PLATES.

TOP SURFACE

BOTTOM SURFACE

VIEW SHOWING SKIN COVERING

OUTER PLANE (BROWNING GUNS)

FIG. 3

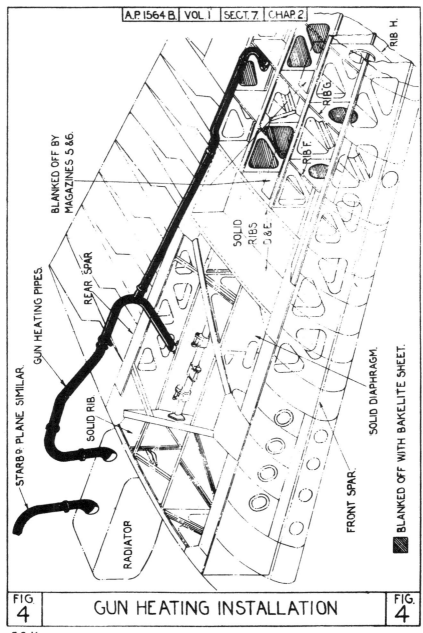

RIB H.

RIB G.

RIB F.

BLANKED OFF BY
MAGAZINES 5 & 6.

SOLID
RIBS
D & E.

REAR SPAR

GUN HEATING PIPES.

STARBD. PLANE SIMILAR.

SOLID RIB.

RADIATOR

SOLID DIAPHRAGM.

FRONT SPAR.

BLANKED OFF WITH BAKELITE SHEET.

| FIG. 4 | GUN HEATING INSTALLATION | FIG. 4 |

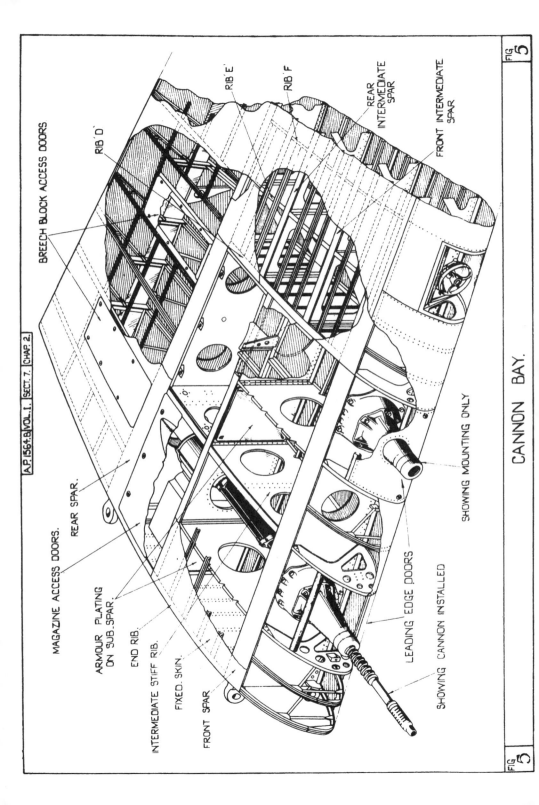

BREECH BLOCK ACCESS DOORS

RIB 'D'

RIB 'E'

RIB 'F'

REAR INTERMEDIATE SPAR

FRONT INTERMEDIATE SPAR

MAGAZINE ACCESS DOORS.

REAR SPAR.

ARMOUR PLATING ON SUB. SPAR.

END RIB.

INTERMEDIATE STIFF RIB.

FIXED. SKIN.

FRONT SPAR.

SHOWING MOUNTING ONLY

LEADING EDGE DOORS

SHOWING CANNON INSTALLED

CANNON BAY.

FIG. 5

FIG. 5

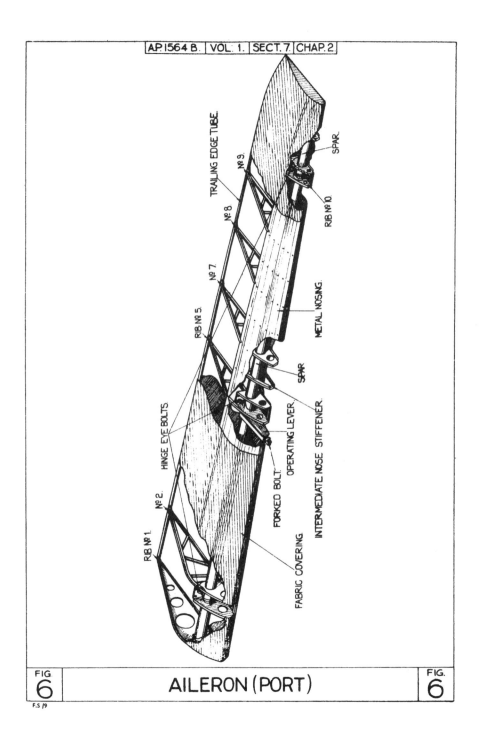

TRAILING EDGE TUBE.

Nº 9.

SPAR.

Nº 8.

RIB Nº 10.

Nº 7.

METAL NOSING.

RIB Nº 5.

SPAR

HINGE EYE BOLTS

OPERATING LEVER.

Nº 2.

INTERMEDIATE NOSE STIFFENER.

FORKED BOLT.

RIB Nº 1.

FABRIC COVERING.

FIG. 6

AILERON (PORT)

FIG. 6

F.S 19

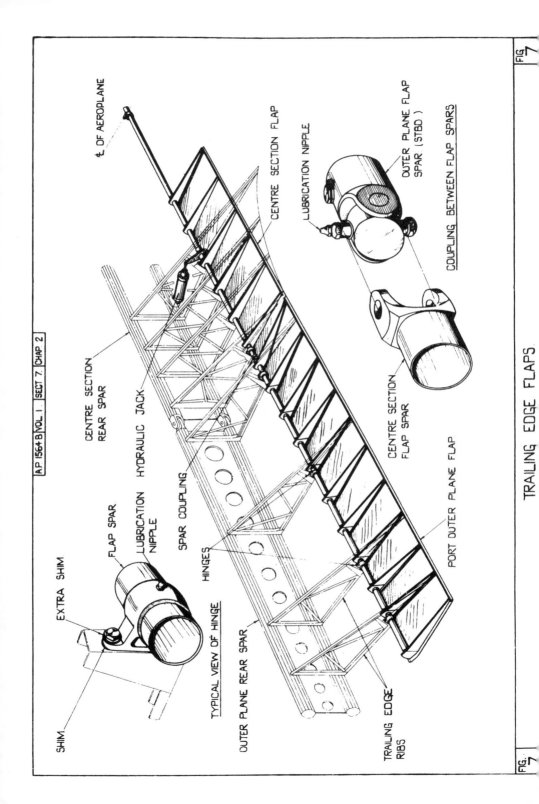

FIG. 7

TRAILING EDGE FLAPS

SHIM

EXTRA SHIM

FLAP SPAR

LUBRICATION NIPPLE

SPAR COUPLING

HINGES

TYPICAL VIEW OF HINGE

OUTER PLANE REAR SPAR

TRAILING EDGE RIBS

PORT OUTER PLANE FLAP

CENTRE SECTION FLAP SPAR

COUPLING BETWEEN FLAP SPARS

OUTER PLANE FLAP SPAR (STBD)

LUBRICATION NIPPLE

CENTRE SECTION FLAP

CENTRE SECTION REAR SPAR

HYDRAULIC JACK

₵ OF AEROPLANE

CHAPTER 3

TAIL UNIT

LIST OF CONTENTS

LIST OF ILLUSTRATIONS

CHAPTER 3

TAIL UNIT

General

1. The tail unit (*see* fig. 1) is of conventional design without external bracing; it is of metal construction and covered with fabric except for the trimming tabs on the elevator and rudder. A fixed tail plane, mounted over the rear end of the fuselage, carries a horn-balanced elevator with trimming tabs incorporated in the trailing edge, the inboard tabs being controllable whilst in flight. The fin, situated over the tail plane, is secured to the fuselage by its two finposts. The rear finpost, the bottom of which forms the fuselage sternpost, carries a mass and horn-balanced rudder; the rudder incorporates a tab in its trailing edge which is controllable from the cockpit and has also an automatic balance action. The surfaces of the tail plane and fin are faired into the fuselage and into one another.

Tail plane

2. The tail plane has front and rear spars which are continuous and parallel to one another over the span and joined by diagonal inter-spar drag bracing. The plane is secured to the tail bay of the fuselage by four high-tensile steel bolts at fuselage joints R and T (*see* Chap. 1, para. 11).

3. *Spars and drag bracing.*—The spars are of dumb-bell section and built up from high-tensile steel strip; they taper in elevation toward the tips, the same section and taper being employed for both front and rear spars. The booms are rolled to a 12-sided section and are joined to the plate webs by pop rivets placed 1 in. apart, except for 6 in. on either side of the tail plane centre line where they are placed $\frac{1}{2}$ in. apart. The drag struts are of similar construction to the spars but smaller sections are employed; the struts are bolted to U-plates which in turn are bolted to the spars in the positions shown in fig. 1. At each end of the innermost diagonal bracing strut, the joint with the spar incorporates two high-tensile steel plates, one on each face of the spar, and bolted together through the spar booms. On the front spar, each pair of plates is bolted by a single bolt to an eye projecting upwards from fuselage joint R, and on the rear spar each pair is bolted by a single bolt to a forked plug on fuselage joint T.

4. On the rear face of the tail plane rear spar, five hinges of the self-lubricating type are provided for the elevator. The hinge side plates (*see* para. 9) are bolted to brackets which are bolted between the spar booms, the central bracket being offset to port; the remainder are symmetrically disposed opposite each drag strut joint. The tail plane-to-elevator gap is reduced to a minimum by fairing strips riveted to the rear spar booms; the strips incorporate eyelets to which the fabric is attached by a long wire pin on each side of the tail plane centre line.

5. For the passage of the duplicate elevator cables through the front spar, a hole is provided in the spar web, and two pulleys are bracketed to the rear faces of the spar booms; the ends of the elevator cables are connected to a

double-ended lever which is carried on a bearing tube between the innermost drag struts. For the passage of the cables to the trimming tabs on the elevator, fibre fairleads and short metal conduits are fitted in the front spar web and in the webs of the innermost drag struts, respectively; also for this purpose, special fairleads are attached to the front face of the rear spar and holes are provided in the rear spar web.

6. *Ribs.*—Except for the innermost ribs and those in the detachable tip (for the latter, *see* para. 7), the ribs are constructed of duralumin with tubular bracing riveted to booms of a special channel section; the ribs are riveted to the spar booms through angle plates. The innermost ribs are composed of L-section booms joined by channel-section bracing, the upper booms incorporating Simmonds double-anchor nuts for the attachment of the upper fin fairing; the lower fin fairing is similarly attached to a channel-section boom just outboard of the innermost rib bottom boom. The nose ribs are placed one opposite and one between each inter-spar rib; they are constructed of duralumin channel-section except the innermost nose ribs which are of flanged and lightened duralumin plate. The leading edge is protected with duralumin sheet pop-riveted to the rib booms, the whole of the tail plane then being covered with fabric secured to the rib booms by channels. Access to the cable connector for the elevator trimming tabs is provided by a woods frame which is fitted into the upper surface at the rear inner corner on either side of the fin.

7. *Detachable tip.*—Outboard of the outermost drag strut and in front of the elevator horn balance, the tip of the tail plane is detachable after the removal of the fabric covering and 18 bolts and 10 rivets. The tip (*see* fig. 1) comprises a subsidiary spar, a front spar extension and two outer ribs of lightened flanged plate, an inner rib of the same construction as the inter-spar ribs, a leading edge tube and a bracing tube, the leading edge being protected with sheet aluminium.

Elevator

8. The port and starboard halves of the elevator (*see* fig. 1) are built up on single tubular steel spars bolted together at their inner ends to form one continuous spar. The ribs are arranged in alignment with those in the tail plane, being attached to the spar through spools and riveted to the leading and trailing edge tubes; the trailing edge tube and the leading edge tube of the horn balance portion are of streamline-section duralumin. Apart from ribs 4, 6 and 10, which are constructed from channel-section duralumin, the ribs are of flanged plate construction with lightening holes in the web. The elevator is fabric covered, the fabric being stitched to the ribs and over the nose fairings; a woods frame is incorporated in the lower surface at the front inner corner of each half-elevator to provide access to the trimming tab cables.

9. The five elevator hinges are mounted on the elevator spar and are of the self-lubricating type; the starboard intermediate is the locating hinge and is shown in fig. 1. Two annular-shaped pieces of self-lubricating bronze, housed between the inner and outer races, provide the bearing surfaces. The inner race of the locating hinge is formed with a flange on one side and is sweated to the spar. The outer race is clamped between the retaining plates by three equally-spaced bolts; two of these bolts engage with each bracket on the tail plane rear spar. The hinge is located by the retaining plates between the flange on the inner race and a loose collar secured to the spar by a taper pin. The remaining hinges are of identical construction except that the inner races are not provided with a flange and the loose collar is omitted.

10. The spar is fitted with duralumin nose fairings, except for a short distance on either side of the centre line and also where small wooden boxes are fitted round the outer and intermediate hinges. The elevator operating lever extends upwards near the inner end of the port spar tube and is connected to the double-ended lever in the tail plane as described in Chap. 4, para. 11; these two levers are enclosed by the fin.

11. *Trimming tabs.*—Between ribs 2 and 8 on each half-elevator (*see* fig. 1), the trailing edge is replaced by a trimming tab, controllable from the cockpit and made to a stream-line section from duralumin tube and plate. The elevator houses an irreversible worm gear in a gear box shaped to conform with the elevator profile and bolted between ribs 7 and 8 (*see* fig. 1, and Chap. 4, fig. 6), the gear providing the outer hinge for each tab; the inner hinge is provided by an end plug which rotates in a bearing in rib 2. The spindle of the worm gear is bolted directly to the tab and the worm wheel is fitted with a sprocket for the control chain (*see* Chap. 4, para. 15). Two other sprockets for the control chain are mounted on a diagonal strut between ribs 7 and 8, and conduits for the cables are fitted between the booms of ribs 2, 4 and 6. A fixed trimming tab is secured to the trailing edge just outboard of each controllable tab.

Fin

12. The fin structure (*see* fig. 1) comprises two vertical finposts and six horizontal ribs braced by one intermediate vertical tube, two diagonal bracing channels, a leading edge tube and aluminium sheet nosing. The front and rear finposts, of high-tensile steel are constructed from rolled polygonal boom riveted to plate webs; the front finpost is tapered at each end but the rear post is tapered only at the upper end. The .front finpost is extended at the top by two steel tubes which are bolted into the finpost booms and meet at the top in a saddle-piece which carries the leading edge tube. The rear finpost is extended upwards by a tapered and flanged duralumin plate which is bolted to the rear faces of the finpost booms, as are also the four rudder hinge brackets and the duralumin fillets for the fin-to-rudder gap.

13. The bottom rib, of flanged duralumin plate with flanged lightening holes, carries Simmonds double anchor nuts inside its flanges for the attachment of the fin-to-tail plane fairing fillets. The top rib, forming part of the leading edge fairing, is also of duralumin plate but all other ribs are built up of channel-section booms and tubular bracing in a similar manner to the tail plane ribs. A small-sectioned bracing tube of duralumin, to which each rib is attached, is fitted between the top and bottom ribs in a vertical position between the front and rear finposts; the structure is also braced by two flanged duralumin strips, lightened with flanged holes, which are fitted between the front and rear finposts as shown in fig. 1.

14. The leading edge tube joins the front ends of each rib, except the uppermost rib, and is covered by a deep duralumin nosing which is pop riveted to the ribs and rear finpost extension. The nosing is reinforced internally by ply-covered spruce formers which are attached to the nosing with duralumin woodscrews, two formers lying between the top two ribs and one between the third and fourth ribs down from the top. The whole fin is covered with fabric.

Rudder

15. The rudder (*see* fig. 1) is of the horn-balanced type, mass-balanced at the point of the horn. The structure consists of a tubular steel rudder post, on which four hinges are mounted, connected by ribs to a leading and trailing edge tube of streamline-sectioned duralumin; there is also an intermediate vertical duralumin tube which braces the ribs together and a short diagonal duralumin tube bracing the lower corner of the rudder.

16. Numbering from the top, ribs 2, 3, 4, 6, 8 and 9 consist of special section tubular booms with ribbed-plate bracing struts, whilst ribs 1, 5 and 7 are of flanged-plate construction; ribs 5 and 7 are lightened with flanged holes. The ribs are riveted to flanged spools which are sweated and tubular-riveted to the rudder post. Saddle plates, riveted round the leading and trailing edge tube, attach the tube to the ribs; at the top, the tube passes through a hole in an extension of the rudder post. The trailing edge is replaced between ribs 5 and 7 by a rudder tab (*see* para. 18). Above the tab a wooden mounting for the tail navigation lamp is carried by the trailing edge and a small channel-section between ribs 4 and 5; the cable from the lamp is carried in a conduit which runs down to a clip on the rudder post just above rib 7. The lead mass-balance weight is housed between the leading edge tube and the top rib, a small channel-section strut being fitted immediately behind the weight between the tube and the rib.

17. As stated above, the rudder is provided with four hinges, the lowest but one being the locating hinge; except for the locating hinge to which the rudder balance tab cables are attached (*see* fig. 2), these hinges are identical with those used on the elevator spar and are similarly surrounded by wooden boxes. At the bottom, the rudder post and the trailing edge tubes are encased in a duralumin fairing which extends approximately half-way up to rib 9; the rudder post is also fitted with duralumin nose fairing strips as used on the elevator spar. The double-ended rudder operating lever is fitted on either side at rib 7 and is bolted between flanged spools which are sweated and riveted to the rudder post. The whole rudder is fabric covered, the fabric being stitched to the ribs in the normal manner.

18. *Tab.*—The rudder balance tab (*see* figs. 1 and 2) is of streamline section and is constructed from duralumin sheet wrapped around a leading-edge tube. The tab is hinged on plugs which are riveted within each end of the tube, the plugs being received in small bearings riveted to the webs of ribs 5 and 7. At the bottom and at right-angles to the tab centre line are two arms to which the tab mass-balance weights and operating cables are fitted; the rear ends of the cables are attached to the inner holes in the arms. As shown in figs. 1 and 2, the cables are taken from the arms forward to two eyes on the rudder locating hinge, being crossed on either side of two co-axial pulleys; the pulleys are mounted through the web of rib 7, the mounting being braced to rib 8 by a small lightened channel-section.

19. The cables give the tab an automatic balance action, its trailing edge moving to port when the rudder moves to starboard. For trimming purposes, the tab is controllable from the cockpit *see* Chap. 4) but, when the cockpit control is in the neutral position, the tab remains approximately parallel with the centre line of the aeroplane through all movements of the rudder.

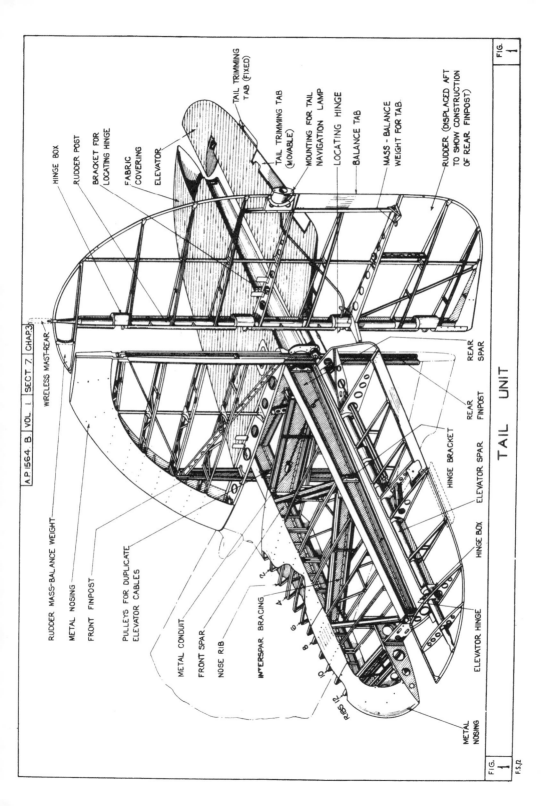

HINGE BOX

RUDDER POST

BRACKET FOR
LOCATING HINGE

FABRIC
COVERING

ELEVATOR

TAIL TRIMMING
TAB (FIXED)

TAIL TRIMMING TAB
(MOVABLE)

MOUNTING FOR TAIL
NAVIGATION LAMP

LOCATING HINGE

BALANCE TAB

MASS - BALANCE
WEIGHT FOR TAB.

RUDDER (DISPLACED AFT
TO SHOW CONSTRUCTION
OF REAR FINPOST)

WIRELESS MAST-REAR

RUDDER MASS-BALANCE WEIGHT

METAL NOSING

FRONT FINPOST

PULLEYS FOR DUPLICATE
ELEVATOR CABLES

METAL CONDUIT

FRONT SPAR

NOSE RIB

INTERSPAR BRACING

RIBS

METAL
NOSING

ELEVATOR HINGE

HINGE BOX

ELEVATOR SPAR

HINGE BRACKET

REAR FINPOST

REAR
SPAR

TAIL UNIT

FIG. 1   F.S./2

FIG.
1

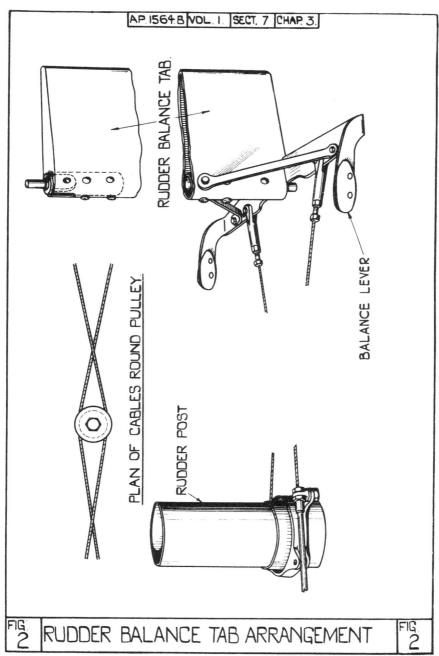

RUDDER BALANCE TAB.

BALANCE LEVER

PLAN OF CABLES ROUND PULLEY

RUDDER POST

FIG. 2 | RUDDER BALANCE TAB ARRANGEMENT | FIG. 2

F.S./4

CHAPTER 4

FLYING CONTROLS

LIST OF CONTENTS

LIST OF ILLUSTRATIONS

CHAPTER 4

FLYING CONTROLS

General

1. The controls for the ailerons, elevator and rudder are constructed as a single unit (*see* fig. 1), fitted centrally within the cockpit; the unit is mounted on a pair of tubes running parallel with the centre line of the aeroplane and secured between the centre section front and rear spars. For elevator control, the control column is rocked fore-and-aft from the bottom and, for aileron control, the top of the control column is rocked sideways on a hinge situated approximately 8 in. below the spade grip; the rudder bar is of the centrally-pivoted type and is adjustable for leg reach. The aileron, elevator and rudder controls may be locked by means of the gear shown in fig. 8. The main plane flaps are operated hydraulically, being controlled by the selector lever mounted on the starboard side of the cockpit (*see* Sect. 9). The trimming tabs on the elevator and the rudder balance tab are controlled by means of handwheels on the port side of the cockpit; the rudder balance tab is also operated automatically by cables from the rudder post (*see* Chap. 3, paras. 18 and 19).

Control column and rudder bar unit

2. The upper portion of the control column is provided at its upper end with a spade grip, which incorporates the control button for the pneumatic operation of the guns and a lever for the application of the pneumatically-operated brakes; the lower end of the upper portion is forked and pinned to the upper end of the lower portion to provide a knuckle joint. A sprocket is fitted to the front end of the joint pin and rotates with the upper portion of the control column; this rotation is transmitted by means of chains and tie-rods to a second sprocket mounted in a socket fitting at the base of the control column. This lower sprocket is keyed to a spindle carried in two ball bearings within the socket fitting, the spindle being forked at its rear end to form the front part of a Hooke type universal joint; the rear part of the universal joint is formed by the forked front end of the aileron torque tube. Thus, when the upper portion of the control column is rocked sideways, the aileron torque tube rotates in a similar direction.

3. The control column is mounted on two cranks which are bolted at their inner ends to spigots on the socket fitting at the base of the control column and supported at their outer ends by bearings on the two parallel mounting tubes (*see* para. 1); the control column may, therefore, rock fore-and-aft on these bearings about an axis at right-angles to the centre line of the aeroplane. Since the axis of rotation is arranged to be in line with the centre of the Hooke type universal joint, fore-and-aft movement of the aileron torque tube is eliminated.

4. Keyed to the aft end of the aileron torque tube is the aileron cable drum from which the aileron cables are taken to the control gear in each outer plane; the drum incorporates two grooved sectors to which the cables are attached as shown in fig. 1. The rear bearing on the aileron torque tube is of the self-aligning ball-bearing type and is mounted on a bracket secured to the flying control unit mounting tubes and to the rear face of the top boom of the centre section rear spar.

5. The fore-and-aft movement of the control column is transmitted by a connecting rod to an elevator lever to which the operating cables are attached. The front end of the connecting rod is hinged to a lug bolted to the control column a few inches above its base, and the rear end is hinged on a bolt between the side plates of the elevator lever at its upper end; the connecting rod is bowed downwards in the centre to provide sufficient clearance for the bottom of the cockpit seat. The elevator lever is hinged on a cross tube mounted between the rear ends of the flying control unit mounting tubes. A bracket plate is bolted to the cross tube on either side of the elevator lever, two rubber buffer tubes being fitted between their rear ends to provide stops for the travel of the elevator lever.

6. The rudder bar is fitted (indirectly) to the top of a spindle mounted almost vertically in a pedestal bearing which is supported by two cross struts between the mounting tubes of the flying control unit, one cross tube being fitted above the mounting and the other below. The rudder bar spindle is flanged at the top to receive a steel slide upon which the rudder bar may move fore-and-aft. The movement is controlled by a star wheel operated by the pilot's foot, the star wheel being fitted to a screw which engages with the centre forging carrying the rudder bar; a movement of $4\frac{1}{2}$ in. is provided, increase in leg reach being obtained by counter-clockwise rotation of the star wheel.

7. Below the pedestal bearing, the lower end of the rudder bar spindle carries the double-ended rudder lever to which the operating cables are attached; a stop for the rudder lever is provided by a fibre block carried on a bracket which is slung from the lower cross tube supporting the rudder pedestal bearing. At the upper end of the spindle immediately beneath the slide, a short lever is fitted which projects slightly forward and to starboard. To the end of this lever is attached a·rod which operates the dual relay valve of the pneumatic brake control. Two-position foot pedals are attached to each end of the rudder bar, the top position of each being provided with a rubber toe strap. The bottom position is used during normal flying and the top position is for use during fighting or aerobatics.

Aileron control

8. From the cable drum on the rear end of the aileron torque tube, cables are taken to port and starboard (*see* fig. 2) to pulleys mounted on the outermost trailing edge ribs of the centre section (*see* Chap. 2, para. 8); for adjustment purposes, the cables are provided with turnbuckles just outboard of the cable drum. From the pulleys in the centre section, the cables pass into the outer planes where they are connected to tie-rods which run outboard behind the rear spar to a point just inboard of the control gear. The outboard ends of the tie-rods are connected to cables which pass around pulleys on the aileron control gears (*see* fig. 3). In the cannon plane the lower tie-rod is replaced by a cable which runs over a pulley situated just outboard of the cannons; adjustment of this cable is provided by means of a turnbuckle which is accessible through the breech block doors.

9. Each aileron control gear is bolted between the bracket for the aileron centre hinge and a similarly-built bracket approximately 8 in. inboard of the centre hinge bracket; the brackets are constructed and secured to the outer plane rear spar as described in Chap. 2, para. 13. Each control gear housing is bolted between two square-section tubes fitted between these brackets by means

of U-plates; withing each housing a spindle is carried in two ball bearings. The control gear pulley is secured to the front end of the spindle and, at the rear end, is a flanged plate lever on which is mounted a ball-end; the ball-end is joined to the aileron operating lever by a short connecting rod (see fig. 4). The ball joint, together with the rotatable fork-end in the extremity of the aileron operating lever, provide the necessary freedom of movement between the rotary motion of the control gear pulley and the linear motion of the aileron operating lever. There is no adjustment for the length of the connecting rod between the ball-end and the aileron operating lever, all adjustments being made by means of the cable turnbuckles within the fuselage. In the port outer plane the mounting for the pressure head is fitted between the square-section tubes carrying the aileron control gear and the inboard bracket supporting these square-section tubes.

10. The aileron control gear gives a differential movement to the ailerons by causing the up-going aileron (on the down-going plane) to move through approximately equal angles for equal displacements of the control column, and the down-going aileron (on the up-going plane) to move through progressively smaller angles at each successive displacement, thus lessening the drag on the up-going plane. The degree to which this effect is present is governed by the angle at which the control gear lever and pulleys are set when the ailerons are in their neutral position. The normal angular movement of the aileron is shown in fig. 4.

Elevator control

11. The duplicate elevator cables are attached in pairs to shackles which are bolted between the side plates of the elevator lever (see figs. 1 and 2), the cables being attached to the shackles through turnbuckles, which provide the necessary length adjustment for the cables. From the ends of the elevator lever, the two pairs of cables run aft along the centre line of the aeroplane to fairleads mounted on fuselage cross strut PP; within this run, the upper pair of cables passes through a fairlead on the underside of the rear sliding tray for the wireless crate, and both pairs pass through fairleads mounted on transverse L-section members attached to fuselage struts LM (see Chap. 1, para. 10). From the fairleads on cross strut PP, the cables run through a hole in the web of the tail plane front spar, over double pulleys mounted on the rear face of the spar, and are then connected to the ends of a double-ended lever. The upper end of the double-ended lever is joined by a connecting rod of fixed length to the elevator operating lever (see Chap. 3, para. 10).

Rudder control

12. The front ends of the duplicate rudder cables are attached through shackles to each end of the rudder bar lever (see para. 7). Each pair of cables runs aft over the upper boom of the centre section rear spar (which is fitted with protective fibre rubbing strips), through fairleads at the outer ends of the cross shaft carrying the elevator lever, and through fairleads mounted on support angles just aft of the flare launching chute. For length adjustment, turnbuckles are fitted into the cables between these latter fairleads and the fairleads mounted on the lower of the two pairs of L-section members attached to fuselage struts LM (see Chap. 1, para. 10). From this point, the cables run through fairleads on cross strut PP through slots in the sides of the fuselage tail bay to the ends of the rudder operating lever; the slots fitted with small light-alloy fairing plates

Flap control

13. The flaps are hydraulically operated by a single hydraulic jack anchored to the centre section rear spar and acting directly on a lever on the centre section flap spar; they are controlled by means of the selector lever described under the hydraulic system in Sect. 9. An indicator, marked in degrees of flap movement to show the position of the flaps at any time is mounted on starboard fuselage side strut CF, beneath the hydraulic selector gear. The indicator is operated by a bowden cable, the lower end of which is clipped to an eyebolt on the centre section flap spar (*see* Chap. 2, para. 32).

Elevator trimming tab control

14. The elevator trimming tabs, one in the trailing edge of each half-elevator, are controlled from the port side of the cockpit by means of a handwheel (*see* Sect. 1) bracketed to fuselage side strut CF. The tabs are coupled to the handwheel by a system of chains and cables (*see* fig. 5) in such a manner that when the top periphery of the handwheel is pushed forward the aeroplane trims nose down, and vice versa. The handwheel incorporates an indicating device, consisting of a pointer carried on a screwed thread and sliding in a slotted scale.

15. A sprocket mounted on the outboard end of the handwheel spindle, carries a short length of chain, the ends of which are attached to the trimming tab cables. From their junctions with the chain, the cables are taken along the port side of the fuselage through fairleads mounted on the outboard side of fuselage joints E and G, through fairleads on the inboard side of joint J and thence through a fairlead at the mid-point of cross strut NN. The cables diverge rearwards from this fairlead, the upper to starboard and the lower to port, and then pass through fairleads in the webs of the tail plane front spar and innermost bracing struts. A little forward of the tail plane rear spar, each cable is connected to an encased cable which is led through the rear spar web and the nosing of the elevator to a bracket on the rear side of the elevator spar; thence the cable passes through a conduit running outboard and parallel with the elevator spar (*see* Chap. 3, para. 11). Just within the outboard end of the conduit, the cable is attached to a chain which passes round the outboard sprocket (*see* Chap. 3, para. 11), and thence aft around the sprocket fitted to the worm wheel at the outer end of the respective trimming tab (*see* fig. 6).

16. The return ends of the chain pass over the inboard sprockets (*see* Chap. 3, para. 11) and are attached to two balance cables that run inboard within other conduits mounted just behind those mentioned in para. 15; the balance cables continue in a straight line across the gap between the ribs of each half-elevator and are joined by an acorn-type connector. Adjustment for the length of the tab control cables is provided by means of turnbuckles near their forward ends; the turnbuckle for the upper cable is situated in fuselage bay EG, and that for the lower cable in bay GJ.

Rudder balance tab control

17. The rudder balance tab is controlled from the cockpit by means of a handwheel bracketed to fuselage port strut C.F1. The handwheel operates a cable drum, which is mounted concentrically at the other end of a spindle; two and a half turns of the control cable are wrapped round the drum and are positioned on it by a small spigot. From the drum, both ends of the cable run through pulleys mounted in a bracket on C.F1. and are connected by turnbuckles to a further pair of cables which pass through fairleads to another pair of pulleys

mounted on fuselage port strut R.U, at which point the cables turn upwards and the ends are joined to a chain (*see* fig. 5). The chain passes over the sprocket of the rudder trimming gear (*see* fig. 7) and operates a lever to the ends of which are pinned two short cables that run in fairlead tubes which are clipped to eye-bolts on a sleeve just below the rudder locating hinge. From this point the cables are passed over pulleys mounted within the rudder and are pinned to the tab mass balance arm.

18. The cockpit control enables the pilot to trim the rudder, but the arrangement of cables within the rudder produces a balance **action** so that the tab tends to remain in the same position in relation to the **line of flight** for all movements of the rudder.

Locking gear

19. The primary flying controls can be interlocked by means of a bracket on the control column and by struts to each end of the rudder bar (*see* fig. 8). The aileron control is locked by a bracket which is clipped to the control column just below the spade grip; the bracket is fitted so that the undersides of the locknuts on the aileron control tie rods bear against the top of a specially-profiled plate incorporated in the bracket. The bracket also embodies a pair of lugs to which two struts are attached by means of shackles. The struts extend downward and forward and, at their lower ends, engage with pegs clipped to the rudder bar just inboard of the foot pedals; these struts lock the rudder bar and also prevent fore-and-aft movement of the control column. To prevent the pilot from sitting in his seat until the controls are unlocked, a spring-loaded interference bar is fitted to a bracket on the control column. its rear end being inserted through a hole in the back of the pilot's seat. In order to facilitate fitting and assembling of the locking gear, the bracket is fixed to the control column by means of a swivel bolt and wing nut. When not in use, the locking strut s, interference bar and bracket are placed in a canvas container and clipped to : . fuselage strut in the starboard side of the wireless bay.

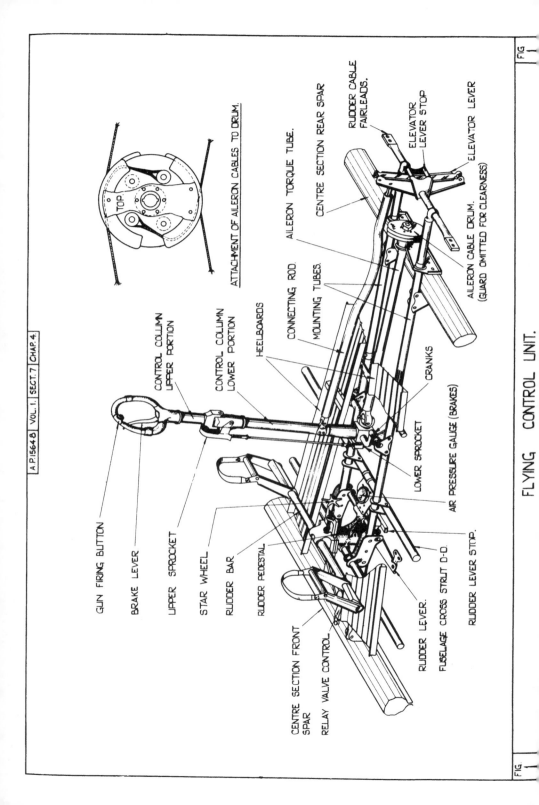

GUN FIRING BUTTON

BRAKE LEVER

UPPER SPROCKET

STAR WHEEL

RUDDER BAR

RUDDER PEDESTAL

CENTRE SECTION FRONT SPAR

RELAY VALVE CONTROL

RUDDER LEVER.

FUSELAGE CROSS STRUT D-D.

RUDDER LEVER STOP.

AIR PRESSURE GAUGE (BRAKES)

LOWER SPROCKET

CRANKS

CONTROL COLUMN UPPER PORTION

CONTROL COLUMN LOWER PORTION

HEELBOARDS

CONNECTING ROD.

MOUNTING TUBES.

ATTACHMENT OF AILERON CABLES TO DRUM.

TOP

AILERON TORQUE TUBE.

CENTRE SECTION REAR SPAR

RUDDER CABLE FAIRLEADS.

ELEVATOR LEVER STOP

ELEVATOR LEVER

AILERON CABLE DRUM.
(GUARD OMITTED FOR CLEARNESS)

FLYING CONTROL UNIT.

FIG. 1

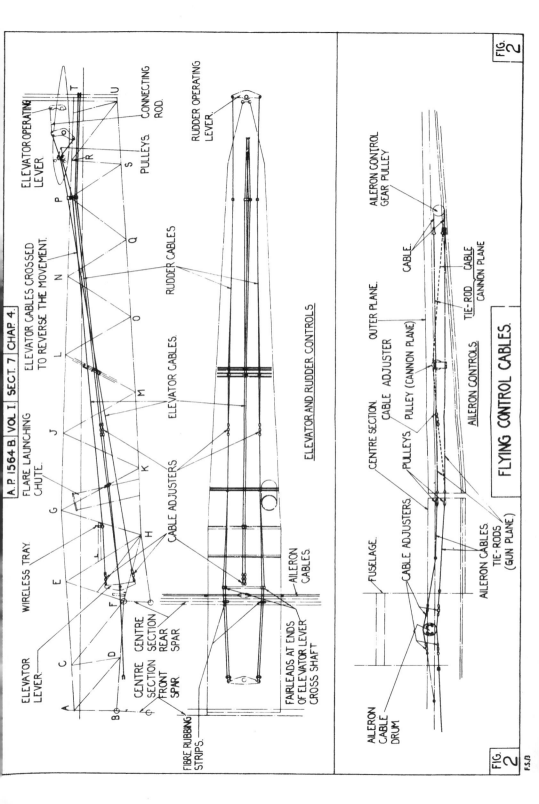

A.P 1564 B. VOL I. SECT. 7. CHAP. 4.

ELEVATOR OPERATING LEVER.

CONNECTING ROD.

PULLEYS.

RUDDER OPERATING LEVER.

ELEVATOR CABLES CROSSED TO REVERSE THE MOVEMENT.

RUDDER CABLES

ELEVATOR CABLES.

FLARE LAUNCHING CHUTE.

WIRELESS TRAY.

CABLE ADJUSTERS

ELEVATOR LEVER.

CENTRE SECTION FRONT SPAR

CENTRE SECTION REAR SPAR

FIBRE RUBBING STRIPS.

AILERON CABLES

FAIRLEADS AT ENDS OF ELEVATOR LEVER CROSS SHAFT

ELEVATOR AND RUDDER CONTROLS

OUTER PLANE.

CENTRE SECTION.

CABLE ADJUSTER

AILERON CONTROL GEAR PULLEY

CABLE.

PULLEY (CANNON PLANE)

TIE-ROD CABLE
CANNON PLANE

PULLEYS.

CABLE ADJUSTERS.

AILERON CONTROLS

FUSELAGE.

AILERON CABLES.
TIE-RODS
(GUN PLANE)

AILERON CABLE DRUM

FLYING CONTROL CABLES.

FIG. 2

FIG. 2

F.S.J3

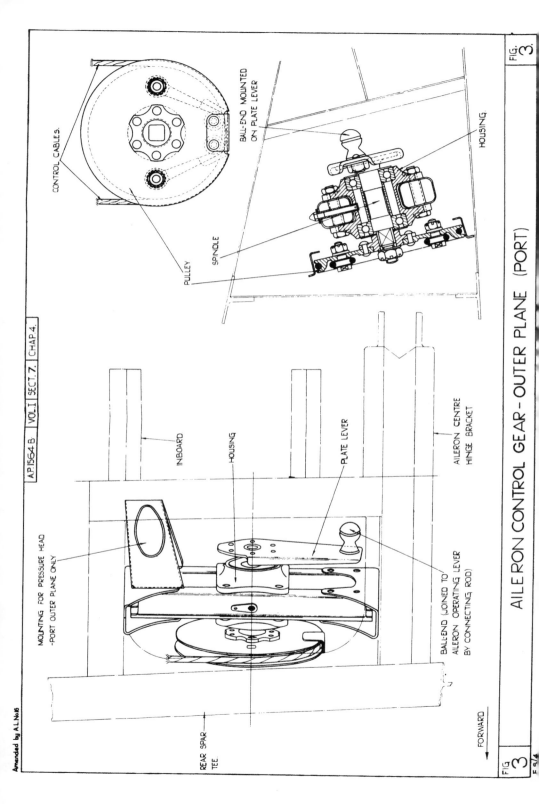

A.P.1564.B | VOL.I | SECT.7. | CHAP.4.

CONTROL CABLES.

BALL-END MOUNTED ON PLATE LEVER

HOUSING.

PULLEY

SPINDLE

MOUNTING FOR PRESSURE HEAD -PORT OUTER PLANE ONLY

INBOARD

HOUSING

PLATE LEVER

AILERON CENTRE HINGE BRACKET

BALL-END (JOINED TO AILERON OPERATING LEVER BY CONNECTING ROD)

REAR SPAR TEE

FORWARD

FIG. 3

AILERON CONTROL GEAR - OUTER PLANE (PORT)

FIG. 3

F.S/4

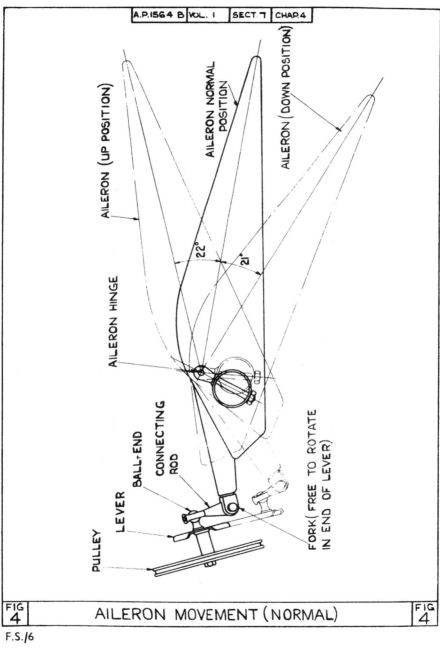

AILERON (UP POSITION)

AILERON NORMAL POSITION

AILERON (DOWN POSITION)

22°

21'

AILERON HINGE

PULLEY

LEVER

BALL-END

CONNECTING ROD

FORK (FREE TO ROTATE IN END OF LEVER)

FIG 4

FIG 4

AILERON MOVEMENT (NORMAL)

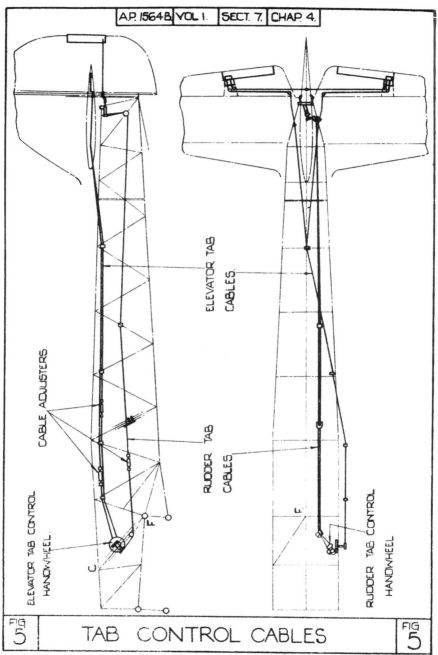

ELEVATOR TAB CABLES.

RUDDER TAB CABLES

CABLE ADJUSTERS

ELEVATOR TAB CONTROL HANDWHEEL.

RUDDER TAB CONTROL HANDWHEEL

FIG 5

FIG 5

TAB CONTROL CABLES

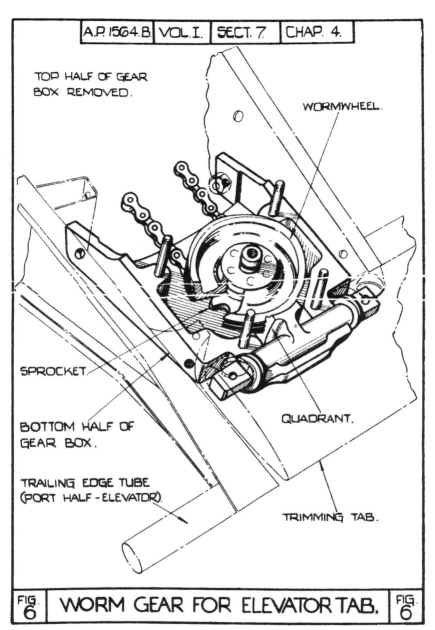

TOP HALF OF GEAR
BOX REMOVED.

WORMWHEEL.

SPROCKET.

BOTTOM HALF OF
GEAR BOX.

QUADRANT.

TRAILING EDGE TUBE
(PORT HALF - ELEVATOR).

TRIMMING TAB.

FIG. 6 | WORM GEAR FOR ELEVATOR TAB. | FIG. 6

F.S./8

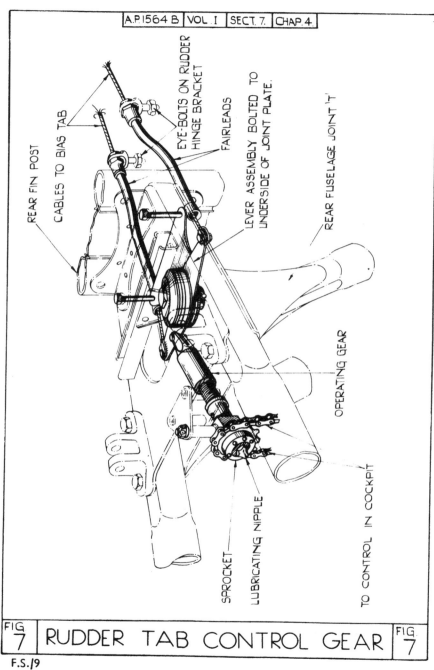

REAR FIN POST

CABLES TO BIAS TAB

EYE-BOLTS ON RUDDER HINGE BRACKET

FAIRLEADS

LEVER ASSEMBLY BOLTED TO UNDERSIDE OF JOINT PLATE.

REAR FUSELAGE JOINT 't'

OPERATING GEAR

TO CONTROL IN COCKPIT

SPROCKET

LUBRICATING NIPPLE

FIG 7 | RUDDER TAB CONTROL GEAR | FIG 7

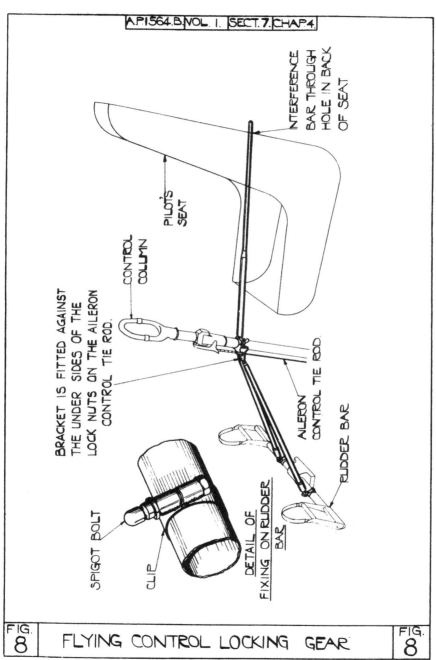

INTERFERENCE BAR THROUGH HOLE IN BACK OF SEAT

PILOT'S SEAT

CONTROL COLUMN

BRACKET IS FITTED AGAINST THE UNDER SIDES OF THE LOCK NUTS ON THE AILERON CONTROL TIE ROD.

AILERON CONTROL TIE ROD.

RUDDER BAR

SPIGOT BOLT

CLIP

DETAIL OF FIXING ON RUDDER BAR

FIG. 8

FIG. 8

FLYING CONTROL LOCKING GEAR

CHAPTER 5

UNDERCARRIAGE

LIST OF CONTENTS

LIST OF ILLUSTRATIONS

CHAPTER 5

UNDERCARRIAGE

General

1. The wide-track undercarriage comprises two oleo-pneumatic shock-absorber struts which retract inwards and backwards into a recess beneath the fuselage and between the centre section spars. The raising and lowering of the undercarriage units is carried out hydraulically, mechanical locking and electrical indicating devices being provided for both the "up" and "down" positions; there is also an audible warning buzzer which operates should the undercarriage be retracted with the throttle lever less than one-third open. A wheel with a medium-pressure tyre is carried on a stub axle on the inboard side of each shock-absorber strut and each wheel is fitted with a pneumatically-operated brake. The brakes are controlled by a lever on the control column spade grip, differential action being obtained in conjunction with the rudder bar.

2. The tail wheel unit is not,retractable but is faired into the rear underside of the fuselage. The unit comprises a spring-loaded or oleo-pneumatic shock-absorber strut which is fully-castoring and self-centring and a wheel carried on an axle in a fork at the lower end of the strut; the wheel is fitted with a self-earthing tyre.

Main wheel units

General

3. The upper end of.the shock-absorber strut (*see* fig. 1) is attached to the forward end of the lower boom of the centre section outer girder (*see* Chap. 2) and is braced both longitudinally and laterally from points approximately one-third down the strut. The longitudinal bracing is provided by a radius rod which is connected to the rear end (F) of the upper boom of the centre section outer girder; the rod is universally jointed at (D) and is provided with a sleeve and trunnion joint at its intersection with the lower boom of the girder. The lateral bracing is provided by a side stay which is connected to the forward end (B) of the centre section inner girder; the stay is knuckle-jointed at (J) and a triangulated lever is attached to its upper portion. For raising and lowering the undercarriage, a hydraulic jack is attached at one end (H) to the triangulated lever and at the other end (C) to the web of the centre section front spar.

4. For freedom of movement in the required directions, the undercarriage components are provided with the following movements:—

(i) *Shock-absorber strut.*—The shock-absorber strut can rotate about the lower boom of the centre section outer girder upon a sleeve block and can also swing fore-and-aft upon its attachment bolt to the sleeve block.

(ii) *Side stay.*—The bottom joint (A) is made through a universal block with rotational freedom just above the block, but the knuckle joint (J) has freedom in the plane of the triangulated lever only. At the top joint the side stay can pivot up and down at (B) and can swing about a line through (B) and (H) (the inboard side of the triangulated lever).

(iii) *Radius rod.*—Moving only in the plane of the shock-absorber strut, the lower portion of the radius rod can swing about joint (E) and about its trunnion (G) with the sleeve on the girder lower boom; the sleeve, and therefore the lower portion of the radius rod, may also rotate about and slide along the girder boom. The knuckle joint (D) provides rotational freedom for the forked attachment to the upper portion of the radius rod and freedom about the attachment bolt. The upper end attachment of the radius rod (joint F) is made through a universal block, with rotational freedom just below the block.

Operation

5. *Raising.*—When the piston of the hydraulic jack moves inboard the side stay folds at joint (J) and forces the shock-absorber strut to rotate about its bearing on the girder lower boom until the leg is horizontal; at the same time the radius rod folds at joint (D) and its lower portion rotates about the girder lower boom. Whilst this inward and upward movement is in progress, the jointed radius rod is also providing a rearward component of movement, the lower portion sliding along the girder lower boom on its sleeve. This rearward movement is caused by the outward swing of the upper portion of the radius rod from joint (F), necessitating a proportional rearward movement of its lower end; the movement is transferred at joint (D) to the lower portion of the radius rod which, in turn, pulls the shock-absorber strut behind the centre section front spar.

6. *Lowering.*—The operations described above in para. 5 occur in reverse when the undercarriage is lowered. In the "down" position the two portions of the side stay are co-linear as are the two portions of the radius rod; the strut is then braced in its landing position. In order that the side stay joint shall not pass through the dead centre, the upper portion is extended past the joint pin to bear upon the lower portion when the two portions are co-linear, and, to ensure that the joint pin reaches dead-centre, an assisting compression spring is fitted between the strut upper attachment and the side stay just below joint (J). These two devices ensure the lateral stability of the strut, upon which condition the longitudinal stability follows automatically.

Locking devices and indicators

7. *"Up" position.*—To retain the undercarriage in the retracted position, automatic catches (*see* fig. 2) are bracketed to the bottom longerons in the foremost bay of the centre fuselage, close to fuselage joints D. The catches engage with stirrups fitted to the inboard ends of the undercarriage wheel stub axles (*see* fig. 1). The complete engagement of each stirrup with its catch actuates a micro-switch (with an on-and-off range of 0·01 in) which illuminates a red lamp on the undercarriage position indicator fitted to the port side of the instrument panel.

8. *"Down" position.*—As soon as the two portions of each undercarriage side stay are co-linear, the stay is automatically locked by a spring-loaded latch which positively prevents the side stay from folding until the latch is released; the latch is hinged at its attachment to the centre section front spar and engages with a projection on the apex (H) of the triangulated lever. The complete engagement of the latch with the side stay actuates a second micro-switch which illuminates a green lamp on the undercarriage position indicator.

9. *During operation.*—The "up" and "down" positions of each undercarriage unit are indicated by independent lamps, intermediate positions of the units not being shown. The latches are automatically released by the operation of the selector lever of the hydraulic system, the release being effected by the action of a system of cables and pulleys connecting the catch gears to a subsidiary arm on the selector lever. The jaws of the catches are automatically closed when the stirrups engage with spring-loaded plungers within the catches, but are opened by the action of a hydraulic jack (*see* fig. 2). When the selector lever is set to WHEELS UP the latches are disengaged, and when it is set to WHEELS

DOWN the catches are opened. In the event of the catches jamming or the cables stretching, the undercarriage units may be released by foot pressure on the emergency release plunger shown in fig. 2; the undercarriage units will then fall under their own weight assisted by the action of the compression spring attached to each side stay.

Indicators

10. *Audible.*—Should the undercarriage units not be locked "down" when the engine throttle lever is less than one-third open, the pilot will immediately be warned by the sounding of a horn which is situated on the port side of the decking. The horn is operated by a switch on the throttle lever, bracket.

11. *Visual.*—The lighting circuit of the undercarriage indicator is in duplicate, the alternative circuits being controlled by means of a change-over switch; the green lamps, which are illuminated when the undercarriage is locked "down", may be switched off at the indicator when the aeroplane is at rest on the ground. The change-over switch is in one unit with the cut-out switch and is located on the instrument panel adjacent to the undercarriage indicator; the red lamps and the buzzer are always in circuit. Two small rectangular windows in the top surface of the fuselage underfairing enable the pilot to see each wheel when retracted.

Shock-absorber strut

12. Each oleo-pneumatic shock-absorber strut comprises an inverted cylinder (*see* fig. 3) in which slides a cylindrical piston rod carrying the wheel stub axle at its lower end; the piston rod is prevented from turning in the cylinder by splines. Compressed air in the upper portion provides a springing medium for absorbing light landing shocks and the necessary damping for heavier shocks is obtained by a form of hydraulic loading which forces oil through an orifice as the piston rod moves upwards.

13. *Construction.*—At its upper end, the cylinder (*see* fig. 3) is forked externally to provide attachment to the sleeve block on the forward end of the lower boom of the centre section outer girder; a gland for the piston rod is fitted at the lower end. The gland comprises a packing stop ring screwed into the cylinder, a single U-sectioned leather packing ring, a tubular capping ring and an externally screwed gland retaining nut. An oil seal (which also acts as a scraper ring) is fitted beneath the gland and is maintained in contact with the piston tube by a cap screwed to the bottom of the gland retaining nut. A nipple is screwed into the bottom end of the cylinder tube to provide means for lubricating the gland. At approximately one-third of the way down the cylinder tube, an external lugged collar is held against a stop ring by a ring nut; the radius rod and side stay, which retain the shock-absorber strut in position, are attached to the lugs on this collar. For receiving the splines which are integral with the tubular piston rod, a splined guide ring is secured inside the cylinder tube (by set-screws with jointing washers) at a position approximately midway between the gland and the collar used for the attachment of the radius rod and side stay.

14. Within the upper end of the cylinder tube, an axial cone-seated plug secures a hollow plunger to the upper end of the tube. In the case of strut Part No. 90274, the plunger is slightly tapered over the greater part of its length and is sharply tapered at the end near the piston; in the case of strut Part No. 91205, the plunger is parallel-sided throughout its length. A vertical oil-lever tube is sweated to the bottom of the plug and extends almost to the bottom of the hollow plunger. The interior of the hollow plunger is put into communication with the interior of the cylinder tube by a series of holes drilled through the

wall around its upper end and by a small leak hole at the lower end. At the upper end, and at right angles to the axis of the attachment bolt to the centre section, the head of the cylinder tube is fitted with an air valve on one side and with an oil-level plug on the other. The air valve is in communication with the inside of the upper end of the cylinder tube, and the oil-level valve is put into communication with the oil-level tube within the hollow plunger by means of the cone-seated plug which is drilled to suit.

15. The tubular piston rod has a wheel stub axle bolted on the inboard side at the bottom end and a composite piston screwed to the upper end; at approximately mid-length, the tube is closed by a transverse partition (integral with the piston tube) which forms the base of the oil chamber. The piston comprises upper and lower halves which are drilled with a ring of vertical holes, a steel damper valve ring (of a lipped cross section and with one $\frac{1}{8}$ in. dia. hole) being housed in the outer annular space between the upper and lower halves. The piston is shouldered internally around its upper periphery, the central hole being slightly larger than the diameter of the hollow plunger above. Below the piston, the piston rod is machined with six external splines which engage with the splined guide ring fixed inside the cylinder tube. Immediately below these splines is a splined collar (integral with the piston rod) which butts against the gland stop ring; this collar acts as a limit stop to the downward movement of the piston rod.

16. *Operation.*—When the shock-absorber strut is fully extended, the oil is at a level determined by the position of the bottom of the oil level tube. On the compression stroke, the air above the oil is further compressed and the hollow plunger tube displaces oil from the upper end of the piston tube, producing a damping effect due to the escaping oil being restricted by the annular space between the plunger tube and the internal lip on the piston. In the case of strut Part No. 90274, the internally-lipped piston shrouds the hollow plunger tube within the first inch or two of movement and thus provides a delayed damping effect which increases progressively due to the external taper of the hollow plunger tube; in the case of strut Part No. 91205, the damping comes into effect immediately but does not vary as the plunger tube is parallel. The tendency for the pressures within the strut to equalize also causes the oil to flow (a) into the hollow plunger tube through the small leak hole at the bottom (exit for the imprisoned air being provided by the holes at the top of the tube) and (b) through the vertical holes in the piston and round the outside of the damper.valve ring into the increasing annular space between the piston tube and the cylinder tube.

17. When the energy·of landing has been absorbed by the compressed air and oil displacement, the compressed air energizes the outward stroke of the piston tube. · The oil within the annular space beneath the piston is now forced up through the holes in the lower half of the piston and, due to the lipped cross section of the damper valve ring, moves the ring upwards into contact with the lower face of the upper half of the piston; in this position, the damper valve ring stops the flow around its lip and only permits the oil to return through its single hole. The passage of oil through the piston is therefore restricted more on the outward than on the inward stroke, thereby ensuring a steady recovery from the compression stroke and eliminating any tendency to violent oscillation.

Wheels and brakes

18. The cast magnesium-alloy wheels are of the small hub type and are fitted with medium-pressure balloon tyres. Each wheel is carried on two ball-bearings on the stub axle at the bottom of each shock-absorber strut; a stirrup, for engagement with the catch gear in the fuselage when the undercarriage is retracted, is fitted at the inner end of each stub axle. The wheels include a

friction surface for the Dunlop pneumatic brake unit fitted into the outer side of each wheel; general information on the brake units may be found in A.P.1464B, Vol. I. For the method of operation of the brakes and a description of the pneumatic brake system, reference should be made to Sects. 1 and 9 respectively.

Fairing

19. When the undercarriage is retracted, the gaps between each under-carriage unit and the wheel recess in the underside of the centre section are closed by fairings on the shock-absorber struts. A large fairing is bolted around the shock-absorber strut through four brackets, a small fairing being clipped to the radius rod through two brackets. The large fairing is of sheet duralumin riveted to one main and two subsidiary duralumin members of flanged plate lightened with flanged holes; to allow adequate ground clearance, the fairing does not extend below the axle centre line, and, consequently, the underside of the centre section is not faired-in completely when the undercarriage is retracted.

Tail wheel unit

Dowty spring type

20. *General.*—The wheel unit (*see* fig. 4) is mounted in the tail bay of the fuselage as described in Chap. 1, para. 11, and comprises a castoring shock-absorbing strut and a pneumatic-tyred wheel; compression coil springs, with friction dampers, are mounted inside an assembly of sliding tubes, the lower tube carrying the wheel fork. The wheel runs on ball bearings on an axle tube located in the fork by two bolts, the wheel being fitted with self-earthing tyre. Four small arms, fitted two at each end of the axle tube, are drilled to take the hooks of the special tail-wheel steering arm which is used when manœuvring the aeroplane on the ground without the aid of the engine.

21. *Construction.*—The shock-absorber strut (*see* fig. 4) comprises two telescoping members K and P, in which a spring and self-centring mechanism are housed. The outer or stationary member K is anchored in the fuselage by an end fitting Q, attached at its upper end, and a bracket U riveted to its lower end. The bracket U also houses an anti-shimmy device, consisting of a friction band O and a clip F. An end plug W and centre tube Y are held in the top end of the outer tube by the bolt A which secures the end fitting Q. At the lower end of the centre tube a self-centring cone N, secured by the pin E and operating in a slot in the centre tube, mates with a second cone M which is secured to the lower sliding member P. These cones are in contact only when the tail is clear of the ground and they ensure that the wheel is maintained in the true fore-and-aft position for landing. When they engage, the resultant "shock" is absorbed by a secondary spring L assembled inside the centre tube. The main spring H is fitted between the plug W and two friction cones, C and D.

22. *Operation.*—Landing and taxying loads caused the sliding member P to be thrust up into the outer tube against the main spring H. The spring partially or fully extends the strut when the loads are released. The friction cones C and D are for the purposes of retarding the movement during compression and extension. Each one is slotted (*see* fig. 4) so that, when the loads drive them together, the outer one expands against the inner surface of the outer tube, while the inner one contracts, to grip the centre tube. While the aeroplane is standing on its wheels, the self-centring cones are disengaged, thereby allowing the wheel to castor against the action of the friction band O.

Dowty oleo-pneumatic type

23. *Construction.*—The Dowty tail wheel unit (*see* figs. 5 and 5A) comprises four assemblies, as follows:—outer casing, self-centring mechanism and pivot bracket, fork, wheel and axle, and the shock-absorber.

(i) The outer casing consists of a tubular member B to which is attached a socket A at the top and an attachment fitting H at the lower end; these fittings provide the attachment points of the unit to the aeroplane. A bearing bush H1 is incorporated in the attachment fitting H.

(ii) The self-centring mechanism is anchored inside the outer member B by a bolt B1 which passes through a spring stop C and the torque fitting D. Two cams E1 and F, whose contact faces are of a helical form, are urged into full contact by a spring C1. The upper cam E1 is indirectly attached to the torque fitting D, being held in position by a pin on which are fitted two rollers D1. These rollers operate in a slot in the torque fitting, thus limiting the movement of the cam to a vertical sliding movement. The lower cam F rotates in unison with the pivot bracket I, to which it is secured by screws. A thrust race G is fitted to facilitate rotary movement.

(iii) The wheel fork L is hinged to the lower end of the pivot bracket, and is also connected to the link K by a pin K1. An eye-end is formed on each arm of the fork to receive the axle L1 and towing brackets N.

(iv) The shock-absorber is either a type C.6595 (*see* fig. 5) or a type C.7941 as shown in fig. 5A. The outer and stationary cylinder Q of the type C.6595 shock-absorber (*see* fig. 5) is held inside the pivot bracket I by two bolts A1, while the inner cylinder V is connected to the wheel fork L by link K. At the inner end of the cylinder V, a diaphragm R, carrying a gland ring Q1, is assembled and is sealed by the synthetic rubber ring Y. The diaphragm also houses a bolt X, which provides a guide for the valve R1. Inside the inner cylinder V is a floating piston T with two gland rings Z; it is subjected to oil pressure on the inner side and air pressure on the outer side. The air is pumped in through an inflation valve W and the outer cylinder Q is filled with oil through a hole normally sealed by a plug P. The inner cylinder is maintained inside the outer cylinder by the screwed sleeve U, which is locked in position by a circlip. The type C.7941 shock-absorber (*see* fig. 5A) is of very similar construction but the inner cylinder V is closed by an end-fitting O, sealed by the ring S1 and secured by the locking-screw L. This end-fitting is formed with a bearing for the shock-absorber attachment pin and carries an inflation valve W. The difference in construction of the diaphragm R is shown in fig. 5A.

24. *Operation.*—Loads induced on landing or taxying are transferred to the sliding cylinder V through the wheel fork and link K, causing it to be thrust further into the outer cylinder Q. This action forces the oil in the outer cylinder through the diaphragm R, lifts the valve R1, and causes the floating piston T to compress the air in cylinder V still further until the movement has been damped. Subsequent reversal of the movement of the floating piston under the action of the increased air pressure causes the oil to close the valve R1 and flow back to the outer cylinder Q through restriction holes in the valve and the holes in the diaphragm, and the recoil movement is retarded. As the oil is returned, the inner cylinder V is forced outwards again until restrained by the screwed sleeve U.

25. The self-centring mechanism operates as follows:—When the wheel castors, the lower self-centring cam F is rotated due to the form of the contact face and causes the cam E1 to ride upwards against the spring C1. When the side load has been expanded, the energy conserved in the spring forces the two cams into full contact again and the lower cam F (and consequently the pivot bracket I) is rotated until the wheel is once more centralised.

Lockheed oleo-pneumatic type

26. *Construction.*—The Lockheed tail wheel unit (*see* fig. 6) comprises four main assemblies as follows, a plunger tube and piston, the cylinder tube assembly, the self-centring mechanism, and the wheel fork assembly.

(i) The plunger tube (1) slides in the cylinder tube (2) and the exposed end of the former carries an air head (3) which is fitted with a rubber seal (4) and an air valve assembly (5). The inner end of the plunger tube is equipped with a piston (6) which is retained in position by four dowels (7); the latter are surrounded by a retaining sleeve (8) and secured by a countersunk screw (9) screwed into one of the dowels. The piston has two rubber seals (10) in contact with the cylinder tube (2) and one rubber seal (11) in contact with the plunger tube. The piston is fitted with a spring (12) and a flutter plate (13), both components being retained in position by a piston cap (14) which is secured by a circlip (15). The piston cap has four holes equally spaced about a smaller hole in the centre and the flutter plate has one hole in the centre. Inside the plunger tube are a floating separator (16), with two rubber seals (17) which isolate the fluid from the air, and a distance ring (18) to limit the travel of the separator towards the bottom of the plunger tube.

(ii) The cylinder tube (2) carries a hinge fitting (19) at the lower end, which is secured in the tube by four dowels (20), the latter being surrounded by a bearing ring (21) which is positioned by a plug (22). The bore of the hinge fitting is fitted with a split Tufnol block (23) behind a rubber seal (24), the two being positioned by a retaining ring (25) secured by a circlip (26). The hinge fitting (19) is attached to the fork (27) by a bolt (28) and the fork is attached to the plunger tube by a bolt (29) which also secures the air head (3) in the plunger tube. The fork pivots on these two points and lubrication is provided for by grease nipples (30). Surrounding the lower end of the cylinder tube is an attachment bracket (31) fitted with two flanged bushes (32), the lower bush making contact with the bearing ring (21) and the upper bush abutting against a retaining ring (33) secured to the cylinder tube by four dowels (34). The dowels pass through the cylinder tube to lock a stop ring (35) which limits the travel of the piston and plunger tube in the downward direction; they are retained externally by a clip (36). Approximately midway in the bore of the cylinder tube is a fluid head (37), which is secured by two taper pins (38) and carries two fluid plugs (39) and a rubber seal (40).

(iii) The self-centring assembly is carried in the upper end of the cylinder tube and comprises a cam (41) which is secured in the tube by four dowels (42), the latter being surrounded by a clip (43). The bore of the cam is fitted with an oilite bush (44) which acts as a bearing for a top attachment (45), the cylinder tube and cam being free to rotate about the top attachment. Two slots are cut in the top attachment and the outer diameter carries a sleeve (46) which is positioned by a cam pin (47), the latter having a roller (48).   The roller is loaded on the cam by a spring (49), one end of which bears on the sleeve and the other on a spring retainer (50), the latter being secured inside the top attachment by a split taper pin (51).

(iv)   The wheel fork (27) carries an axle (52), which bears on the extensions of two towing spools (53), to which are welded two hooks (54), the whole being retained in position by two bolts (55).

27.   *Operation.*—Loads induced on landing or when taxying result in the plunger tube (1) together with the piston (6) being forced upwards so that fluid above the piston is displaced through the holes in the piston cap (14) and past the flutter plate (13), thereby forcing the separator (16) downwards and further compressing the air in the plunger tube.   When the loads are reduced or released, the compressed air in the plunger tube forces the separator upwards and the fluid above the separator drives the flutter plate on to the piston cap, thus restricting the flow of fluid through the holes in the piston cap.

28.   The self-centring mechanism operates as follows:—When the strut is deflected rotationally from the centre position, the cam (41), by contact with the roller (48), compresses the spring (49).   When the rotational load on the strut is removed the spring forces the roller down the face of the cam and returns the strut to the central position.

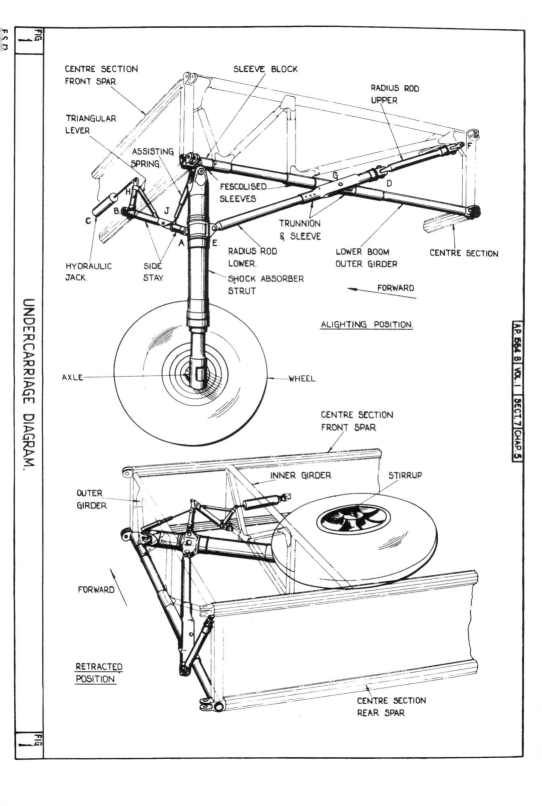

FIG 1

UNDERCARRIAGE DIAGRAM.

CENTRE SECTION
FRONT SPAR.

SLEEVE BLOCK

RADIUS ROD
UPPER

TRIANGULAR
LEVER

ASSISTING
SPRING.

FESCOLISED
SLEEVES

F

G

D

TRUNNION
& SLEEVE

H

B

J

C

A

E

RADIUS ROD
LOWER.

LOWER BOOM
OUTER GIRDER

CENTRE SECTION

HYDRAULIC
JACK.

SIDE
STAY

SHOCK ABSORBER
STRUT

FORWARD

ALIGHTING POSITION.

AXLE

WHEEL

CENTRE SECTION
FRONT SPAR

INNER GIRDER

STIRRUP

OUTER
GIRDER

FORWARD

RETRACTED
POSITION

CENTRE SECTION
REAR SPAR

FIG 1

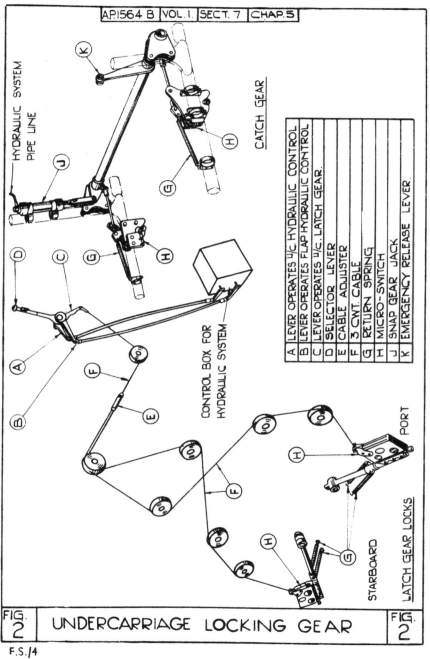

A	LEVER OPERATES U/C. HYDRAULIC CONTROL
B	LEVER OPERATES FLAP HYDRAULIC CONTROL
C	LEVER OPERATES U/C. LATCH GEAR.
D	SELECTOR LEVER
E	CABLE ADJUSTER
F	3 CWT. CABLE
G	RETURN SPRING
H	MICRO-SWITCH
J	SNAP GEAR JACK
K	EMERGENCY RELEASE LEVER.

HYDRAULIC SYSTEM
PIPE LINE

CATCH GEAR

CONTROL BOX FOR
HYDRAULIC SYSTEM

PORT

STARBOARD

LATCH GEAR LOCKS

FIG. 2	UNDERCARRIAGE LOCKING GEAR	FIG. 2

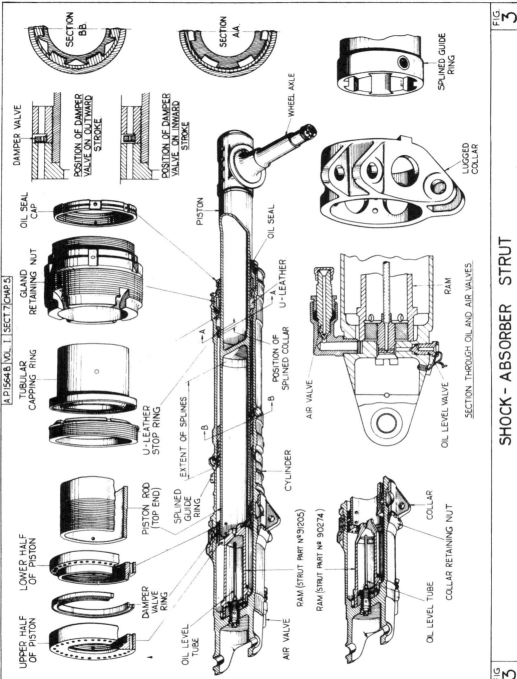

SECTION BB.

SECTION AA.

SPLINED GUIDE RING

DAMPER VALVE

POSITION OF DAMPER VALVE ON OUTWARD STROKE

POSITION OF DAMPER VALVE ON INWARD STROKE

WHEEL AXLE

OIL SEAL CAP

GLAND RETAINING NUT

TUBULAR CAPPING RING

U-LEATHER STOP RING

PISTON ROD (TOP END)

SPLINED GUIDE RING

LOWER HALF OF PISTON

UPPER HALF OF PISTON

DAMPER VALVE RING

OIL LEVEL TUBE

AIR VALVE

RAM (STRUT PART Nº 91205)

RAM (STRUT PART Nº 90274)

PISTON

OIL SEAL

U-LEATHER

POSITION OF SPLINED COLLAR

EXTENT OF SPLINES

CYLINDER

LUGGED COLLAR

RAM

AIR VALVE

OIL LEVEL VALVE

SECTION THROUGH OIL AND AIR VALVES

COLLAR

COLLAR RETAINING NUT

OIL LEVEL TUBE

SHOCK - ABSORBER STRUT

FIG. 3

FIG. 3

F S K

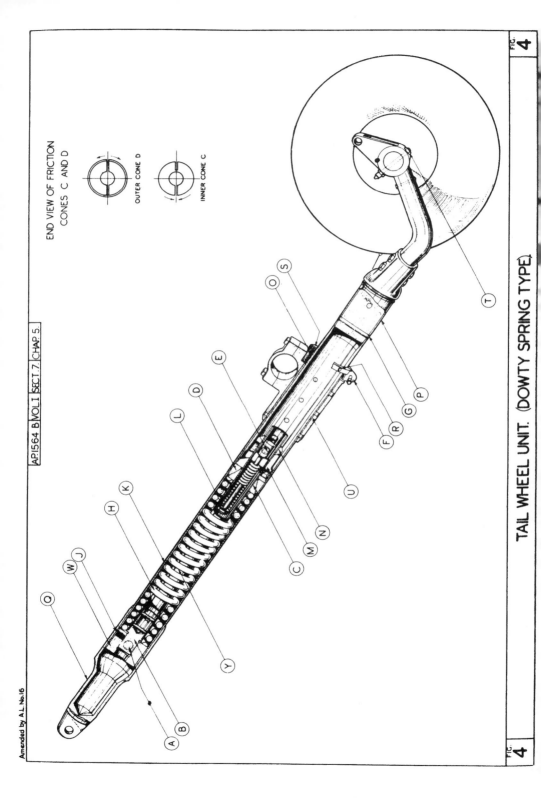

END VIEW OF FRICTION
CONES C AND D

OUTER CONE D

INNER CONE C

TAIL WHEEL UNIT. (DOWTY SPRING TYPE)

FIG. 4

FIG. 4

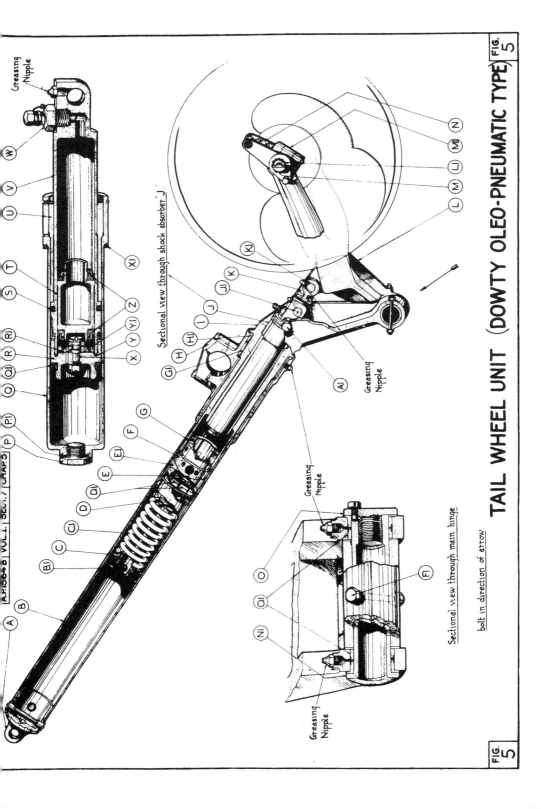

Greasing Nipple.

Sectional view through shock absorber 'J'.

Greasing Nipple

Greasing Nipple

Greasing Nipple

Sectional view through main hinge

bolt in direction of arrow.

TAIL WHEEL UNIT (DOWTY OLEO-PNEUMATIC TYPE)

FIG. 5

FIG. 5

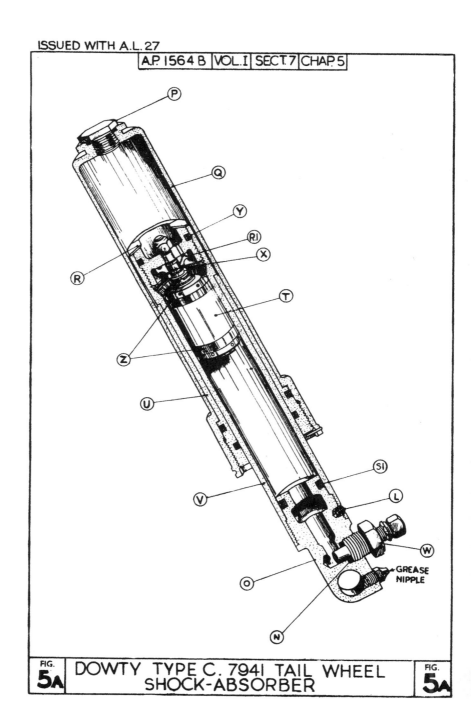

FIG. 5A — DOWTY TYPE C. 7941 TAIL WHEEL SHOCK-ABSORBER

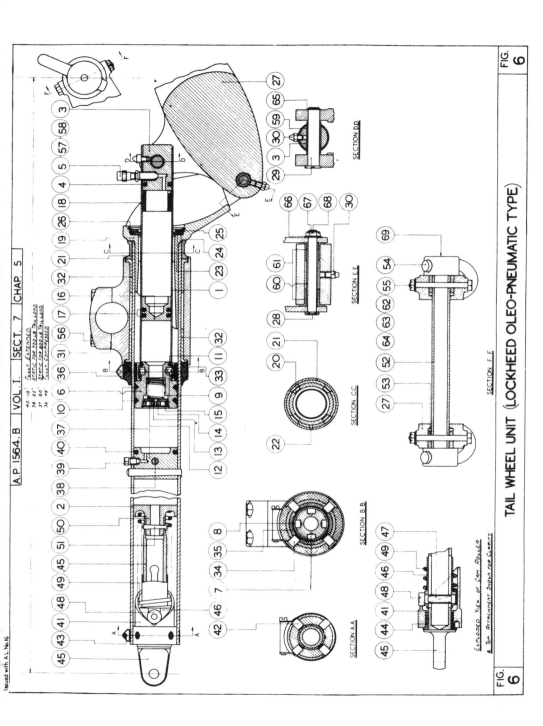

FULLY EXTENDED
STATIC FOR 700 LB. TAIL LOAD
STATIC FOR 800 LB. TAIL LOAD
FULLY COMPRESSED

SECTION D.D

SECTION E.E

SECTION C.C

SECTION F.F

SECTION B.B

SECTION A.A

EXPLODED VIEW of CAM ROLLER
& TOP ATTACHMENT SHOWN FOR CLARITY

TAIL WHEEL UNIT (LOCKHEED OLEO-PNEUMATIC TYPE)

FIG. 6

Section 8: Engine installation — Description.

SECTION 8

ENGINE INSTALLATION—DESCRIPTION

LIST OF CONTENTS

LIST OF ILLUSTRATIONS

SECTION 8

ENGINE INSTALLATION—DESCRIPTION

Engine

1. The aircraft is powered with a Merlin XX, two-speed supercharged, ethylene-glycol-cooled engine of the twelve cylinder 60 deg.V type; for full particulars of its construction and for methods of operation, *see* A.P.1590G, Vol. I. A variable pitch propeller is driven through reduction gearing and is provided with constant-speed control. Boost pressure is controlled automatically in relation to throttle position and altitude but the automatic control can be cut out under emergency conditions and maximum boost obtained. The carburation system normally employs an automatic mixture control but on some aeroplanes this is replaced by a mixture control lever in the cockpit. The throttle control lever is interconnected with the ignition advance and retard control, permitting progressive automatic advance in relation to the degree of throttle opening employed. Ejector-type exhaust manifolds are normally fitted, but are replaced on certain aeroplanes by the flame-damping type.

2. An air compressor is driven from the rear end of the starboard camshaft and an engine-speed indicator is driven from the rear end of the port camshaft. An electrical generator is mounted on the port side of the crankcase and an electric starting motor is mounted vertically on the right-hand lower side of the wheelcase. Hand starting gear, with an operating handle on each side of the engine, is incorporated with the gear train for the electric starting motor. Dual gear-type fuel pumps are driven in tandem from the left-hand side of the wheelcase. A hydraulic system pump is mounted at the base of the crankcase and a coolant pump is fitted at the bottom of the wheelcase. The suction for the suction-operated instruments on the instrument-flying panel is obtained from a vacuum pump mounted on the lower right side of the reduction gear casing, and the constant-speed unit for the airscrew control is mounted on the lower left side of the reduction gear casing. Gauges in the cockpit show engine speed, boost pressure, oil pressure and temperature, coolant temperature and fuel feed pressure; on later aircraft, a warning lamp is fitted in place of the fuel feed pressure gauge.

Fuel system

General

3. Fuel is normally drawn by the dual engine-driven pumps in approximately equal quantities from each main fuel tank in the centre section, a reserve tank being fitted in the fuselage immediately in front of the pilot's instrument panel; this latter tank also provides a supply for the engine priming pump. The supply from the main tanks or from the reserve tank is governed by a three-way cock remotely controlled from the cockpit; a fuel filter is fitted between the three-way cock and the engine. On later aircraft the pipes from the main and reserve tanks have self-sealing coverings. To prevent failure of the fuel supply at high altitudes, air pressure is applied to the tanks. One of four different types of long-range tanks may be fitted. The fuel system installation is shown in fig. 1 and a diagram of the system is given in fig. 2. The fixed long-range tank installation is shown in fig. 4.

4. *Main tanks.*—Each main fuel tank is of approximately rectangular form and has an actual capacity of 34½ gallons and an effective capacity of 33

gallons; it is constructed of sheet aluminium and is protected by Linatex self-sealing covering and fabric; four attachment feet are bolted to the tank shell. The top surface is strengthened by small swaged troughs which accommodate eight specially-housed Simmonds nuts for the attachment of the upper aerofoil surface, seven similar nuts being incorporated in the tank lower surface for the attachment of the lower aerofoil surface. Within the tank there are two longitudinal baffles and three transverse baffles, with two tunnels between the inboard and outboard sides for the passage of the centre-section inter-girder bracing tubes (*see* Sect. 7, Chap. 2).

5. The screwed filler cap, situated in the upper front outboard corner of the tank, is fitted with an internally-secured chain and is deeply slotted to facilitate its removal. Access to the filler cap is obtained through a door in the centre-section top covering and the door is attached internally to the door frame by a length of balloon cord. The outlet connection is situated in a recess in the inboard lower edge of the tank. Two handholes are provided for inspection of the interior of the tank, one in the outboard face towards the rear and one in the underside towards the front. A flush-type electric fuel contents gauge (*see* A.P.1275, Vol. I) is situated in a recess in the centre of the upper rear edge of the tank; on some aeroplanes, a calcium chromate inhibitor to prevent corrosion is fitted immediately below the gauge at the bottom of the tank.

6. Each main tank is housed between the centre-section inner and outer girders (*see* Sect. 7, Chap. 2) and is carried by four brackets, two on each girder upper boom. Each of these brackets has an internally-tapped spigot with a circular rubber pad to form a seating for the tank foot. A similar pad is fitted on the upper side of the tank foot; the pads are of such a thickness that the spigot does not project through the total thickness. The uppermost pad is held by a washer and a bolt inserted in the spigot; the bolt is screwed down as far as the end of the spigot to compress the pads.

7. *Reserve tank.*—The reserve fuel tank is of approximately semi-circular form and has a capacity of 28 gallons; it is constructed of sheet aluminium, and is protected by Linatex self-sealed covering and fabric. The tank is fitted internally with one longitudinal baffle, in the centre of which is a large approximately-rectangular flanged hole. A channel-section bearer, lightened with flanged holes, is fitted at each end across the bottom of the tank and four tank feet are bolted externally to these cross bearers. The front tank feet are mounted on fuselage cross strut AA and the rear feet on longerons AC, port and starboard. Each tank foot comprises upper and lower semi-circular portions hinged together, with the front feet at their front ends and the rear feet at their outboard ends. The ends of the tank feet which are remote from the hinges are bolted together and rubber blocks are interposed between the feet, and the tubes on which they are mounted. Baffles are fitted aft of and underneath the tank to afford protection to the pilot while leaving the aeroplane in the event of fire; they are attached to the rear face of the firewall and to the decking front former.

8. The screwed filler cap, situated in the top of the tank near the front end and slightly to starboard, is fitted with an internal retaining-chain and has a deep slot to facilitate removal. Access to the cap is obtained through the upper rear door in the top rear panel of the engine cowling; the door is attached internally to one of the fastener springs with a length of balloon cord. The sump, incorporating outlet and drain connections, is on the underside of the

tank. A priming pipe connection is situated in the rear face of the tank near the top and a flush-type electric fuel contents gauge (*see* A.P.1275, Vol. I) is situated in a pocket in the upper rear edge of the tank, slightly to starboard.

9. *Fuel contents gauge transmitters.*—The electric fuel contents gauge transmitter in each fuel tank is of the float and potentiometer type; a selector switch, in conjunction with a meter, both fitted on the starboard side of the instrument panel, enables the contents of any tank to be determined at will. A wiring diagram is given in Sect. 6.

10. *Pipe-lines.*—A two-way cock is fitted at each tank outlet connection, the cocks being normally locked in the "open" position, except in special circumstances, i.e. to remove a tank. The two main tanks are interconnected through a T-piece with a non-return valve on each side, the valves being fitted to prevent any flow from one tank to the other whatever the attitude of the aircraft. From the third arm of the T-piece a pipe is taken to the three-way fuel cock mounted on the port lower longeron just aft of joint B. The supply pipe from the reserve tank is joined to the opposite connection on the cock; the cock is remotely controlled by a handle, mounted on the port side of the fuselage in the angle between struts CF and CF.1. On later aircraft the four pipes connecting the main and reserve tanks to the main three-way cock are self-sealing. From the three-way cock a flexible pipe runs to the rear face of the centre-section front spar web, where it is coupled to the inlet connection of a filter mounted on the front face of the spar, the connection projecting through the spar web.

11. At the top of the filter is the outlet branch, which is connected by a flexible pipe to the inlet connection of the engine fuel pump; from the outlet connection of the pump, another flexible pipe runs to the carburettor. To reduce the risk of vapour locks, the fuel pump is cooled by air led through a duct which connects to an air scoop on the port leading-edge fillet.

12. From a banjo fitting at the priming connection on the reserve tank a supply pipe runs to the inlet connection of the manually-operated priming pump, which is mounted on a bracket on fuselage joint C, on the starboard side. The priming delivery pipe runs directly from the pump to the engine-priming connection, from which it is distributed by four pipes to the induction manifolds.

13. A fuel feed pressure gauge, mounted on the starboard side of the instrument panel in the cockpit, is connected by a capillary tube to the outlet side of the engine pump. On later aircraft a warning lamp, which is illuminated when the fuel feed pressure falls below a predetermined figure, is fitted in place of the pressure gauge. The pressure unit, which is mounted on the reducing valve on the engine and operates the lamp, is described in A.P.1275, Vol. I, and a wiring diagram is given in Sect. 6.

14. From a connection on the engine induction manifold a small diameter tube runs to a fuel trap mounted on the port side of the front face of the firewall, whence a similar tube continues to a boost pressure gauge on the starboard side of the instrument panel in the cockpit.

Long-range tanks installations

15. *General.*—Some aircraft are adapted to carry long-range tanks, of which there are four types—two fixed types, either non-operational or operational, and two jettisonable types of either 45 gallons or 90 gallons capacity. The two types of fixed tanks are similar; the operational types are Linatex-covered, gun firing is not interfered with, and the mountings are strengthened to permit combat manœuvres. Fuel from the fixed long-range tanks is delivered into the main tanks by means of an electrically-driven immersed fuel pump (*see*

A.P.1464B, Vol. I) in each long-range tank; the pumps are switched on to "top up" the main tanks, as required. Fuel from the jettisonable long-range tanks is forced out of the tanks direct to the engine pump by means of air pressure from the fuel tanks air pressure system (see para. 24). The fixed long-range tanks are also under pressure as a vent pipe from each tank is connected to the main tanks. There are no contents gauges for the long-range tanks.

16. *Fixed non-operational tanks.*—The tanks, which are of cylindrical shape with faired ends (*see* fig. 4), are made of light-alloy sheet with welded joints and have two circular baffles, one at each of the attachment straps. Towards the back of each tank is an electrically-driven, centrifugal, immersed pump (*see* A.P.1464B, Vol. I) with a delivery connection at the top, from which a pipe runs into the centre-section tank at a point about two-thirds up the outboard side. An overflow pipe, which also acts as a filler pipe, connects this point with the long-range tank just forward of the pump. The bottom of the pump is positioned by means of a locating clip inside the bottom of the tank and the electrical lead is connected opposite the supply pipe at the top, where the pump protrudes through the tank skin. Towards the front in the top skin of the tank is a plug, which is removed to form a vent when the tank is being filled. The tanks, when fitted, are each held by two straps against two brackets bolted to the front and rear lower spar booms below No. 2 gun in the gun bay, the brackets being braced by a stay. The brackets, stay and pipes are faired into the main plane by panels secured by washer-headed bolts.

17. The immersed pumps are controlled by switches on the port side of the cockpit (*see* Sect. 1); a wiring diagram is given in fig. 4. The tanks are under pressure (see para. 15).

18. *Fixed operational tanks.*—For the fixed operational long-range system, the same pipe system and tanks are used as for the non-operational system but the tanks are self-sealing and the vent plugs at the forward ends are replaced by cocks, the run of the pipes is different, the straps are modified, stronger stays are fitted, and the case and link chutes are extended down through the side fairings to permit the No. 2 ·303 in. guns, or the inboard 20mm. guns, to be fired. For the ·303 in. gun the case and link chute is extended through the outboard side fairing and for the 20 mm. gun the inboard and outboard fairings are modified to incorporate a case deflector and an extension to the link chute. There are also slight differences in the fairings and access doors and in the run of the pipes to the centre-section tank.

19. *Jettisonable tanks.*—The jettisonable tanks are of tinned steel and have a filler cap at the forward end. Each tank is strapped to a pair of mounting brackets. Rollers on the brackets fit into two hooks mounted on the underside of the outer planes with their open sides facing aft. When the tank is in position, the open side of the rear hook is closed by a pawl, which is pivoted on the rear hook bracket and connected by cable to the jettison lever in the cockpit. The pawl is held in the closed position by the spring-loaded latch attached to the rear mounting bracket. When the jettison lever is operated, the pawl rotates and forces the rear mounting out of engagement with the hook, assisted by the force of the airstream; the latch also disengages from the release-cable end of the pawl and the tank falls away, breaking the glass tubes (*see* para. 21) of the fuel delivery and air pressure pipes. The tank fairings, constructed of plywood on spruce stiffeners in the case of the side fairings and papier mâché in the case of the nose and tail fairings, are attached to the mounting brackets on the tank. Along the top edge of the fairings is a double-over strip of sponge rubber which seals the gap between the fairings and the undersurface of the plane when the

tank is in position. An extension for the case and link chute for the No. 2
·303 in. gun (or a deflector plate for the inboard 20 mm. gun) is attached to the
fairing. A streamer is fitted at the aft·end of each tank; these streamers
extend in the airstream behind the trailing edges of the planes, where they are
visible to the pilot until the tanks are jettisoned.

20. The tanks are of either 45 or 90 gallons capacity; the two systems
are similar except that, with the 90 gallon tanks, slightly different nose and tail
fairings are necessitated by the larger size of the tanks, and the tanks are bolted
direct to the mounting brackets; when the 90 gallon tanks are used an auxiliary
oil tank (*see* para. 31) is provided.

21. *Pipe-lines.*—The fuel from the jettisonable tanks is forced up into
the main system between the main fuel cock and the filter (*see* fig. 2) by air
pressure from the exhaust of the vacuum pump, a tapping being taken from the
system supplying internal pressure to the main fuel tanks (*see* para. 24). The
air pressure control valve (*see* para. 26) vents to atmosphere at altitudes below
20,000 ft. but the fluid resistance of the long vent pipe generates a pressure of
about 1 lb./sq. in. which is sufficient to force fuel up to the filter. Both the
air pressure and the fuel delivery pipes are connected to the tank by rubber
tubes and L-shaped glass tubes; when the tank starts to fall away the glass
tubes break and free the tank. The fuel is drawn from a small compartment
formed by two baffles across the bottom of the tank. The pipes from each
tank join at a three-way cock under the cockpit and a connection is taken from
this cock to the main system, between the main fuel cock and the filter.

22. *Jettisonable tanks control cock.*—The 3-way cock in the jettisonable
system is remotely controlled from a fuel and jettison control box mounted on the
starboard side strut CF, just below the flare release control (if fitted) and windscreen de-icing pump, which have been re-positioned to accommodate the control
box. The fuel cock control consists of a Teleflex control box (*see* A.P.1464B, Vol. I)
operated by a handwheel attached to it by means of a spindle incorporating a
spring-loaded plunger; the plunger can engage with one of three holes in a
mounting plate fitted beneath it to provide positive PORT, STARBOARD
and OFF positions. From the remote control box a Teleflex conduit runs
down strut CF and across the centre-section to another control box, mounted
on the rear wall of the wheel housing and connected to the 3-way cock.

23. *Jettisoning lever.*—The jettisoning lever is mounted in a gated slot
on the side of the fuel and jettison control box and is connected by cables running
along the rear spar, port and starboard, to the release pawls on the tank rear
hooks. When the fuel control handwheel is in either of the "on" positions,
the jettison-lever gate is obstructed by a spring-loaded trigger, but when the
handwheel is turned to OFF a projection on the handwheel spindle engages
the trigger and moves it away from the gate. To prevent air being vented to
atmosphere when the tanks are jettisoned, a cock in the air pipe-line to the tanks
is interconnected with the jettison lever and is automatically shut when the
lever is moved to the JETTISON position. If the jettisonable tanks are not
fitted, the jettison lever is locked in the JETTISON position by removing the
forward fixing screw for the gate and replacing it in the inboard fixing hole
provided, thus clamping the lever in position.

Fuel tanks air pressure system

24. *General.*—The reduction in density of the atmosphere at high altitudes
results in partial breakdown of the fuel supply to the suction side of the fuel
pump, due to expansion of air which has been trapped in the fuel. To obviate

fuel starvation from this cause, air pressure is applied to the tanks at an altitude of 20,000 ft. and is increased thereafter in proportion to further increase in altitude. Pressure is derived from the exhaust side of the vacuum pump, and controlled by a pressure control valve (*see* para. 26) mounted aft of the pilot's seat on the port side of the fuselage.

25. The exhaust from the vacuum pump is connected from the air outlet on the oil separator to the pressure control valve (*see* para. 26). The control valve starts to close at about 20,000 ft. and the pressure built up is applied to the tanks through a pipe leading from the pressure side of the control valve to a 4-way union under the reserve fuel tank, from which connections are made to the top of the main and reserve fuel tanks. Pressure can be released to atmosphere, if required, by a release cock fitted on the port side of the cockpit, in a pipe-line which is tapped into the pipe to the pressure control valve and which leads direct to atmosphere, aft of the radiator.

26. *Pressure control valve.*—The pressure control valve (*see* fig. 3) consists of a disc valve controlled by an aneroid capsule. The aneroid capsule G is enclosed in the top chamber of the valve housing H and the top chamber is connected to atmosphere through the small top connection M, from which a vent pipe leads to the vicinity of the radiator. The top chamber is sealed off from the lower chamber by the plate C, which is held in position by the spring A. An operating rod B connects the capsule to the disc valve D. At about 20,000 ft. the reduced atmospheric pressure causes the capsule to extend and the valve D begins to close until, at a height of 35,000 ft., a pressure of about $2\frac{1}{2}$ lb./sq. in. is built up in the system; in fig. 3 the valve is shown in the closed position. At altitudes below 20,000 ft., the valve opens fully and air escapes to atmosphere through the large outlet connection, and a second vent pipe to the rear of the radiator.

27. In order that excessive pressure is not built up, a safety valve L, controlled by a spring F, is fitted within the control valve (*see* fig. 3); the relief pressure is 5 lb./sq. in. The valve is in the form of a flanged cup, the flange forming the valve seat while the cup accommodates a piston K which forms a damping device for both the main valve and safety valve. Under certain conditions (for example, if the vacuum pump fails at a high altitude with the main valve on its seat) a partial vacuum would be formed in the system as the fuel level dropped; to overcome this, a series of holes drilled in the flange of the valve L are covered by a ring seating E, normally held in the closed position by the pressure of air on the seating. If a vacuum tends to form in the tank, the ring lifts and allows air to be drawn into the system.

Oil system

General

28. The lubrication system of the engine is of the conventional dry sump type, necessitating the use of an external oil tank, the engine pumps maintaining oil in constant circulation from the tank, through the engine, through the cooler and back to the tank; a viscosity valve and an oil filter are included in the circuit (*see* figs. 5 and 6). The oil tank forms part of the port leading edge of the centre section (*see* Sect. 7, Chap. 2) and is attached to the front spar by means of two pairs of feet on the upper and lower rear edges of the tank; insulation against vibration is similar to that used for the main fuel tanks in the centre section (*see* para. 6). At the top and bottom the tank skin projects rearwards beyond the rear tank wall; the upper edge meets the forward edge

of the outer cover over the port main fuel tank and is screwed to the cover, whilst the lower edge engages with a fairing strip beneath the spar. The flanges of the inner and outer end walls of the tank project sufficiently beyond the tank skin to provide seatings for the leading edge fillet and the gap fairing between the centre section and the port outer plane. On certain aeroplanes the front of the tank is self-sealing.

29. *Main oil tank.*—The tank has an actual capacity of 10½ gallons and an effective capacity of 9 gallons (*see* para 31) and is constructed of light-alloy sheet to the profile of the centre-section leading edge at its point of attachment. Two baffles are fitted within the tank parallel to the centre line of the aeroplane. The outboard baffle has seven flanged holes, approximately evenly spaced; the inboard baffle has two oval-shaped holes, placed approximately one-third of the depth of the tank from the top, and is drilled along the bottom edge with thirteen holes of small diameter. The enclosed portion between the inboard baffle and the inboard end of the tank acts, when necessary, as a partial-circulation chamber for quick warming of the oil and is of approximately 1¾ gallons capacity.

30. The filler cap is situated in the leading edge profile of the tank towards the outer end, and is fitted with a short length of chain attached to a screw securing the filler seating in position. The cap is deeply slotted to facilitate its removal. The oil inlet and outlet connections are situated in the inboard wall of the tank, the former at the top; internally, the inlet connection is extended forward by a short tube with a flared end and the outlet connection is continued by a plain tube pointing downwards. The oil inlet connection is incorporated in a circular plate, which may be removed for cleaning and inspection of the interior of the tank; for the same purpose, a circular hand-hole is provided in the outboard wall. The vent pipe connection is near the top of the rear wall, about half-way along the length of the tank and below it, in the bottom rear edge of the tank, a drain connection incorporating a screw valve is fitted.

31. *Auxiliary oil tank.*—The auxiliary oil tank is only fitted when the 90 gallon jettisonable fuel tanks are installed; it has a capacity of 4 gallons and is mounted in the decking behind the pilot's seat. When the tank is used, the main oil tank (see para. 29) is filled with 8 gallons of oil.

32. *Oil cooler—early type.*—The oil cooler on early aeroplanes is of cylindrical form and is housed in the centre of the coolant radiator. The matrix casing and baffles are constructed of sheet brass and the tubes are of copper. The matrix area is divided into four parts by three vertical flow plates, one of which is centrally disposed. The matrix casing has three inlet ports on the starboard side and three outlet ports on the port side. The central flow plate has two ports at its rear end, while the remaining two flow plates have two ports each at their front ends. An extension plate on each side of the cooler extends forward to enable four fixing bolts to pick up the front of the radiator and, towards the rear, three pads, equally spaced, provide bearing surfaces for the cooler inside the coolant radiator.

33. The oil inlet and outlet connections are mounted at the top rear end of the cooler, the inlet branch connecting with the starboard, and the outlet branch with the port, side. The oil flows into the cooler casing, through the inlet ports in the matrix casing, between the cooling tubes to the forward end, and through the ports of the flow plates back to the rear end of the cooler. Through the ports in the centre flow plate it passes forward and then rearwards to the outlet connection. A drain plug is situated at the bottom rear end of of the cooler.

34.   *Oil cooler—later type.*—The oil cooler on later aeroplanes is also housed within the centre of the coolant radiator and consists of a cylindrical casing of sheet brass; brazed to it, at the rear end, is an eccentric duct, under which are situated the inlet and outlet ports to the cooler matrix.   Three branch con-nections are brazed to the outside of the duct and three baffles to the inside, two of which isolate the by-pass, while the third baffle separates the inlet portion of the duct from the outlet portion; in the outlet portion a drain connection is fitted at the lowest point of the cooler.   Two flow plates and a central by-pass baffle divide the matrix into four compartments or flows, suitable ports being provided at the front end of the flow plates and the rear end of the by-pass baffle for inter-communication.   Each compartment houses a bank of round tubes, the ends of which are expanded to a hexagon shape, of larger size than the diameter of the tube, to form a honeycomb; oil flows along the outside of the tubes in the space between them from the inlet or starboard branch, travers-ing each flow along its length, to the outlet or port branch (*see* fig. 5).

35.   The central by-pass baffle consists of two plates held apart by distance pieces and brazed together at the front and rear edges.   To divide the chamber thus formed into two connected compartments a baffle is provided approx-imately one-third of the way along from the front.   On each side of the two plates, at the top, are two passages, one in direct communication with the by-pass connection and the other with the outlet connection.   Intercommunication is effected by a series of holes along the top front portion of the baffle side plate, next to the by-pass inlet passage, and by a series of holes in the rear part of the side plate to the by-pass outlet passage.   When the viscosity valve diverts the oil to the by-pass pipe-line it flows from the centre branch on the cooler into the by-pass inlet passage and along this to the front of the cooler, thence through the holes, down the forward lower compartment of the central by-pass, under the baffle, up the rear after compartment to the communicating holes of the by-pass outlet passage, and out through the outlet branch (*see* fig. 5).

36.   The cooler is fitted in the centre of the coolant radiator and is connected to the radiator by means of four bolts, two through each of two forward ex-tension pieces attached to the cooler casing; at the rear it is held against move-ment by three bearing pads sweated to the cooler casing.

37.   *Oil filter.*—The filter (*see* fig. 7) is mounted on the front face and to the starboard side of the firewall.   The cylindrical filter body has an upper branch for the inlet, and a lower branch for the outlet, connection, a drain plug being incorporated at its lower end; two locating shoulders are provided to receive the securing cap.   A gauze-covered filter element is held within the body by a retaining spring, a sealing cap, and a securing cap fitted with an adjusting screw.

38.   *Pipe-lines.*—The oil system installation is shown in fig. 5 and a diagram of the system is given in fig. 6.   From the outlet connection on the inboard wall of the tank a pipe is taken through a gland in a small bulkhead fitted in the port leading edge fillet to the upper inlet connection of the oil filter, mounted on the front face of the firewall on the starboard side; from the lower connection on the filter a flexible pipe runs to the inlet connection of the engine suction pump.   From the engine scavenge pump connection a small flexible pipe con-nects with a pipe leading to a double-ended union fitted in the firewall, on the port side just above the centre-section spar.   From the rear face of the firewall a pipe is taken along the port side of the fuselage to the viscosity valve mounted on fuselage strut FH.1.

39. With the early type of oil cooler, when the oil is cold and viscous the viscosity valve (*see* A.P.1464B, Vol. I) by-passes the oil from the engine back to the oil tank. When the oil has warmed up, the valve causes oil to flow through the cooler and then back through the viscosity valve to the oil tank. From the viscosity valve, the oil is returned to the oil tank through two lengths of pipe joined together by a union fitted in the firewall.

40. With the later type of cooler, the connection previously used for the pipe to the oil tank is blanked off and oil by-passed by the viscosity valve flows through the by-pass circuit of the cooler (*see* fig. 5); when the oil has warmed up it is diverted to the normal circuit of the cooler. The oil is returned from the cooler to the tank by three lengths of pipe, joined together at a point adjacent to the rear spar, and by a union in the firewall.

41. From the vent connection in the upper edge of the oil tank a vent pipe is taken to the double-acting valve (*see* para. 45) and thence to a T-piece, one branch of which is connected to the engine breather, and the other to the oil separator on the vaccum pump installation (*see* Sect. 9). The oil pressure gauge on the starboard side of the instrument panel is joined by a capillary tube to a banjo fitting on the engine, and a similar tube connects the thermometer bottle on the engine with the oil temperature gauge, situated on the instrument panel beneath the oil pressure gauge.

42. The auxiliary oil tank (*see* para. 31) for the 90 gallon jettisonable tanks installation, is connected to the main oil tank by a pipe (*see* fig. 6) in which a pilot-controlled cock is fitted. To keep the auxiliary oil warm during flight and to ensure that a pressure greater than that in the main oil tank is built up in the auxiliary tank, a small-bore pipe is connected from the bottom of the auxiliary tank to the main delivery pipe to the oil cooler. Before the cock in the main pipe is opened, oil displaced from the auxiliary tank by the warm oil from the main delivery pipe escapes through a stack pipe extending up to the filler neck and into the main pipe on the main oil tank side of the cock. When the cock is opened, after sufficient oil has been consumed from the main tank, the auxiliary oil gradually flows into the main tank.

43. *Auxiliary oil tank cock control.*—The control handle for the cock is mounted on a bracket above the radiator flap control quadrant. It incorporates a ratchet mechanism that allows the cock to be turned "on" but not to be turned "off" subsequently during flight; four gallons of oil from the main system would gradually be transferred back to the auxiliary tank if the cock were turned off during flight after the tank had drained.

Oil tank pressure system

44. *General.*—The reduction in density of the atmosphere at high altitudes results in partial breakdown of the oil supply to the suction side of the oil pump, due to expansion of air which has been trapped in the oil. To obviate oil starvation from this cause, an air pressure of approximately 4 lb./sq. in. is maintained in the oil tank under all conditions of flight, by means of a pressure control valve (*see* para. 45).

45. *Pressure control valve.*—The double-acting valve which controls pressure in the oil tank (*see* para. 44) is fitted in the pipe-line from the oil tank to the engine breather and vacuum pump oil separator and is situated forward

of the firewall on the starboard side. The unit has (*see* fig. 8) two spring-loaded valves, assembled within a circular body consisting of two halves screwed together. The valve B is normally held in its seat by the spring A and, as air is thus prevented from venting from the tank, pressure is built up as the oil level rises in the tank; the valve B lifts to release air from the tank if the pressure exceeds 4 lb./sq. in. To prevent a partial vacuum in the tank under certain conditions, the valve C opens against the action of spring D.

Oil dilution system

46. On some aircraft a dilution system is fitted to enable the viscosity of the oil to be reduced by the introduction of a small quantity of fuel, thus facilitating starting of the engine under the coldest weather conditions. The system is described in A.P.1464B, Vol. I and instructions for its use are given in Sect. 4, Chap. 2 and in A.P.2095; a wiring diagram is given in Sect. 6.

47. The oil dilution valve is operated electrically by a push-button in the cockpit and is mounted on the front face of the firewall (*see* fig. 5). Two pipes are connected to it (*see* fig. 6); one pipe connects the valve to the engine fuel pump and the other connects the valve to the feed pipe from the oil tank to the filter.

Cooling system
General

48. The engine is cooled with a mixture of 70% distilled water and 30% ethylene glycol D.T.D.344A (Stores Ref. 33C/559) and the whole cooling system (*see* fig. 9) is sealed so that the vapour generated by heating the coolant exerts pressure on the coolant, thus raising its boiling point and therefore its capacity for absorbing heat from the engine. The coolant is circulated by means of a pump driven from the base of the engine wheelcase. From the engine, the coolant is passed through two outlets to the header tank, mounted on the front face of the firewall; a thermostatic or spring-loaded relief valve (*see* A.P.1464B, Vol. I) is fitted in the tank to control the pressure on the system. From the tank the coolant passes to the radiator, which is situated under the fuselage, and then forward to the single inlet connection on the engine pump. A thermostat is incorporated in the system to by-pass the radiator when the coolant·temperature is low. The quantity of air passing through the radiator is controlled from the cockpit by a flap fitted to the radiator fairing.

49. *Header tank.*—The header tank is constructed of sheet brass; it is carried on two brackets on the front face of the firewall and is secured by a single bolt through each of the four tank feet. Rubber packings are interposed between the tank feet and the brackets and between the brackets and the bolt heads, to provide insulation against vibration. On the top transverse cowl rail a sheet of armour plating is attached, to protect the tank.

50. Two vertical baffles, running fore and aft, divide the tank so that approximately one quarter of its capacity is outboard of each; the baffles extend nearly to the top of the tank and are provided with nine flanged holes. The coolant from the engine passes through inlet pipes, riveted through flanged spools into the lower front face of the tank; the conical sump is bolted into the bottom surface of the tank and provides the outlet connection. The pipes forming the inlet connection are continued internally to the centre of the tank where they turn upwards; near the top they bend outwards and change to a rectangular section, the upper side being riveted to the top skin of the tank.

A slightly smaller pipe is brazed into each inlet pipe where it turns upwards, these pipes projecting downwards into the top of the tank sump.

51. Six tie-rods are fitted through the tank between the front and rear faces. At the top on the centre line is a small steam dome and in line with this on the front face of the tank is mounted the thermostatic or spring-loaded relief valve; a pipe from the relief valve connection runs into the steam dome. A splash plate bent to a triangular shape is riveted at its two ends to the top of the tank, immediately underneath the dome.

52. The capacity of the tank is four gallons, but only half this quantity of coolant is carried. When the coolant is cold it flows through the smaller tubes on the inlet pipes to the sump and through the outlet connection, thus mixing with the minimum quantity of low-temperature coolant and ensuring rapid warming-up of the engine. If the expansion of the coolant causes the internal pressure to exceed atmospheric by more than $2\frac{1}{4}$ lb./sq. in. during warming-up, the relief valve (*see* A.P.1464B, Vol. I) will open and relieve this pressure. Under cruising conditions the direction of flow is the same as during warming-up and the relief valve maintains the pressure at the saturated steam pressure appropriate to the temperature of the coolant; if, owing to the presence of air or incondensable gas in the system, the pressure in the tank exceeds the saturated steam pressure by more than $3\frac{1}{4}$ lb.sq.'in., the relief valve will open and purge the system of the incondensable gas. Under high-power conditions, the rate of flow is increased and a certain amount of steam is generated; in consequence the steam and some of the coolant surges up to the top of the vertical pipes. The steam rises to the top of the tank and the coolant is sprayed over the baffles into the lower-temperature coolant on their outboard sides. The steam is condensed in the steam dome, but, if the pressure in the tank exceeds approximately 30 lb./sq. in. above the atmospheric pressure corresponding to the height of the aircraft, the relief valve will open. During cooling-off, should the pressure in the tank be reduced below $-2\frac{1}{4}$ lb./sq. in., the relief valve will open to admit air and prevent collapse of the tank. The splash plate minimises the possibility of coolant being swirled into the steam dome.

53. On later aircraft, a re-designed type of relief valve is fitted, in which the warming-up and purge pressures have been raised to between 8 and $10\frac{1}{2}$ lb./sq. in. and between 8 and $12\frac{1}{4}$ lb./sq. in. respectively, to prevent local boiling of the coolant and also to ensure a pressure at the pump inlet.

54. The filler neck, fitted with a screwed filler cap and retaining chain, is situated in the starboard side of the tank; access to the filler cap is obtained through the forward and lower of the two doors in the top rear cowling panel on the starboard side. A vent pipe, connected to the relief valve on the front face of the tank, is taken down inside the engine cowling on the starboard side to vent directly to the atmosphere through a rubber connection in the top front corner of the starboard intermediate side panel of the engine cowling. In the front face of the tank, between the inlet pipes, a connection for a thermometer bulb is riveted to the tank, a capillary tube being taken from the bulb to the gauge on the starboard side of the instrument panel.

55. *Thermostat.*—The thermostat (*see* A.P.1464B, Vol. I) serves to decrease the time taken in warming-up the engine by returning the coolant through the by-pass directly back to the engine, until such time as the coolant has reached a temperature necessitating the use of the radiator; it also prevents

cavitation in the engine pump, which would result from increased flow resistance in the radiator at low temperatures.

56. *Radiator.*—The combined coolant radiator and oil cooler (*see* fig. 9) is suspended beneath the fuselage just aft of the centre-section rear spar; at the front it is bolted to brackets on the rear face of the rear-spar lower boom and at the rear to brackets on the radiator support tubes, which are fitted between fuselage joints H and the lower boom of the centre-section rear spar. To protect the radiator from excessive vibration, thick rubber liners are inserted in the attachment bolt housings; the housings are bolted to the attachment brackets, which are riveted to the radiator at each end of each outboard side. The oil cooler is mounted through the centre of the radiator and is secured by four bolts at the front and supported on three pads at the rear.

57. The coolant enters, under pressure from the engine pump, through a cone-shaped branch on the top starboard side and passes through the honeycomb in this half of the radiator to the bottom, whence it passes across to the other half of the honeycomb and up through the tubes to the outlet branch. A drain plug is fitted in the rear undersurface, on the centre line of the radiator.

58. *Radiator flap control.*—The radiator is enclosed in a tunnel-type fairing beneath the fuselage, the quantity of air passing through the radiator being controlled by a flap, hinged along its front edge, which forms the rear part of the fairing undersurface. The flap is operated by two rods (*see* fig. 10), the upper ends of which are adjustable and attached to levers mounted on each end of the countershaft. The countershaft is supported at each end by a bearing, just inboard of the levers, secured to the lower longeron FH, port and starboard; at its port end, the countershaft carries another lever, the upper end of which is connected by a tube of fixed length to the lower end of the control lever mounted in the cockpit. The control lever is mounted on the port side of the pilot's seat, between quadrant plates bracketed to fuselage cross strut FC.FC and is supported by a stay tube from port joint F.

59. The control lever may be set in any one of five positions by depressing a knob at the top of the lever (on tropical Hurricanes the range of movement from the normal position is increased and a different stop is fitted on the control quadrant to allow seven positions to be used), moving the lever to the required position, and then releasing the knob; the knob is spring-loaded internally and operates a catch pin engaging with the notches in the quadrant plates. Movement of the lever to the two extreme positions sets the flaps either fully "down" or "up", respectively; in the "up" or "normal" position the flap follows the line of the radiator fairing and a stop is fitted on the control lever quadrant to prevent movement of the flap beyond this position.

60. On early aeroplanes, just inboard of the port bearing, the countershaft carries a small lever, the upper end of which is connected through a bowden cable with a flap-position indicator mounted on port strut CF1.

61. *Pipe-lines.*—The outlet pipe from the header-tank sump (*see* fig. 9) runs to the starboard side and then down almost to the bottom of the firewall, where it is joined to another length of pipe which passes rearwards through a gland in the firewall; the pipe continues along the starboard side of the fuselage beneath the plane-to-fuselage fairing fillet and is clipped to fuselage side strut CF. Just aft of joint F the pipe is joined to another short length of pipe, the aft end of which is coupled to the thermostat bracketed to fuselage side strut FC.H. Two pipes run from the thermostat, one continuing rearward and then

forward to the starboard inlet branch to the radiator and the other passing across the fuselage to the return pipe from the radiator. The former pipe is in two parts coupled together at the rear extremity of the run and is clipped to fuselage cross strut HH between the coupling and the radiator, whilst the latter pipe is coupled to a T-joint in the return pipe from the radiator.

62. From the port branch connection on the radiator the return pipe-line is taken along the centre line of the aeroplane, through a gland in the web of the centre-section rear spar, to a clip on fuselage cross strut DD and then to port through a gland in the web of the centre-section front spar. A separate length of pipe is used between the spars and through the front spar, the joints in the pipe-line being adjacent to each spar; a vent plug is fitted between the clip on fuselage cross strut DD and the front joint. From the joint just in front of the centre-section front spar a short length of pipe connects directly with the centrifugal pump on the engine. After the coolant has been pumped round the engine it is returned through two parallel pipes, which are connected to branches on the front face of the header tank by rubber hose and jubilee clips. All pipe connections in the cooling system, except the inlet connections to the header tank, are of non-rigid type.

Ignition system

63. The diagram of the ignition system (*see* fig. 11) shows the connections between the main magnetos, the starting magneto, and the control switches; for operation of the system and the connections between the magnetos and the distributors, reference should be made to A.P.1590G, Vol. I. The starting magneto is mounted on the starboard engine mounting strut XZ. On later aeroplanes the starting magneto is replaced by a booster coil mounted on strut YZ (*see* also Sect. 10); a wiring diagram for the ignition system with booster coil is given in Sect. 6.

Engine controls

64. *Throttle and mixture controls.*—These engine controls are mounted on the port top longeron CE, close to the pilot's left hand. The longer (inboard) lever is the throttle control and the shorter (where fitted) is the mixture control; the levers are moved forward to open the throttle and to weaken the mixture. The knob on the mixture control lever projects in the way of the throttle control lever to ensure that the mixture control is pulled back to RICH on closing the throttle, thus preventing the mixture from being excessively weakened at small throttle openings. On some aeroplanes, the mixture is automatically set at all throttle openings for the best possible consumption and a mixture control lever is not provided.

65. In those aeroplanes having a mixture control lever, throttle and mixture levers are mounted outboard of the longeron on concentric spindles and are retained in any required position by tightening a series of friction discs mounted on the outer spindle. The spindles project inboard below the longeron, the inner being fitted with a knurled cap, whilst the outer carries a small wheel just behind the knurled cap. By turning the knurled cap the friction on the mixture control lever may be adjusted, the wheel providing a similar adjustment for the throttle control lever.

66. Below the spindles a small box contains a micro-switch unit for the undercarriage warning buzzer, the switch being operated by a cam plate pivoting

about a pin at the lower rear corner of the box; this cam plate is actuated by a roller mounted on the bolt attaching the throttle control rod fork-end to the throttle lever.

67. The two control levers project upward through a plate mounted on the decking shelf; adjustable stops are fitted at the forward ends in the path of travel of the levers. Pinned to the lower end of each control lever is a fork-end, into which is screwed the end of a flexible push-pull member operating in a conduit; the conduit runs forward and downwards along the port side of the fuselage structure, passes through a gland in the firewall, and is anchored to a bracket on the front face of the firewall. A rod, attached to the flexible member, emerges from the conduit at its anchorage and is connected to its appropriate lever on the engine by means of a fork-end and pin.

68. *Automatic boost control cut-out.*—Automatic boost control is provided to maintain a constant boost pressure without continual manipulation of the throttle lever by the pilot. In conditions of emergency, the boost control cut-out may be used to render the automatic boost control inoperative, thus enabling full boost to be obtained at any altitude; the cut-out control is located on the port side of the instrument panel. A boost pressure gauge, connected with the induction manifold, is mounted on the starboard side of the instrument panel.

69. *Supercharger two-speed control.*—The supercharger two-speed gear is controlled from the cockpit through a Teleflex cable. A sliding fork is attached at one end to the lever on the engine and its other end is connected to the Teleflex cable by a swivel coupling, which is clamped to the side of the engine. The cable passes through the firewall in the region of port joint A and runs to a cockpit control mounted on joint C.

70. *Slow-running cut-out control.*—The control to stop the engine when it is ticking over consists of a bowden cable connected to the cut-out control lever on the carburettor; the cable runs through the firewall, is clipped to starboard strut AD, and connects to the pilot's control mounted on a bracket which picks up with the hydraulic selector gear bracket on strut CF.

71. *Propeller control.*—The constant-speed propeller control is mounted on the port side of the decking just above the throttle control. The control consists of a housing A (*see* Sect. 4, Chap. 3, fig. 15) provided with a central boss and three mounting lugs, the larger of which is drilled and split to provide an inlet for the control cable and its conduit; the conduit is locked in position by means of a split pin and a locking screw.

71A. A gear plate M, provided with two sets of teeth, is a sliding fit on the boss in the housing. The castle teeth C on the upper face of this plate engage corresponding teeth B attached to the control lever D. The other teeth round the circumference of the gear plate engage with the helix winding on the control cable. A hexagonal nut K screws on to the threaded boss of the gear plate, thereby clamping the castle teeth on the gear plate and control lever together.

71B. A spindle L, screwed only on the upper part, passes through the whole assembly and is prevented from turning by two plates on its head which fit into a groove on the bottom of the housing. A knurled damper wheel E, a keyed washer H and a spring washer G are fitted on to this spindle, the washer and spring washer being placed between the boss on the gear plate and the knurled damper wheel, which is prevented from being screwed off the spindle by a locking

D ring F. A circular plate J is placed over the control unit and picks up with the mounting bolts passing through the lugs on the housing. Two adjustable stops are provided in this plate and operational instructions are inscribed on it.

71C.   The teleflex conduit and cable are used between the control in the cockpit and the control box, which is fitted to the governor unit on the starboard bottom side of the reduction gear casing of the engine. From the cockpit control the conduit runs forward and downwards through a gland in the firewall and along the port top longeron of the engine mounting, to the front of the engine.

Hand starting equipment

72.   Two starting handles are stowed in the wheel recess beneath the centre-section (*see* Sect. 7, Chap. 1), one on each side wall.   In use, the handles are engaged with the ends of a countershaft carried in brackets on the engine mounting struts XZ.   A sprocket at the starboard end of the countershaft is connected, by means of a chain, with a sprocket on the inboard end of a small countershaft mounted on the starboard engine mounting strut XY.   The outboard end of this latter countershaft carries a double sprocket connected to the starter sprocket on the engine, and in early aircraft, to the starting magneto.

73.   Later aircraft are fitted with a booster coil in place of a starting magneto and only a single sprocket is carried on the outboard end of the small

countershaft. The sprocket is connected by a chain to the starter-sprocket on the engine.

Electric starting equipment

74. A wiring diagram for the electric starting system is given in Sect. 6; the power for the system is supplied by the aeroplane accumulator only when an external supply is not available. The external supply plug is connected with a socket in the aeroplane in which is combined an isolating switch for automatically cutting out the aeroplane accumulator; the cover over the socket must be rotated before the plug can be inserted, the rotation operating a switch which isolates the negative pole of the aeroplane accumulator. The combined socket and isolating switch is situated on the starboard lower strut of the engine mounting and is accessible through a door in the engine cowling; a hook is provided on the door for the attachment of the lanyard of the ground cable. When the power supply has been connected the engine may be turned by depressing a press-button switch, situated on the port side of the instrument panel; this switch operates a relay switch, mounted adjacent to the external supply socket, which in turn operates an electric starting motor mounted on the starboard side of the engine wheel case. Later aeroplanes are fitted with a booster coil in place of the starting magneto (*see* para. 72 and Sect. 10).

Oil drain collector

75. Used oil from the fuel pump, hydraulic pump, and supercharger is conducted by pipes to a small reservoir which has both a vent pipe and a drain pipe leading through the bottom of the engine cowling (*see* fig. 12). The drain pipe is fitted with a cock so that the reservoir may be emptied when the aeroplane is on the ground. Used oil from the engine breather is led to the tail end of the fuselage or, on certain later aeroplanes, to the trailing edge of the main plane at the gap fairing between the centre section and starboard outer plane.

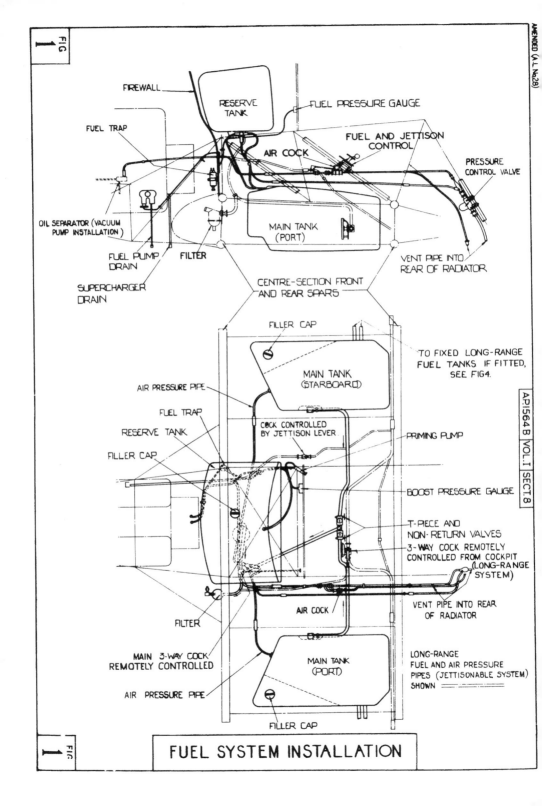

FIG 1

FIREWALL

FUEL TRAP

RESERVE TANK

FUEL PRESSURE GAUGE

AIR COCK

FUEL AND JETTISON CONTROL

PRESSURE CONTROL VALVE

OIL SEPARATOR (VACUUM PUMP INSTALLATION)

MAIN TANK (PORT)

FUEL PUMP DRAIN

FILTER

VENT PIPE INTO REAR OF RADIATOR

SUPERCHARGER DRAIN

CENTRE-SECTION FRONT AND REAR SPARS

FILLER CAP

MAIN TANK (STARBOARD)

TO FIXED LONG-RANGE FUEL TANKS IF FITTED, SEE FIG 4.

AIR PRESSURE PIPE

FUEL TRAP

RESERVE TANK

FILLER CAP

COCK CONTROLLED BY JETTISON LEVER

PRIMING PUMP

BOOST PRESSURE GAUGE

T-PIECE AND NON-RETURN VALVES

3-WAY COCK REMOTELY CONTROLLED FROM COCKPIT (LONG-RANGE SYSTEM)

VENT PIPE INTO REAR OF RADIATOR

FILTER

AIR COCK

MAIN 3-WAY COCK REMOTELY CONTROLLED

MAIN TANK (PORT)

LONG-RANGE FUEL AND AIR PRESSURE PIPES (JETTISONABLE SYSTEM) SHOWN ═══

AIR PRESSURE PIPE

FILLER CAP

FUEL SYSTEM INSTALLATION

FIG 1

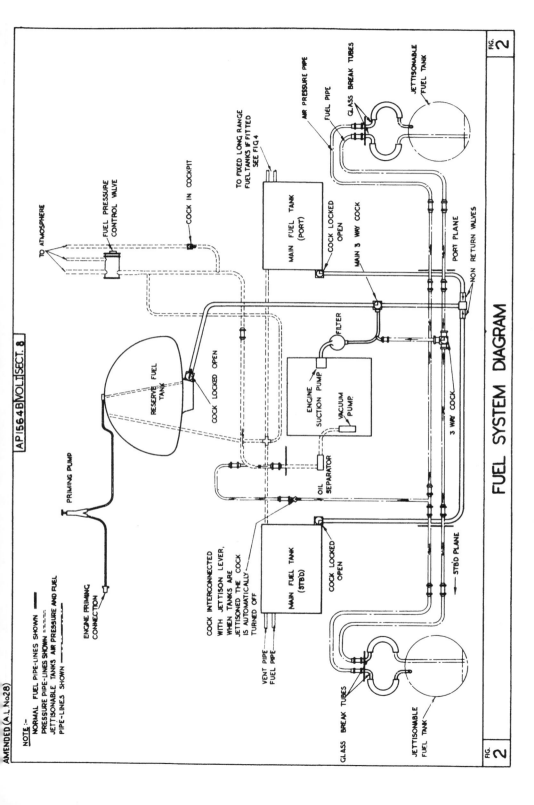

AMENDED (A.L No 28)

AP1564B|VOL|SECT. 8

NOTE:-
NORMAL FUEL PIPE-LINES SHOWN ▬▬▬
PRESSURE PIPE-LINES SHOWN ▬▬▬
JETTISONABLE TANKS AIR PRESSURE AND FUEL
PIPE-LINES SHOWN ▬▬▬

ENGINE PRIMING
CONNECTION

PRIMING PUMP

TO ATMOSPHERE

FUEL PRESSURE
CONTROL VALVE

COCK IN COCKPIT

TO FIXED LONG RANGE
FUEL TANKS IF FITTED
SEE FIG 4

AIR PRESSURE PIPE

FUEL PIPE

GLASS BREAK TUBES

JETTISONABLE
FUEL TANK

MAIN FUEL TANK
(PORT)

COCK LOCKED
OPEN

MAIN 3 WAY COCK

PORT PLANE

NON RETURN VALVES

RESERVE
FUEL
TANK

COCK LOCKED OPEN

FILTER

ENGINE
SUCTION PUMP

VACUUM
PUMP

3 WAY COCK

OIL
SEPARATOR

COCK INTERCONNECTED
WITH JETTISON LEVER,
WHEN TANKS ARE
JETTISONED THE COCK
IS AUTOMATICALLY
TURNED OFF

VENT PIPE
FUEL PIPE

MAIN FUEL TANK
(STB'D)

COCK LOCKED
OPEN

STB'D PLANE

GLASS BREAK TUBES

JETTISONABLE
FUEL TANK

FUEL SYSTEM DIAGRAM

FIG.
2

FIG.
2

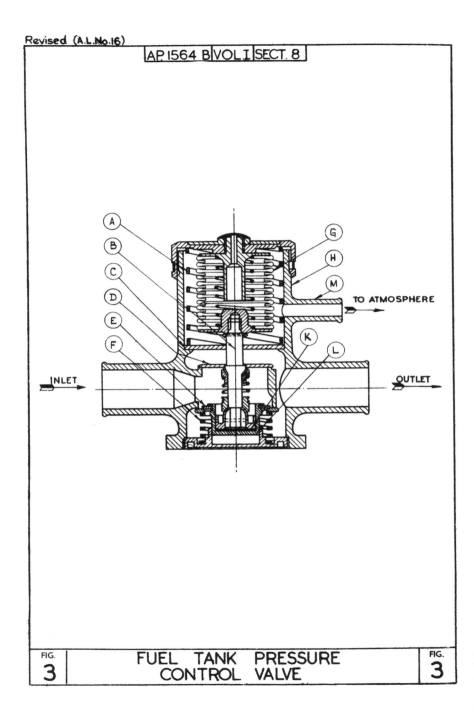

TO ATMOSPHERE

INLET

OUTLET

FIG.
3

FUEL TANK PRESSURE
CONTROL VALVE

FIG.
3

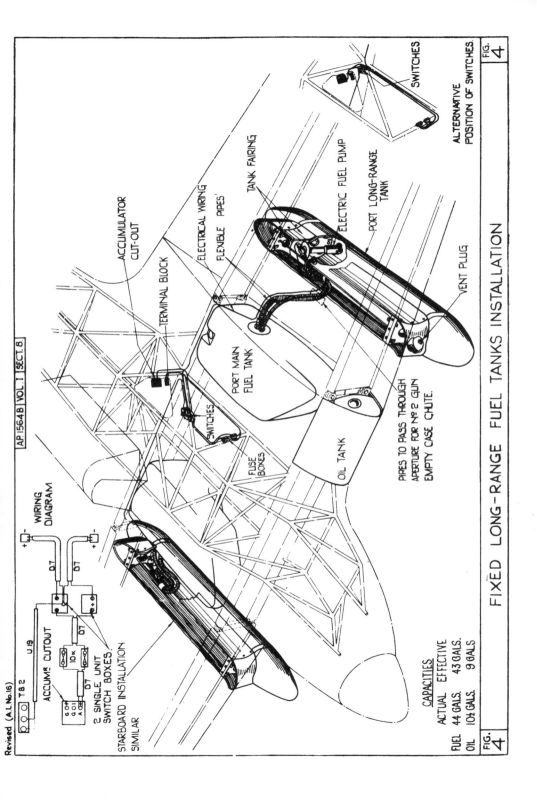

WIRING DIAGRAM

TB 2

ACCUM: CUTOUT

U 19

2 SINGLE UNIT SWITCH BOXES.

STARBOARD INSTALLATION SIMILAR

CAPACITIES

	ACTUAL	EFFECTIVE
FUEL	44 GALS.	43 GALS.
OIL	10½ GALS.	9 GALS

ACCUMULATOR CUT-OUT

TERMINAL BLOCK

ELECTRICAL WIRING

FLEXIBLE PIPES

TANK FAIRING

ELECTRIC FUEL PUMP

PORT LONG-RANGE TANK

SWITCHES

FUSE BOXES

PORT MAIN FUEL TANK

OIL TANK

VENT PLUG

PIPES TO PASS THROUGH APERTURE FOR Nº 2 GUN EMPTY CASE CHUTE.

SWITCHES

ALTERNATIVE POSITION OF SWITCHES.

FIXED LONG-RANGE FUEL TANKS INSTALLATION

FIG. 4

FIG. 4

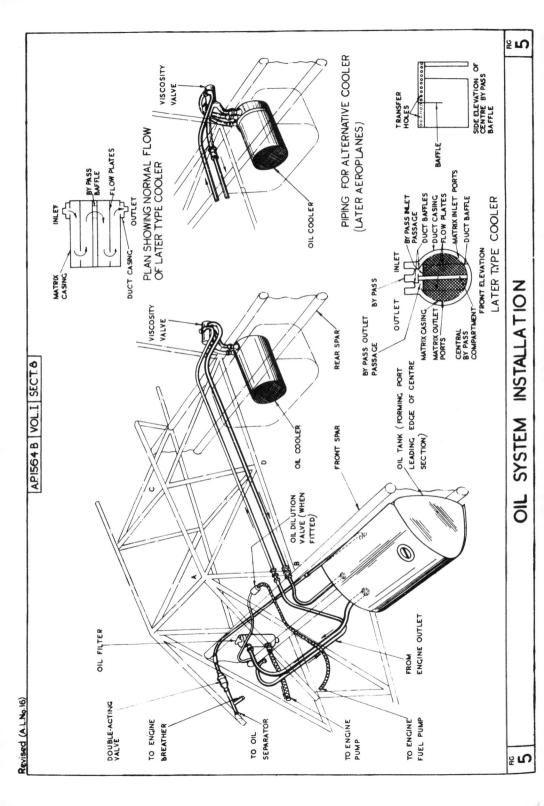

OIL SYSTEM INSTALLATION

PLAN SHOWING NORMAL FLOW OF LATER TYPE COOLER

INLET
BY PASS BAFFLE
FLOW PLATES
OUTLET
MATRIX CASING
DUCT CASING

VISCOSITY VALVE
OIL COOLER

PIPING FOR ALTERNATIVE COOLER (LATER AEROPLANES)

TRANSFER HOLES
BAFFLE
SIDE ELEVATION OF CENTRE BY PASS BAFFLE

BY PASS INLET PASSAGE
DUCT BAFFLES
DUCT CASING
FLOW PLATES
MATRIX INLET PORTS
DUCT BAFFLE
INLET
OUTLET
BY PASS
MATRIX CASING
MATRIX OUTLET PORTS
CENTRAL BY PASS COMPARTMENT
BY PASS OUTLET PASSAGE
FRONT ELEVATION

LATER TYPE COOLER

VISCOSITY VALVE
OIL COOLER
REAR SPAR
FRONT SPAR
OIL TANK (FORMING PORT LEADING EDGE OF CENTRE SECTION)
OIL DILUTION VALVE (WHEN FITTED)
OIL FILTER
DOUBLE-ACTING VALVE
TO ENGINE BREATHER
TO OIL SEPARATOR
TO ENGINE PUMP
TO ENGINE FUEL PUMP
FROM ENGINE OUTLET

FIG 5

A.P.1564 B | VOL.I | SECT.8

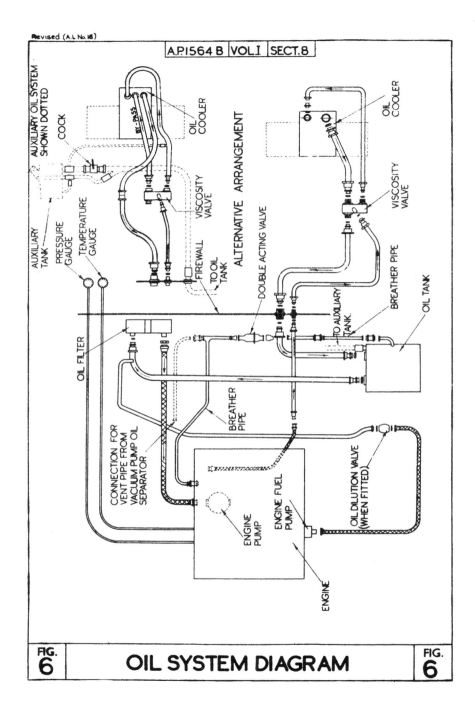

AUXILIARY OIL SYSTEM
SHOWN DOTTED

COCK

BY-PASS

OIL COOLER

OIL COOLER

VISCOSITY VALVE

VISCOSITY VALVE

ALTERNATIVE ARRANGEMENT

DOUBLE ACTING VALVE

BREATHER PIPE

OIL TANK

AUXILIARY TANK

PRESSURE GAUGE

TEMPERATURE GAUGE

FIREWALL

TO OIL TANK

TO AUXILIARY TANK.

OIL FILTER

CONNECTION FOR
VENT PIPE FROM
VACUUM PUMP OIL
SEPARATOR

BREATHER PIPE

ENGINE PUMP

ENGINE FUEL PUMP

OIL DILUTION VALVE
(WHEN FITTED)

ENGINE

FIG. 6

OIL SYSTEM DIAGRAM

FIG. 6

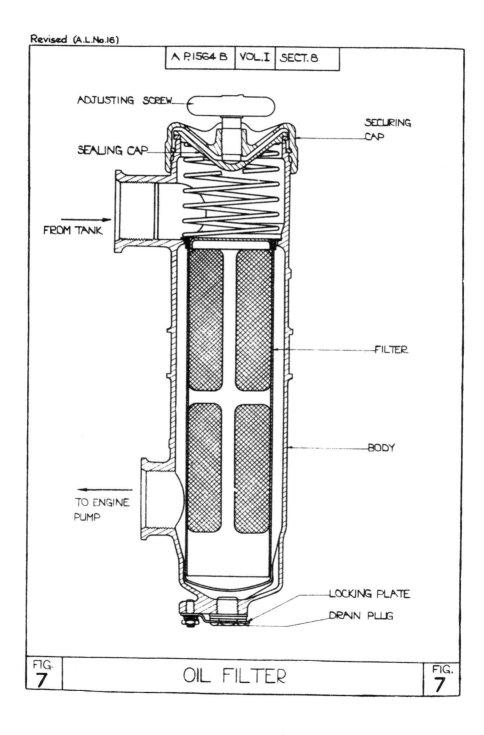

| A.P.1564 B | VOL.I | SECT.8 |

ADJUSTING SCREW

SECURING CAP

SEALING CAP

FROM TANK

FILTER

BODY

TO ENGINE PUMP

LOCKING PLATE

DRAIN PLUG

FIG.
7

OIL FILTER

FIG.
7

A
B
C
D

FIG.
8 | OIL TANK PRESSURE CONTROL VALVE | FIG.
8

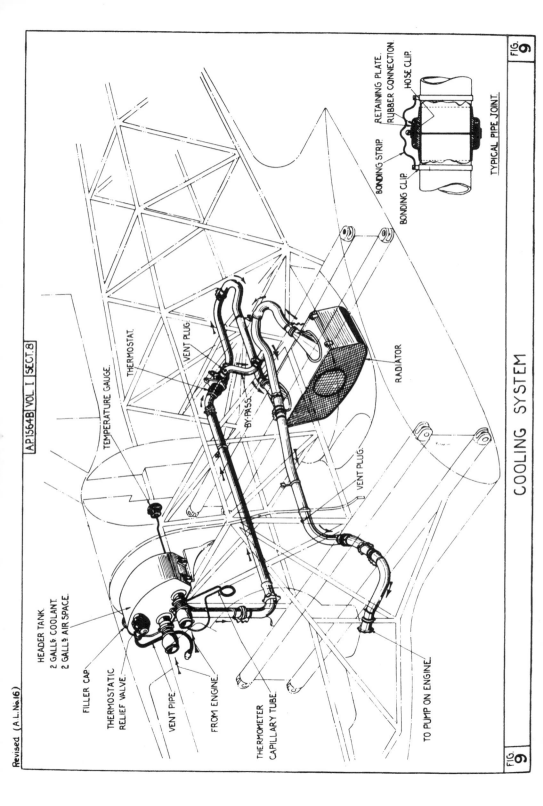

AP1564B VOL. I SECT. 8

HEADER TANK.
2 GALLS COOLANT.
2 GALLS AIR SPACE.

TEMPERATURE GAUGE.

THERMOSTAT.

VENT PLUG.

FILLER CAP.

THERMOSTATIC
RELIEF VALVE.

VENT PIPE.

FROM ENGINE.

BY-PASS.

VENT PLUG.

RADIATOR

THERMOMETER
CAPILLARY TUBE.

TO PUMP ON ENGINE.

COOLING SYSTEM

RETAINING PLATE.
RUBBER CONNECTION.
HOSE CLIP.

BONDING STRIP

BONDING CLIP.

TYPICAL PIPE JOINT.

FIG.
9

FIG.
9

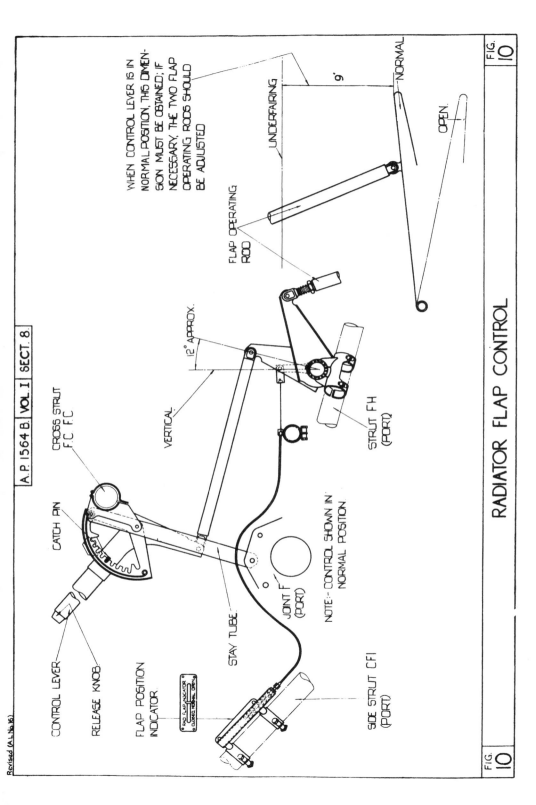

WHEN CONTROL LEVER IS IN NORMAL POSITION, THIS DIMENSION MUST BE OBTAINED; IF NECESSARY, THE TWO FLAP OPERATING RODS SHOULD BE ADJUSTED

UNDERFAIRING

9°

NORMAL

OPEN

FLAP OPERATING ROD

12° APPROX.

VERTICAL

STRUT FH (PORT)

CONTROL LEVER

RELEASE KNOB

FLAP POSITION INDICATOR

CATCH PIN

CROSS STRUT F.C F.C

STAY TUBE

JOINT F (PORT)

NOTE:- CONTROL SHOWN IN NORMAL POSITION

RAD. FLAP INDICATOR
CLOSED NORMAL OPEN

SIDE STRUT CFI (PORT)

RADIATOR FLAP CONTROL

FIG. 10

FIG. 10

A.P. 1564 B | VOL.I | SECT.8

STARBOARD MAG.

BONDING TERMINAL.

STARTING MAG SWITCH.
(STORES REF 5 C./547.)

ISOLATING
SPARK GAPS.

STARTING MAG.

PORT MAG.

—— H.T. BRAIDED UNIPLUG
----- L.T. BRAIDED UNISHEATH 7
■■■ UNISHEATH 7
—·— H.T. CABLE (RUBBER INSULATED)
—— BONDING WIRE

D.P. ENGINE SWITCH.
(STORES REF. 5 C./548)

FOR IGNITION DIAGRAM WHEN BOOSTER COIL IS FITTED SEE SECT. 6.

FIG.
11

IGNITION DIAGRAM.

FIG.
11

A.P. 1564B | VOL. I | SECT. 8

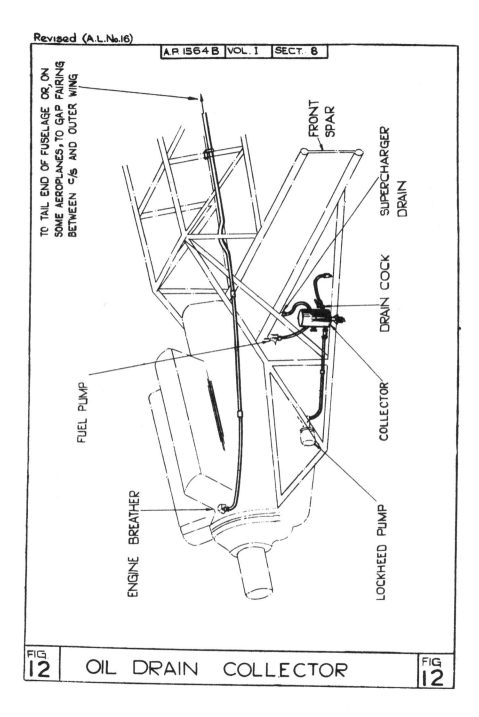

TO TAIL END OF FUSELAGE OR, ON SOME AEROPLANES, TO GAP FAIRING BETWEEN C/S AND OUTER WING

FRONT SPAR

SUPERCHARGER DRAIN

DRAIN COCK

FUEL PUMP

COLLECTOR

ENGINE BREATHER

LOCKHEED PUMP

FIG. 12

OIL DRAIN COLLECTOR

FIG. 12

Section 9:
Hydraulic and pneumatic systems — Description.

SECTION 9
HYDRAULIC AND PNEUMATIC SYSTEMS—DESCRIPTION

LIST OF CONTENTS

LIST OF ILLUSTRATIONS

Note.—Figs. 3, 6, 16 and 17 have been deleted.

SECTION 9

HYDRAULIC AND PNEUMATIC SYSTEMS—DESCRIPTION

Introduction

1. This Section is limited to a description of features of the hydraulic, pneumatic and vacuum systems, peculiar to this aeroplane.

Hydraulic system

General

2. Raising and lowering of the undercarriage and of the main plane flaps are effected hydraulically and the system is automatic in operation, selection of the desired operation of undercarriage or flaps, by means of the selector gear, being sufficient to commence the operation. The latches locking the undercarriage "down" are operated by cables connected to the selector gear, and the catches locking it in the "up" position are operated by a small jack. A pressure relief valve is fitted in the flaps "down." circuit to relieve excessive pressures caused by air loads acting on the flaps. Relief valves for the remaining circuits are incorporated in the control box. A control valve is fitted in some aeroplanes as an alternative to the control box; it is not illustrated. A pressure gauge is incorporated in the main supply circuit and is mounted on the starboard side of the cockpit. The hydraulic system installation is illustrated in fig. 1 and a diagrammatic arrangement is given in fig. 2. The following paragraphs describe the components and their function in detail, where these are peculiar to this aeroplane. Reference should be made to A.P.1803, Vol. I for information relating to any of the components not described below, including the handpump (Part No. C.3585), the control unit (Part No. C.4917D) and the rotary control valve (Part No. C.6165).

Engine-driven pump

3. The pump, which is of the annular displacement type, is situated below the crankcase on the centre-line of the engine, and is attached to the crankcase by six studs passing through a vertical circular flange at its rear end. The suction and delivery connections are on the starboard side of the pump, the upper connection being the delivery; a drain plug is fitted at the bottom. A full description of the pump, which is of the Lockheed Mk. IV, Series IF or IIF, is given in A.P.1803, Vol. I.

Filter

4. The filter (*see* fig. 10) is mounted on a bracket attached to starboard fuselage strut EH. It comprises a body A, a screwed cap E, and a composite gauze and felt filter element C. The upper end of the filter element is centralized in the body by means of a washer B, which has a lip engaging the interior of the element. A dished washer F, assembled on a stem integral with the cap, centralizes the lower end of the element. The element is gripped between the washers by the action of a coiled spring assembled on the stem between the cap and the washer F. A split pin through the end of the stem prevents loss of the spring and washer when the cap is removed from the body. To prevent the spring from crushing the element, another spring is assembled inside the element.

Fluid enters at the connection D, which communicates with the exterior of the filter element, and after passing through the element, emerges through the connection G.

Selector gear

5. The selector gear (*see* fig. 4) is mounted on the inboard side of starboard fuselage strut CF, to which it is clamped by a split bracket C. It consists essentially of a number of levers assembled on a hollow shaft M, and selectively operated by a lever B mounted on a spherical bearing N on the shaft. Two levers, one on each side of the selector lever, are connected by rods to the control box or rotary control valve, the lever H on the inboard side operating the valves in the flap circuit and the lever G, on the outboard side, operating the valves in the undercarriage circuit. Outboard of the undercarriage lever are two more levers D and F, which are also operated by the selector lever B through the medium of a pin L, which engages in slots formed in the levers. Lever D is coupled by cables to the latch gear which locks the undercarriage "down", and the lever F provides an attachment for the spring E which is stretched between it and lever D. The spring maintains the levers against stops which prevent their movement in one direction. Movement of the operating lever to the WHEELS UP position moves the lever D, thereby releasing the latch gear. Movement to the WHEELS DOWN position moves the lever F, which increases the tension in the spring, thereby maintaining the lever D against the stop. The undercarriage and flap levers are locked in their neutral positions by latches J engaging notches K in the levers; a spring, passing through the hollow shaft and coupling the latches together, urges them into engagement with the levers.

6. The selector lever, which, on certain aeroplanes, has a pin projecting from the handgrip to facilitate operation, projects through an indicator plate which is gated and inscribed with operating instructions; movement of the selector lever about its spherical bearing is guided by a plunger engaging a corresponding H-shaped recess in the bearing. The plunger is totally enclosed within the selector lever, and to disengage it from the holes the catch P on the side of the lever must be depressed. When the selector lever is in the central NEUTRAL position the plunger engages a dimple in the bottom of the recess to locate the lever non-positively, but when the lever is moved sideways and then forwards or rearwards so that the plunger enters one of the holes at the extremities of the recess, the lever is locked positively and the plunger release must be operated before moving the lever.

7. When the handle of the selector lever is moved to starboard from the neutral position, a dog O on the lever enters the notch K in the flap lever and disengages the latch J; forward or rearward movement of the handle then imparts movement to the flap lever and the valves in the control box are set to raise or lower the flaps. When the handle is moved to port a dog on the selector lever engages the undercarriage lever; forward or rearward movement of the handle then results in the lever D or F being moved to release the appropriate locking device and the valves in the control box are set to raise or lower the under-carriage. Since the selector lever must pass through neutral in moving from one side of the gate to the other, the flap lever is returned to neutral and locked by its latch when the selector lever engages the undercarriage lever; similarly, the undercarriage lever is left in neutral when the selector lever is in engagement with the flap lever. In order to prevent accidental raising of the undercarriage, a spring-loaded catch is provided, which obstructs the WHEELS UP position;

this necessitates operation of the catch before the selector lever can be moved to that position.

Automatic cut-out valve

8. The automatic cut-out valve (*see* fig. 5) is clipped to starboard fuselage struts FC,H and EH; its purpose is to enable the engine-driven pump to circulate fluid round a by-pass circuit at low pressure when none of the jacks in the main circuit are being operated. There are three pipe connections to the cut-out valve; an inlet F for fluid from the engine-driven pump, an outlet L leading to the control box in the main circuit, and a by-pass outlet E leading through the filter to the reservoir. The fluid is diverted from the main circuit to the by-pass circuit by means of a piston C carrying a plunger N, which opens a by-pass valve G when the fluid pressure in the main circuit rises at the end of an operation. The plunger slides in the piston and is urged towards the valve by a spring O housed in the piston and held in place by a cap P. Distance pieces Q are fitted between the spring and the cap to produce the correct initial compression of the spring; the cap also holds a gland ring B and a distance piece A on the piston. The length of the plunger is made adjustable by providing it with a screwed extension M. The piston assembly, as a whole, is urged away from the valve by a spring D. In the outlet K a non-return valve J is fitted. The outlet side of the valve communicates through the passage L with the space at the side of the piston remote from the by-pass valve. When the undercarriage units are being raised or lowered, fluid entering the connection F from the engine-driven pump passes straight through the cut-out to the control box, opening the non-return valve and holding the by-pass valve closed. The fluid pressure on the piston is not sufficient to move it against the spring D and the plunger is therefore kept out of contact with the by-pass valve. When the jacks reach the end of their stroke, the pressure in the pipeline, and consequently the pressure on the piston, rises and the piston assembly moves as a unit until the plunger engages the by-pass valve. Owing to the fluid pressure on the by-pass valve and the comparative weakness of the spring O, movement of the plunger is then arrested and continued movement of the piston compresses the spring. When the spring is fully compressed, the plunger again moves with the piston and slightly opens the valve. Fluid then flows out of the connection E to the reservoir and the pressure in the pipeline from the engine-driven pump to the cut-out falls to a low value. Immediately this occurs, the non-return valve J closes and holds the high pressure in the main circuit; since this pressure is acting on the piston, the latter is held in the position to which it was moved by the fluid. The plunger, however, is now free to move under the action of the spring O, since there is no longer any fluid pressure on the valve and the valve spring H is weaker than the spring O; the plunger therefore pushes the valve fully open. The parts remain in these positions until the valves in the control box are set for another operation of the undercarriage or flaps. The pressure in the pipeline between the connection K and the control box is then released and the spring D returns the piston to its original position; the spring H closes the by-pass valve and the sequence of operations described above is repeated.

9. The same sequence of operations takes place when the flaps are being raised, but when they are being lowered the fluid is not diverted to the by-pass circuit until the selector lever is returned to NEUTRAL (*see* para. 17).

Undercarriage jacks

10. The jacks which raise and lower the undercarriage units are mounted behind the web of the centre-section front spar (*see* Section 7, Chap. 5), the closed

ends of the jack cylinders being attached to the webs by universal joints; the piston rods are coupled to the triangulated levers of the undercarriage unit side stays. The jacks are illustrated in fig. 7 and have a forged cylinder K, closed at one end by an end fitting A screwed to the cylinder. The end fitting is locked by a screwed ring C which, in turn, is locked to the boss for the pipe connection by means of wire; a sealing ring is interposed between the end fitting and the ring to prevent leakage of fluid. A pair of lugs on the end fitting provides the means for anchoring the jack to the centre section and an eyebolt O, screwed into the end of the piston rod J, provides the connection to the undercarriage unit; the eyebolt is locked in position by a nut and tabwasher. Two pipe connections B and L, for connecting the jack in the hydraulic circuit, are screwed into the end fitting and the gland end of the cylinder, respectively. The piston has a body D screwed into the end of the piston rod and locked by a pin; a circlip is also fitted to guard against loss of the pin. A support ring H and a cup ring G are assembled between the piston body and a shoulder on the piston rod and another cup ring F is held on the piston by a nut E locked by a split pin. The packing ring M, which seals the piston rod, is held in position by a gland nut N.

Flap jack

11. The flap jack (*see* fig. 7) is connected between the centre-section rear spar and an arm on the flap spar. The jack consists of a forged cylinder D, the closed end of which has a pair of lugs by which the jack is anchored to the centre-section spar; a pipe connection A is screwed into this end of the cylinder. The other end of the jack has an end fitting J screwed to the cylinder and locked by a screwed ring F, a sealing ring being fitted to prevent leakage; the screwed ring is locked to the pipe connection G by means of wire. A bush H is fitted at the base of the union G for locating the end fitting J relative to the cylinder D. The gland assembly consists of a gland ring, a spacer ring, another gland ring and a support ring, the whole assembly being held in position by a gland nut K, which is locked by a grubscrew. An eyebolt L is screwed into the end of the piston rod E and locked by a nut and tab washer, thus enabling the pin centres to be adjusted when necessary. The piston body is integral with the piston rod and the cup rings B, one on each side of the piston body, are held in place by nuts C, locked by circlips.

Catch gear jack

12. The catch gear jack (*see* fig. 8) is mounted on starboard fuselage strut CD and its purpose is to release the catches which lock the undercarriage units in the "up" position. The jack consists of a light-alloy cylinder C, in which slides a combined piston rod and piston D; a gland ring B is held in place on the piston by a nut H, locked by a split pin. The jack is extended by fluid which enters the cylinder by a banjo pipe connection A and is retracted by a spring G housed in the cylinder. An end plug E, screwed into the cylinder, provides an abutment for the spring, and also limits the stroke of the piston by acting as a stop against which a shoulder F on the piston rod bears when the jack is extended. The jack is connected to the pipeline leading to the anchored ends of the undercarriage jack so that when the selector gear is set to lower the undercarriage units, the jack extends and releases the catches. When the undercarriage is being raised, the pressure in the jack is released and the spring retracts the piston; the catches then automatically engage when the undercarriage units reach the "up" position.

Pressure relief valve

13. The pressure relief valve (*see* fig. 9) is clipped to the front of the centre-section rear spar. Its function is to allow the flaps to rise automatically if the speed of the aeroplane exceeds a pre-determined value when the flaps are down. The valve consists of a body E, provided with a seat G which is screwed into the body and locked by a grubscrew. The valve F is maintained on its seat by the spring K, which is fitted between two centralizing washers C, the top one bearing against the adjusting stud M and the lower one bearing against a shoulder on the spindle B and maintaining it in a hole in the top of the valve F. The adjusting stud M is screwed into the spring housing L and leakage past this point is prevented by a gland A held in position by a gland nut. The spring housing is screwed into the valve body and locked by the locking plate J. The inlet connection D of the valve is connected to the pipeline leading to the anchored end of the flap jack and the outlet connection H leads through the filter to the reservoir.

Non-return valves

14. Two non-return valves are used in the system; one with ⅜ in. B.S.P. connections and the other with ½ in. B.S.P. connections. The ⅜ in. B.S.P. valve (*see* fig. 10) consists of two parts A and D, screwed together, with a sealing washer interposed to make a fluid-tight joint. The valve element consists of a cruciform valve B with a rubber washer C sprung over a protuberance on the valve; the whole assembly is maintained on its seat by a spring E. This valve is assembled in the pipeline from the delivery connection on the handpump; when the pump is operated, the valve opens to allow fluid to pass into the system.

15. The ½ in. B.S.P. valve (*see* fig. 10) is similar to the ⅜ in. B.S.P. valve, with the exception that the valve element consists of a cruciform valve B with a rubber washer C attached by means of a special bolt and nut. There is no spring in this unit. The valve is connected, in effect, between the main supply and return pipelines to the control box; its purpose is to enable fluid to by-pass from the return pipeline to the supply pipeline when the demand made by the undercarriage jacks on the engine pump (during lowering operations) is too great, thereby causing a partial vacuum in the system. The valve ceases to operate when the engine pump resumes effective operation of the jacks.

Variable-flow valve

16. The variable-flow valve (*see* fig. 10) is connected in the pipeline between the control box and the gland ends of the undercarriage jacks. Its purpose is to restrict the flow of fluid when the undercarriage is being lowered and so reduce the speed at which the undercarriage tends to fall under its own weight; when the undercarriage is being raised, the valve permits free flow of fluid. The valve is similar in construction to the ⅜ in. B.S.P. non-return valve (*see* para. 14) except for a small hole through the valve member through which fluid flows when the valve is seated. No spring is fitted.

Operation of system

17. A diagram of the hydraulic system is given in fig. 2. When the system is idle, the engine-driven pump circulates fluid round a by-pass circuit which includes the automatic cut-out valve, the filter, and the reservoir. When the

selector lever is moved to the flaps UP or DOWN position, the appropriate valves in the control box or rotary control valve are opened and the automatic cut-out valve diverts fluid from the by-pass circuit to the control box from whence it is directed to one end of the flap jack; fluid displaced from the other end of the jack is directed by the control box or valve through the filter to the reservoir. If the flaps are being raised, the cut-out valve automatically diverts the fluid supply to the by-pass circuit when the jack reaches the end of its stroke. When the flaps are being lowered, a pressure relief valve comes into operation. This valve is connected between the pipeline leading to the anchored end of the jack and the pipeline leading from the control box or valve to the filter, and its purpose is to limit the amount by which the flaps can be lowered when the aeroplane is travelling at more than a certain speed. If the aeroplane is travelling at less than this speed, the pressure relief valve does not blow-off until the flaps are fully "down", but if this speed is exceeded the air pressure on the flaps causes the hydraulic pressure in the jack to rise above the value at which the valve is set; the valve therefore opens and the flaps do not reach the fully "down" position. Similarly, if the flaps are already fully "down" when the speed becomes excessive, the flaps will be blown partially "up". Since the relief valve is set to blow-off at a lower pressure than that at which the cut-out operates, the fluid is not diverted to the by-pass circuit when the selector lever is at FLAPS DOWN. Should the flaps take up an intermediate position owing to the speed of the aeroplane being excessive, they will automatically move to the fully "down" position when the speed is reduced sufficiently, provided that the selector lever is left at FLAPS DOWN. If it is desired to only partially lower the flaps, the selector lever must be returned to NEUTRAL when the flaps reach the desired position.

18. When the selector lever is moved to the WHEELS UP position, the latches which lock the undercarriage units "down" are released by a mechanical connection to the selector lever, and the valves in the control box or rotary control valve are set to cause the jacks to retract the undercarriage units. When the selector lever is moved to the WHEELS DOWN position, the control box or valve directs fluid to the undercarriage jacks and also to the catch gear jack which is connected to the pipeline leading to the anchored ends of the undercarriage jacks. The catch gear jack releases the catches which lock the undercarriage units "up" and the units fall under their own weight. To prevent the units being damaged by falling too quickly, a variable-flow valve, which restricts the flow of the fluid, is inserted in the pipeline through which fluid returns to the control box or valve. A non-return valve, fitted between the two four-way pieces, allows fluid to pass directly from the main return connection of the control box or valve to the main supply connection to make up any lack of fluid if the demand of the jacks, when the undercarriage is falling, exceeds the output of the pump.

19. If the engine-driven pump has failed or the engine is not running, the undercarriage and flaps can be raised and lowered by setting the selector lever in the usual way and operating the handpump.

Pneumatic system

General

20. The wheel brakes and the gun-firing mechanism are operated pneumatically. The ·303 in. gun-firing installation is illustrated in fig. 11 and piping diagrams for the ·303 in. and 20 mm. installations are given in fig. 12 and 13,

respectively. The Dunlop brake system is fully described and illustrated in A.P.1464B; the following paragraphs give the location of each component, but only describe those peculiar to this aircraft. Reference should be made to A.P.1519 for a description of the air compressor, to A.P.1641E for a description of the gun-firing control and to A.P.1749 for information relating to the ciné-camera.

21. The pneumatic system is fitted with either a B.T.H. type A.V.A., or with a Heywood, engine-driven air compressor. With the B.T.H. compressor, and oil reservoir and a non-return valve are fitted, while the charging connection is situated in the port side of the front face of the firewall; with the Heywood compressor no reservoir or non-return valve is fitted, but a pressure regulator is incorporated either on the starboard side of the air cylinder or on the starboard side strut AY and the charging connection is situated either on the port side of the front face of the firewall or on the starboard side of the air cylinder sealing cover. These circuits are illustrated in fig. 11, 12 and 13. The engine-driven compressor is mounted on the engine at the rear end of the starboard cylinder block. The air supplied by the compressor is stored in a cylinder at a maximum pressure of 300 lb./sq. in.; the cylinder can be charged on the ground by means of a handpump or a compressed-air cylinder attached to the charging connection.

Oil reservoir
22. The oil reservoir (*see* fig. 14) is mounted on the starboard side of the front face of the firewall. It consists of a cylindrical container with a pipe connection in each end, and is mounted vertically so that the inlet is at the bottom and the outlet at the top. A filler neck, provided with a cap projects upwards from near the bottom of the reservoir at an angle of 45 deg., an d an overflow connection, provided with a plug, is fitted, adjacent to the filler ı eck and part way up the side of the reservoir; the overflow connection enabl ıs the level to be adjusted when the oil content of the reservoir is being replenished. Air from the compressor enters the inlet at the bottom of the reservoir, bubbles through the oil, and leaves by the outlet at the top of the reservoir. The outlet connection is extended by a pipe projecting downwards to the centre of the reservoir in order to prevent the escape of oil whatever the attitude of the aircraft.

Oil trap
23. The oil trap, if fitted, is mounted on the front face of the firewall and serves to trap any oil carried by the air.

Oil and water trap
23A. On certain aircraft an oil-water trap is incorporated in lieu of an oil trap; it is mounted on the front face of the firewall on the port side.

Air cylinder
24. The air cylinder is supported by two straps against four brackets which form a cradle; the two upper brackets are bolted to the mounting tubes for the flying controls, and the lower brackets are secured to channel stiffeners on the centre-section front spar. The inlet connection is at the starboard end of the cylinder and the outlet is at the port end.

Air filter
25. The air filter is mounted on the rear face of the firewall.

Brakes relay valve
26. The brakes relay valve is mounted on the port flying controls mounting tube. immediately above the air cylinder; its purpose is to provide differential

operation of the brakes in response to movement of the rudder bar. The valve is controlled by a rod extending to starboard and coupled to an arm on the rudder bar spindle; the length of the rod is adjustable by means of its screwed fork-ends.

Pressure gauge

27. A triple pressure gauge, showing the pressure in the air cylinder and in each brake, is mounted on a plate fixed at its forward end to the rudder bar pedestal and at its rear end to a fuselage cross strut.

Pressure-reducing valve

28. The pressure-reducing valve is mounted on the rear face of the firewall. A full description is contained in A.P.1641E. Early aircraft have valve No. A.H.O.5119 and later aircraft have valve No. A.H.O.16313.

Ammunition counter

28A. On certain aircraft an ammunition counter is fitted on the decking above the starboard cockpit floodlamp. This counter is pneumatically-operated when the guns are fired.

Operation of system

29. The operation of the system is slightly different according to the type of compressor fitted (*see* para. 21). From the B.T.H. compressor, compressed air passes through the oil reservoir and the oil trap to the air cylinder. If the pressure in the cylinder exceeds 300 lb./sq. in. a valve in the compressor opens to permit the compressor to idle; the delivery valve of the compressor is then closed by the pressure in the pipeline and oil from the oil reservoir is forced along the pipeline to seal the valve. From the cylinder, air passes through the filter to the pressure-reducing valve, which delivers it to the system at working pressure. From the Heywood compressor, compressed air passes through the oil trap and the pressure regulator into the air cylinder. If the pressure exceeds 300 lb./sq. in. a valve in the pressure regulator opens to permit the compressor output to be discharged to atmosphere; a non-return valve fitted in the pressure regulator prevents the pressure in the air container from escaping through the regulator. From the cylinder, air passes through the filter to a pressure-reducing valve, which delivers it to the system at the working pressure required.

30. When the brakes control lever on the control column spade grip is operated, the brakes relay valve directs air to the wheel brakes. If the rudder bar is in the neutral position, equal pressures are produced in the two brakes; if the rudder bar is moved from neutral, the pressure in one brake is increased and the pressure in the other brake is decreased.

31. When the pushbutton on the spade grip is depressed air is directed to the gun-firing circuit to fire the guns or to operate the ciné camera. Successive ciné camera exposures are made during the whole time the button is depressed, the electrical circuits of the camera being controlled by a pneumatically-actuated switch in the gun-firing circuit.

Vacuum system

General

32. Power for the suction-operated flying instruments is provided by a vacuum system incorporating an engine-driven pump. A perspective view of the installation is given in fig. 15. The following paragraphs deal briefly with the components of the system, the instruments themselves being fully described in A.P.1275, Vol. I, and the pump, relief-valve and oil separator, in A.P.1519, Vol. I.

Pump

33. The Mk. III type Pesco B3 engine-driven pump has a square flange by means of which it is bolted to a mounting pad on the starboard side of a gearbox at the front end of the engine. The pump receives lubricating oil through a hole in the engine mounting pad, which aligns with one of four holes provided in the pump flange.

Relief valve

34. The relief valve is mounted on a bracket bolted to starboard joint **W** of the engine mounting and is connected in the pipeline on the suction side of the pump. If the suction produced by the pump exceeds the correct value the valve opens and permits air to enter the system.

Oil separator

35. The oil separator is clipped to the starboard engine mounting strut **WY**. Air from the pump enters the separator by a pipe connection near the bottom of its front face and leaves by an outlet at the rear end of its upper face. The oil drains out of a pipe connection at the forward end of the bottom face of the container and is led into the vent pipe connected between the oil tank and the engine breather.

Test adaptor

36. A test adaptor is provided in the suction pipeline just forward of the instrument panel. The adaptor has two branches, one for connecting a suction gauge and the other for connecting an external pump to enable the instruments to be tested when the engine is not running; the branches are normally blanked off by knurled caps.

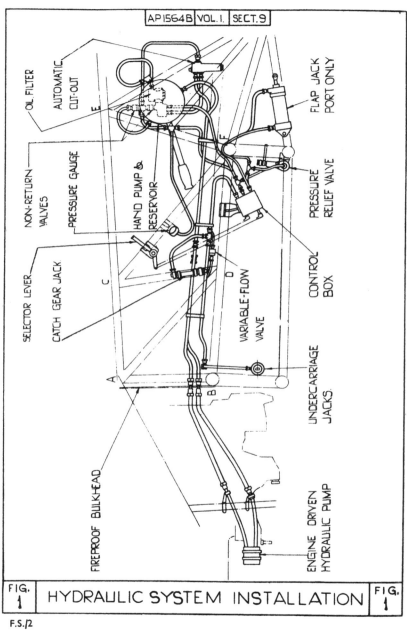

OIL FILTER

AUTOMATIC CUT-OUT

E

FLAP JACK PORT ONLY

NON-RETURN VALVES

PRESSURE GAUGE

HAND PUMP & RESERVOIR

PRESSURE RELIEF VALVE

SELECTOR LEVER

CATCH GEAR JACK

C

D

VARIABLE-FLOW VALVE

CONTROL BOX

A

B

UNDERCARRIAGE JACKS

FIREPROOF BULKHEAD

ENGINE DRIVEN HYDRAULIC PUMP

| FIG. 1 | HYDRAULIC SYSTEM INSTALLATION | FIG. 1 |

F.S./2

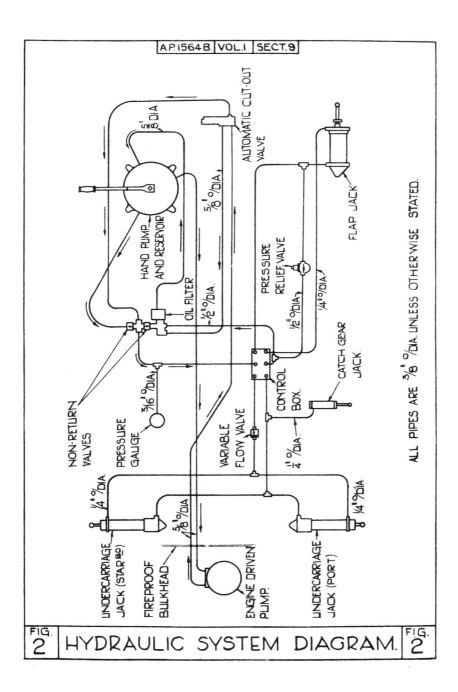

ALL PIPES ARE $\frac{3}{8}$"/DIA. UNLESS OTHERWISE STATED.

AUTOMATIC CUT-OUT VALVE

$\frac{5}{8}$"/DIA

$\frac{5}{8}$"/DIA

HAND PUMP AND RESERVOIR

OIL FILTER

$\frac{1}{2}$"/DIA.

$\frac{5}{8}$"/DIA.

FLAP JACK

PRESSURE RELIEF VALVE

$\frac{1}{2}$"/DIA.

$\frac{1}{4}$"/DIA.

NON-RETURN VALVES

PRESSURE GAUGE

$\frac{3}{16}$"/DIA.

CATCH GEAR JACK.

CONTROL BOX.

VARIABLE FLOW VALVE

$\frac{1}{4}$"/DIA.

$\frac{1}{4}$"/DIA.

$\frac{1}{4}$"/DIA

$\frac{5}{8}$"/DIA

UNDERCARRIAGE JACK (STAR.BD)

FIREPROOF BULKHEAD

ENGINE DRIVEN PUMP.

UNDERCARRIAGE JACK (PORT)

| FIG. 2 | HYDRAULIC SYSTEM DIAGRAM. | FIG. 2 |

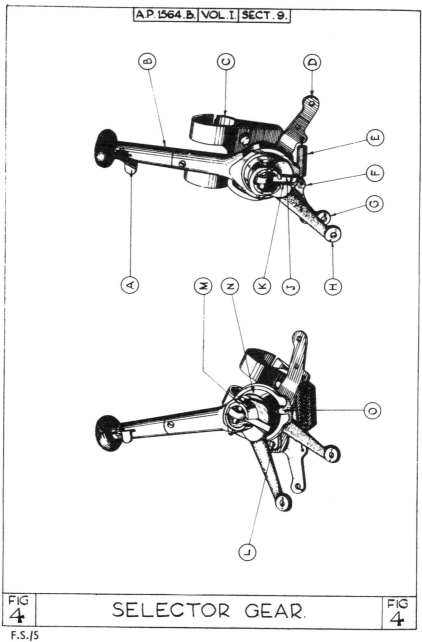

FIG
4

SELECTOR GEAR.

FIG
4

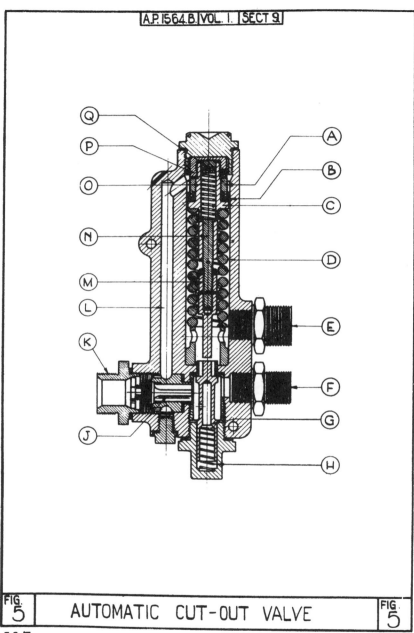

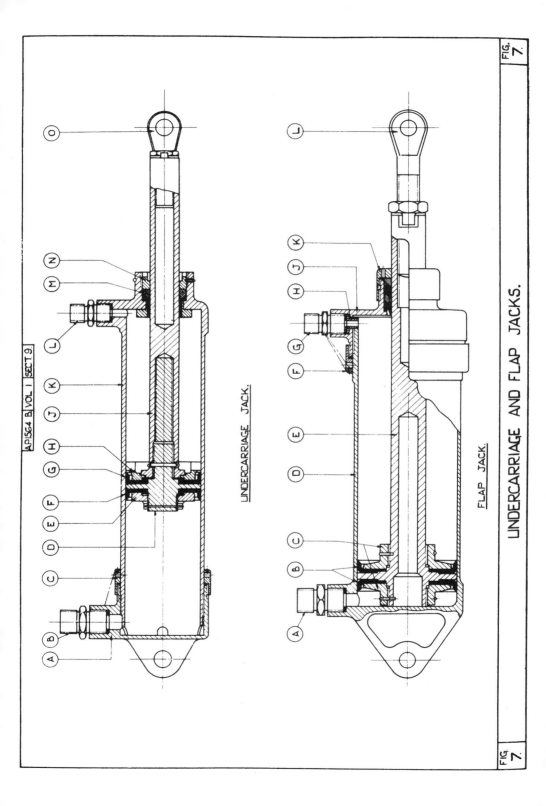

UNDERCARRIAGE JACK.

FLAP JACK.

UNDERCARRIAGE AND FLAP JACKS.

FIG.
7.

FIG.
7.

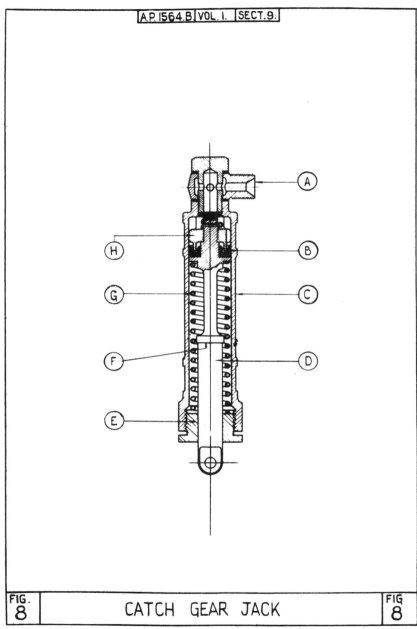

FIG. 8

FIG 8

CATCH GEAR JACK

F.S./11

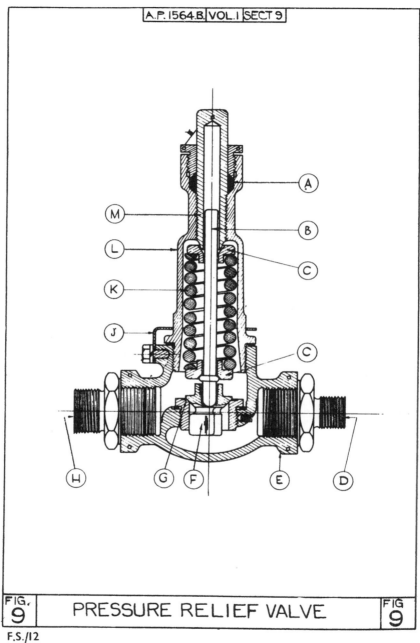

FIG. 9

PRESSURE RELIEF VALVE

FIG 9

F.S./12

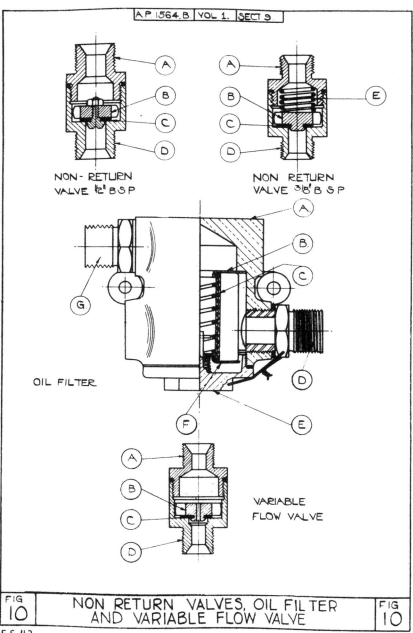

NON - RETURN
VALVE ½" BSP

NON RETURN
VALVE ⅜" BSP

OIL FILTER

VARIABLE
FLOW VALVE

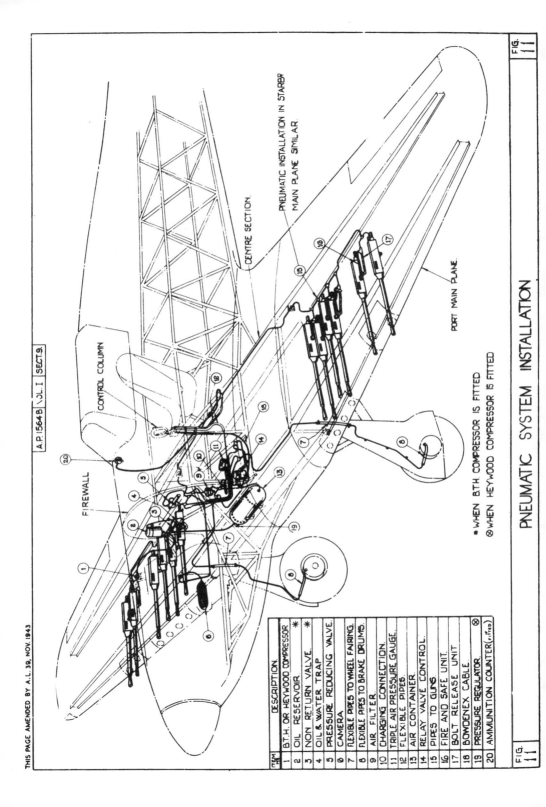

PNEUMATIC INSTALLATION IN STARB.
MAIN PLANE SIMILAR.

CENTRE SECTION.

CONTROL COLUMN

FIREWALL

PORT MAIN PLANE.

* WHEN B.T.H. COMPRESSOR IS FITTED
⊗ WHEN HEYWOOD COMPRESSOR IS FITTED

ITEM	DESCRIPTION
1	B.T.H. OR HEYWOOD COMPRESSOR ＊
2	OIL RESERVOIR. ＊
3	NON RETURN VALVE. ＊
4	OIL & WATER TRAP
5	PRESSURE REDUCING VALVE.
6	CAMERA
7	FLEXIBLE PIPES TO WHEEL FAIRING.
8	FLEXIBLE PIPES TO BRAKE DRUMS.
9	AIR FILTER.
10	CHARGING CONNECTION.
11	TRIPLE AIR PRESSURE GAUGE.
12	FLEXIBLE PIPES.
13	AIR CONTAINER
14	RELAY VALVE CONTROL.
15	PIPES TO GUNS
16	FIRE AND SAFE UNIT.
17	BOLT RELEASE UNIT
18	BOWDENEX CABLE.
19	PRESSURE REGULATOR. ⊗
20	AMMUNITION COUNTER (IF FITTED)

PNEUMATIC SYSTEM INSTALLATION

FIG. 11

FIG. 11

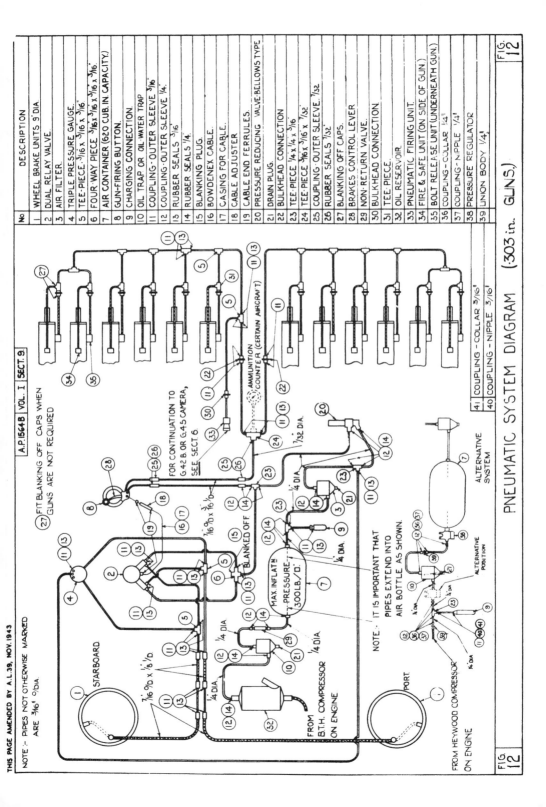

THIS PAGE AMENDED BY A.L.39, NOV. 1943

A.P.1564B | VOL. I | SECT. 9

NOTE :- PIPES NOT OTHERWISE MARKED ARE 3/16" O/DIA

(27) FIT BLANKING OFF CAPS WHEN GUNS ARE NOT REQUIRED

No	DESCRIPTION
1	WHEEL BRAKE UNITS 9" DIA
2	DUAL RELAY VALVE.
3	AIR FILTER.
4	TRIPLE PRESSURE GAUGE.
5	TEE-PIECE 3/16 x 3/16 x 3/16"
6	FOUR-WAY PIECE 3/16 x 3/16 x 3/16 x 3/16.
7	AIR CONTAINER (620 CUB. IN. CAPACITY.)
8	GUN-FIRING BUTTON.
9	CHARGING CONNECTION.
10	OIL TRAP OR OIL WATER TRAP
11	COUPLING-OUTER SLEEVE 3/16"
12	COUPLING-OUTER SLEEVE 1/4.
13	RUBBER SEALS 3/16
14	RUBBER SEALS 1/4.
15	BLANKING PLUG.
16	BOWDENEX CABLE.
17	CASING FOR CABLE.
18	CABLE ADJUSTER
19	CABLE END FERRULES.
20	PRESSURE REDUCING VALVE-BELLOWS TYPE
21	DRAIN PLUG.
22	BULKHEAD CONNECTION
23	TEE- PIECE 1/4 x 1/4 x 3/16.
24	TEE-PIECE 3/16 x 3/16 x 7/32
25	COUPLING OUTER SLEEVE 7/32
26	RUBBER SEALS 7/32
27	BLANKING OFF CAPS.
28	BRAKES CONTROL LEVER
29	NON-RETURN VALVE.
30	BULKHEAD CONNECTION.
31	TEE- PIECE.
32	OIL RESERVOIR.
33	PNEUMATIC FIRING UNIT.
34	FIRE & SAFE UNIT (ON SIDE OF GUN.)
35	BOLT RELEASE UNIT (UNDERNEATH GUN.)
36	COUPLING - COLLAR 1/4"
37	COUPLING - NIPPLE 1/4"
38	PRESSURE REGULATOR
39	UNION BODY 1/4"
40	COUPLING - NIPPLE 3/16"
41	COUPLING - COLLAR 3/16"

PNEUMATIC SYSTEM DIAGRAM (.303 in. GUNS.)

FIG. 12

AMMUNITION COUNTER (CERTAIN AIRCRAFT)

FOR CONTINUATION TO G.42 B. OR G.45 CAMERA, SEE SECT. 6.

STARBOARD

FROM B.T.H. COMPRESSOR ON ENGINE

FROM HEYWOOD COMPRESSOR ON ENGINE

PORT.

MAX INFLATN PRESSURE 300 LB./□.

NOTE:- IT IS IMPORTANT THAT PIPES EXTEND INTO AIR BOTTLE AS SHOWN.

ALTERNATIVE SYSTEM

ALTERNATIVE POSITION

Nº	DESCRIPTION
1	WHEEL BRAKE UNITS 9" DIA.
2	TRIPLE PRESSURE GAUGE
3	GUN-FIRING BUTTON
4	BRAKES CONTROL LEVER.
5	DUAL RELAY VALVE
6	BOWDENEX CABLE
7	COCKING VALVE
8	BULKHEAD CONNECTION
9	BLANKING PLUG.
10	
11	OIL TRAP
12	DRAIN PLUG
13	PRESSURE REGULATOR
14	AIR CONTAINER (620 CUB IN CAPACITY)
15	CHARGING CONNECTION
16	AIR FILTER
17	DRAIN PLUG
18	PRESSURE REDUCING VALVE (BELLOWS TYPE)
19	BLANKING OFF CAPS.

FOR CONTINUATION TO G 42 B
CINE CAMERA, SEE SECTION 6.

NOTE :- PIPES NOT OTHERWISE
MARKED ARE 3/16"Ø.

⑲ FIT BLANKING OFF CAPS WHEN
CINÉ CAMERA OR GUNS
ARE NOT REQUIRED.

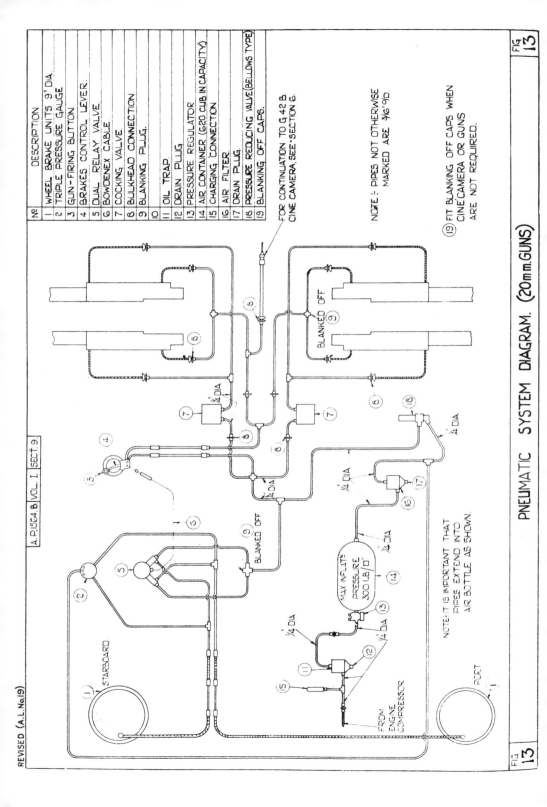

PNEUMATIC SYSTEM DIAGRAM. (20m.m.GUNS)

FIG 13

FIG 13

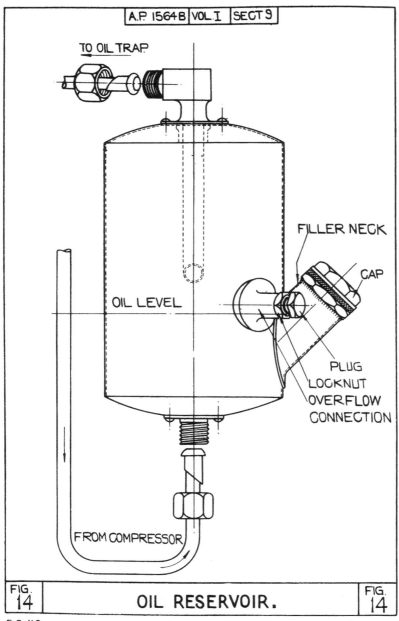

TO OIL TRAP

FILLER NECK

CAP

OIL LEVEL

PLUG

LOCKNUT

OVERFLOW

CONNECTION

FROM COMPRESSOR

FIG.
14

OIL RESERVOIR.

FIG.
14

F.S./18

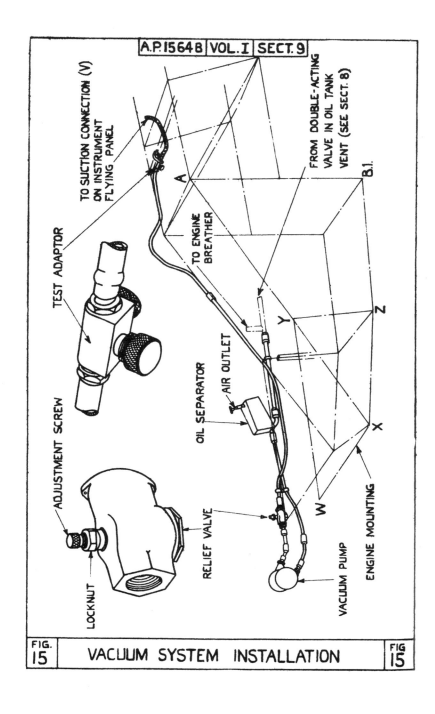

TO SUCTION CONNECTION (V)
ON INSTRUMENT
FLYING PANEL

TEST ADAPTOR

ADJUSTMENT SCREW

LOCKNUT

RELIEF VALVE

TO ENGINE
BREATHER

OIL SEPARATOR

AIR OUTLET

FROM DOUBLE-ACTING
VALVE IN OIL TANK
VENT (SEE SECT. 8)

A

B.1.

Z

Y

X

W

VACUUM PUMP

ENGINE MOUNTING

FIG.
15

VACUUM SYSTEM INSTALLATION

FIG
15

Section 10:
Electrical and radio installations — Description.

SECTION 10

ELECTRICAL AND RADIO INSTALLATIONS—DESCRIPTION

LIST OF CONTENTS

General

1. A brief description of the position of the main electrical components and of their accessibility is given in this Section. Wiring and theoretical diagrams are given in Section 6, and the majority of the components are fully described in A.P.1095, Vol. I.

Generator circuit

2. The power supply for the electrical components is obtained from a 12-volt 500 or 750-watt engine-driven generator, type L, B or LX, situated on the port side inside the engine cowling and charging a 12-volt 40 amp. hr. type B or D accumulator, carried on the starboard side of the wireless bay on a tray mounted between the side struts EH and GH. The generator is of the shunt-wound type, and in the case of types L and LX a carbon pile voltage regulator, type B or F, is fitted on the back of the armour plating behind the pilot's seat to maintain a constant voltage irrespective of engine speed and load fluctuations. The type B generator is self regulating. On later aircraft a warning lamp mounted on the decking near the undercarriage warning horn has been introduced to give the pilot indication of power failure. The lamp is in parallel with the main fuse and the accumulator cut-out, a rectifier being incorporated in the wiring.

3. A suppressor, type O or W, is fitted below the generator to prevent interference with the radio equipment. A cut-out, which prevents reverse feed from the accumulator to the generator, is fitted on the outboard side of the electrical panel on the port side of the cockpit and on early aircraft the main fuse (40 amp.) is fitted on the port strut E.F.; on later aircraft the fuse (60 amp.) is mounted on the inside bottom corner of the electrical panel. On the port decking shelf in the cockpit are mounted an ammeter, range 50–0–50 amps., a voltmeter, range 0–20 volts, and a switch box, type B, which is included in the shunt field as a safety measure.

Landing lamps

4. Two landing lamps, type G, are fitted, one in the centre of the leading edge of each wing in a housing covered by acetate sheet. Each lamp has a completely independent electrical circuit and is controlled, through a magnetic relay, type B, by a single-pole, two-way and "off", tumbler switch, which is on the decking shelf at the extreme port corner of the instrument panel. The relays are mounted either on the strut below the electrical panel (early aircraft) or on the forward end of the electrical panel (later aircraft. The lamp beam can be dipped by a lever at the port side of the cockpit. One contact at each end of the controlling switch is connected to the rear negative terminal on T.B.15 and the other contacts are connected to the middle terminals S on the respective relays. When the switch is moved to close the circuit of one landing lamp, a coil, connected between terminals S and A inside the corresponding relay, is energized, and the relay contacts close to connect terminals A and A and thus complete the lamp circuit.

Engine starting circuits

5. Early aircraft are fitted with a hand starting magneto; in later aircraft a booster coil takes the place of the hand starting magneto. These circuits are described separately below.

6   *Engine starting and ignition circuits (with booster coil).*—The electric motor is mounted towards the rear of the engine /on the starboard side, while the booster coil is fitted on starboard engine mounting strut XZ. Two push switches are mounted side by side on the port side of the instrument panel, one of these energizing the relay coil fitted on the starboard engine mounting strut AZ and the other completing the circuit for the booster coil; when starting the engine, these two switches must be depressed at the same time. The magnetos are controlled by a double pole switch which is mounted close to the push switches on the instrument panel. A B.T.H. socket is located beneath the relay on the starboard strut B1.Z, permitting an external source of power to be plugged in across terminals B+ and M2 after the face of the socket has been rotated; the rotation operates a switch which breaks the internal connection between M2 and B−, so that the aeroplane accumulator is cut out of the circuit.

7.   *Engine starting (with hand starting magneto).*—The starting motor is mounted towards the rear of the engine on the starboard side. The push switch on the port side of the instrument panel energizes the relay coil on the starboard engine mounting strut A.Z., which completes the motor circuit. A B.T.H. socket is located beneath the relay on the starboard strut B1.Z, permitting the use of an external source of power; a hand starting magneto is mounted on the starboard engine mounting strut.

Station-keeping lamps

8.   Certain aeroplanes are fitted with station-keeping lamps and these are mounted on the port and starboard fuselage struts G.H. so that their beams are directed along the trailing edges of the main planes. The ON-OFF switch is mounted on the decking shelf on the port side of the cockpit. On later aeroplanes, with a modified form of wiring, no provision is made for fitting these lamps.

Reflector gun-sight

9.   The switch for the reflector gun-sight lamps is situated on the starboard end of the instrument panel. Near it, on the starboard decking, is a dimmer switch and a three-way socket into which is plugged the connection to the sight. The lamp has two filaments, one giving a bright light for use in daylight and the other a dim light for use at night. The dimmer switch enables either filament to be selected and also enables the low-power filament to be dimmed. For a description of the gun-sight, *see* A.P.1730B, Vol. I.

Cockpit lighting

10.   Four lamps are provided to illuminate the cockpit, each of which is controlled by a separate switch. One lamp is situated at each side of the instrument panel; a third lamp, to illuminate the compass, is located below the instrument-flying panel, with its dimmer switch near the port lamp, and the fourth lamp is at the port side near the pilot's seat, with its dimmer switch just forward of the lamp.

Navigation lamps

11.   Three navigation lamps are provided, one in the tip of each outer plane in a housing covered by acetate sheet, and one on the rudder. They are controlled by the middle unit of the three-unit switchbox at the port end of the instrument panel.

Identification lamps

12. The indentification lamp switchbox is situated at the front end of the starboard side of the cockpit, and provides for steady illumination or morse signalling from either or both lamps. The upward and downward identification lamps are situated about midway along the fuselage in the upper and lower surfaces respectively, the upward lamp just aft of the sliding hood in its rearmost position and the downward lamp at the flare structure. The circuit is protected by the same fuse as the fuel contents gauges circuit.

Fuel contents gauges

13. A transmitter is fitted in each of the main fuel tanks carried in the centre section and in the reserve tank forward of the cockpit. One indicator only is provided and is situated at the starboard side of the instrument panel. A 3-way selector switch is situated immediately above the indicator. The circuit is protected by the same fuse as the identification lamps. For details of the selector switch, transmitter and indicator, *see* A.P.1275.

Undercarriage indicator

14. The undercarriage indicator is situated on the port side of the instrument panel, adjacent to the master switch which has two tumblers. Operation of the right-hand tumbler puts the reserve or normal lamps into circuit, and the left-hand one is used to switch off the green lights which indicate that the under-carriage is locked in the "down" position. The red lights ("up" locked position) and the horn cannot be switched off. The indicator lamps are operated by micro-switches in the wheel recesses in the wings, the switches being actuated by the undercarriage mechanism. The horn, which sounds when the under-carriage is not locked in the "down" position and the throttle lever is in a position less than one-third open, is mounted on the port side of the cockpit. The micro-switch in the horn circuit is operated by a cam at the end of the throttle lever.

Heated pressure head

15. The heated pressure head is situated midway along the lower side of the port outer plane. The heater element is switched on by the left-hand unit of the three-unit switchbox at the port side of the instrument panel.

Ciné camera

16. The ciné camera is situated in the leading edge of the starboard outer plane where it adjoins the centre section. It is operated by the closing of a push switch, to the rear of the ciné camera, which is pneumatically-operated when the gun-firing button on the control column is pressed. The ciné camera may also be operated independently of the guns by means of the push switch mounted on the side of the control column spade grip below the gun-firing button.

Oil dilution valve

17. The oil dilution valve is mounted on the port front face of the fire wall and the push switch, which controls the valve, is fitted to the port decking shelf in the cockpit.

Ignition system

18. A diagram of the ignition system is given in Sect. 8, fig. 10, and shows the connections between the main magnetos, the hand starting magneto and the control switches; for a description of the operation and the connections between the magnetos and the distributors, reference should be made to A.P.1590G, Vol. I.

Heated clothing

19. A socket for the supply to the electrically-heated boots and gloves is stowed in clips on the electrical panel in the cockpit. The current is taken from terminal G+ on the accumulator cut out and the negative return is taken to T.B.26 via a 10 amp. fuse.

Radio installations

20. Provision is made for the installation of either a T.R.9D or T.R.1133B or D radio in the bay immediately behind the pilot's seat, wiring diagrams for which are given in Sect. 6. For the T.R.9D installation the remote control is of the mechanical type and an aerial wire is fitted between the rudder and the aerial mast. In the case of the T.R.1133B or D, the controller is of the electrical type, but no aerial wire is fitted; the aerial mast acts as an aerial and a matching device is incorporated between the set and the mast. Provision is also made for fitting the A.R.I.5000 or A.R.I.5025 installation; the set is mounted on support channels behind the T.R.9D or T.R.1133B or D and the control unit just above the fuselage joint H. The radio supply is taken from the accumulator in the generator circuit, but in aircraft with the later method of wiring, the supply can also be drawn from an external supply plugged into the external supply socket. This additional source of supply obviates the use of the aircraft accumulator when the radio is required for use on the ground. Certain aircraft are provided with beam-approach equipment; a wiring diagram for this is included in Sect. 6. The amplifier, type A.1271, is mounted on the top longeron close to joint C, and the aerial is mounted on the underfairing near the downward identification lamp.

Section 11: Equipment installations — Description.

SECTION 11

EQUIPMENT INSTALLATIONS—DESCRIPTION

LIST OF CONTENTS

LIST OF ILLUSTRATIONS

Note.—In captions to illustrations, for "cannon" read 20 mm. gun or guns.

SECTION 11

EQUIPMENT INSTALLATIONS—DESCRIPTION

Introduction

1. This Section is limited to a description of certain items of equipment not dealt with in detail elsewhere in this publication; the disposition of the equipment is shown in fig. 1, and a diagram of access doors is given in Sect. 4, Chap. 3. The navigational equipment and the stowage of the first-aid outfit and hand starting handles are described in Sect. 1, and the flying controls locking gear, picketing rings, and weatherproof covers are described in Sect. 4, Chap. 2. The instruments are described in A.P.1275, Vol. I, and their disposition is illustrated in Sect. 1. The location of fuselage members, called up in the following paragraphs, will be found in Sect. 7.

·303 in. gun installation

2. *Guns.*—Mk. IIA aircraft have eight Browning ·303 in. guns and Mk. IIB aircraft twelve Browning ·303 in. guns (*see* fig. 2). Sets of 'four are mounted at the inboard ends of each outer plane, and the remaining guns are mounted in pairs outboard of the landing lamps, the ammunition being carried in boxes situated near the guns. The mountings for each set of guns comprise two steel tubes, one carrying the rear mounting brackets and the other carrying the front mounting brackets. The rear brackets provide lateral and vertical adjustment of the rear ends, the front brackets providing the necessary freedom of movement of the front ends of the guns. The firing of the guns is pneumatically controlled by a pushbutton on the control column (*see* Sect. 1), and the gun compartments are heated by warm air taken from the rear of the radiator (*see* Sect. 7, Chap. 2). Certain aircraft have an ammunition counter, operated pneumatically when the guns are fired.

3. *Blast tubes.*—The guns fire through blast tubes which extend through holes in the front spar web and align with corresponding holes in the nosing. At their rear ends the blast tubes are located by means of spherical adaptors on the guns themselves; the tubes are spring-loaded and bear against catches in the blast tube doors at their front ends.

4. *Rear mountings.*—The rear end of each gun is located by a mounting fork H (*see* fig. 3) supported by an adjustable bracket D fixed on the mounting tube referred to in para. 2. The stem G of the fork slides in a split sleeve F and is positioned by a screw fitted with a knurled knob E; by turning the screw the fork can be raised or lowered to alter the elevation of the gun. The split sleeve is carried between a pair of lugs on the bracket by a headed pin L, on which is freely mounted a two-part hollow screw J and K; the holes in the wall of the sleeve are threaded to receive the screw and the stem G is slotted to clear the screw throughout its range of adjustment. The two parts of the screw are coupled by a tongue-and-slot joint, which transmits rotary motion whilst permitting relative longitudinal movement of the two parts. The screw can be turned by means of a knurled knob B which rotates in a bearing in the bracket, a projection on the end of its shank engaging a recess in the end of the screw; by turning the knob the fork H is adjusted laterally. Both the vertical and lateral adjustments can be locked by tightening the nuts C on the end of the pin L; tightening the nuts squeezes the two parts of the screw together, thus

compressing the split sleeve and causing it to grip the stem G; rotation of the screw is prevented by the friction produced between the threads in the sleeve and on the screw.　The gun is attached to the fork H by a pin having a knurled head A, the periphery of which, as well as the peripheries of the knobs B and E, is provided with holes to enable it to be turned by a tommy bar if it is too stiff to be turned by the fingers.

5.　*Front mountings.*—The front end of each gun is attached by means of a pin G to a fork D (*see* fig. 3) which, in turn, is carried by a bracket F fixed on the mounting tube referred to in para. 2.　The pin has a knurled head C provided with holes in its periphery so that it can be turned by a tommy bar if it is too stiff to be turned by the fingers; a locknut is fitted at the end of the pin projecting through the fork.　When the rear end of the gun is raised or lowered the gun pivots about the pin; if it is required to move the rear end laterally, the nut E clamping the fork must be slackened off to permit the fork to turn in the bracket.

6.　*Magazines.*—Two magazines are situated on each side of the inboard sets of guns and one on each side of the outboard sets, the ammunition belts being fed to the guns over rollers in the magazines and through feed necks attached to the top edges of the magazines.　The two outer guns of each set of four are fed from their outboard sides, and the remaining two from their inboard sides; similarly the outer gun of each outboard pair is fed from its outboard side and the innermost gun of the pair from its inboard side.　The magazine lids are fastened by pins and spring clips in the case of the inboard sets of guns and by spring-loaded catches in the case of the outboard sets.

7.　The maximum normal capacities of the magazines are as follows:—

No. 1 magazine	...	...	...	...	338 rounds
No. 2　,,	...	...	...	...	324　,,
No. 3　,,	...	...	...	...	338　,,
No. 4　,,	...	...	...	...	338　,,
No. 5　,,	...	...	...	...	328　,,
No. 6　,,	...	...	...	...	328　,,

Some aeroplanes have magazines of increased capacity for Nos. 1–4 guns, as follows:—

No. 1 magazine	...	...	...	...	370 rounds
No. 2　,,	...	...	...	...	490　,,
No. 3　,,	...	...	...	...	380　,,
No. 4　,,	...	...	...	...	395　,,

8.　*Case and link chutes.*—Empty cartridge cases are jettisoned into the airstream through apertures in the bottom surface of the outer planes beneath the guns; the cases are conducted by metal chutes, bolted to reinforcing angles and plates attached to the bottom skin, the chutes being provided with felt pads where they are in contact with the undersides of the guns.　The links are ejected on the opposite sides of the guns to the magazine feed necks, and, in the case of the three inboard and two outboard guns in each plane, are conducted by means of chutes into the case chutes; the link chute for the outer gun of the inboard set leads to a separate aperture in the bottom of the plane.

20 mm. gun installation

9.　An alternative armament of the aeroplane (*see* fig. 4) consists of four Hispano Mk. I or Mk. II 20 mm. guns, mounted in sets of two in each outer plane. The rear mounting for the outboard gun is assembled between rib D and a channel stiffener attached to the bottom skin, and between the intermediate stiff rib and a corresponding stiffener for the inboard gun. The front mounting is attached to a casting fixed to the forward side of the front spar, and it protrudes through the leading edge of the main plane. The rear mounting provides vertical and lateral adjustment of the rear ends of the guns, the front mountings permitting the necessary freedom of movement at the front end. Firing is pneumatically-controlled by a push-button on the control column (*see* Sect. 1).

10. *Rear mountings.*—The rear end of each gun is bolted to an adaptor A (*see* fig. 6), the end of which is housed in a bearing B and held in position by a screw C. The bearing is assembled to a vertical screwed spindle D, which is housed in a swinging link E; the lower end of the link and a locknut on each side of it runs on a horizontal screwed spindle F mounted between bearings on rib D and a channel stiffener. A locating ring G is assembled to the horizontal screwed spindle to take up end play between the two bearings. An adjustable barrel H is fitted at the top of the swinging link to lock the vertical adjustment of the gun and is in turn locked to the link by means of a locknut.

11. *Front mountings.*—The front end of each gun is housed in a spherical bearing B, which is assembled in the forward end of the gun mounting; the mounting (*see* fig. 5) is a casting and is mounted on another casting which, in turn, is bolted to the front spar. The spherical bearing is positioned on the muzzle between a shoulder on the muzzle and the recoil spring. A bearing block A is attached to the end of the mounting by screws, and the spherical bearing is held against the bearing block by a retaining ring C, which is screwed into the block. When aligning, the retaining ring must be slackened to enable the gun to pivot about the centre of the spherical bearing.

12. *Ammunition boxes.*—One ammunition box is situated on the inboard side of each gun, the ammunition being fed over rollers in the boxes and through feed necks attached to the top edges of the boxes. The locating spigots are fitted at the bottom, and rubber pads are fitted to each foot at the four corners of the box. The lid is hinged to the box and is fastened by two plungers at the roller side.

13. *Case and link chutes.*—Empty cartridge cases and links are jettisoned into the airstream through apertures in the access doors in the bottom surface of the plane adjacent to each gun; the cases and chutes are conducted by sheet-metal chutes, which are riveted to the access doors.

Gun sights

14. Provision is made for fitting a ring and bead sight or an M.G. Mark II reflector sight. A mounting bracket for the reflector sight and the upper end of its dimming screen, and for the ring of the ring and bead sight, is fixed to the handrail behind the windscreen; a mounting for the lower end of the dimming screen is provided on the instrument-panel cross tube. A mounting for the bead is provided on the arch cowl rail over the engine.

15. *Reflector gun-sight.*—The reflector gun-sight is described in A.P.1730B, Vol. I. A dimmer switch on the starboard side of the cockpit (*see* illustration in Sect. 1) enables a high or low power filament of the gun-sight lamp to be selected as required, and also enables the low-power filament to be dimmed until the image of the graticule is only just visible. A dimming screen (*see* illustrations in Sect. 1) is provided to slide up in front of the reflector screen if

the background of the target is too bright. Holders for three spare bulbs are fitted on the starboard side of the instrument panel (*see* Sect. 1).

Ciné camera

16. A mounting for a G.42B or G.45 ciné camera is provided in the inboard end of the starboard outer plane nosing. Exposures are controlled by two separately operated switches; one switch is pneumatically-operated by the gun-firing circuit; this switch is mounted on the inboard side of the inner diagonal girder in the outer plane; the other switch is mounted on the bottom left-hand side of the control-column spade grip. The installation is illustrated in fig. 7; the cockpit controls are described in Sect. 1 and the ciné camera itself is described in A.P.1749, Vol. I.

Parachute flare

17. On early aircraft a 4 in. parachute flare is stowed in a chute on the port side of the fuselage just behind the radio (*see* fig. 8). The flare is launched through a small door in the underside of the fuselage, the latches securing the door being connected by a bowden cable to a handle mounted on a bracket attached to a strut at the starboard side of the cockpit (*see* Sect. 1). The lower portion of the flare contains the candle unit and the larger, upper part, contains the parachute.

Safety harness

18. An F-type or L-type safety harness is fitted to the cockpit seat (*see* fig. 9, and Sect. 1). Two short straps attached to the shoulder straps of the harness extend rearwards and are secured to a metal fitting F carrying a plunger B having a circumferential groove E; the plunger normally engages a socket D in the decking behind the seat and is retained by a locking plunger A engaging the groove. The locking plunger can be withdrawn to permit the pilot to lean forward by operating a control lever mounted on the starboard upper longeron; when the pilot leans back the plunger on the harness is drawn into the socket by a cable C passing over a pulley and attached to a spring housed in a tube behind the bulkhead. The pull of the harness is transmitted to fuselage joints J by anchorage cables attached to the fittings on the bulkhead.

Oxygen equipment

19. *Early aircraft.*—A high pressure oxygen cylinder is mounted below the pilot's seat on the right-hand side, with the outlet connection at the top (*see* fig. 10).* From this connection, the high pressure pipeline forms a loop and runs forward, clipped to a hydraulic pipe, then up the starboard side-strut C–D, and across the fuselage at the cross strut C–C, being clipped to both of these struts, and to the regulator mounted on the instrument panel. The low pressure pipe from the regulator runs along the port side of the cockpit near member CE, passing through holes in an instrument panel support bracket and the decking shelf, to the bayonet union socket mounted on the shelf. The regulator is described in A.P.1275, Vol. I.

20. *Later aircraft.*—On later aircraft two high-pressure oxygen cylinders are mounted, one behind and one below, the pilot's seat (*see* fig. 10). On some aircraft these cylinders are wire-wound as a protection against sudden bursting if they should be hit by a shell. From the outlet connections of the cylinders, high pressure pipes run to a T-piece near port joint C; both of these pipes have non-return valves incorporated at the T-piece. A pipe from the third branch of the T-piece runs to a control valve mounted on the port decking shelf. From this valve a pipe incorporating a filter is taken to a regulator mounted on the instrument panel. The low pressure pipe from the regulator runs to an oxygen economiser mounted on longeron D.F. and a feed pipe from the economiser is taken to a bayonet socket attached to the pilot's harness. On some aircraft the filter, control valve, and economiser may not be fitted; when the economiser is not fitted, the low pressure pipe from the regulator is taken to a bayonet socket mounted on the port decking shelf.

Landing lamps dipping control

21. Each lamp unit is mounted on a gimbal so that its beam may be dipped under the control of the pilot; it is returned to the "up" position by a spring. Dipping is controlled by a control lever mounted on the port side of the cockpit (*see* Sect. 1) and connected to the lamp by bowden cable. When the lever is in its rearmost position, the lamp points downwards at an angle of 15½ deg.; by pushing the lever forward the lamp is depressed further. The lever may be clamped in any position by means of a small knurled wheel mounted on its spindle; when free it returns automatically to its rearmost position under the action of the return spring on the lamp. From the control lever the bowden cable (*see* fig. 11) runs downwards to a double pulley unit which is bolted to the port front mounting bracket of the coolant radiator, behind the centre-section rear spar. The pulleys rotate together, the cable being wound round, and secured to, the smaller pulley; attached to opposite sides of the larger pulley are cables running outboard to port and starboard behind the rear spars of the main plane. Each of these cables passes through a fairlead at the centre-section outer rib and is connected by means of a turnbuckle to the cable within the root end of the wing. The cable then passes outboard through a conduit behind the rear spar, around a pulley at rib G, forward to a fairlead at the front spar, and thence to the outboard side of the periphery of the lamp; the length of each cable may be adjusted at the turnbuckle. An adjustable stop for the cable, between the cockpit lever and the double pulley unit, is mounted in a bracket on the electrical panel, just below the lever.

Desert equipment

22. Certain aircraft are provided with desert equipment stowed in the fuselage aft of the wireless unit (*see* fig. 12); access to the equipment is obtained by removing the detachable panel on the port side of the fuselage. All the items are stowed in the tray, except the signal pistol and cartridges, which are clipped to a fuselage strut.

Air cleaner

23. On aircraft supplied for use in the tropics an air cleaner is fitted to prevent extraneous matter entering the air intake. It consists of a streamlined fairing riveted underneath the lower engine panel, containing a Vokes Multi

"V" air filter (*see* A.P.1464B). Within the fairing in front of the air filter a shutter is incorporated which is controlled by the pilot, thus enabling warm or cold air to be sucked into the carburettor. When the shutter is in the lower position it blanks off the inlet in the front of the fairing and the air passes through the engine cowling and is warmed by being in contact with the engine before passing through a hole in the bottom of the lower engine panel and into the fairing. In the upper position the shutter blanks off the hole in the lower engine panel and the air passes directly through the front of the fairing.

Windscreen de-icing installation

24.   The windscreen de-icing installation (*see* fig. 13) consists of a de-icing fluid tank with a capacity of 4 pints, mounted on the starboard side of the fuselage, and a handpump in the cockpit, which is connected to the tank by a pipe clipped to the starboard strut CD. The pump draws the de-icing fluid from the tank and delivers it to the windscreen through a pipe which is clipped to the cockpit decking and instrument pane! and which passes through the decking to the bottom edge of the front panel of the windscreen. The pump may be either a Rotax or Ki-gass; both types are described in A.P.1464B.

Cockpit air conditioning

25.   Some aircraft have air-conditioning ventilators which enable the pilot to admit fresh air to the cockpit, as required. They are fitted through each side of the decking just aft of the instrument panel, in the form of a fixed casing bolted to the decking and containing a rotating louvre to regulate the air flow. When the ventilators are rotated to the forward setting air is cut off but when they are in the aft setting a stream of fresh air is directed towards the pilot's face. In addition, the temperature in the cockpit is reduced by asbestos lagging at the top of the radiator, the thermostat and the coolant pipes aft of the firewall.

Upward firing recognition device

26.   For the purpose of recognition at night an upward-firing recognition device is fitted in the rear fuselage adjacent to the aerial mast; it is operated by a remote control (*see* Sect. 1) on the port side of the pilot's seat. The control is connected by a bowden cable, adjustable at the rear end, to a signal discharger. The discharger is mounted on two cross tubes attached by U-bolts to the top longerons near joint J. The flare is fired from the cartridge in the discharger drum and is ejected through the blast tube. Initial operation of the control rotates the cartridge case and brings one cartridge into line with the blast tube. The last part of the control movement fires the cartridge and, on release, the control returns to its original position under the action of a spring mechanism incorporated in the discharger. Some aircraft are fitted with a control to enable the pilot to select an individual cartridge; the selector lever is mounted beside the control handle and is connected by cable to the signal discharger.

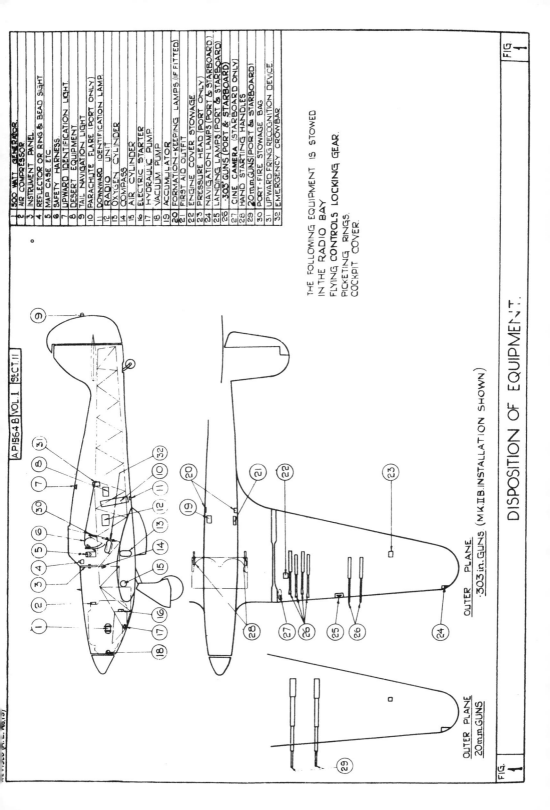

AP1564B VOL. I SECT. II

1	500 WATT GENERATOR
2	AIR COMPRESSOR
3	INSTRUMENT PANEL
4	REFLECTOR OR RING & BEAD SIGHT
5	MAP CASE ETC
6	SAFETY HARNESS
7	UPWARD IDENTIFICATION LIGHT
8	DESERT EQUIPMENT
9	TAIL NAVIGATION LIGHT
10	PARACHUTE FLARE (PORT ONLY)
11	DOWNWARD IDENTIFICATION LAMP
12	RADIO UNIT
13	OXYGEN CYLINDER
14	COMPASS
15	AIR CYLINDER
16	ELECTRIC STARTER
17	HYDRAULIC PUMP
18	VACUUM PUMP
19	ACCUMULATOR
20	FORMATION-KEEPING LAMPS (IF FITTED)
21	FIRST AID OUTFIT
22	ENGINE COVER STOWAGE
23	PRESSURE HEAD (PORT ONLY)
24	NAVIGATION LAMPS (PORT & STARBOARD)
25	LANDING LAMPS (PORT & STARBOARD)
26	.303 GUNS (PORT & STARBOARD)
27	CINE CAMERA (STARBOARD ONLY)
28	HAND STARTING HANDLES
29	20mm.GUNS (PORT & STARBOARD)
30	PORT-FIRE STOWAGE BAG
31	UPWARD FIRING RECOGNITION DEVICE
32	EMERGENCY CROWBAR

THE FOLLOWING EQUIPMENT IS STOWED
IN THE RADIO BAY
FLYING CONTROLS LOCKING GEAR.
PICKETING RINGS.
COCKPIT COVER.

OUTER PLANE.
.303 in. GUNS (MKIIB.INSTALLATION SHOWN)

OUTER PLANE
20mm.GUNS

DISPOSITION OF EQUIPMENT.

FIG. 1

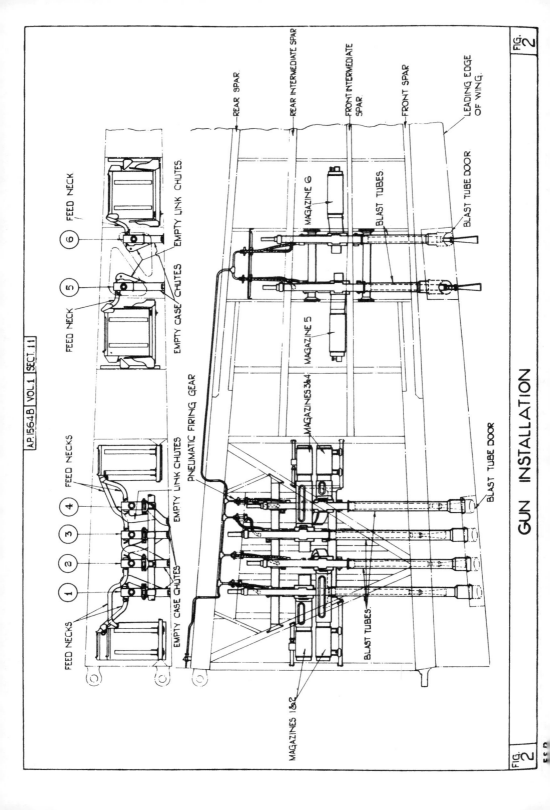

FEED NECK

FEED NECK 5

FEED NECK 6

EMPTY LINK CHUTES

EMPTY CASE CHUTES

FEED NECKS

FEED NECKS 1 2 3 4

PNEUMATIC FIRING GEAR

EMPTY LINK CHUTES

EMPTY CASE CHUTES

REAR SPAR

REAR INTERMEDIATE SPAR

FRONT INTERMEDIATE SPAR

FRONT SPAR

LEADING EDGE OF WING.

MAGAZINE 6

BLAST TUBES

BLAST TUBE DOOR

MAGAZINE 5

MAGAZINES 3&4

BLAST TUBE DOOR

MAGAZINES 1&2

BLAST TUBES

GUN INSTALLATION

FIG. 2

FIG. 2

ES.D

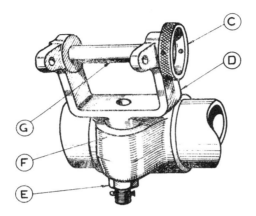

FRONT MOUNTING.

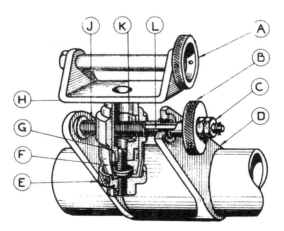

REAR MOUNTING.

FIG. 3

GUN MOUNTINGS.

FIG 3

F.S./4

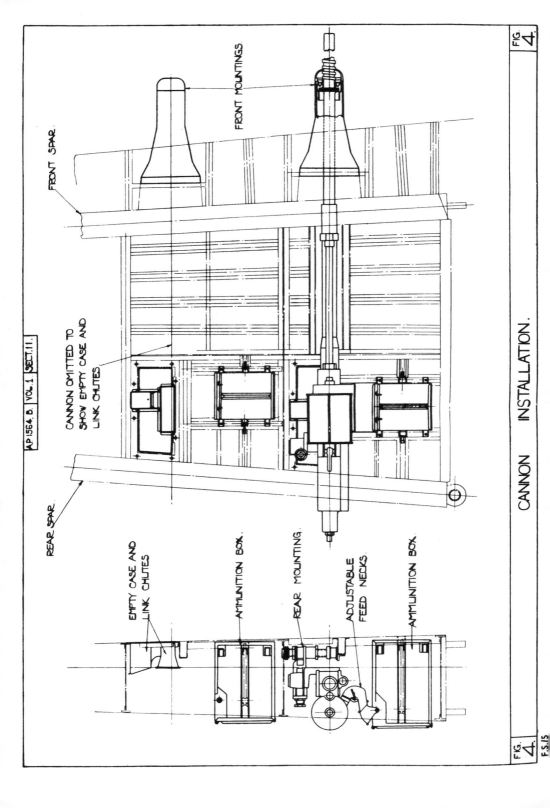

AP.1564.B. | VOL.1. | SECT.11.

FRONT SPAR.

FRONT MOUNTINGS.

CANNON OMITTED TO
SHOW EMPTY CASE AND
LINK CHUTES.

REAR SPAR.

EMPTY CASE AND
LINK CHUTES.

AMMUNITION BOX.

REAR MOUNTING.

ADJUSTABLE
FEED NECKS.

AMMUNITION BOX.

FIG.
4.

CANNON   INSTALLATION.

FIG.
4.

F.S.15

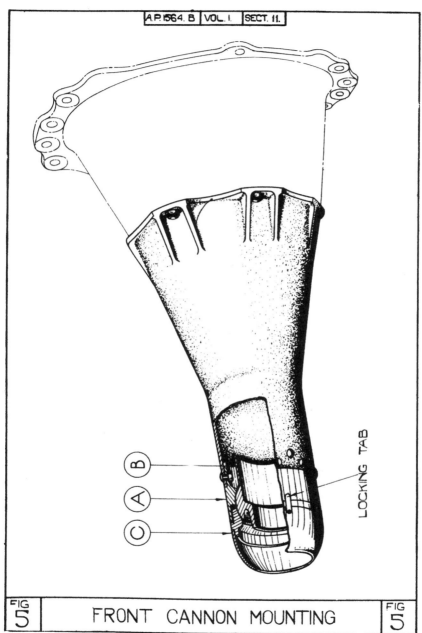

LOCKING TAB

B

A

C

FIG 5

FRONT CANNON MOUNTING

FIG 5

F S. 17

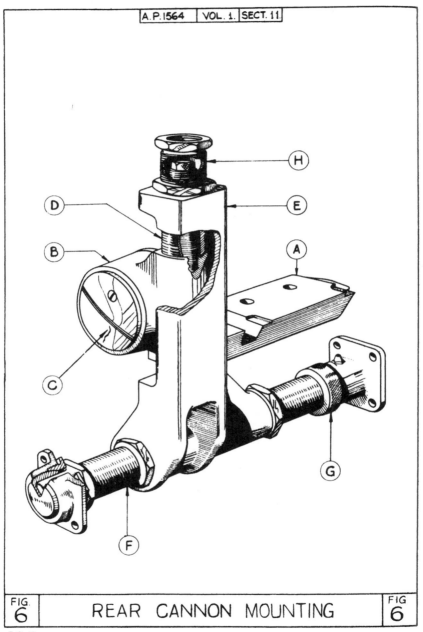

FIG. 6

REAR CANNON MOUNTING

FIG 6

F.S./8

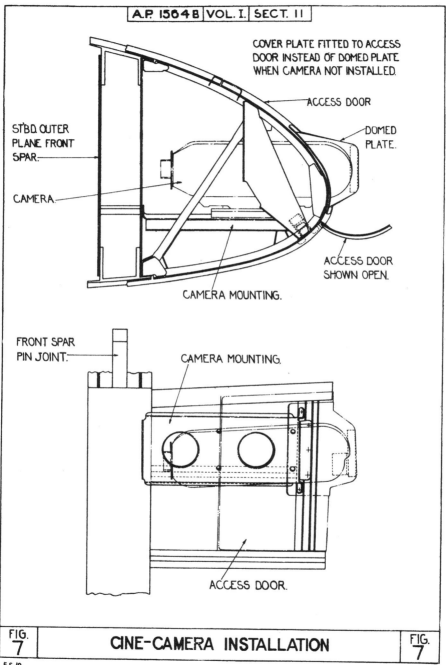

COVER PLATE FITTED TO ACCESS
DOOR INSTEAD OF DOMED PLATE
WHEN CAMERA NOT INSTALLED.

ACCESS DOOR

ST'BD. OUTER
PLANE FRONT
SPAR.

DOMED
PLATE.

CAMERA.

ACCESS DOOR
SHOWN OPEN.

CAMERA MOUNTING.

FRONT SPAR
PIN JOINT.

CAMERA MOUNTING.

ACCESS DOOR.

FIG.
7

CINE-CAMERA INSTALLATION

FIG.
7

F.S./9

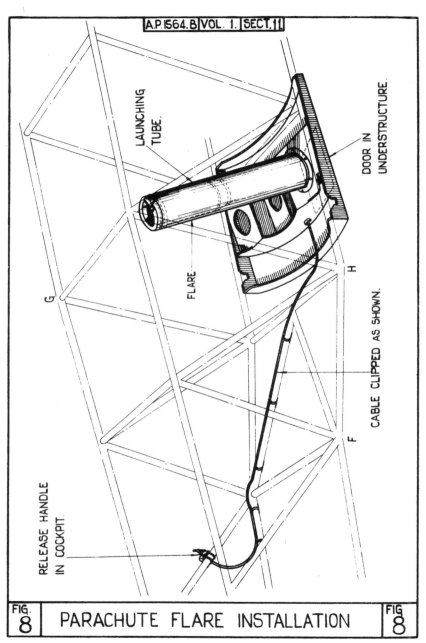

LAUNCHING TUBE.

DOOR IN UNDERSTRUCTURE.

FLARE

RELEASE HANDLE IN COCKPIT.

CABLE CLIPPED AS SHOWN.

G

H

F

FIG. 8

PARACHUTE FLARE INSTALLATION

FIG. 8

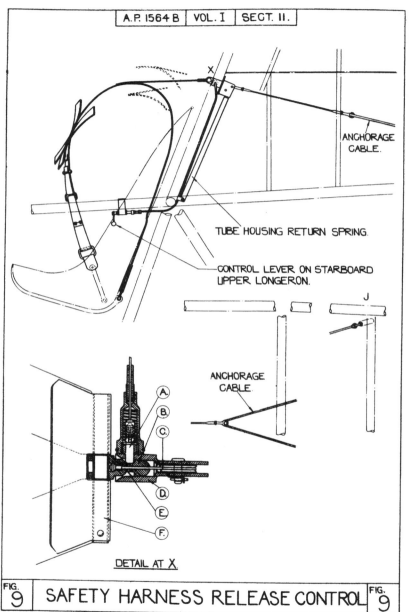

X

ANCHORAGE CABLE.

TUBE HOUSING RETURN SPRING.

CONTROL LEVER ON STARBOARD UPPER LONGERON.

J

ANCHORAGE CABLE.

(A)
(B)
(C)
(D)
(E)
(F)

DETAIL AT X.

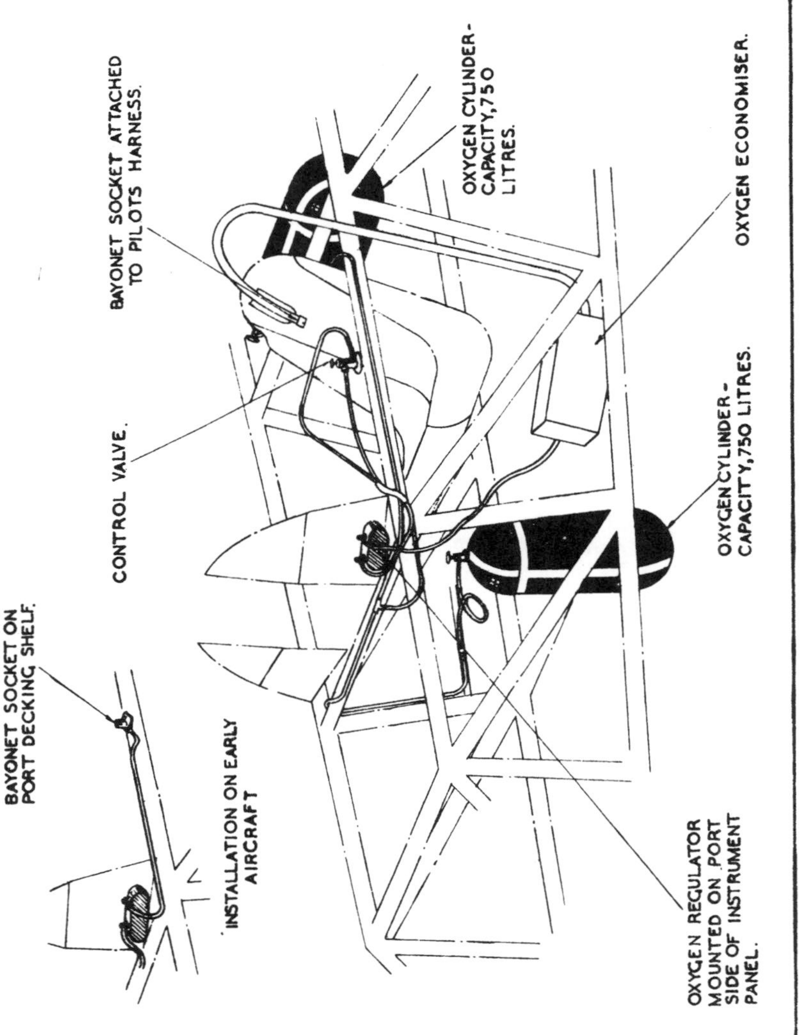

A.P. 1564.B. VOL I. SECT II.

BAYONET SOCKET ATTACHED TO PILOTS HARNESS.

OXYGEN CYLINDER - CAPACITY, 750 LITRES.

OXYGEN ECONOMISER.

CONTROL VALVE.

OXYGEN CYLINDER - CAPACITY, 750 LITRES.

BAYONET SOCKET ON PORT DECKING SHELF.

INSTALLATION ON EARLY AIRCRAFT

OXYGEN REGULATOR MOUNTED ON PORT SIDE OF INSTRUMENT PANEL.

FIG. 10

OXYGEN INSTALLATION

FIG. 10

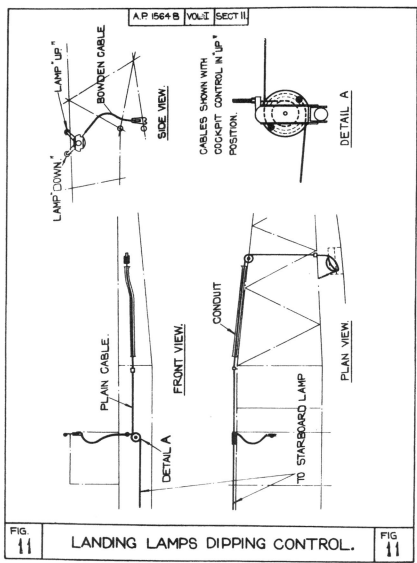

LAMP "UP"

BOWDEN CABLE

LAMP "DOWN."

SIDE VIEW.

CABLES SHOWN WITH COCKPIT CONTROL IN "UP" POSITION.

DETAIL A

PLAIN CABLE.

FRONT VIEW.

DETAIL A

CONDUIT

PLAN VIEW.

TO STARBOARD LAMP

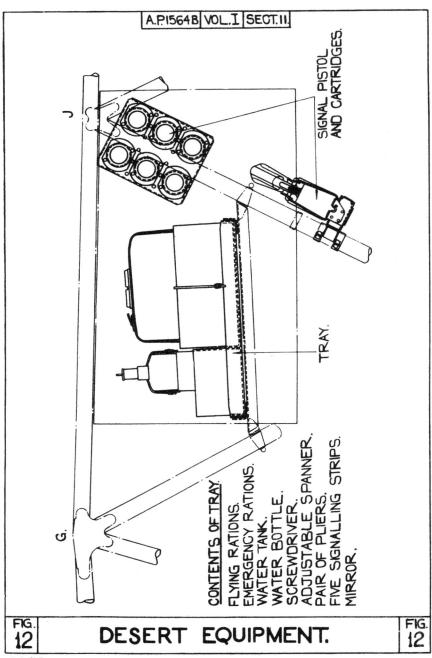

SIGNAL PISTOL AND CARTRIDGES.

J

TRAY.

G.

CONTENTS OF TRAY.
FLYING RATIONS.
EMERGENCY RATIONS.
WATER TANK.
WATER BOTTLE.
SCREWDRIVER.
ADJUSTABLE SPANNER.
PAIR OF PLIERS.
FIVE SIGNALLING STRIPS.
MIRROR.

FIG. 12 | DESERT EQUIPMENT. | FIG. 12

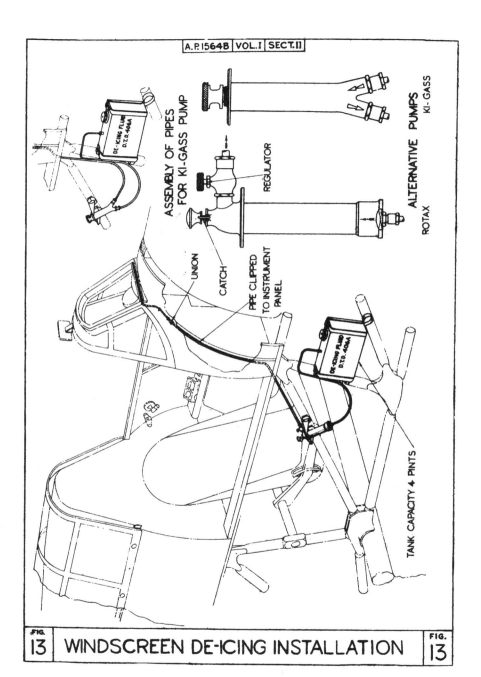

ASSEMBLY OF PIPES
FOR KI-GASS PUMP

ALTERNATIVE PUMPS

KI-GASS

ROTAX

KI-GASS

REGULATOR

UNION

CATCH

PIPE CLIPPED
TO INSTRUMENT
PANEL

DE-ICING FLUID
D.T.D.406A

DE-ICING FLUID
D.T.D.406A

TANK CAPACITY 4 PINTS

FIG.
13

WINDSCREEN DE-ICING INSTALLATION

FIG.
13

Addendum I:
Sea Hurricane IIB & IIC, Hurricane IIB & IIC (with arrester hook).

ADDENDUM I

SEA HURRICANE IIB AND IIC
AND
HURRICANE IIB AND IIC
(with arrester hook)

LIST OF CONTENTS

Loading and C.G. data—*cont.*

LIST OF ILLUSTRATIONS

Arrester hook

8. The hook (*see* fig. 2) is of the 10,500 lb. fixed wide-nose type. It consists, basically, of two steel side plates B, to which two catch plates A are riveted, and a steel nose J is bolted. The nose is provided with slots F and K for two operating levers H which pivot about a bolt G passing through the side plates and the nose of the hook. The operating levers are pinned at the top to a sliding stop E which slides in grooves in the side plates, the forward portion of the stop protruding above the side plates. Normally, the sliding stop is kept in the rear position by a spring D retained in a spring housing C, and the lower parts of the operating levers are then clear of the slots K; in this condition the hook cannot be inserted into the snap gear as the sliding stop catches against a stop plate (*see* para. 9), as shown in detail in fig. 2. When the arrester cable is caught up in the hook it forces the bottom of the levers back into the slots K, causing the top of the levers to move forward. This pushes the sliding stop forward so that it will clear the stop plate and allow the catch plates A to engage in the snap gear.

Snap gear

9. The snap gear (*see* fig. 3) is mounted below two vertical combined channel and saddle assemblies J which are bolted to cross strut Q–Q, registered by four studs H to the ground handling strut below Q–Q, and connected to each other by a stainless steel stop plate K (*see* para. 8). At the bottom of each channel assembly are bolted two extension plates A. Each of these carries at the top a release pawl G, operated by the cable F from the cockpit control, and at the bottom, below the channels, a trigger plate M pivoting on a spigot bolt L. A pin E at the top of the trigger plate fits behind an arm D of the release pawl. When the cable is pulled by the cockpit control the release pawls pivot about their attachments, causing the arms to move outwards, taking the pins E with them, and withdrawing the lips of the trigger plates sufficiently to allow the arrester hook to drop, as shown at the bottom of fig. 3. The release pawls and the trigger plates are returned to their original positions by the action of the springs B and C so that the arrester hook can be snapped home (*see* para. 6).

Arrester hook damper

10. The arrester hook damper (*see* fig. 4) is riveted at the top to a short length of tube which is connected to a pivot point on a bracket attached to fuselage joint L; at the bottom, it is bolted to the port member of the arrester hook V-strut (*see* fig. 1).

11. The damper consists of a plunger rod A sliding in a cylinder E which is divided into two portions. The upper end contains three rubber buffer rings M which are engaged by a stop D secured to the top of the plunger rod and take the weight of the arrester hook when it has fallen; the lower end, which contains a piston H also attached to the plunger rod, is filled with $\frac{1}{3}$rd pint of anti-freezing fluid (specification D.T.D.44D) through the hole opened by removing the upper of the two plugs C. The piston is fitted with a clack valve R and a spring-loaded valve G. When the arrester hook falls, the plunger rod and the piston pulled down and fluid flows freely to the top of the piston round the clack valve R. On striking the deck excessive rebound of the hook is checked by the fluid trapped in the cylinder, which can only escape back to the bottom of the piston through holes J and the spring-loaded valve G.

Fitting arrester hook in "up" position

12. To secure the arrester hook in the snap gear as a ground operation, lift the arrester hook V-strut nearly into position and then depress by hand the projecting levers in the nose of the hook (*see* para. 8) while the hook is raised the last few inches into the snap gear. If this is not done, the hook cannot be received by the snap gear, and therefore will not remain up.

Adjustment of snap gear control cable

13. Just forward of the point where the control cable divides into two is a turnbuckle, access to which may be obtained by removing the rear underfairing panel (*see* para. 18). The turnbuckle should be adjusted to take up any slack in the cable, but not so tightly as to cause the trigger plates in the snap gear to be withdrawn or the hook will not be securely held. The correct adjustment may be found by checking that the T-grip in the cockpit is just home on its support tube and that when the T-grip is pulled up, the trigger plates on the snap gear just clear the catch plates on the hook.

Lubrication

14. The bearings of all moving parts of the arrester gear and snap mechanism, and the control cable, are lubricated with anti-freezing oil (D.T.D.417A). *The mixture of one part grease to two parts paraffin (D.T.D.539), or of one part oil to one part paraffin, must not be used as a lubricant on any part of the Hooked or Sea Hurricane, the aileron differential gearbox included.*

Damper

15. *Topping up.*—The oil cylinder of the damper should be kept filled with Intavia utility oil or anti-freezing oil to specification D.T.D.44D. This should be inserted through the upper of the two plugs C shown in fig. 4.

16. *Dismantling.*—To dismantle the damper, proceed as follows (*see* fig. 4) :—

(i) Unscrew the locknut N which locks the top half of the cylinder to the centre bearing sleeve L.

(ii) Unscrew the top half of the cylinder.

(iii) Remove the split-pin from the top stop and unscrew the disc D.

(iv) Remove the rubber buffer rings M and spacing washers.

If it is required to fit new rubber buffer rings, this can be done without further dismantling. Should damage have occurred in the lower portion of the damper, proceed as follows:—

(v) Remove the drain plugs C and drain the fluid from the cylinder into a clean receptacle.

(vi) Remove the grubscrew K from the centre bearing sleeve L.

(vii) Unscrew the centre bearing sleeve and remove it from the plunger rod A, when the packing gland O and clamp P may be removed by unscrewing the setscrews securing them to the sleeve.

(viii) Remove the grubscrew B from the bottom bearing cap F.

(ix) Unscrew the cap and remove it complete with the plunger rod assembly.

(x) Remove the fork end and lock nut from the plunger rod A and slide off the bottom bearing cap F.

ADDENDUM I—HOOKED HURRICANE AND SEA HURRICANE

Note.—In general, information is given only when it differs from or is additional to that for the normal Hurricane of corresponding mark.

General

1. *Hurricane, with arrester hook.*—The Mk. II variants of the hooked Hurricane are the Mk. IIB and IIC. These carry the same armament as their corresponding normal Hurricane marks, from which they differ mainly in the provision of deck arrester gear and a position indicator for the arrester hook; normal R.A.F. radio equipment is installed.

2. *Sea Hurricane.*—The main differences between the Sea Hurricane IIB and IIC and their corresponding hooked Hurricane marks are that Sea Hurricanes are fitted with radio equipment of the type used in the Fleet Air Arm, and are provided with stowage for a signal pistol and cartridges.

3. The information in this addendum is applicable to both the hooked Hurricane and the Sea Hurricane except where the contrary is specifically stated.

PILOT'S CONTROLS AND EQUIPMENT

General

4. The controls and equipment for the pilot are described in Section 1 of this publication.

CONSTRUCTION AND OPERATION OF ARRESTER GEAR

General

5. The arrester gear consists, basically, of a hook, a V-strut, snap mechanism and a damper.

6. To provide additional local strength for the arrester gear, new side struts L–M 1 and a cross strut M 1–M 1 are provided. The arrester hook is carried on the V-strut (*see* fig. 1), which is pivoted at joints M 1, and attached to a damper which acts as a buffer for the hook at the end of its travel, and also checks the rebound of the hook when it hits the deck. The rebound is not fully damped out and when the hook picks up the cable, the arrester gear returns to its original position and is secured by the snap gear; if the cable should not be picked up, the hook is rejected by the snap gear and falls again to the limit of its travel.

7. When the arrester hook is in the "up" position, the V-strut fits into recesses provided in the rear underfairing A (*see* fig. 1), gaps at the forward end being covered by two small fairing panels. The snap gear is mounted on two brackets secured to cross strut Q–Q and to the handling bar tube D, which is below this strut. The release cable for the control in the cockpit runs along the port side of the fuselage and divides into two just forward of the release gear. An indicator lamp in the cockpit shows a green light when the arrester gear is in the "down" position.

(xi) Remove the packing gland and clamp ring from the bottom bearing cap F, after taking out the screws attaching them to the cap.

The plunger rod can be dismantled further but, as the limits on the valve are very critical, the complete rod assembly should be replaced if any part is damaged.

17. *Re-assembling.*—When re-assembling the damper, it is essential that the centre lines of the plugs O are not offset from each other by more than 0·17 in. To ensure that this is so, extra jointing washers may be used at the centre bearing sleeve L. If damage to the damper has necessitated removal of the clack valve R, the damper must be subjected to two tests on re-assembly. The first is a mechanical test which should be carried out as shown in fig. 4; the second test is to impose a hydraulic pressure of 100 lb./sq. in. and watch for leakage.

REMOVAL AND ASSEMBLY OPERATIONS

Rear underfairing panel

18. Before starting to remove the rear underfairing panel (A in fig. 1), which is of wood and fabric construction, it is necessary first to release the arrester gear by operating the cockpit release handle, and to lower the hook by hand; if the aircraft is standing on a muddy or sandy surface a block of wood or a metal sheet should be provided for the hook to rest on, to prevent grit and dirt from fouling the mechanism. When the arrester gear has been released, the six fasteners which hold the fairing in place should be unscrewed, the fairing being supported while this is done, after which the fairing may be gently eased off backwards.

Damper

19. To remove the damper proceed as follows:—

(i) Remove the rear underfairing panel.

(ii) Detach the bottom of the damper from the port side of the arrester hook V-strut by removing the $\frac{5}{16}$ in. dia. bolt (C in fig. 1), with nut, split pin and distance tube, which secures the fork end on the damper rod to the attachment lug bolted to the V-strut.

(iii) Remove the $\frac{5}{16}$ in. dia. bolt (B in fig. 1), with nut and washer, attaching the plug end at the top of the damper to joint L.

V-strut

20. *Removal.*—The arrester gear V-strut can only be detached when the rear underfairing panel and the $\frac{5}{16}$ in. bolt securing the damper to the strut have been removed. It is then only necessary to take out the eyebolt E with its castle nut and split pin, which attaches the V-strut to joint M 1 at each side of the fuselage; the rivets attaching the bush F to the side plate should *not* be removed.

21. *Assembly.*—When the V-strut has been re-assembled, it is essential to check that the sliding stop on the hook clears the stop plate by at least 0·1 in. when in the forward position, and that the indicator lamp operates when the strut is down.

ELECTRICAL INSTALLATIONS

Arrester hook indicator lamp

22. A wiring diagram for the arrester hook indicator lamp is given in fig. 5. The supply for the lamp is taken from a terminal block on the electrical panel and the lamp is operated by a micro-switch mounted on side strut L–M 1.

LOADING AND C.G. DATA

Introduction

23. For the determination of the C.G. position the aircraft is considered standing with the thrust line (or rigging datum line) horizontal and the under-carriage down.

24. The distance of the C.G. aft of the C.G. datum point, which is called the moment arm of the C.G., is given by the expression

$$\frac{(\text{Tare wt.} \times \text{tare C.G. moment arm}) \pm (\text{Wts. of loads} \times \text{respective moment arms})}{\text{Tare weight} + \text{total weight of loads}}$$

$$= \frac{\text{Tare moment} \pm \text{load moments}}{\text{total weight}}$$

25. The moment arm (in inches) is positive when the load considered lies aft of a vertical line through the C.G. datum point and is negative when the load considered lies forward of a vertical line through the C.G. datum point. The weight (in pounds) is in all cases positive.

Datum point

26. The datum point is the centre of the engine starting handle shaft and is marked on the port side of the aircraft. The position of this point is based on the assumption that the centre-line of the bracket supporting the starting shaft is 6 in. from the centre-line of joint "X" measured along strut "XZ" (*see* Loading Diagram, fig. 6).

27. When determining the aircraft C.G. position by weighing, any variation in the position of the C.G. datum point from the nominal should be noted and the necessary correction made. For example, if the dimension referred to above differs from the nominal by 0·5 in. (i.e. actual measurement gives 5·5 or 6·5 in.) this correction should be made to the calculated dimension of the C.G. aft of the C.G. datum point, the correction being added if the centre-line of the bracket is aft of its nominal position.

C.G. travel limits

28. Approved limits of C.G. travel are 56 in. to 60·4 in. aft of the C.G. datum point, measured parallel to the thrust line. The C.G. position must be kept within the specified range, even with the fuel consumed and with ammu-nition expended. For example, if the loaded aircraft has a C.G. position 56 in. aft of the C.G. datum point at the commencement of flight, then in a short time the consumption of the fuel load will move the C.G. position beyond the approved forward limit.

Examples on the determination of the C.G. position

29.   To determine the C.G. position for an aircraft with any particular load (*see* para. 24) the total moment for that loading, as shown on the loading diagram, is divided by the corresponding total weight.   The resultant quotient is the distance of the C.G. behind the C.G. datum point.

30.   *Normal loading.—*

	Weight (lb.)	Moment (lb./in.)
Mk. IIC aircraft (*see* fig. 6)	7,891	475,831

C.G. moment arm $= \dfrac{475,831}{7,891} = 60\cdot3$ in. aft of datum.

31.   *With main fuel consumed and ammunition expended—*

	Weight (lb.)	Moment (lb./in.)
Mk. IIC aircraft	7,891	475,831
Deduct main fuel	−497	35,386
Deduct ammunition	−226	15,549
Total	7,168	424,896

C.G. moment arm $= \dfrac{424,896}{7,168} = 59\cdot2$ in. aft of datum.

32.   *Embodiment of modifications.—*Assume modifications Nos. **388, 400, 411** and **441** have been incorporated and refer to para. 34 for the respective weight and moment values.

	Weight (lb.)	Moment (lb./in.)
Mk. IIC aircraft at tare weight ...	5,847	328,601
Mod. No. 388	+ 1·43	111
Mod. No. 400	+21·75	941
Mod. No. 411	+ 4·5	608
Mod. No. 441	− 2·5	−163
Total	5,872·18	330,098

The above totals represent the new tare condition of the aircraft after the embodiment of the modifications.   To this condition the desired operational load should be added, including all or part of the change in load affected by the modifications introduced.

	Weight (lb.)	Moment (lb./in.)
Aircraft at modified tare weight ...	5,872·18	330,098
Total removable load for Mk. IIC aircraft as on Loading Diagram ...	2044·0	147,230
Mod. No. 411	+2·5	+326
Mod. No. 411 existing removable equipment moved	*	+ 39
Total	7,918·68	477,693

For new all-up weight

$$\text{C.G. moment arm} = \frac{477,693}{7,918 \cdot 68} = 60 \cdot 3 \text{ in. aft of datum.}$$

Modifications included

33. The tare weight and loading shown on the loading diagram include the following modifications:—

(i) *Mk. IIB aircraft*—Modification Nos. 1, 2, 3, 4, 5, 6, 7, 8, 9, 10, 11, 12, 14, 15, 16, 17, 18, 19, 20, 21, 22, 23, 24, 25, 26, 27, 28, 29, 30, 31, 32, 33, 34, 35, 36, 37, 38, 39, 40, 41, 42, 43, 44, 45, 46, 47, 48, 49, 50, 51, 52, 53, 54, 55, 56, 57, 58, 59, 60, 61, 62, 63, 64, 65, 66, 67, 68, 69, 71, 72, 74, 75, 76, 77, 78, 79, 80, 81, 82, 83, 84, 85, 86, 88, 92, 94, 95, 96, 97, 98, 99, 100, 101, 102, 103, 104, 105, 106, 107, 108, 109, 110, 111, 112, 113, 114, 116, 117, 118, 119, 120, 123, 124, 125, 126, 127, 128, 129, 130, 131, 133, 134, 135, 136, 137, 138, 139, 140, 141, 142, 143, 144, 145, 146, 147, 148, 149, 151, 152, 153, 154, 155, 156, 157, 158, 159, 160, 163, 164, 165, 167, 170, 172, 173, 174, 176, 177, 178, 179, 180, 181, 182, 183, 185, 186, 187, 188, 189, 190, 191, 192, 193, 194, 195, 197, 198, 199, 201, 202, 204, 206, 207, 208, 209, 210, 214, 215, 216, 217, 218, 220, 222, 223, 224, 225, 227, 228, 229, 231, 233, 234, 235, 236, 237, 239, 241, 242, 243, 244, 245, 246, 249, 252, 253, 254, 255, 257, 258, 259, 265, 267, 268, 271, 273, 278, 279, 280, 282, 286, 288, 289, 292, 293, 296, 297, 298, 301, 302, 303, 304, 305, 308, 309, 310, 311, 312, 314, 316, 318, 319, 322, 323, 327, 328, 329, 331, 332, 333, 336, 339, 342, 351, 352, 362, 364, 367, 368, 370, 376, 378, 381, 384, 393, 394, 401, 411, 412, 413, 414, 415, 431, 432.

(ii) *Mk. IIC aircraft.*—Modification Nos. 1, 2, 3, 4, 5, 6, 7, 8, 9, 10, 11, 12, 13, 14, 15, 16, 17, 18, 19, 20, 21, 22, 23, 24, 25, 26, 27, 28, 29, 30, 31, 32, 33, 34, 35, 36, 37, 38, 39, 40, 41, 42, 43, 44, 45, 46, 47, 48, 49, 50, 51, 52, 53, 54, 55, 56, 57, 58, 59, 60, 61, 62, 63, 64, 65, 66, 67, 68, 69, 71, 72, 74, 75, 76, 77, 78, 79, 80, 81, 82, 83, 84, 85, 86, 88, 92, 94, 95, 98, 99, 100, 101, 102, 103, 104, 105, 106, 107, 108, 109, 110, 111, 112, 113, 114, 116, 117, 118, 119, 120, 123, 124, 125, 126, 127, 128, 129, 130, 131, 133, 134, 135, 136, 137, 138, 139, 140, 141, 142, 143, 144, 145, 146, 147, 148, 149, 151, 153, 154, 155, 156, 157, 158, 159, 160, 163, 165, 167, 170, 172, 173, 174, 176, 177, 178, 179, 180, 181, 182, 183, 185, 186, 187, 188, 189, 190, 191, 192, 193, 194, 195, 197, 198, 199, 201, 202, 204, 206, 207, 208, 209, 210, 214, 215, 216, 217, 218, 220, 222, 223, 224, 225, 227, 228, 229, 231, 232, 233, 234, 235, 236, 237, 239, 241, 242, 243, 244, 245, 246, 249, 252, 253, 254, 255, 257, 258, 259, 265, 267, 268, 271, 273, 275, 278, 279, 280, 282, 288, 289, 292, 293, 297, 298, 301, 302, 303, 305, 308, 309, 310, 311, 312, 314, 317, 318, 319, 322, 323, 325, 327, 328, 329, 331, 332, 333, 336, 340, 342, 351, 352, 355, 362, 363, 364, 367, 368, 370, 376, 378, 381, 384, 393, 394, 401, 411, 412, 413, 414, 415, 431, 432.

Changes of weight and moment due to modifications

34. Any modifications that are incorporated on the aircraft but are not shown on the appropriate list in para. 33, are additional to those included on the Loading Diagram and must be allowed for when calculating the total weight and C.G. position (*see* para. 32); the following table gives changes of weight and moment due to such additional modifications.

Mod. No.	Description	Tare weight		Removable load	
		Weight (lb.)	Moment (lb./in.)	Weight (lb.)	Moment (lb./in.)
70	Hydraulic pressure gauge introduced	+ 1·0	72	—	—
91	Desert equipment (removable) introduced	—	—	+ 56·8	8,570
230	Air intake cover modified	—	—	+ 0·25	18
251	Engine couplings at header tank improved	+ 0·13	3	—	—
262	Tropical cooling introduced	− 0·02	− 2	—	—
263	Cockpit air conditioning introduced	+17·0	1,275	—	—
264	Air cleaner for air intake introduced	+28·92	347	—	—
272	Oil tank immersion heater introduced	+11	319	—	—
306	45 gall. drop tanks—removable (Mk. IIB)	—	—	+ 751·0	46,800
307	45 gall. drop tanks—removable (Mk. IIC)	—	—	+ 751·0	46,800
341	2–500 lb. bombs introduced	—	—	+1048·0	59,500
346	Air cleaner, rear portion strengthened	+ 0·41	11	—	—
359	2–250 lb. bombs, removable parts in wings (Mk. IIB)	—	—	+ 542·63	30,950
361	2–250 lb. bombs, removable parts in wings (Mk. IIC)	—	—	+ 540·63	30,850
369	Rear view mirror, type "B" introduced	+ 0·25	20	—	—
372	Power failure warning light introduced	+ 0·53	40	—	—
373	New material for walkways introduced	− 1·0	− 80	—	—
374	Spring-loaded relief valve on header tank	− 0·67	− 18	—	—
383	(i) S.B.C. removable parts	—	—	+ 737·75	41,000
	(ii) S.C.I. removable parts	—	—	+ 655·75	38,300
386	S.B.C. and S.C.I. provision on 500 lb. carriers	—	—	+ 0·27	11
388	Self-sealing fuel pipes introduced	+ 1·43	111	—	—
400	U/c wheel type A.148213 as an alternative to A.H.10019	+21·75	+941	—	—
407	Guard for rear oxygen cylinder introduced	+ 0·25	+ 24	—	—
408	(i) Downward ident. light, three-colour introduced	+ 2·5	+348	—	—
	(ii) Existing equipment moved	*	− 25	—	—

* A weight figure is not given here because the moving of existing equipment involves no change in weight.

Mod. No.	Description	Tare weight		Removable load	
		Weight (lb.)	Moment (lb./in.)	Weight (lb.)	Moment (lb./in.)
411	Provision for R.3067 type 90 aerial	+ 4·5	+608	+ 2·5 *	+ 326 + 39
412	T.R.1196A, removable parts introduced	− 0·75	− 81	− 44	−5016
416	R.10A installation introduced	+ 0·5	+ 51	—	—
417	(i) R.10A installation introduced	—	—	+ 4·0	+ 456
	(ii) Existing equipment moved	—	—	*	+ 109
418	Incendiary bomb stowage introduced	+ 0·5	+ 72	—	—
419	Throttle lever of improved type introduced	+ 0·5	+ 59	—	—
421	Conversion from Rotol to D.H. C/S propeller	+25·0	−865	—	—
433	R.P.M. indicator drive, shortened type introduced	− 0·25	− 7	—	—
441	Sun screen for gun sight deleted	− 2·5	− 163	—	—

* A weight figure is not given here because the moving of existing equipment involves no change in weight

The following modifications have been omitted from the previous table, because their effect on weight and C.G. position is negligible:—

Nos.—291, 326, 338, 344, 347, 371, 382, 424, 430, 438.

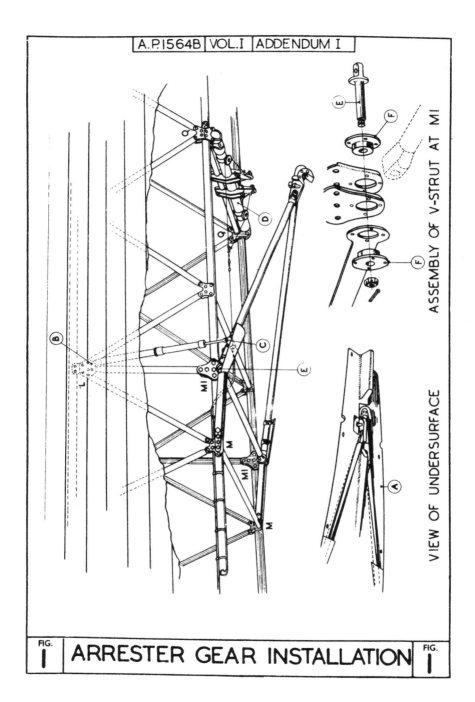

ASSEMBLY OF V-STRUT AT MI

VIEW OF UNDERSURFACE

FIG. I   ARRESTER GEAR INSTALLATION   FIG. I

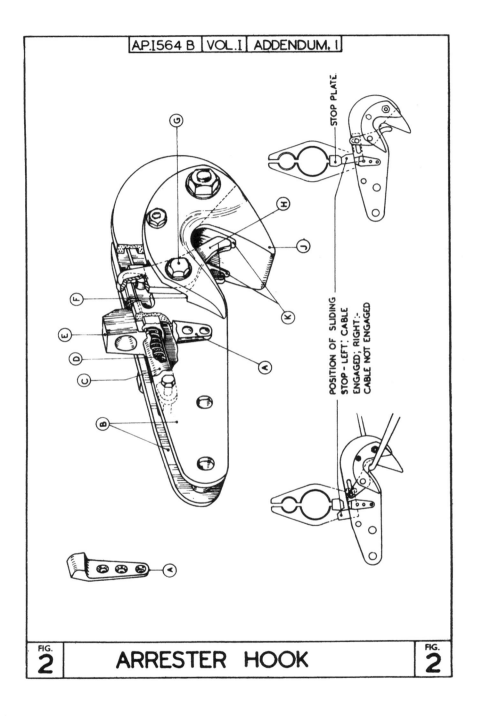

STOP PLATE.

POSITION OF SLIDING STOP – LEFT: CABLE ENGAGED; RIGHT:- CABLE NOT ENGAGED

FIG. 2   ARRESTER HOOK   FIG. 2

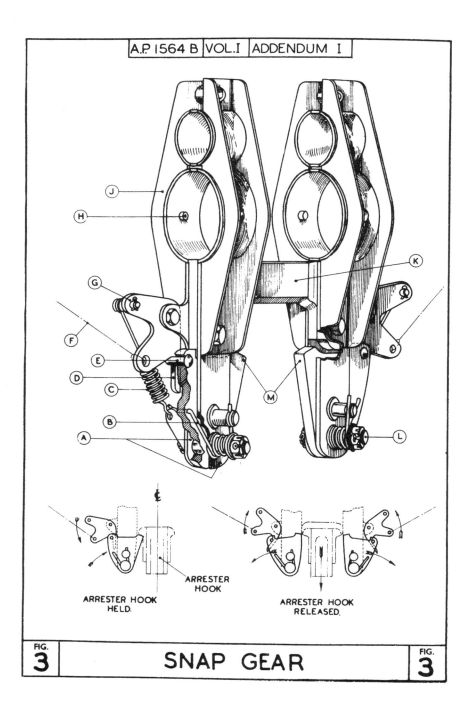

ARRESTER
HOOK

ARRESTER HOOK
HELD.

ARRESTER HOOK
RELEASED.

FIG.
3

FIG.
3

SNAP GEAR

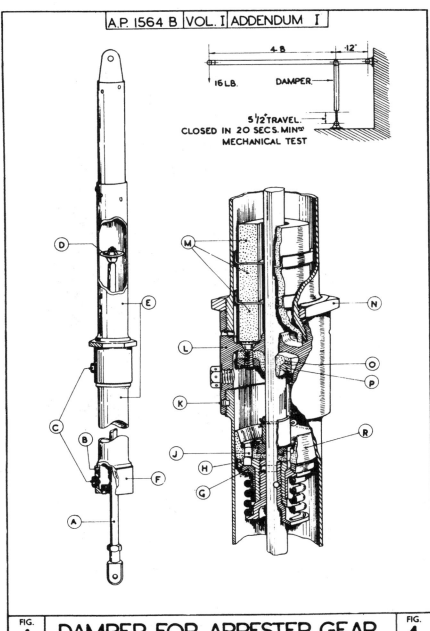

4 B

.12"

16 LB.   DAMPER.

5 ½" TRAVEL.
CLOSED IN 20 SECS. MIN∞
MECHANICAL TEST

FIG. 4 | **DAMPER, FOR ARRESTER GEAR** | **FIG. 4**

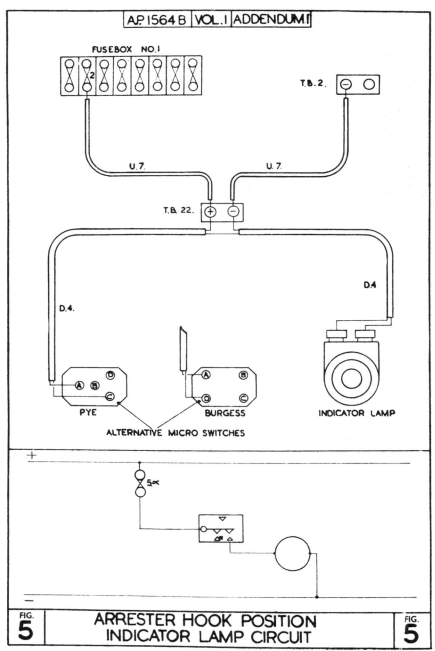

FUSEBOX NO.1

T.B.2.

U.7. U.7.

T.B. 22.

D.4.

D.4

PYE

BURGESS

INDICATOR LAMP

ALTERNATIVE MICRO SWITCHES

| FIG. 5 | ARRESTER HOOK POSITION INDICATOR LAMP CIRCUIT | FIG. 5 |

PP2216 M   /256 5/43 9450 C & P Gp. 959 (4)

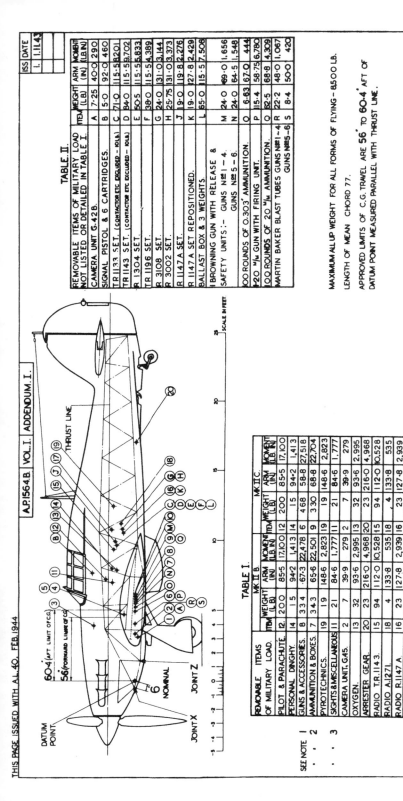

ISS 1. — DATE 1.11.43

TABLE II.

REMOVABLE ITEMS OF MILITARY LOAD NOT LISTED OR DETAILED IN TABLE I.

	ITEM	WEIGHT (LB)	ARM (IN)	MOMENT (LB.IN)
CAMERA UNIT G.42B.	A	7.25	40.0	290
SIGNAL PISTOL & 6 CARTRIDGES.	B	5.0	92.0	460
TR1133 SET. (CONTACTOR ETC EXCLUDED - 10LB.)	C	7.0	115.5	8201
TR1143 SET. (CONTACTOR ETC EXCLUDED - 10LB.)	D	84.0	115.5	9,702
R1304 SET.	E	50.5	115.5	5,833
TR1196 SET.	F	38.0	115.5	4,389
R3108 SET.	G	24.0	131.0	3,144
R3002 SET.	H	25.75	131.0	3,373
R1147A SET.	J	19.0	119.8	2,276
R1147A SET REPOSITIONED.	K	19.0	127.8	2,429
BALLAST BOX & 3 WEIGHTS.	L	65.0	157.0	7,508
BROWNING GUN WITH RELEASE & SAFETY UNITS:- GUNS Nos 1 - 4.	M	24.0	69.0	1,656
GUNS Nos 5 - 6.	N	24.0	64.5	1,548
100 ROUNDS OF 0.303" AMMUNITION.	O	6.63	67.0	444
20 m/m GUN WITH FIRING UNIT.	P	115.4	58.75	6,780
100 ROUNDS OF 20 m/m AMMUNITION. GUNS Nos 1 - 4.	Q	82.5	68.8	4,309
GUNS Nos 5 - 6.	R	22.2	48.0	1,067
MARTIN BAKER BLAST TUBES	S	8.4	50.0	420

TABLE I.

REMOVABLE ITEMS OF MILITARY LOAD.	ITEM	MK II B WEIGHT (LB)	ARM (IN)	MOMENT (LB.IN)	ITEM	MK II C WEIGHT (LB)	ARM (IN)	MOMENT (LB.IN)
PILOT & PARACHUTE.	12	200	85.5	17,100	12	200	85.5	17,100
PERSONAL DINGHY.	14	15	94.2	1,413	14	15	94.2	1,413
GUNS & ACCESSORIES.	8	334	67.3	22,478	8	468	58.8	27,518
AMMUNITION & BOXES.	7	34.3	65.6	2,501	6	330	68.8	22,704
PYROTECHNICS.	19	19	148.6	2,823	19	19	148.6	2,823
SIGHTS & MISCELLANEOUS.	11	21	84.6	1,777	11	21	84.6	1,777
CAMERA UNIT, G45.	2	7	39.9	279	2	7	39.9	279
OXYGEN.	13	32	93.6	2,995	13	32	93.6	2,995
ARRESTER GEAR.	20	23	216.0	4,968	20	23	216.0	4,968
RADIO T.R.1143.	15	94	112.0	10,528	15	94	112.0	10,528
RADIO A.1271.	18	4	133.8	535	18	4	133.8	535
RADIO R.1147 A.	16	23	127.8	2,939	16	23	127.8	2,939
RADIO R.3108.	17	28	129.0	3,612	17	28	129.0	3,612
TOTAL REMOVABLE ITEMS OF MILITARY LOAD.		1,143		93,948		1,264		99,191
FUEL. MAIN.	10	497	71.2	35,386	10	497	71.2	35,386
FUEL. RESERVE.	3	202	47.8	9,656	3	202	47.8	9,656
OIL.	1	81	37.0	2,997	1	81	37.0	2,997
AIRCRAFT AT TARE WEIGHT	5	5,656	56.6	320,248	5	5,847	56.2	328,601
TOTALS.		7,579		462,235		7,891		475,831

SEE NOTE 1, 2, 3.
SEE NOTE 4.

MAXIMUM ALL UP WEIGHT FOR ALL FORMS OF FLYING - 8,500 LB.

LENGTH OF MEAN CHORD 77.

APPROVED LIMITS OF C.G. TRAVEL ARE 56" TO 60.4" AFT OF DATUM POINT MEASURED PARALLEL WITH THRUST LINE.

NOTE 1: { (ITEM 8 INCLUDES BROWNING GUNS, FIRE & SAFETY UNITS, REAR SEAR RELEASE UNITS, BLAST TUBES, CASE & LINK CHUTES.) (ITEM 6 INCLUDES 20 m/m GUNS, FIRING UNITS, CASE & LINK CHUTES.) }

NOTE 2: (ITEM 7 INCLUDES AMMUNITION, MAGAZINES, FEED NECK & FEED MECHANISM. ITEM 7 = 580 RDS. ITEM 9,382 RDS.)

NOTE 3: (ITEM 11 INCLUDES REFLECTOR GUN SIGHT & FILAMENTS, NAVIGATIONAL COMPUTOR, CONTROL LOCKING DEVICE, PICKETING EYES, COVERS FOR AIR INTAKE, PROPELLER, ENGINE, & HOOD, CROWBAR & FIRST AID.)

NOTE 4: (ITEM 10 90 GALLS. AT 7·2 LB/GALL. ITEM 3·28 GALLS AT 7·2 LB/GALL. ITEM 1 9 GALLS AT 9 LB/GALL.)

DATUM POINT. — 60.4" (AFT LIMIT OF CG) — 56" (FORWARD LIMIT OF CG) — NOMINAL — JOINT Z — JOINT X — F.6 — THRUST LINE — SCALE IN FEET.

LOADING & C.G. DIAGRAM.

FIG 6.

Addendum II: Hurricane IID & IV.

ADDENDUM II

HURRICANE IID AND IV

LIST OF CONTENTS

LIST OF ILLUSTRATIONS

ADDENDUM II—HURRICANE IID AND IV

Note.—In general, information is given only when it differs from or is additional to that for the normal Hurricane II, and applies to both Marks IID and IV except where the contrary is specifically stated.

General

1. *Hurricane IID.*—The Hurricane IID is similar in general construction to the other Hurricane II variants which are described in this publication, but it is provided with wings which have been modified to carry two Vickers Type "S" 40 m/m guns or two Rolls-Royce Type "B–H" 40 m/m guns (*see* fig. 1), and two ·303 in. Browning guns. The Browning guns are mounted, one on each side, outboard of the 40 m/m guns.

2. On all but very early aircraft the pilot, radiator and engine are protected against small arms fire from the ground, by armour plate on the forward part of the aircraft. The pilot is additionally protected by windscreen side panels of bullet-proof glass and heavy gauge duralumin panels on the forward part of the decking. The oil tank has a self-sealing covering; a wire-mesh stone guard is fitted in front of the radiator fairing and the starboard landing lamp is blanked off. On later aircraft, the carburettor air scoop has been removed, a gauze filter being provided at the air intake entry under the fuselage.

3. When the 40 m/m guns are not fitted, 45 or 90 gallon drop fuel tanks can be installed; these tanks are the same as those fitted to normal Hurricane aircraft and will not therefore be described in this addendum. Some early aircraft were equipped to carry 45-gallon fixed operational overload fuel tanks instead of drop tanks.

4. *Hurricane IV.*—This is similar in most respects to the Hurricane IID, but is provided with a "low-attack" wing, which enables the aircraft to be fitted with either two Vickers Type "S" 40 m/m guns *or any one set* of the following items (*see* fig. 1), in addition to two ·303 in. Browning guns:—

    2 40 m/m Rolls-Royce Type "B–H" guns (early aircraft only).
    Bombs (two 250 or 500 lb.).
    2 S.B.C.
    2 S.C.I.
    2 Drop fuel tanks.

The Rolls-Royce and Vickers guns are mounted in the same position under the wing, the only difference being in the method of mounting. Additional armour protection is incorporated as for the Hurricane IID (*see* para. 2).

5. It should be borne in mind that Mk. IV wings may be obtained as spares for either mark of aircraft, and that the fitting of such wings to a Mk. IID does not convert it into a Mk. IV as the corresponding controls and equipment are not installed in the fuselage.

6. *Additional structure in wings (both marks).*—The Hurricane IID wing and the "low attack" wing are similar in general construction to the normal Hurricane wing but are provided with certain additional structure. This structure comprises a number of nut plates and Simmonds anchor nuts, to

provide attachment points for the armament or tanks slung beneath the wings. The mountings for the ·303 in. guns are in the wing just outboard of the 40 mm. guns, and are similar to the normal ·303 in. gun installation.

7. Additional access doors are incorporated in the top and bottom skin, to provide access to the mountings of the ·303 in. guns and the magazines of the 40 mm. guns. The landing lamp windows are covered with a detachable panel.

DESCRIPTION OF ALTERNATIVE INSTALLATIONS AND CONTROLS.

Vickers Type "S" 40 m/m guns

8. *General.*—The Vickers 40 m/m guns are electro-pneumatically controlled by a push-button incorporated in the throttle-lever. They cannot be fired, however, until a master switch, which is mounted on the decking shelf forward of the throttle, is switched on. A pneumatic cocking valve is fitted on the inboard face of the electrical panel, and in the event of a misfire the lever should be pushed down. Each gun (*see* fig. 2) is supported by means of a mounting attached to the rear spar and a gun bearer attached to the sub-spar in the gun bay, and when in position is enclosed in a streamlined fairing. The magazine provided with each gun on all Hurricane IID and early Mk. IV aircraft carries 15 rounds, but on later Mk. IV's each magazine has a capacity of 30 rounds.

9. *Front mounting.*—The front mounting (*see* fig. 3) consists of two brackets A, bolted to the gun bearers just forward of the sub-spar; each bracket incorporates a bearing shoe C which is held in place by means of a small grub screw F. A long attachment bolt B passes through the brackets, shoes and the lugs on the gun and is secured in position by means of a castle nut D and split pin.

10. *Rear mounting.*—The rear mounting (*see* fig. 4) consists of an upper bracket G bolted to the rear spar, a lower bracket N to which the rear end of the gun is attached, and a link E connecting the two brackets and providing lateral and vertical adjustment. The central hole of the lower bracket is threaded on the inside and a screwed plug D is fitted into it and locked by two bolted half clips C round the outside of the housing. For vertical adjustment, the plug is screwed in or out of the bracket, as required. Inside the screwed plug is a ball-end B for the lower end of the link between the upper and lower brackets to allow rotation for lateral adjustment. The link is secured in the upper bracket by a spindle F, which can be adjusted for lateral alignment by means of an adjuster bolt H which is screwed into the inboard lug of the bracket. In order to lock the adjuster bolt, this lug is split and fitted with a locking bolt K.

Rolls-Royce Type "B-H" 40 m/m guns

11. *General.*—The 40 m/m Rolls-Royce guns (*see* fig. 5) are fired in a similar manner to the Vickers "S" guns (*see* para. 8) and are mounted one underneath each wing like the Vickers gun, the chief difference being that the rear mounting is removed from the rear spar and bolted into position on the front spar, forming the front mounting for this installation, while its rear mounting is at the sub-spar; in addition fairings are not provided for this gun. The magazine is of the hopper type and holds 12 rounds.

12. *Front mounting.*—The front mounting for this gun is the same as that used at the rear for the Vickers gun and is described in para. 10.

13. *Rear mounting.*—The rear mounting (*see* fig. 3) is the same as the front mounting used on the Vickers gun (*see* para. 9), the only difference being that the long attachment bolt is replaced by two small attachment studs H.

·303 in. guns

14. The two ·303 in. guns are fired pneumatically from the push-button on the spade grip of the control column, in the usual manner. The mountings are standard as described for the Hurricane Mk. I and IIB in A.P.1564A, Vol. I, and Mk. IIB in this publication.

Alternative equipment controls (Hurricane IV only)

15. The S.B.C. and S.C.I. installations (*see* fig. 1) are operated by the push-button on the throttle lever, which is also used to release the bombs. The fuzing of the bombs and the jettisoning of the drop fuel tanks are as for other Hurricane variants, and, consequently, are fully described elsewhere in this publication.

Drop tanks

16. The installation of drop fuel tanks on both marks of aircraft is exactly as described in A.P.1564B, Vol. I, Section 4, Chapter 2.

Camera unit

17. The camera unit operates only when the 40 m/m guns are fired, or when the camera firing push-button at the bottom of the control column spade grip is pressed. A lag adaptor is fitted in the pneumatic system so that the camera unit will continue to operate for a short period after the guns have ceased firing.

GROUND HANDLING AND PREPARATION FOR FLIGHT

Vickers Type "S" 40 m/m guns

18. *Installation.*—The Vickers 40 m/m guns are referred to as port and starboard and must not be confused, i.e. the port gun bears an even number and the starboard gun an odd number. When the guns are to be fitted, the front mountings will be in the correct position under the wings; the rear mountings may be in the correct position, they may be mounted on the front spar or they may be stowed on the board in the ·303 in. gun bay. As the magazine is an integral part of the gun, feed necks are not required. The spent cases are ejected through a chute which is built into the gun fairings; each gun ejects inboard. The following procedure should be used when installing each gun:—

(i) Remove the access doors between the gun mountings in the under-surface of the wings and store them.

(ii) Remove the rear drop tank hook and inboard stabilising pad, if fitted, and stow in the ·303 in. gun bay.

(iii) Attach the lower half of the rear mounting N complete with ball B, plug D and link E (*see* fig. 4) to the receiver of the gun and lock the four attachment studs M in position with 18 s.w.g. soft iron wire L. *Important.*—When the mounting is in position a careful inspection must be made to ascertain that the ends of the studs do not project on the inside of the gun.

(iv) Insert the bearing shoes C (stowed in the gun bay) into position in the front gun mounting (*see* fig. 3) and secure them in place by means of the grub screws F provided.

(v) Offer up the gun. Place a profile washer on the long attachment bolt B (Part No. A.116074) and insert the bolt through the front gun mounting A and the lugs on the guns; place a second profile washer E on the end of the bolt and screw on a castle nut D. If the hole for the split pin has not been drilled, drill a hole through the bolt in the appropriate place and insert a split pin thereby locking the castle nut in place.

Note.—It is most important that the hole for the split pin should be drilled accurately, and the split pin inserted.

(vi) Still supporting the gun, insert the spindle F (*see* fig. 4) through the rear gun mounting bracket G, the link E and adjuster H. Place a washer on the spindle and screw on the G.K.N. nut J originally removed from the spindle.

(vii) Align the gun (*see* para. 19), not omitting to replace the split pin on the front mounting.

(viii) Connect the flexible pipe of the Dunlop firing and re-cocking unit, which is attached to the guns, to the pneumatic connections on the firing valve.

19. *Alignment.*—The rear mounting of each gun is adjustable vertically and laterally to enable the guns to be converged on to a point 200 yds. ahead on the centre-line of the aircraft, the front mounting being provided with bearing shoes that make it self-aligning. To align the guns, proceed as follows:—

(i) Remove the split pin from the front mounting bolt B (*see* fig. 3) and slacken off the castle nut D and the grub screws F.

(ii) At the rear mounting (*see* fig. 4) slacken the G.K.N. nuts on the half clips C which clamp the plug D in the housing N. Vertical adjustment may now be made by adjusting the plug in the housing with the special combination spanner (Stores Ref. 8D/2423) provided for this purpose. When the necessary adjustment has been made, re-tighten the G.K.N. nuts on the half-clips.

(iii) For lateral adjustment, at the rear mounting, unlock the adjuster H on the spindle F by slackening the G.K.N. nut K on the split lug of the mounting bracket G. Next loosen the G.K.N. nut J on the spindle. Adjustment may now be made by turning the adjuster in the required direction. When the necessary adjustment has been made, first re-tighten the G.K.N. nut on the split lug and then the G.K.N. nut on the spindle.

(iv) On the front mounting tighten the grub screws F which hold the bearing shoes C in place, also tighten the castle nut bolt B and replace the split pin to lock it in position.

20. *Loading.*—Instructions for loading are given in P.Arm.P. No. 32, Chap. 2. The magazine access doors in the side of the fairings must first be moved by disengaging the three Dzus fasteners in the lower edge of each. These doors must be replaced when loading is completed.

21. *Assembly and removal of gun fairing.*—To fit the fairings to the gun, the following instructions should be followed:—

(i) Assemble the fairing support brackets in position on the lower lugs on the gun. Pass the special stud (Part No. A.117212) through the brackets and lugs, place a washer at each end and secure in place with Simmonds nuts.

(ii) Place the end cap over the end of the gun and tighten the two screws in the fixing ring of the cap.

(iii) Offer up the fairings, making sure that port parts are used on the port wing. Secure the fairings in place by engaging the two "butterfly" type Dzus fasteners.

(iv) Join the two halves of the fairing together by engaging the Dzus fasteners along the edges, dealing with the top edges first.

(v) Check that the "Fire" and "Safe" access door is in place and properly secured.

To remove the gun fairings, the procedure described above should be reversed. Additional information to that given here is given in P.Arm.P. No. 33.

Rolls-Royce Type "B-H" 40 m/m guns

22. *Installation.*—The Rolls-Royce 40 m/m guns are referred to as port and starboard. Feed necks and chutes for links and empty cases are not required and the gun is not provided with a fairing. To install each gun proceed as follows:—

(i) Remove the top and bottom access doors aft of the rear spar (*see* fig. 6). As the top door will be replaced by a door with a blister (Part No. C.121638–9) and the magazine enters the wing through the space originally covered by the lower access door, both doors should be stored.

(ii) Assemble the front mounting in its correct position as shown in fig. 5, if it is not already in place. If a Vickers gun has just been removed from the aircraft, the mounting will be found attached to the under-surface of the wing at the rear spar. If drop tanks have been fitted, the mounting will be attached to the front spar but swung aft.

(iii) Bolt the housing of the mounting (*see* fig. 4) complete with ball, plug and link to the attachment plate on the gun, inserting the bolts from the inside of the plate, and using bolts, washers and G.K.N. nuts supplied with the gun.

Note.—The studs M employed when the mounting is attached to the Vickers gun, may not be used with the Rolls-Royce gun, when the bolt A is used.

(iv) Insert the bearing shoes into position in the rear gun mounting (*see* fig. 3) and secure them in place by means of the grub screws provided in the base of the mounting.

(v) Present up the gun. Place a profile washer on the attachment studs H which are provided with the gun and insert the studs through the side brackets of the rear mounting and into the appropriate fittings on the gun.

Note.—The long attachment bolt used on the Vickers installation cannot be used on this installation.

(vi)   Still supporting the gun, insert the spindle through the front gun mounting brackets, the link and the adjuster.   Place a washer on the spindle and screw on the G.K.N. nut originally removed from the spindle.

(vii)   Align the gun (*see* para. 23), not forgetting to lock the studs on the rear mounting with 18 s.w.g. soft iron wire G.

(viii)   Connect the flexible pipe lines of the firing and re-cocking unit, which is attached to the gun, to the pneumatic connections in the firing valve.

(ix)   Fit the new magazine access door in position (*see* sub-para. (i)).

23.   *Alignment.*—The procedure for aligning this gun is basically the same as for the Vickers gun, except for slight variations caused by the reversal of the mountings and minor differences in detail of attachment.   The full procedure is as follows:—

(i)   Slacken the attachment studs and grub screws at the rear mounting.

(ii)   At the front mounting, slacken the G.K.N. nuts on the half-clips C which clamp the plug D in the housing N.   Vertical adjustment may now be made by adjusting the plug in the housing with the special spanner (Stores Ref. 8D/2423) provided for this purpose.   When the necessary adjustment has been made, re-tighten the G.K.N. nuts on the half-clips.

(iii)   For lateral adjustment, at the front mounting, unlock the adjuster H on the spindle F by slackening the G.K.N. nut K on the split lug of the mounting bracket G.   Next loosen the G.K.N. nut J on the spindle. Adjustment may now be made by turning the adjuster in the required direction.   When the necessary adjustment has been made, first re-tighten the G.K.N. nut on the split lug and then re-tighten the G.K.N. nut on the spindle.

(iv)   Tighten up the grub screws F and attachment studs at the rear mounting and lock the studs with 18 s.w.g. soft iron wire.

24.   *Loading.*—Access for loading ammunition is obtained through the door in the top surface of the wing.

Access to auxiliary electrical equipment

25.

   Note.—The numbers in brackets refer to the access panel numbering in Sect. 4, Chap. 3, fig. 1.

Mk. IID

Master switch Throttle switch Fuse box, 20-amp. Gun firing relay	... ...	Port rear side panel (12)
T.B.31 T.B.32	... ...	Access door (26)
Firing valve	... ...	Through undersurface of wing after removing gun fairings

Master switch		
Throttle switch		
Gun firing relay	... ...	Port rear side panel (12)
T.B.15		
T.B.2		
Bomb switches	...	Starboard rear side panel (14)
Subsidiary electrical panel		
Socket mounting panel		
Fuse boxes—20-amp.	...	Port access door (6)
10-amp.		
5-amp.		

Bomb carriers (Hurricane IV only)

26. *Installation.*—The bomb carriers are mounted underneath the wings, one on each side, and are referred to as port and starboard. When in position they are enclosed in streamlined fairings. The following installation procedure covers the details which are peculiar to this aircraft but for fuller instructions reference should be made to A.P.1664, Vol. I, Chap. 3:—

(i) Remove and stow the drop tank hooks, if fitted.

(ii) Check that the carriers have been modified for use with Hurricane aircraft. (The modified racks are shorter than standard ones and have side plates and fairing brackets bolted to them).

(iii) Offer up the carriers and bolt them in position at the points shown in the relevant detail of fig. 6. inserting washers and packing between the brackets and the wing as follows:—
At front bracket, washer A.122338 and A.Std.915 G/18.
At intermediate brackets, packing 22G L.3 or D.'.'.D.390 1·5 in. × 3 in. as necessary.
At rear bracket, washer A.122338.
At each mounting bracket lock the bolt heads together with 18 s.w.g. soft iron wire.

(iv) Fit the 5-way plugs of the carriers into the aircraft 5-way sockets situated in the undersurface of the wing.

(v) Remove the port access door in the side fairing aft of the pilot's cabin and remove the two 5-way plugs from the subsidiary electrical panel and replace them in the 5-way socket labelled BOMB.

(vi) Remove the 5-way plug from the socket mounting pawl above the subsidiary panel and replace it in the socket marked BOMBS.

(vii) Remove the hoist doors from the carrier fairing. Offer up the fairing, making sure that a port fairing is used on the port wing, etc., and secure it in place by means of the nine washer-headed bolts provided. Repeat the operation with the other carrier.

(viii) Assemble the hoist doors in position and engage the four Dzus fasteners.

27. *Loading.*—The loading of the bombs is described in A.P.1664, Vol. I. Before the bombs can be loaded it is necessary to remove the hoist doors from the bomb carrier fairings. When the bombs are in position the crutches must be adjusted to suit, using the special box spanner A.Std.1219, which is stowed in the case for the control locking gear. The hoist doors must then be replaced.

S.C.I. and S.B.C. (Hurricane IV only)

28. *Installation and loading.*—The smoke curtain installation and small bomb containers are mounted underneath the wings, one on each side, suspended on the same carriers as those employed for bombs, and using the same type of hook attachment. The method of installation is as described in para. 26 and in A.P.1664, Vol. I, Chap. 3, A.P.2457A, Vol. I, Sect. 1, Chap. 2, except that bomb carrier fairings are not fitted with S.B.C. in position and the electrical lead from the S.C.I. or S.B.C. should be attached to the adaptor box at the front of the bomb carrier. For instructions concerning loading, reference should be made to A.P.2457A, Vol. I, Sect. 1, Chap. 2.

Pneumatic installation

29. The two ·303 in. guns on all three marks are controlled pneumatically by the push button on the control column spade grip and the two 40 mm. guns are electro-pneumatically controlled by a master switch mounted on the port decking shelf and a push-button incorporated in the throttle lever (*see* fig. 7). For the operation of the electro-pneumatic firing valve *see* A.P.1641E, Vol. I. The air for cocking the 40 m/m guns is controlled by a cocking valve (*see* A.P.1641E, Vol. I) mounted on the electrical panel in the cockpit. The camera unit pneumatic switch, which controls the operation of the camera unit, is operated by air taken from the pipe between the firing valve and the gun and passes through a lag adaptor and a small pneumatic reservoir which, together with the pneumatic switch, are mounted forward of the firing valve. The lag adaptor acts as a restrictor valve and, when the 40 mm. guns cease firing, it ensures that sufficient pressure is held in the pneumatic reservoir to keep the camera unit in operation for a further 1 to 1½ seconds.

Electrical installation

30. *40 m/m guns.*—Operation of the push-button firing unit for the 40 m/m guns, after the master switch has been closed, closes the contacts of the gun-firing relay (*see* fig. 8), mounted on the port side behind the pilot's seat, and energizes the solenoids of the electro-pneumatic firing valves, fitted one in each wing, inboard of the guns. The solenoid opens an air valve within each firing valve and allows the pneumatic pressure to operate the guns and camera unit pneumatic switch.

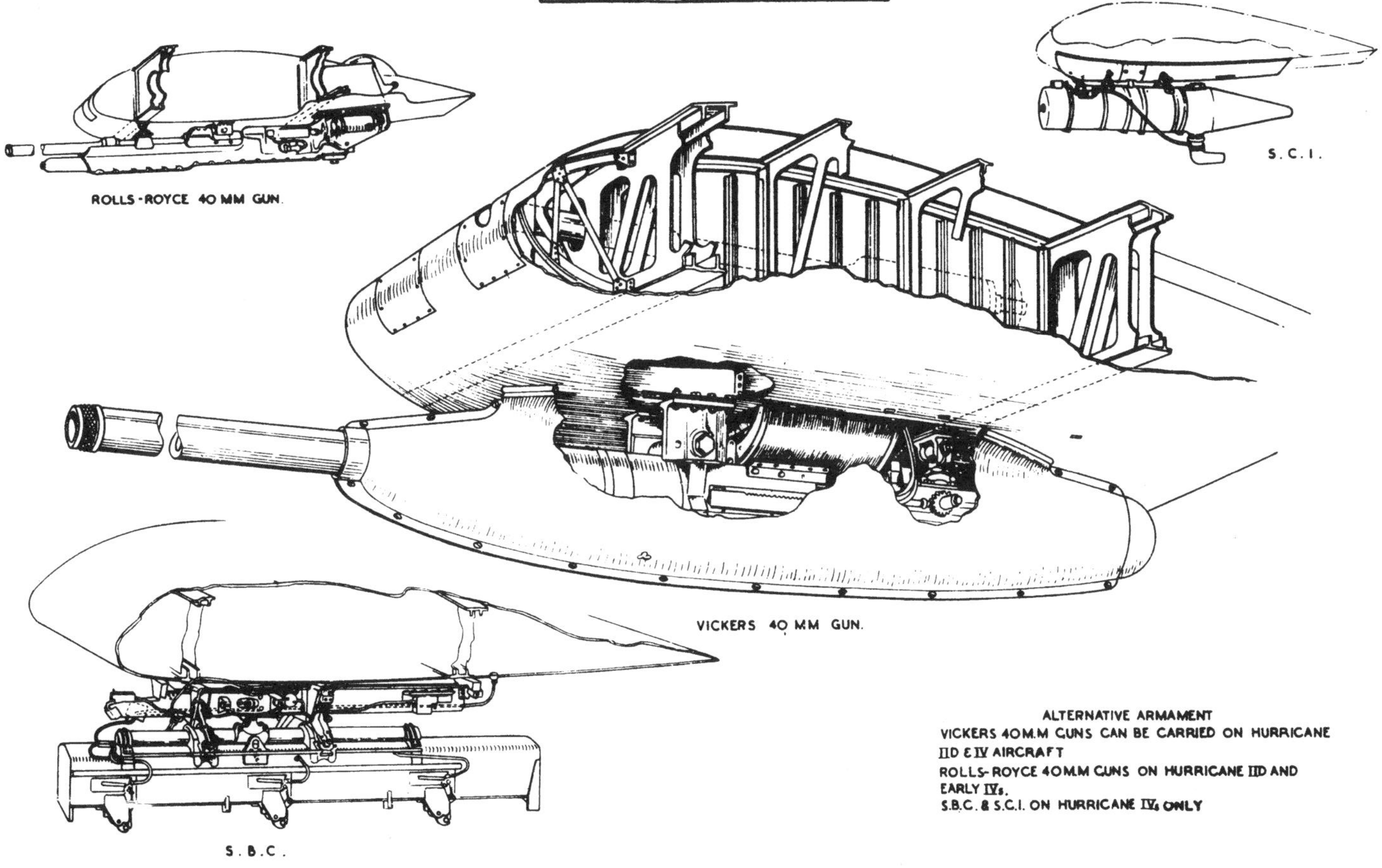

A.P.1564B,C &D VOL.1 ADDENDUM II

S.C.I.

VICKERS 40 M.M. GUN.

ROLLS-ROYCE 40 MM GUN.

S.B.C.

ALTERNATIVE ARMAMENT
VICKERS 40M.M GUNS CAN BE CARRIED ON HURRICANE
IID & IV AIRCRAFT
ROLLS-ROYCE 40MM GUNS ON HURRICANE IID AND
EARLY IVs.
S.B.C. & S.C.I. ON HURRICANE IVs ONLY

HURRICANE IID & IV WING ALTERNATIVE ARMAMENT

FIG. 1

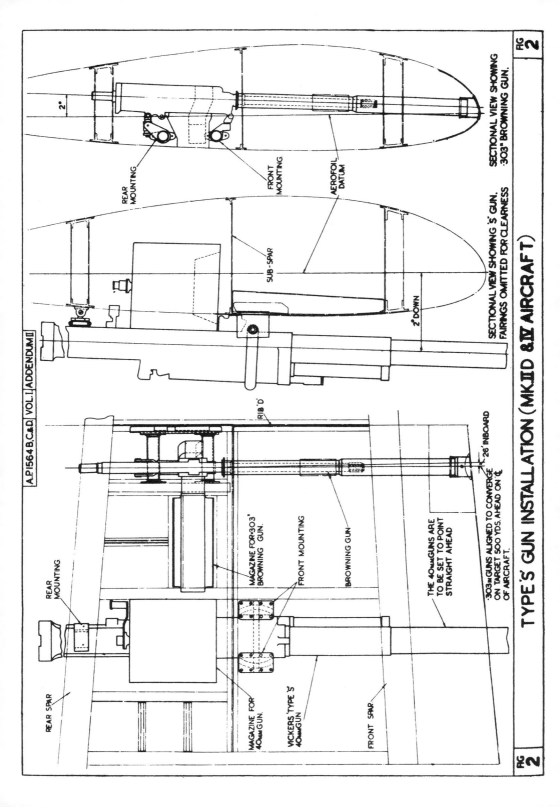

FIG 2

REAR
MOUNTING

FRONT
MOUNTING

AEROFOIL
DATUM

SECTIONAL VIEW SHOWING
.303" BROWNING GUN.

SUB-SPAR

2° DOWN

SECTIONAL VIEW SHOWING 'S' GUN,
FAIRINGS OMITTED FOR CLEARNESS

RIB 'D'

REAR
MOUNTING

MAGAZINE FOR.303"
BROWNING GUN.

FRONT MOUNTING

BROWNING GUN

THE 40mm GUNS ARE
TO BE SET TO POINT
STRAIGHT AHEAD

.303mm GUNS ALIGNED TO CONVERGE
ON TARGET 500 YDS. AHEAD ON ₵
OF AIRCRAFT.

26" INBOARD

REAR SPAR

MAGAZINE FOR
40mm GUN.

VICKERS TYPE 'S'
40mm GUN.

FRONT SPAR

TYPE 'S' GUN INSTALLATION (MK.II D & IV AIRCRAFT)

FIG 2

A.P.1564 B,C&D VOL. I ADDENDUM II

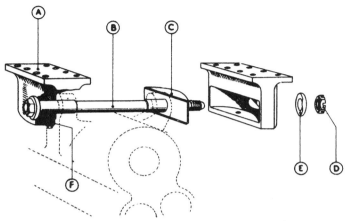

VICKERS 40 M.M. GUN ATTACHMENT (FRONT)

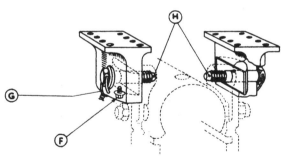

ROLLS-ROYCE 40 MM. GUN ATTACHMENT (REAR)

| FIG. 3 | 40 M.M GUN MOUNTING | FIG. 3 |

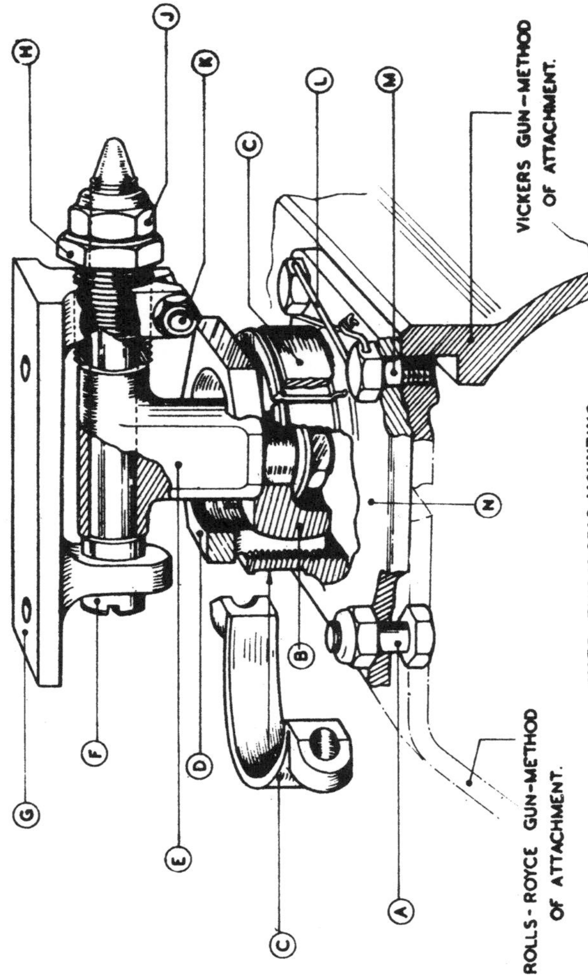
VICKERS GUN—METHOD OF ATTACHMENT.
NOTE – THIS IS REAR MOUNTING OF 'S' GUN AND FRONT MOUNTING OF 'B-H' GUN.
ROLLS-ROYCE GUN-METHOD OF ATTACHMENT.
A
B
C
C
D
E
F
G
H
J
K
L
M
N

FIG. 4 **40 M.M GUN MOUNTING** FIG. 4

This leaf issued with A.L. No. 43, March 1944

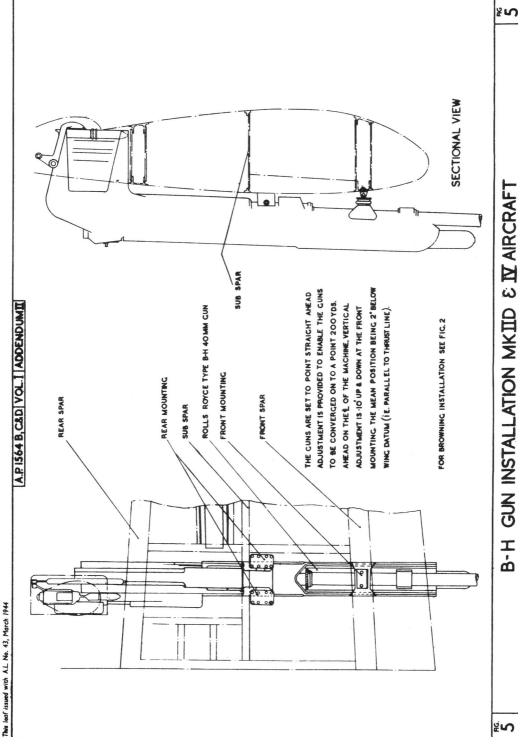

SUB SPAR

SECTIONAL VIEW

REAR SPAR

REAR MOUNTING
SUB SPAR
ROLLS ROYCE TYPE B-H 40 MM GUN
FRONT MOUNTING

FRONT SPAR

THE GUNS ARE SET TO POINT STRAIGHT AHEAD
ADJUSTMENT IS PROVIDED TO ENABLE THE GUNS
TO BE CONVERGED ON TO A POINT 200 YDS.
AHEAD ON THE ₵ OF THE MACHINE. VERTICAL
ADJUSTMENT IS ·I0⁰ UP & DOWN AT THE FRONT
MOUNTING, THE MEAN POSITION BEING 2⁰ BELOW
WING DATUM (I.E. PARALLEL TO THRUST LINE).

FOR BROWNING INSTALLATION SEE FIG. 2

B-H GUN INSTALLATION MKIID & IV AIRCRAFT

FIG. 5

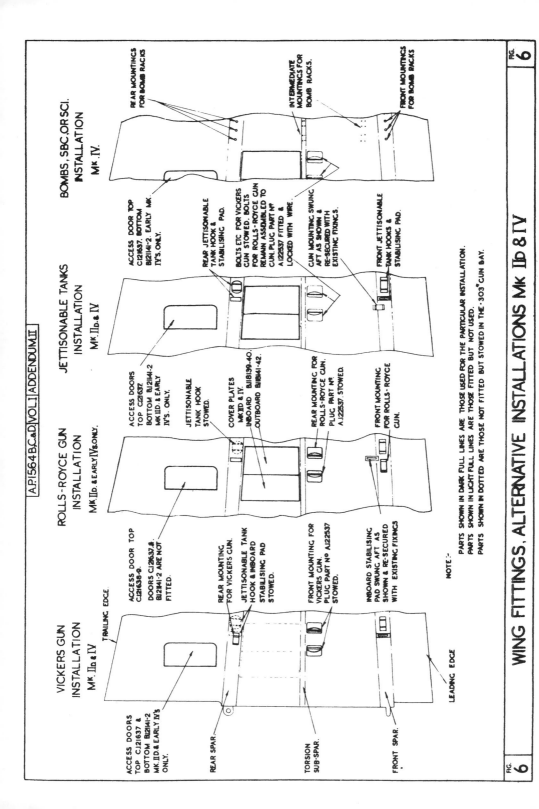

WING FITTINGS, ALTERNATIVE INSTALLATIONS Mk IIᴅ & IV

FIG. 6

A.P.1564B,C,D VOL.I ADDENDUM II

·303 GUN FIRING
BUTTON

COCKING
VALVE

FROM PRESSURE
REDUCING VALVE.

FOR CONTINUATION
SEE SECT. 9 FIG.13

TO BRAKE RELAY
VALVE.

ROOT RIB

FIRING VALVE
FOR ELECTRICAL
CONNECTIONS SEE
FIG. 8

·303 GUN   40mm GUN   40mm GUN   ·303 GUN
   PORT   STARBOARD

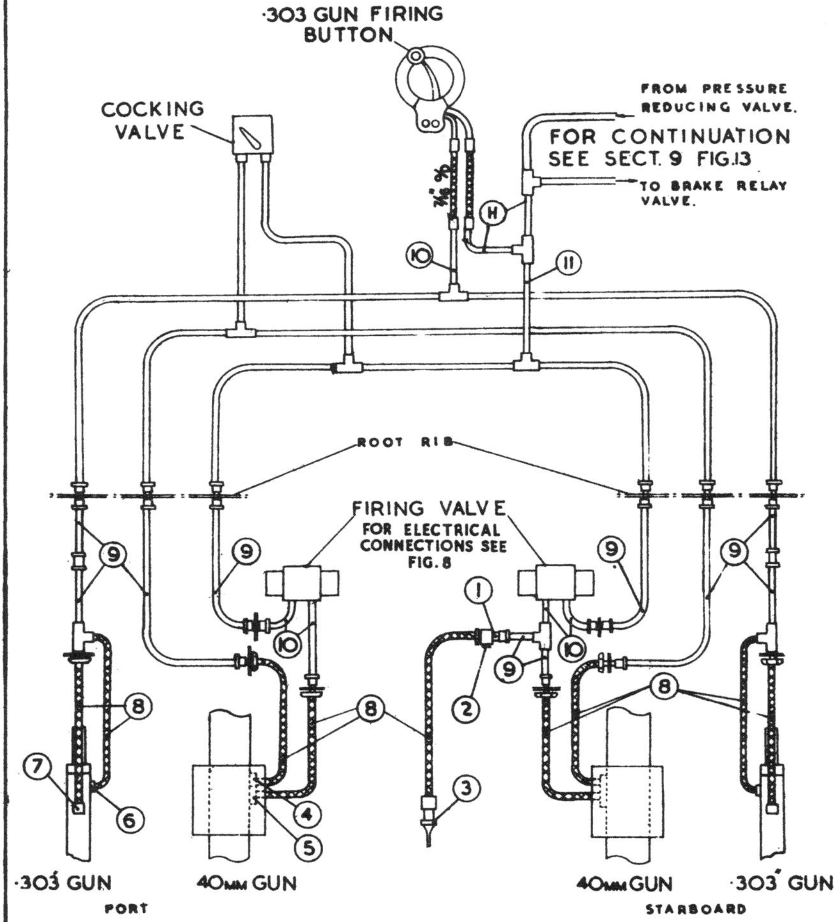

No	DESCRIPTION
1	LAG ADAPTOR
2	PNEUMATIC RESERVOIR
3	CAMERA FIRING UNIT
4	COCKING CONNECTION (40mm GUN)
5	FIRING CONNECTION (40mm GUN)
6	BOLT RELEASE UNIT
7	FIRE AND SAFE UNIT
8	FLEXIBLE HOSE
9	3/16 x 22G TUNGUM
10	5/16 x 22G TUNGUM
11	1 3/8 x 22G TUNGUM

| FIG. 7 | PNEUMATIC SYSTEM DIAGRAM MK IID & IV | FIG. 7 |

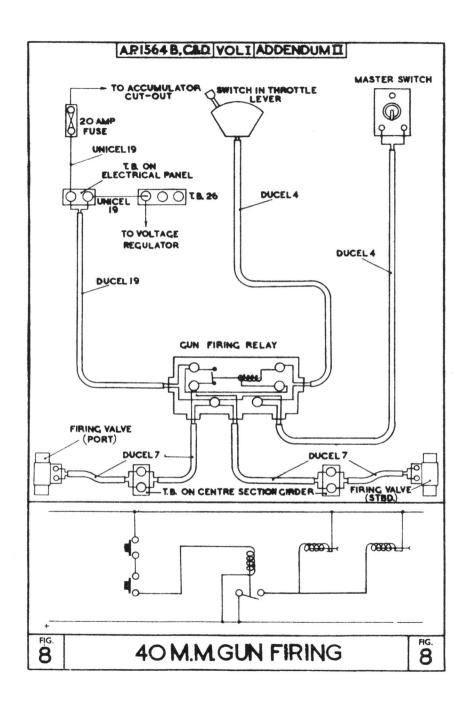

TO ACCUMULATOR CUT-OUT

SWITCH IN THROTTLE LEVER

MASTER SWITCH

20 AMP FUSE

UNICEL 19

T.B. ON ELECTRICAL PANEL

UNICEL 19

T.B. 26

TO VOLTAGE REGULATOR

DUCEL 4

DUCEL 4

DUCEL 19

GUN FIRING RELAY

FIRING VALVE (PORT)

DUCEL 7

DUCEL 7

T.B. ON CENTRE SECTION GIRDER

FIRING VALVE (STBD.)

+

FIG. 8

40 M.M. GUN FIRING

FIG. 8

A.P.I564B,C & D,VOL.I,ADDENDUM II

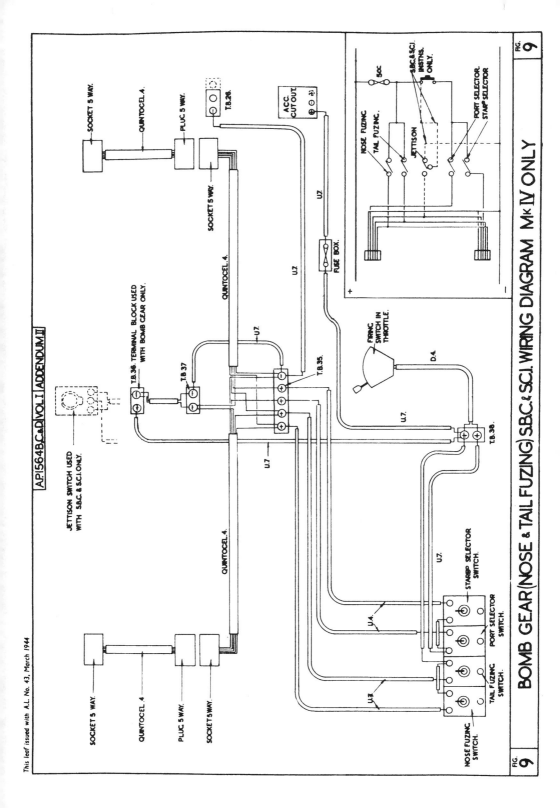

SOCKET 5 WAY.

QUINTOCEL. A.

PLUG 5 WAY.

T.B.26.

SOCKET 5 WAY.

ACC. CUT OUT

QUINTOCEL. 4.

U.7.

FUSE BOX.

JETTISON SWITCH USED WITH S.B.C. & S.C.I. ONLY.

T.B.34. TERMINAL BLOCK USED WITH BOMB GEAR ONLY.

T.B 37

U.7.

T.B.35.

U.7.

U.7.

T.B.38.

FIRING SWITCH IN THROTTLE.

D.4.

U.7.

QUINTOCEL. 4.

U.7.

SOCKET 5 WAY.

QUINTOCEL. 4

PLUG 5 WAY.

SOCKET 5 WAY.

STAR'BD SELECTOR SWITCH.

U.4.

PORT SELECTOR SWITCH.

U.7.

TAIL FUZING SWITCH.

NOSE FUZING SWITCH.

5cc

S.B.C. & S.C.I. INSTNS. ONLY.

NOSE FUZING

TAIL FUZING.

JETTISON

PORT SELECTOR

STAR'B'D SELECTOR

FIG. 9

FIG. 9

BOMB GEAR (NOSE & TAIL FUZING) S.B.C.& S.C.I. WIRING DIAGRAM MkIV ONLY